GURU NANAK DEV

THE GREAT GURUS OF THE SIKHS SERIES

GURU NANAK DEV

Editor-in-Chief

O. P. RALHAN

ANMOL PUBLICATIONS PVT. LTD.
NEW DELHI-110002 (INDIA)

ANMOL PUBLICATIONS PVT. LTD.
4374/4B, Ansari Road, Daryaganj
New Delhi-110 002

Guru Nanak Dev

First Edition 1998

ISBN 81-7488-670-2

PRINTED IN INDIA

Published by J. L. Kumar for Anmol Publications Pvt. Ltd., New Delhi-110 002 and Printed at Mehra Offset Press, Delhi.

Preface

'Great Gurus of the Sikhs' in six volumes is a monumental work by the editor drawing every succinct information on each of the ten Gurus from unapproachable historical and religious sources.

These volumes should not be treated simply in biographical sketches of their lives or travelogue of their lives, but an account of their teachings, philosophies, travelogue, their sufferings and sacrifices for the country, their mythological and theological aspects, socio-economic reforms, their political contention and wars with the autocracy at their times and many more touching incidents of their lives, miracles which they manifested on several occasions—all have been contained in them. These volumes are treasures of religious wealth enshrined in their sacred *Vanis*—viz. Guru Granth Sahib and on political scenario of their times.

The sufferings of the Gurus were immense during Mughal period. Guru Arjun Dev, Guru Teg Bahadur and Guru Gobind Singh sacrificed every thing for the sake of their sincere love for humanity and reforming zeal. Repressive policies and numerous maneuvre could not bend them, instead. The rulers have to bow before them for their unparallelled and unmatched chivalry shown by them in spite of great emotional hurdles.

These volumes are faithful and sincere narration of the political conditions, social conditions, religious fanaticity of the rulers, prevailing at that times and how all those Great Gurus not only fought against heavy odds but simultaneously never allowed to fade away the spiritual lamp lighted by them which even today imparts eternal peace to thousands of people not only of Sikh people but all other religions.

These volumes on Great Gurus of the Sikhs advocate tenaciously a superb, enchanting study for each and every one. Highly recommended for teachers, students, social reformers, historians. A useful and worthy of acquisition for each library. Section of Sikh history in each library remain incomplete without such a marvellous set.

Preface

[illegible]

[illegible]

[illegible]

[illegible]

[illegible]

[illegible]

Contents

1

Early Life

Guru Nanak born in April 15, 1469 in Rai Bhoe Ki Talwandi, now known as Nankana Sahib in the Sheikhupura district of West Pakistan. His father Mehta Kalu, was a Patwari which was fairly high in the revenue department in olden times. His mother's name was Tripata, and he had an elder sister, named Nanki, four years to him.

EFFECTS OF TEACHINGS

Parents Perturbed

Mehta Kalu was troubled sorely over the strange ways of Guru Nanak. In spite of the love-inspired efforts of Mata Tripata, the Mehta could not but detect his son's gifts to beggars and sadhus. How could a man whose heart was after storing wealth and riches in this world relish such 'wasteful' conduct of his son? He rebuked the child. The latter promised to obey his father. But what could he do? Charity, open handed charity, was in his grain. The Divine urge would not let him be what his father would make of him. His soul was in constant communion with the Supreme Soul. He could not resist these early calls to a life that was to be his in times to come. The Mehta reproached the astrologer for having predicted a great and glorious future for such an 'idler and spendthrift'. "What a joke," he would say, "you said he would be a great ruler over men and lands; he would win untold wealth and honour for himself and his people. Yet he has begun the other way. He seems bent upon throwing away what little I have honesty gathered. Was it a joke or an error on your part?" The astrologer would not given in. How could he let it be supposed that his science, on which he depended for his sustenance, was false, or that he was not well versed in it? "Have patience," he would say, "I still hold that Nanak is to be even greater than rulers of men and lands. Judge him not too hastily, nor measure him with your own standards."

The Pandha's Strange Pupil

At last the fond father, intent on moulding his son after his own heart, decided to send the 'refractory' child to school. "That", though he, "will at least keep him away from home for the day-time and thus stop his wasteful conduct. He'll also have no time to go about hunting after sadhus his faqirs and imbibe their ways. Perhaps, thus weaned from such distractions, he may learn the three R's and qualify himself for stepping into my shoes when I am gone."

Like a dutiful son that he was, Guru Nanak readily agreed to do as bidden. On an 'auspicious' day Mehta Kalu took his son, the would-be world-teacher to a *Pandha*, a Brahmin schoolmaster, "Take good care of him," said he to the *Pandha*, "for he is rather troublesome!" The *Pandha*, however, discovered no such trait in his new pupil. He found him quick to learn and ready to obey. The *Pandha* felt not a little puzzled over what appeared to him either an unheared of precocity in the child or a most wonderful miracle. All his life he had seen no such pupil. The child learnt to write in an amazingly short time. But a great wonder was still in store for the schoolmaster. One day Guru Nanak sat a little apart, apparently engrossed in writing on the *Patti*, or the wooden tablet. The schoolmaster watched him with interest. He had already discovered that this new pupil of his was no ordinary child. He had seen him at play leading the whole band. He had often watched him close his eyes and sit for hours as if in ecstasy. He was sure it was not sleep. He had looked into the mysterious eyes of his strange coach. Sometimes they would shrine with unbounded mirth; at others they seemed to be deep unfathomable wells at the bottom of which was seen reflected all the agony that afflicted the world. His pupils had also told him, "Whenever you leave the school room for a white, Nanak gathers us round him and makes us all repeat after him the name of the Omnipotent, Formless Lord. At such times, his face always appears to be radiant with an unearthly light." The teacher had heard, seen, and felt, all this; so it was with a strange, heart-quivering expectation that he watched Guru Nanak as he sat apart, calm and concentrated, writing on the *Patti* and humming to himself a soft, low tune as he wrote. At last, the watchful eyes of the schoolmaster discovered that Guru Nanak had laid aside his pen and was looking at his work in mute joy and admiration. Later, when he was in his full glory as a world-teacher, Guru Nanak revealed the secret of his matchless compositions. It was not he that wrote or composed. He was simply an amanuensis of the Supreme Lord, an organ wherewith the World of God was proclaimed to humanity. Here was a sample, the first one, of such composition. The great amanuensis sat watching his work in joy and wonder. The schoolmaster thought that his pupil, having finished his writing, would come up to him and show it. But Guru Nanak did not move. The *Pandha* waited for him till he could wait not longer. A strange urge was in his heart. The like of it he had never felt before. He rose, went up to where his strange pupil sat, and said, "Nanak, thou has been writing something. I should like to see it."

The Teacher Taught

Guru Nanak rose at the bidding of the schoolmaster and gave the *Patti* into his hands. Great indeed was the amazement of the Pandha. He found that the writing on the *Patti*, was not what he had expected, or what his pupils generally wrote at that stage of their educational career. Not disconnected, independent words and figures, but sentences and paragraphs. He began to read. He bowed again and again as he read.It was a hearty discourse on God, man, and the universe. It was an acrostic on the alphabet. But what an acrostic it was to be written by a child! It contained an essence of the message of hope, joy, and deliverance which the Guru had to proclaim to the suffering, despairing, misguided humanity; a burden of the Divine Song by which Guru Nanak had, later, to wean people from their soul-killing habits and inclinations, to lift them up to the level of gods, to the feet of the Lord. A few lines of the acrostic are given below:

"Why art thou misled, O fool? Why cherish so tall conceit of thy talents vain?
Then alone canst thou a learned may be deemed,
When a good account of the life to the Lord thou canst give.
Remember that He, who created the universe is the Supreme Lord of all.
They alone can achieve the true object of their coming into the world.
Who, fixing their hearts and minds on Him, keep always engaged in the service of God is all...
Praise the All-pervading, Boundless Lord alone.
True merit and reward they alone shall win
Who meekly serve, who in their lives realized and practise truth.
He alone can be deemed to scholar true
Who, in his life halt realized the love and knowledge of God.
If the same Lord pervading in all he could see,
Who then could man a proud egotist be?
The servant who exerteth himself is service, and love,
Who is ever busy in executing the commands of the Guru,
And who is equally poised amid good and evil, in grief and joy,
Such a one shall attain a union with the Lord.
Why die of grief and anxious care, O mortal fool?
Ever doth He give to all what he hath ordained.
Why all this bustle for show and deceit, my friend?
In a whole or two wilt hence thou go; this show will end.
Why gamble thy life thus idly away?
Hie to the Lord; at His feet thy self thou lay.
Calm cool, and happy are they whose souls to His feet are linked;
Those whose souls are thus attached are truly saved.
And though favour Divine, true happiness they get.
He in whose heart the Supreme Lord doth ever abide,
Every moment His praises doth he sing;
The Creator blendeth such a one with Himself
And he entereth not the cycle of birth and death again...
The Creator of all the worlds pervadeth everywhere.
What is doubt and what is illusion?
Whatever pleaseth Him is good.
Impute no blame to others, my soul,
On they *Karma* the blame doth lie in whole.
As did I sow so now I reap.

I'd blame none else for this my grief.
No other Giver is there but He
Who has created all things and sustains them all,
Mediate on God's name, get absorbed in Him;
Day and night strive for the merit that His Name will give.

The *Pandha* had heard from Mehta Kalu and his own pupils of the strange ways of his pupil. He had also learnt about the astrologer's prophecy about him. The writing on the wooden tablet confirmed the belief that was then germinating in several pious hearts—namely that Mehta Kalu's son was destined to be the promised Deliverer. But the *Pandha*, like a worldly man of learning, would not believe without a further test. "This is all right," said he to his pupil, "but what I have to teach is also essential. You are a Khatri's son. You should also learn accountancy, so that, after your father, you may take up his place. That will ensure you honour, riches, and a happy, comfortable life. It will also please your father."

The Way of True Knowledge

"That may be true," replied Guru Nanak, "but what of the life to come? Will all that you wish to teach help me at the time when an account of this life must need be rendered? No friend, such knowledge of accounts will be of no avail hereafter." The answers that the Guru gave to these and other questions of the *Pandha* are embodied in a hymn which may be translated as follows:

"Burn thy earthly cravings, grind their ashes well,
and make they ink therefrom;
Let a pure, high mind thy paper be:
Make love thy pen and heart thy write;
Then write as a Teacher true doth guide thee.
Write the Name of God, write his praises,
Write of the Lord that hath no limit, end, or measure;
O Friend, learn to write this account,
So that, when and where an account is called from thee,
Thou mayest win a mark of honour true.
There, in the life to come, true honour and greatness, everlasting joys and
eternal
delights are attained;
There shall marks of honour and acceptance be on the brows of those
Whose hearts enshrine the Sacred, True Name.
Not by idle words but through Grace Divine can such honour be won.
Some come unto the world and others depart therefrom,
Yet what high sounding names they give themselves;
Some are beggars born and some have courts both royal and great;
In the life to come full well shall they know
That if their lives here he devoid of the Love of God,

All else of no account shall be.
In loving fear of Thee, my Lord, I ever do live,
So doth my body pine and waste away;
For, those who were known as lords and kings,
Have I seen get mingled into dust and clay.
When a man will depart from hence, O Nanak,
All attachments false shall sundered be."

(Sri Rag)

The schoolmaster found his Master. He acknowledged that he himself, and not the Divine pupil before him, was in need of instruction. He bowed to Guru Nanak and retired.

Change of Mood and School

Guru Nanak attended the school for some days more and then ceased. He had learnt all that the schoolmaster could teach him. Again, there came over him the same phase which erstwhile had started his father. Sometimes he would run and jump, frisk and gambol, with children of his age; but more often he would sit at home, lost in profound thought, or would visit *Sadhus* and *Faqirs* in the neighbouring forests and have talks with them. The father was perturbed again. The family priest and astrologer, Hardial, now advised the Mehta to send his son to a Sanskrit scholar. "He does not like," said he, "to learn accounts and such other things. He has a religious bent of mind. Put him to school with a *Pandit.* Let him learn *Vedas* and *Shastras* and be a scholar of repute."

Communion with Nature and Creator

This was agreed to. Guru Nanak was taken to a Sanskrit scholar named Brijnath. Here, too, the child was as quick at learning as before. In a short time this pupil, who was to be a World-teacher, convinced his new school-master that he had little need for such scholastic training as the Brahmin scholar could give. Having learnt from Brijnath as much as he deemed necessary, and having taught him what was most essential for a man of religion, Guru Nanak took to his former ways—meditations at home and association with *Sadhus* and *Faquirs,* interrupted, now and then, by jubilant, mirthful pranks with his playmates. He would retire to the seclusion of the forests and sit there in complete abandonment. His heart would become one with Nature. Her beauty charmed him. It took his heart captive and, for hours at a stretch, he sat with wide open eyes, drinking deep with every pore of his body the joy and harmony of the scene before him. From Nature his heart rose to the feet of the Creator. His eyes would then close. A quiet glory would overspread his countenance. For hours he would sit thus enjoying the beauties of Nature and an unbroken communion with the Creator of these beauties. At such time his heart was in complete harmony with Nature and his whole being in tune with the Lord of creation. A supreme, unearthly joy filled him, body and soul, as he sat there watching the play of the Infinite in the finite Nature all round him.

Company of Ascetics

At other times he would visit ascetics and anchorites, bands of whom frequented the dense forests around Talwandi "for the combined objects of undisturbed prayer and escape from the persecution of bigoted Moslem rulers." He heard their learned discourses on *Vedas* and *Shastras.* But he was there not only to receive. He gave them glimpses of the Infinite Fount of knowledge Divine that intuitively flowed into his heart at all time. He learnt from them no doubt, but he learnt far more from his "undisturbed communings with nature, with his own soul, and with his Creator. The voice that had spoken to many a seer again became vocal in that wilderness, and raised (Guru) Nanak's thoughts to the summit of religious exaltation. In summer's heat and winter's frost, in the glory of the firmament, in the changeful aspects of nature, as well as in the joys and sorrows of the inhabitants of his little natal village, he read in bright characters and repeated with joyous iteration the name of the Formless Creator. The Name henceforth became the object of his continual worship and meditation and indeed one of the distinctive features of his creed."

Set to Learn Persian

But Mehta Kalu was ill pleased at the ways of Guru Nanak. When he found his only son thus turning a truant, sore indeeed was his grief. Rai Bular, who had heard of Guru Nanak's devotional temperament and had thereby taken a liking to him, sympathised with his father and said, "Don't grieve or despair Mehta. Your son is possessed of great ability. Set him to learn Persian. I could then put him in charge of my office. He will do well there. He has no doubt refused to learn accountancy and Sanskrit; but perhaps he might take to Persian. Anyhow, there is no harm in trying."

This was done. Guru Nanak was now sent to a *Mulla*, or a Muslim teacher. There, too he astonished his teacher by the quickness with which he learnt all that the Mulla taught him. But the Mulla, too, soon found that his pupil was greater than he himself. After learning from the teacher as much as pleased his heart, Guru Nanak initiated him into a knowledge of God and made the teacher his pupil. He then kept away.

The Early Call of Duty

Once more, he was free to enjoy God and Nature. Long and frequent were now his communions with these inexhaustible founts of Infinite joy. But sad, depressing moments intervened between these hours of bliss. The world around him was burning with fires excited by the low, ignoble passions of fallen man. It was groaning under a heavy load of suffering that was increasing day by day. How could this plight be ended? This thought filled him with compassion. He sat sad and mute. Then his compassionate heart would melt in a deep real sympathy for the down-trouble humanity. Thus swayed by these two opposite moods, Guru Nanak passed his days, pining for the time when he would not only make the whole human race partakers of the Boundless Joy that filled his heart and soul to the very core, but when he would himself share and lighten the burden of grief and suffering, of passion and anguish, that was crushing the very life of men. The supreme call of humanity and God was ever ringing in his soul. But the time for the response had not yet come.

BOYHOOD—SECULAR OCCUPATIONS

The Divine Cow-herd

His scholarstic career thus came to an early end. All the three teachers to whom he had been sent has acknowledged him their teacher. He had learnt a little from all of them no doubt, but had taught them a good deal more. Mehta Kalu was puzzled. His only son had shown aversion to qualifying himself for earning a living. At last he thought within himself, "Nanak loves to live in the forests. He is fond of solitude. Why not send him to tend cattle? He will be free to roam and muse, and will also to engaged in some useful work. Perhaps he may take to this sort of work and be able to eke out a living, howsoever humble."

Guru Nanak was anxious to obey and please his father as far as he could. It was no lack of such hearty intention that provided his father with food for grief. It was the strong, mysterious urge for the great duty charged with which he had come into the world that took him captive in the midst of his secular occupations. It was the vision of the great humane task which waited him that made him merge deep in soul-stirring thought. It was the call of the care-laden, suffering humanity that permitted him no leisure for the tasks that his father would yoke him to.

So, when his father told him what his new task was to be, Guru Nanak gladly obeyed. Thus for a time the great World-teacher, who was to tend and feed with the bread of God the souls of men and lift and lead them to the Abode of the Infinite Lord, tended his father's cattle. As they grazed in the forest, he would sit or roam as duty would demand or as his impulse would dictate. He had ample opportunities of giving reins to his master passion. Nature, with all her grandeur and beauty, was now his companion for the whole day. He was happy. Every evening he returned home with a joyous beaming face. This pleased the heart of Mehta Kalu. His only son, who had played almost a truant at school, was now taking to an occupation which, thought not likely to yield honour and riches, could yet be honest and profitable.

In tune with the Infinite

For some time things went on all right. One day, as he sat under a tree, opening out his heart and soul to the Beloved that he found pervading the wide stretch of Nature before him, his eyes closed. The Great Charmer had entered his heart and locked Himself in. Guru Nanak became thus captive in the life-giving embrace of his Beloved Lord. He saw nothing, he heard nothing, he thought nothing of the outer world. The cattle grazeed as they would. They strayed into a neighbour's field. The owner of the field drove out the cattle and came in great rage to the place where Guru Nanak sat in the lap of his Maker. Finding him 'asleep', he began to mutter, "What a wary herdsman, this! Himself he sleep and lets his cattle graze at will and ruin poor people's crops. Little does he realize the grief that grips the hearts of us tillers of the soil when our crops, raised with great toil and labour, are thus ruined by stray cattle. See how free of care he sleeps! Get thou up, O sluggard!"

Guru Nanak came to himself. He uttered *'Dhann Nirankar,* O Sublime, Formless Lord,' and opened his eyes. He saw the farmer and heard his remonstrances. With smile on his lips he said, "Let go, my friend. Be not enraged. What it God's dumb creatures have taken a few bites from thy crops? The Bountiful Lord who is the creator not only of thyself and thy fields and crops, but also for these cattle, will bless you with plenty. You will have no cause to grieve." But the owner of the field was not to be appeased. He took the Divine Child to Rai Bular and told him of what had happened. The by-standers informed the Rai that Mehta Kalu's son was rather insane; hence there was no good remonstrating with him. So the Mehta was sent for. Rai Bular told him to compensate the farmer for the damage done to his crops. We can imagine what must have passed in the heart of the father. His only son having proved a 'failure' at school, had now done something worse. He had made him receive a public reproach from is employer. There was also the compensation that had to be paid. The Divine Child read the mind of his father. He addressed Rai Bular and said, "But before pronouncing judgment, would not examine the crops that are said to have been damaged? God is merciful. How could a few bites by His creatures be the cause of injury to a poor man's crop?" The Rai sent his men. They came running back and said, "The crop is untouched. It seems richer and greener in the place where this man reported the cattle to have caused a damage."

Rai Bular Enters the Path

All were astonished. The Rai, who had already heard of Guru Nanak's budding greatness and of his having taught his teachers, besought the Divine Child to grant him a little light. "You are surely a Yogi," said the Rai, "an ascetic or a great saint. Give me a little of this great gift."

Guru Nanak, with half-shut eyes, and in a soft, sweet voice, sang a Divine Song which may be freely translated as under :

Let Yogis practise Yoga; let the Epicureans enjoy their fill; let the Penitents practise penance and rub and bathe themselves in holy waters. They lack the inner vision. I would have none of their manifold practices. Thy call, O Beloved Lord of all, doth ever ring in my heart. I hear Thy call every moment of my life. Other can hear it, too. All can hear it, if they will. Let a man retire within himself, sit in quiet thought and sing the praises of the All-pervading Lord. Then will be surely hear the Divine call. But if a man knew how to do this rightly, he would not sit idle. He will know that whatever he soweth that shall he reap; whatever be earneth that shall he enjoy. So he must engage himself in good and useful deeds. At the same time, he should ever remember and praise the Lord. He should engrave the Name of the Lord on the tablet of his soul. Then will he be honoured in the life to come. There his condition will depend on his acts in this life. Every breath that is drawn without the thought of God is wasted in vain. This body, this life, is of no use if it is not well used in the twofold path of performing good and useful deeds and making a constant remembrance of God the habit of the soul."*

Rai Bular bowed. Others who had the ears to hear the divine message of Guru Nanak also bowed. All went their way. The field which was the cause of all this is now the site of a Gurdwara called the *Kiara Sahib* or the Sacred Field.

The Sacrificial Thread

Kalu now rejoiced to see his son ever in high spirits. Guru Nanak seemed to be taking a keen interest in his occupation. He enjoyed it. The father thanked his stars for this change in his son. He resolved to invest him with the Hindu sacrificial thread. The day was fixed. All friends, relatives, neighbours, and religious men of the locality were invited. When the preliminary rites had been performed, the family priest, Hardial, lifted his hand to put the thread round Guru Nanak's' neck. People were getting ready words of congratulations which were usually showered on the child's father on such occasions. But a surprise was in store for all of them. With a loving, thoughtful smile playing on his lips, the Divine child caught the priest's uplifted hand and asked, "What are you about, dear pandit?" Hardial replied, "This is the sacred thread by wearing which thou wilt be admitted to the position of the Twice-born. Without it a man is a Sudra. This thread will give the honour both here and hereafter. So let me it round thy neck."

"How", said Nanak, "can this thread of thine made from cotton give one honour in the life to come? It remains with the body. It does not accompany the soul in its long journey after death. There every one goes threadless. Give me a thread that will really help my soul in the life to come."

"But," replied Hardial, "the great holy Rishis of old, who had a true knowledge of God as well as of the needs of the soul in its journey to Him, have ordained the wearing of this triple thread for the Twice-born Hindus. They believed that it would help the wearer both in this life and the next. Moreover, if this thread will not satisfy you, what sort of thread would you have? Whence has it to be had?"

The Thread for the Soul

"That I can tell thee," replied the Divine child. "The lasting, sacred thread for the soul should be made from a realization in practical life of noble, lofty ideals of true religion and morality. Let mercy be the cotton, contentment the threat, purity the knots, and truth the needed twist. Blend these virtues together in the every-day life. Thereby the soul will be invested with a threat which will never get old or dirty, burnt or lost, and which will never break. A man who has such a thread round his neck is truly blessed. He needs no other thread. So, not this thread for me which can be had from the bazar so cheap and which gets old, dirty and broken."

Hardial felt his wisdom and learning failing him. To be thus put out by a child in the presence of that pig gathering was too much for him. He had hoped that Guru Nanak would be a great apostle of the decaying Hindu religion. But here was a rude shock for him. Nanak had refused to respect the Hindu initiation ceremony. So he mustered courage and said, "Dear child, we must respect the custom initiated by the great Rishis. A Hindu without the this thread is a man without a religion. I am sure you are to be a man of religion. So wear the thread."

"What religion does thy thread give to the wearer? Around me I see that men who pride themselves on being Twice-born, and round whose necks this cotton threat has been put by learned Brahmins, are committing the foulest deeds. They rob and kill, lie and deceive, give reins to lust and greed, and commit a thousand sins and crimes against their fellow creatures. Their souls are polluted to the core. Is this the religion which they thread has given them? What a religion! I would have none of it."

"True," replied and Brahmin, "people have fallen in character. This thread used to be the mark of a lofty, religious life. This is has ceased to be to a great extent. Still, the remedy lies not in discarding the ancient custom but in reforming men's character. So come, please. Don't shake your head. Do you think all the rishis of old, and all your sires besides, have been mere fools? If this thread does not please you, what sort of thread would you have?"

"I have told you this already. The true thread is to be had by the acquisition and practice of noble qualities, by praising God, and by leading a life of an ever-constant, unbroken consciousness of his presence in and around us everywhere. By realizing the Will of the Supreme Lord in his daily life does a man obtain a thread on which he can rely with confidence. The thread thus obtained will be truly the thread of the soul. It was never get old or fall away. It will ever accompany the wearer in this life and the next. It will take him into the presence of the Blissful Lord and win for him a place of honour in His court. Such a threat would I gladly wear."

The Brahmin could argue no longer. So he said, "What you have said is all true. We are truly without a true thread of the soul; we would wear that too. But you are without a thread of the body. Wear it now, and then we all can strive to have a thread for the soul, too."

All Go Threadless

"Are you sure", said the Divine child, "that even your bodies have the needed string? I find none anywhere. There is no string to blind the sexual organs and restrain them from lust and vice; there is no string to hands and feet which could keep them from evil doing; there is no string for the tongue, nor one for the eyes which would keep them from sensual, sinful pleasures. Yes, the whole body has no string. Nay, the whole community is going threadless. Mark the consequent degradation all round. How high you hold your head in pride of your high caste. The thread has verily proved a curse for the community. Having engendered caste pride, it has broken asunder all ties of union, and chains are now around your necks. All this because you wear not the true thread. Yet you would spin threads of cotton, and, assembling all in one place, enjoy a feast, and put threads, false and now positively harmful, round the necks of others. What a huge joke! And what an unheared of wonder! People who are blind in the soul pose as seers and come audaciously forward to guide others over paths which they themselves cannot see. I for one will not follow such a guide."

Hardial was rendered speechless. All present felt how true was all that the Divine child had said or hinted at. His analysis of the fall of the Hindu community and the advent of tyranny and political subjection was felt to be right. The Brahmin and others, who had come to invest the Divine child with the sacred thread, realized that they themselves were threadless. Hardial bowed to the child and said, "True, child. Our community has fallen very low. There is no help. Each of us should try to save his soul. Who is there to take up the risky, arduous task of uplifting a downtrodden, subject race?"

Who Should Save ?

Guru Nanak's eyes flashed with a heavenly luster and, in the next instant, softly closed. He took a deep breadth and sang, "When the Lord in His Mercy sends Grace to a man. He puts him to the task that He would get performed. It is not for us to choose. That servant and that alone can serve the Lord whom He chooses to follow His commands and to carry out His Will. By obeying his behests, by carrying out His Will, the servant will win His satisfaction and get a place of honour in the Lord's palace. If he does what pleases his Lord, he will certainly obtain all that in his heart he may wish or desire. He would become acceptable to the Father above and, having performed his allotted task in the world, would enter the court divine arrayed in honour."

The Brahmin and the rest had to go away, musing within themselves on the 'miracle' that they had witnessed.

The Twofold Duty

For sometime more the Divine child continued tending his father's cattle as best as he could. He wanted to be a dutiful son and obey his earthly father. But there was the heavenly Father, too, who was every beckoning him to undertake the great task for which He had sent him into the world. This call of the Bewitching Lord come uncalled and at old moments. When it came, the Divine child was gripped like a captive. And the cattle? Well, they grazed where they liked, tended by gods and angels, as the Divine child sat in the lap of his Father. This communion with the Blissful Lord affected the child's visible life. His heart and soul gushed with a strange, abiding joy. He would sing his Master's glory in verses whose appeal went straight in the core of the heart. He held discourses with all who would. To all be appeared to be an active lad with a religious bent of mind.

Nature Sevens and Shades Him

At he sat in the forest, one day, the Divine fingers invisibly touched the strings of his heart; a delicious, inaudible melody broke forth, filled his whole being, and lifted and bound him to the Lotus feet of the Bewitching Lord. For long did he remain in that posture. Then he lay down to rest. The day passed on. The sun descended well to the west. The shadows of the trees veered round to the east. But the sun's rays touched not the body of the Divine youth as he lay there in their path. Something invisible had intervened between him and the sun. It seemed that the shadow of the tree and remained stationary. Rai Bular passing by in the afternoon witnessed this "miracle." On another occasion, while the cattle grazed in the forest tended by gods and angels, Guru Nanak lay down under a tree. After sometime, though a space among the leaves and branches, the sun's rays began to fall on his face. A big, white cobra came out from its hole, spread its wide hood, and protected his face against the sun. By a strange accident Rai Bular passed again that way. As he beheld the cobra with the large out-stretched hood, the Rai's heart was filled with fear lest the youthful saint should be bitten. But, as he hastily approached the place, the cobra smoothly crept away. Guru Nanak awoke. Rai Bular was standing mute in wonder. He had heard much about Mehta Kalu's son but now he had seen far more. He found that the whole Nature, animate and inanimate, loved the Divine youth and did him service and homage. And it could not have been otherwise. He beheld the Creator ever indwelling in all His creation. He was one with Nature and her indwelling Lord. How could Nature let a part and parcel of herself and a dear one of her Lord be exposed to uncomfortable heat? The allembracing love that ever flowed from his heart had charmed the cobra out of its hole and made it shield him with its hood. He had given himself up wholly to the Lord of the Universe and, by His Will, the whole universe was now at his service.

Rai Bular's heart was won. He hugged the youthful saint to his bosom. A sweet, abiding peace and joy filled his heart. He took the youth with him to Mehta Kalu and congratulated him on having such a one of his son. He advised him not to reproach the youth for his indifference to his worldly affairs.

Strange Passive Mood

Days passed on. Guru Nanak gave up tending cattle. A strange, passive mood overcame him. He would either sit alone all day long in the forest, seek out sadhus and have discussions with them, or lie at home, apparently in dejected spirits. For days he would eat nothing. Sometimes he would sing his matchless Divine songs, at others he would shed tears of joy and sorrow. People said that his insanity had now become fully developed. Others, more religious minded, said that his heart had become completely estranged from the world. He would soon renounce his home and be a full-fledged recluse. All attempts made by his fond father and mother to persuade him out of this dejection proved abortive. When they represented to him the necessity of his taking to agriculture, or some trade, he replied that he had already sown the crops to raise and distribute which he had come into the world; he had already begun the trade by which he was to buy out the souls of men from the bondage of sorrow and suffering, from the cycle of life and death. When his mother said that, to disprove the people's talk of his having become insane, he should give up for a few days his religious preoccupation and take to some work, he replied that he could not live even a moment without repeating the Name. He would die the instant that he forgot the Lord and gave up communion with Him. When he was asked to eat and drink, he said that he had but one hunger—that for the true Lord. He was ever striving to satisfy that craving of his soul. He felt no physical hunger or thirst, no discomfort of any kind. How could he forget the True Lord who sustains the whole creation?

A Physician Sent for

For four days at a stretch Guru Nanak lay at home. He spoke with none. He ate or drank nothing. His people thought that something was wrong with his system. A physician was sent for. As he held Guru Nanak's wrist to feel the pulse, the latter smiled a winsome smile, withdrew his arm and said, "What are you about, my friend?" The physician replied that, by feeling his pulse, he was going to diagnose his trouble. He would then prescribe a suitable remedy. The smile on the lips of the Divine child waxed more bright. In a sweet, melodious voice he sang,

> "The physician has been called his art to show;
> Gripping my arm my pulse doth he try;
> But alas, the simple physician doth not know
> That the pain in my heart doth lie."

(Var Malar)

"Go home" continued he, "thou are ill-fitted to know what ails me."

"Then describe thy symptoms thyself. Let me know thy trouble, and I shall choose a proper remedy."

The Real Pain

"O simple physician, don't trouble thyself. Give me no medicine, for no medicine of thine, my friend, can remove the pain that I feel or the suffering that my body undergoes. What ails me, do you ask? Listen. The acutest pain that grips my heart and soul is the sense of separation from my Beloved Lord. Then there is the constant, unsatisfied hunger for His Name that tortures me with its pangs. Still another of my troubles that ever gnaws at my heart is the thought of death. All these pains consume my body and make me pine away. What medicine is there is thy stock against the disease which springs from a forget-fulness of the True Lord and a devotion to sensual pleasures? How can you cure the wicked, blind heart which has thus brought on itself an endless punishment? Thy medicines could perhaps cure the ailments of the flesh and could be taken as long as there is life in it. They have no effect on the soul. I'll tell thee a never-failing medicine which can make the body as bright as gold and the soul most pure and serene. Name, the Blissful Name of the Glorious Lord, is the all curing medicine. Take in but ever so little of this precious drug and thou wilt find thy body and soul not only freed of all pain and suffering, but also rendered pure, radiant, and strong. Gladly shall I take such a medicine if thou hast one, my friend. Physician, first heal thyself; then freely go about healing others."

The Physician Healed

As he said this, he fixed his loving, penetrating look into the eyes of the physician. A quiver went through the body of the letter. He felt that he, and no Guru Nanak, was in need of a remedy. And he had got it. That look and those words had done their work. The physician was healed by the patient, he bowed and went away in silence, musing over the words of the strange youth. He was convinced that the Divine youth for whom he had come to prescribe would heal and render whole the ailing bodies, the aching lacerated hearts, and the afflicted souls of his fellowmen. Before going he said to Mehta Kalu, "Cheer up, good sir, your son is a great one. He is not ill. He has come to heal mankind."

THE UNPARDONABLE OFFIENCE

The Two Phrases

For three months Guru Nanak remained in that passive listless mood. He ate little, he spoke little, and he moved little. His parents were naturally anxious about their only son whom *Pandits* and *Mullas* had failed to teach, whom the physician had failed to heal, and in whom all had discovered signs of some mysterious greatness of which they, his parents, had no inkling. They were helpless, however. They sighed and kept quiet.

The phase then ended. Guru Nanak, who was a youth of about sixteen now, threw aside the lethargy which had, to all appearances, possessed him for over three months. He began to move about, to associate and talk with youths of his own age, and to eat and drink as an ordinary healthy man. His parents were glad. They thought that their son had recovered from the mysterious illness which had laid him how for three long months.

Set to Make a Good Bargain

Mehta Kalu now thought that it was time to make his son engage in some trade or business. So he called Guru Nanak into his presence and said, "Son, it is time that you should learn to earn a living. You have proved a failure at school and also as a cowherd. What will you do? You are no child now. We hope to see you married in the near future Unless you learn a profitable trade, how will you support your family and your parents who are getting old? I have thought of a plan. I shall give you a small sum. With that you should make a good, profitable bargain, I would suggest that to begin with, you should purchase from near-abouts articles that can be sold at a profit here. When, after a few trips you get experienced, and also lay by a little capital, you can go further abroad and engage in greater bargains. How do you like the proposal?"

Guru Nanak replied, "Father, I long to obey and please you. If I fail, it is not for lack of effort or intention. Some mysterious force take hold of me. I shall try my best to do as you bid me."

Men of God in Need of Food

So Guru Nanak was given sum of twenty rupees and told to make a good bargain with it. Bala, a trusted servant of the Mehta, accompanied him. The two started towards Chuharkana, a village about twelve miles from Talwandi. As they wended their way, they noticed a cluster of trees. Guru Nanak turned his steps in that direction. Why? The same mysterious power which ever swayed his body and soul was now directing his steps. He was going to make a mighty good bargain. Bala followed him. In that cluster of trees they found a company of Sadhus. These men of religion had no covering for their bodies excepting the loin-cloths. They were all engaged in diverse forms of penance. Their bodies were weak and lean. Guru Nanak approached one of them and began to talk with him. He learn that the Sadhus had no food for the last several days. Their vows forbade them to go and beg for food. They were given to roaming about the halting in secluded places, away from the haunts of men. In their too great concern for the soul they were altogether neglecting their body. For physical sustenance they relied on God. They were content to eat when and whatever He was pleased to send. The Divine youth was deeply impressed by their faith and trust in God. The pangs of hunger that they had born for several days made a powerful appeal to his heart. He felt the money in his pocket. Here were men of God in great need of food. How could he pass by them unconcerned with a sum in his pocket that could satisfy their want? His compassionate heart urged him to decide and act at once. Could there be a better bargain than that of feeding hungry mouths? He took the money from his pocket and placed it before the Sadhu. The latter declined to touch it. "You are a young man yet," said the Sadhu. "Perhaps your parents may not like this act of yours and you may have to suffer in consequence. You need not worry about us. God, whom we seek and serve, and in whom we trust, will send us food when it pleases Him. We can wait till then."

"Don't mind what happens to me," said Guru Nanak. "I shall bear it. The body has to be ruled by the soul and not the soul by the body. My soul is touched at the sight of your sufferings, voluntary as they are. I can't go away without doing what I can to allay them. God seems to have sent me hither for this very purpose."

Strikes the Good Bargain

The Sadhu thereupon, told the Divine youth that money was of no use to them. They would not touch it. He should, if he was so inclined, bring them articles of food. So Guru Nanak and his companion went and purchased as much provisions as could be had for the sum and carried them to the ascetics. They broke their several days, fast and blessed the youth whom God had sent to feed them. The place where the hungry mouths were fed by Guru Nanak is the site of a Gurdwara called the *Khara Sauda* or the Good Bargain.

The Sacred Tent

Having invested his capital in a bargain which to him appear to be the best and the most profitable, Guru Nanak retraced his steps towards Talwandi. His whole being was related with joy and satisfaction. He had fed the hungry and done his duty by man and God. As they approached Talwandi, Guru Nanak's thoughts reverted to his father. "He sent me to make a good bargain. I was obeyed him according to my own light and capacity. But he will not understand this. He will think that I have thrown away his money. He will be angry. Why not keep away from his wrath as long as possible?" So he sent Bhai Bala to the village but himself he stayed out. He sat concealed under a tree and passed the night there. In the morning Mehta Kalu came to know of the return of Bala. He was naturally perplexed at the non-appearance of his son. He guessed what it meant. Summoning Bala into his presence, he enquired about his son. Bala told him the whole story and added, "I pleaded with him, but he would not listen. He said that he was obeying you. When, last evening, we came near the village, he concealed himself near the tank as perhaps he had began to fear your anger. I did my duty and am not to blame."

The Beating

Mehta Kalu's anger knew no bounds. He ran to the place, dragged out his son from under the hanging branches of the tree, and began to slap him, right and left, till his cheeks were black and blue with the beating. Thus did the Master suffer for having taken pity on the fellowmen. He bore the slaps of his found, worldly father with an unruffled quiet, offering each cheek in turn to receive the fast-falling blows. He showed no anger, he offered no resistance, he evaded no slap. Without a mummer, he let his body bear the consequences of the noble act performed in obedience to its master, the soul.

Rai Bular's Grief

Rai Bular heard of this incident. He had already become an ardent admirer and a true disciple of the Master. When he heard that the Divine youth had been beaten black and blue by Mehta Kalu, very sad was he. He sent for the Mehta and said, "What have you done? Why did you beat this holy man? And what a beating! Look at his cheeks where your hands have played havoc! Didn't I tell you never to ill-treat this great man? You always think of him as your son. You fail to understand him. Was it for twenty rupees that your ire was so excited? You could have double that some from me. You shouldn't have beaten your only son for that. What a father you have proved!"

Mehta Kalu's Remonstrances

Mehta Kalu felt that all present were wrongly accusing him of greed and hard-heartedness. He had to defend and justify himself. So he said "Rai Sahib, it does not become me to gainsay what you say. But you yourself in my place and see how painful it is. He is my only son; hence my sorrow at his foolish conduct is all the greater. He has proved a failure at school. He was too idle to be a good cowherd. He paid no heed to agriculture. He gives away my humble earnings to idlers and beggars. He is of age to look about for a means of livelihood. I sent him to earn something by making a good, profitable bargain. And what has he done? He has thrown away me hard-earned money. The sum is not very big, no doubt. But his has shown me which way the wind blows. He will waste away all that I have earned or shall earn. This thought allows me no rest. It made me angry. As his father, it was my duty to correct him. So I gave him a few slaps. He will behave better in future. Yet you reproached me for having done my duty by him. You may, sir, but you should rather pity me."

Rai Bular's Warning

Rai Bular answered, "Short-sighted Kalu, when will your eyes begin to see? He is not an ordinary man to behave like ordinary people. He has great things to do He has not disobeyed you even. He has carried out your orders to the letter. You sent him to make a good and profitable bargain. That he did. What better bargain could there be? I shall pay you the sum so well invested by him. I wish I could take him to my house and be a slave unto him. But the prevalent usage forbids it. People will talk. Take heed, Mehta. If you ill-treat him again, I shall devise means to get him away from you."

The Unpardonable Offence

The incredulous Mehta was astonished at what seemed to him the simplicity of Rai Bular. But to dispute the point further would have been injudicious. He kept quiet and went away. For some days all went well. The Divine youth was allowed to live as he pleased. He, too, did nothing that could excite the Mehta's anger. But how long could that be? How could the Divine call be silenced or put down? How could the ever-tuned harp of his godly, human, sensitive heart be made dull and irresponsive to the divine melody and the still, sad music of humanity which, for him, surcharged the very air that he breathed? Sometime after, as he was returning home after a bath, he met a mendicant who begged alms from him in name of God. An appeal made in the name of his Lord by a poor, homeless man was too strong for him to resist. He gave the beggar a drinking vessel of brass which he had in his hand and a ring of gold which was on his finger. Mehta Kalu came to know of it. He was exasperated. He bade his son either mend his ways or leave his house.

Rai Bular's Deep Concern

Rai Bular was by now a discipline-in-spirit of Guru Nanak. He heard of the fresh estrangement between the father and son. It made him sad. It set him thinking how best to put an end to these vexatious family quarrels, how best to secure for the Guru a life where he could freely follow the dictates of his heart and soul. He was convinced that as long as Guru Nanak lived with his well-meaning but worldly-wise father, there could be no end to such troubles. It was necessary that Guru Nanak should go somewhere else.

The Rai was thus on the look-out for a suitable lace where he could persuade his Master to go, when an event occurred which promised to solve the problem. Bhai Jai Ram, who was the husband of Bebe Nanaki and a Diwan at the court of Daulat Khan Lodi of Sultanpur, came on a visit to Talwandi. He heard the bitter complaints of his father-in-law against, the idle, squandering habits of Guru Nanak. He heard of the sort of life that Guru Nanak then lived and the great respect in which he was held by many people of the village. He also met Rai Bular who complained of the ill-treatment which Guru Nanak got from his father. They put their heads together and decided that Diwan Jai Ram should find a job for Guru Nanak at Sultanpur and then send for him there. Mehta Kalu gladly agreed. Guru Nanak gave his consent to go when called.

AT SULTANPUR

Divine Storekeeper

Diwan Jai Ram soon succeeded in the mission. So he wrote the promised letter inviting the Guru to Sultanpur. Guru Nanak took leave of his parents and friends and started towards the city of his sister. A few days after his arrival there he was introduced to the Governor of the place. Daulat Khan was pleased at the learning, manner, and bearing of the youth. He gave him a dress of honour in token of having engaged him in the service and put him in change of his *Modikhana* or Storehouse.* Guru Nanak applied himself to his new duties in right food earnest. They were admirably suited to the inclinations of his temperament. He had to deal our provisions. He had ample opportunities of satisfying his master passion, that of open-handed charity. But he was careful not to give away more than what his own pay and allowance could meet. His scrupulously honest, amiable, and straightforward dealings with all who got or bought rations from the Storehouse soon won for him the good opinion of all. He came to be greatly esteemed by all who came in touch with him.

The good report reached the Nawab, too. He came to have full confidence in the storekeeper about whom all spoke so highly.

The Song of Dedication

While executing so well the duties of his office, Guru Nanak did not neglect or forget his divine duties. He was in tune with the Lord now as ever before. He would get up early, about a watch before day-break, and go out into the neighbouring forest to enjoy an un-interrupted communion with the Lord of the Universe. He would bathe in the little stream called *Vein.* Then siting on its banks, he would dive deep into the ocean of ecstasy, and fly on the wings of the soul to the lotus feet of the Blissful Lord. As he watched the heavens above, in set with countless sparkling, twinkling starry gems, as he observed their reflection in the heaving bosom of the slow-moving stream, as he beheld. Nature all around him clothed in a blissful peace, as the cool breeze from the stream gently fanned his worshipful face, a heavenly calm descended upon his heart, a thrill of quiet, refreshing joy imperceptibly passed through his whole being, and his soul expanded to engulf the whole universe in its embrace of love. He sat there charmed by the sublimity of all that he heard, felt, or saw. He would sit their for long, wrap in mute adoration. Then the bliss that filled him through and through would break forth into heavenly music. He would sing the praises of the Lord. This continued till the rise of the sun. Then he would return to his worldly duties. There, too while his body was engaged in the performance of his work, his heart and soul were with his Maker. It is recorded that when, in weighing out rations, he reached the number thirteen—*tera*—, he would pause, his face would assume a look of strange intoxication, and he would several times repeat, in his sweet melodious voice, the world *tera* which also means, "Thine, All is Thine O Lord." If the persons to whom the grain had to be dealt out happened to be poor customers, he would go on weighing it out to them and count each weighing as *tera* or thirteen. Blessed indeed were they on whom was thus bestowed unasked divine food for the soul as they came to have the food for the body! This simple song of dedication composed of one world charmed the hearers. As long as he sang, they all stood mute and spell-bound. In the evening he would retire again to the forest and give himself up to an enjoyment of blissful communion with the Lord. His love for the company of religious men—Sadhus and Faqirs—was fresh and strong as ever. He loved to feat all ascetics and wandering faqirs who came to the city.

Marriage Plans

His open-handed charity won him the love of the poor and the needy. But his sister and brother-in-law felt uneasy; for he was not saving much out of his earnings. They knew that his father would be distressed to learn that his son was throwing away on beggars and faqirs all that the earned. They put their heads together and devised a plan whereby he could probably be induced to be less free with his earnings. They decided to marry him. They were afraid lest the religious zeal which by then was quite clearly visible in his nature should become too strong and lead him to renounce the world altogether and become a recluse. So they decided to yoke him to family life. They believed that conjugal affection would cure him of the slight 'waywardness' which his too frequent meetings with Sadhus had produced in his temperament. All that love and consideration which till then he had been bestowing on others would be diverted towards his wife and children. He would become a thrifty man of the world, laying by a good part of his earnings for the upkeep of his family. They knew how happy Mehta Kalu would be on hearing the good news of his son's reversion to real family life.

Thus did the fond relatives hope to wean him from that life of spirit to which he had come to lead all men. Thus would they imprison in the family circle the affections that were to flow for the whole human race; thus would they tie down with family ties the spirit that was to break the chains from round the necks of millions of his fellow creatures; thus would they enchain his should that even then was given to fly as freely as a bird in the skies and dive deep into the fathomless ocean of ecstasy. They might as well have tried to hold the winds in their grip or bidden the waves of the sea to be still. Even Guru Nanak himself was powerless to resist, divert, or withstand the divine call. When it came, he was himself no longer. In fact, he lived ever in the arms of the Beloved Lord even as a fish ever lives in the bosom of the river or lake. To use his own words, "He was in love with God; he lived, moved, and had his being in the Lord. In his love he would laugh, in his love he would weep and cry like a child, and in His love he would sit dumb and mute. He cared for none except his true, beloved Master at whose door he ever begged for the food of the body and spirit, and partook of it when He was pleased to bestow it."* Not for himself alone was he gathering the spiritual treasures, but for the whole human race.

Marriage

Still Guru Nanak's was to be a path difference from the paths known to the world before. He was to show how true life of religion could be lived amid the ties and duties of family life. So he agreed to get married. At the age of about nineteen he was married to Mala Sulakhni, the daughter of Baba Mula, a resident of Batala in the present district of Gurdaspur. But the marriage was powerless to divert his heart and soul from the path that he had come to lay down for humanity. He tried to be as considerate a husband as was consistent with his life of the spirit.

Mardana gets a Wedding Gift

His parents had come to see him married. They were glad to learn that their son had, by a dilligent discharge of his duties, earned a good name and was to all apperances on a good way to riches. They were happy to hope that thenceforth he would give up his infatuation for Sadhus and Faqirs and divert that love to his wife and family. His loving companions of Talwandi who had become enamoured of him had also come. The first among them was Mardana, the musician. He asked the Master for a wedding gift and got a *rabab* or rebeck. What with his own inborn aptitude for music, and what with the loving favour of his Divine Master, Mardana turned out to be a peerless musician and singer. He would play on the rebeck as the Guru sang his spontaneous divine songs in a sweet melodious voice, or he would sweetly sing those songs stored in a tenacious memory as the Master sat in mute adoration. Others also came. A regular *satsang* gathered there. The Guru fed them all out of the rations that were permitted him with his salary. He had no liking for boarding. His distributed all he got. To many of the persons who had followed him from Talwandi he procured some or other employment at Sultanpur. They were, all of them, his disciples. They adored him. In the evenings all assembled to listen to the divine songs and discourses of the master. Out of them Bahi Bhagirath and Bahi Mansukh are still remembered for their love and devotion to the Guru, Mansukh was the first person to record the Divine songs of the master as they were song by him.

Ideal Life for Youth

Time passed quietly by. Guru Nanak seemed at last to have found an occupation that in every way satisfied him. He seemed to have grown out of his early aversion to the affairs of the world. He seemed to have arranged a compromise between his own love for seclusion and his parents' desire for a busy worldly life for him. He was proving to be an honest and capable employee, a loving and generous friend, a neighbour inspired by active sympathy for all, a citizen of free open-handed charity, an excellent householder, and a pious, holy man of religion. Two sons were born to him, the first, Sri Chand, in 1494, and the second, Lakhmi Das, in 1497 A.D. Respected by the public, trusted and honoured by his employer, loved by his disciples and companions, and adored by his wife, he lived a life of happiness and peace. This seemed to be the ideal life for a young man. But Guru Nanak had a higher mission. The sad still music, the plaintive voice of poor, afflicted humanity that he ever heard in the soul would sometimes catch him in the midst of his songs or reveries. Tears would flow down his cheeks. A quiver would run through his body. A yearing for making an immediate responses to the call of humanity overcame him at such times. He would wish to go at once and cool and soothe the burning world. But the time was not yet. The Divine call had not yet come. He was to wait for that. A circle of disciples gathered round him at Sultanpur, and he contended himself for the time being with kindling their spirits with the heavenly spark that he had got as a gift from God.

Malicious Reports

Evil natures would discover faults even in the faultless. The frame of Guru Nanak excited jealousy in some evil breasts. Some did not like his 'thoughtless' charity; others disliked his free association with men of all castes and creeds; some did not relish his iconoclastic religious views which he disseminated with effective zeal; others could not bear to hear him praised by religious-minded Hindus and Muslims alike; some were jealous because of his being held in high esteem by the Nawab. They did what they thought would ruin his credit with the Nawab, put an end to his charities, and thereby push him to the background. They reported to the Nawab that the storekeeper was squandering away the contents of the storehouse. It would be empty in no time. Twice of thrice, on the basis of such reports, the Nawab checked the accounts. Every time some balance was found due to the Divine storekeeper. One time Guru Nanak was even kept confined in a room pending the examination of his accounts. That room is now the site of a Gurdwara called *Kothari Sahbi* or the Sacred Cell. Each time Guru Nanak's credit with the Nawab increased till the latter gave up listening to the evil reports of ill-meaning persons.

THE CALL

Waiting for the Call

For ten years or so Guru Nanak thus demonstrated to the world that he had come to teach, namely, how a man of religion, loving and serving God through a loving service of his creation, should live in the world, for the world, and yet be above the world—laughing, enjoying, making merry, eating and drinking, and performing all the duties of an official, a householder, and a man of the world, and yet maintaining, all the time, an attitude of aloofness, detachment, and renunciation towards the alluring things of the world; keeping ever in tune with the Infinite Lord. By precept and example, by his divine touch, he initiated many into this life of the Spirit. But for how long could the bush conceal the sun? How could Talwandi or Sultanpur monopolize the precious divine commodity which was meant for the whole world? He was not to save only a few hundred people of these two places. Humanity called him to be its saviour. There was an anguish in the voice of humanity, the confused murmur that arose from the human depths and that, comprising in it all tears, all agonies, all afflictions, became the sigh of the whole creation, a sigh for one who would end the suffering and make all happy and full of joy. Night and day the call of humanity would quietly steal into his heart and, gathering force and volume, grow into a loud lament as that of a child left all alone and lost in a vast, limitless wilderness. But he was waiting for the call from above. He would go forth when bidden. The call came at last.

Drowned?

One day, in the year 1497 A.D. he went out to bathe as usual in the stream. An attendant sat near his clothes. He plunged into the stream, at the place since called the *Sant Ghat*. He delayed too long that day. The servant waited in great anxiety. He then looked into and along the stream, but there was no sign of Guru Nanak. At last the servant sadly concluded that his master must have been drowned. He went and informed Jai Ram. Soon, he news spread in the town. The Nawab also heard it. People flocked to the river. The Nawab also reached the spot. Divers were ordered to search for the body. They failed. All returned to the city in great sorrow.

Why and Where Gone?

His disappearance caused evil tongues to be busy again. It was said that he had squandered away the contents of the store-house; that when he had found his position to have become irretrievable, he had gone and drowned himself. These reports did not fail to reach the ears of the Nawab. He caused the provisions to be weighed, the cash to be counted, and the accounts to be examined. It was found that a handsome balance was due to the Guru. This confounded the people. "Why then has he gone? Where has he gone?" Such questions were on everybody's lips, but there was none who could answer them.

As Bhai Gurdas States it

Well, where had he gone? Not an easy matter for the like of us to comprehend or explain. The earliest record of the event is found in the poetical works of Bhai Gurdas. This great Sikh savant was initiated into the Faith By Guru Amardas, the third Guru. He had thus ample opportunities of meeting many Sikhs who had seen Guru Nanak and had lived with him. We also know that Bhai Gurdas presented his compositions to Guru Arjan Dev who studied them critically. Guru Arjan Dev pronounced the works of Bhai Gurdas to be a key to the Guru Granth Sahib. So we can take it that whatever is recorded by Bhai Gurdas the approval of Guru Arjan Dev.

Bhai Gurdas refers to this event in the following words :

"Penance he did asutere beyond measure.
And lucky was he,
For the gracious Hari
Bestowed on him His fullest pleasure.
The Guru then reached the Gracious Lord's Eternal Seat,
Happy and swift,
And got the gift
Of priceless Name and of Humility sweet.
From there he fixed a steady, thoughtful gaze
On the world below;
What a scene of woe!
We found the earth in dreadful flames, ablaze.

No teacher or guide was there;
Chaotic dark was everywhere.
The whole creation
In deep agitation
Was raising a piteous, woeful moan,
Crying that a way in the dark he shown.
Donning a dress very oddly made
Forth he went, a path he laid
Of true renunciation:
And with determination
Strong he started a huge campaign
To better the world and end the pain."

This is then what Bhai Gudas has recorded about this event. We should bear in mind the fact that this had the approval of Guru Arjan Dev., the fifth Guru.

Puratan Janam Sakhi

The next record that we have of the Guru's life is what is called the Old Chronicle (*Puratan Janam Sakhi*), written about the year 1635 A.D., in the time of Guru Hargobind. In this chronicle the writer has tried to describe the events of the spiritual world in the language of this world. He says that as the Guru look a dip in the stream, angels from God bade him follow them. They took him into the presence of God. The Lord extended to him a cordial welcome and offered him a cup of nectar as a mark of His favour. He quaffed it with humble joy. The Guru was then charged with the duty of going forth into the world and showing the right way of life and worship to the fallen and miguided humanity. He was to remain uncontaminated by the world as before, but he was to exert his utmost to bring others on to the path which he had followed so well. In all this work he was promised to be ever blessed with divine grace and help. The Guru is represented to have humbly accepted the duty thus laid on him by his maker. He thanked and praised the Lord and stood mutely enjoying the Blissful Presence of the Lord. He was then conducted back into the waters of the stream. Full three earthly days had passed by then.

Guru Nanak's Divine Song

Among the Guru's own sacred Songs there is one which is generally believed by the faithful to describe this event. That song may be translated thus :

"A Ministerial out of work was I
To His work He did me apply.
The Mighty Lord to me did say,
'Sing my praises night and day.'
The Master summoned the Minstrel to His Eternal Abode
A robe of Name and eulogy true on me bestowed.
A cup of the Nectar of True Name

By His grace to me there came.
At the bidding of God I took me fill.
I gave me peace which fills me still.
All else can taste it if so, they will......." *(Majh ki Var)*

The Blissful State

Mucauliffe writes, "One day after bathing (Guru) Nanak disappeared in the forest, and was taken in a vision to God's presence." Whatever words we may choose, whatever picture we may form for our limited understanding, the fact remains that for three earthly days Guru Nanak was considered to have been lost or drowned. Listening to the myriads voices of Nature clothed in dawn, with the doleful, piteous moan of humanity ringing in his heart, the call of the Gracious Lord captivating his soul, a sort of charm having overspread his whole being, he went whether the Lord was pleased to draw him. Yes, listening to all these voices and hearkening to the Divine call, he went as far as the thick solitudes where nothing any longer comes to disturb the collected soul. There, away from all, in the eye of the Lord, he sat wrapt in mute adoration. Humanity's doleful cry was in his ears, in his heart and soul, in the form of a dismal song. 'It was the song of mystic bird. This song said, in marvellous modulations, all that man thinks and feels, all that he suffers, all that he seeks, all that falls short of fulfilment for him.' It summed up for him, in sweet harmonies, the destinies of living beings, the distressed agony of a flaming, passion-ridden world, and appealed to him, in the name of the imense pity that filled his soul, to go forth with his message of hope and liberation, and save the world. The song that rang in the heart, inaudible to the bodily ears, lifted his soul softly on light, strong wings, to the heights where dwells the Creator and Sustainer of the universe, and from where the soul can look downwards on the whole creation as on a map spread out. Once in the Blissful presence, Guru Nanak forgot all about earth, sky, and time; he forgot himself.

From this happy state Guru nanak returned when the Lord bade him. He went to the house where he used to take rest and lodge his disciples, guests and friends. All who saw him found that he was a changed man. He opened wide the doors and invited the poor to take away all that was there. To those who hesitated he himself handed over the articles that he found in the house.

A Man Possessed?

The news spread in the city. A large crowd of spectators assembled at the place. Nawab Daulat Khan also came. He enquired from Guru Nanak what had happened to him. But the Guru heard nothing and said nothing. He seemed to be in a strange intoxication, to be like a man possessed. People said that some evil spirit had possessed him. The Nawab shook his head in great sorrow and went away.

The call had come. Having given away all his material wealth to the poor, he was now ready to distribute, with an equally liberal and generous heart, the spiritual riches that he had received from his Lord. He went out in the wilderness. Mardana alone accompanied him with his rebeck.

THE RESPONSE

His Sister's Unfailing Faith

Even when Guru Nanak was generally believed to have been drowned, his sister, Bebe Nanki, had kept alive her faith in the divine nature of her brother. "Rivers can't drown him," she had said. Now, too, when all proclaimed that some evil spirit had come to posses her brother, who in consequence, had given away to the poor all that he had in the rest-house and would speak to none, her heart did not droop, her faith did not waver. "What evil spirit can posses him?" said she. "He has come to drive away the spirit of evil than possesses mankind."

The Exorcism

Some well-meaning, simple folk took a *Mulla* or Muslim priest to the place where Guru Nanak was sitting. The Mulla began to utter some spells and write down some holy words on a paper. This paper was to form an amulet which was to be hung round Guru Nanak's neck. The Guru smiled and sang :

"Crushed are the lives of those
Who write and sell the Name of God."

[*Var Sarang, Shlok* 20(1)]

The *Mulla* heeded not the Guru's objurgation, but continued uttering his incantations and writing out his charm. Having finished what he thought was necessary for the exorcism, he addressed the evil spirit which was supposed to have possessed the Guru and said, "Who art thou?" This was the usual question for such times. The *Mulla* believed that the spirit would speak, disclose his identity, and be prevailed upon to quit the sufferer. But he had a strange patient this time to deal with. The Guru replied,

"Some do call me an evil sprite,
Others in me do a demon descry,
Some declare me a luckless weight,
But Nanak the humble am I."

[*Rag Maru Shlok* 7 (1)]

The *Mulla* was convinced that no evil spirit possessed the Master. He made ready to retire. Other, near him then said that perhaps Guru's view are unconvincing. Thereupon the Guru made a sign to Mardana to play the rebeck and sang a song which may be translated thus :

"Mad is Nanak gone, O totally mad
But mad is he for the Bounteous Dad.
None save God doth the heed or know,
To none save Him doth allegiance show.
Only then may one truly mad be known,

When from fear of God hath his madness grown.
Only then is he mad in south, O brother,
When he doth one thing and doth no other—
Findeth his Master's Order and Will
And obeyeth Him steadily, cheerfully still.
The Will of God with him doth e'er prevail,
Wisdom of every sort be deemeth of little avail.
Then is man truly mad, O friend
His love doth God to him extend.
Unworthy and low doth he himself deem
And holdeth all else in high esteem.
Mad of this type hath Nanak grown
For the sake of Him do let him alone." *(Rag Maru)*

"No Hindu no Muhammadan"

The silenced the *Mulla* and the rest. They were convinced that Guru Nanak was possessed with the spirit of God, and had become a true faqir. All bowed and went away. For the whole of that day and the following night the Guru sat as in a trance. He neither spoke nor moved. On the following day he came to himself. The first words that he then uttered were, "There is no Hindu, there is no Muhammadan." Soon the words were on everybody's lips. The Hindus had really ceased to be true Hindus. Moreover, they had became too deeply demoralized to resent or heed such sayings as that of the Guru. The Muhammadans, however, were at the height of power. They were the rulers. Their religion was spreading everywhere. How could a Hindu dare say in the Muslim raj that no Muhammadan was in the land. The Qazi took the words to the Nawab and complained to him that Guru Nanak was casting a great slum on the whole Muhammadan community. Although the Nawab had come to believe that Guru Nanak was a true lover of God and incapable of injuring any one's feelings, yet the Qazi had his way. The Nawab sent for Guru Nanak. The latter refused to obey the summons. "My Master," said he, "does not permit me to obey any man and more. I must obey my Lord." Thereupon, the Nawab sent another messenger who said with great humility, "The Nawab beseeches you in the name of your Lord God to favour him with your sight. He does not command as a Governor but entreats as a humble admirer of yours."

A call made in the name of God Guru Nanak could not resist. He got up and went into the presence of the Nawab. The latter received him with great respect and expressed his sorrow at having lot such a honest *Modi.* The Guru smile and said, "there is no Hindu; there is no Muhammadan. Upon this the Qazi said, "About Hindus I would say nothing there may or may not be any true Hindus in this land. But how can you say that there is no Muhammadan? There are million of true followers of the Prophet."

The Guru then made a sign to Mardana to play the rebed and sang a song which may be translated thus:

Admonitions to Qazi:—The True Muslim

"To be worthy of being called a Muhammadan is difficult. One should, in the first place, acquire the virtues and qualities of a Muhammadan and then should be boast of being a follower of the Prophet. Let him first truly love the religion preached by men of God and rid himself of vanity and pride of pelf. Resigning himself to God, let him become lowly and humble. Let him put aside the fear of birth and death. Let him joyfully accept the Will of God. Let him believe God to be all in all. Let him quell all thoughts of self. Let him be kind and merciful to all living beings. When a man does all this, and not before, can he be called a true Muhammadan." (*Var Majh, Shlok* 8(1)).

The Qazi was not yet satisfied. He put some more questions. As Mardana played the rebeck, the Guru sang as follows :

> "Make mercy thy mosque. Let faith and sincerity be thy prayer-carpet, and what is just and lawful thy holy book. Let humility be thy circumcision, sweetness of behaviour thy fasting; thus shalt thou a true Muhammadan be. Let virtuous deeds be thy Ka'aba; Truth thy spiritual guide; charity thy creed and prayer; and quiet, unruffled temperament thy rosary. Do all this, my friend, and God will bestow honour on thee." (*Var Majh, Shlok* 7 (1)).

The Forbidden Acts and Things

"Listen further! Let all fully realize that what belongs by right to others should be shunned by Muhammadans as they shun pork and by Hindus as they shun beef, the two things forbidden most peremptorily by their religions. Be sure that only then will the spiritual guides of both Hindus and Muslim intercede for their followers when the latter do not eat what is thus forbidden, when they cease to usurp other people's rights and things, when they cease to coerce others into their faith and views. Mere talk, lip professions, and idle observances will not lake thee to Paradise. It is rather by the practice of Truth in the daily life that thou canst gain emancipation. Whatever is forbidden thee as food cannot become permissible by being spiced. Idle words and pious professions, divorced from right and virtuous conduct, are verily like the spice by which people try to legalize what is unlawful. But all in vain, my friend. False, hypocritical professions can beget falsehood only. No amount of them can make falsehood become truth, just as no amount of spice can make the forbidden for become permissible. So give up mere lip-professions and all vain, deceptive show, and engage thyself in virtuous deeds. (*Var Majh, Shlok* 7(2)).

Five Prayers

"You people have five prayers which are said at five different times in the day and are called by five different names. Listen, I tell you what the five prayers should really be. Unalloyed truth should be the first one. Acquisition permitted by law, religion, and morality should be the second; charity to all in the name of God should be the third; good intentions and a pure heart should be the fourth; and the praise and glorification of God the fifth. Let good and virtuous acts be thy *Kalma* or the creed to be ever repeated. Do all this, my friend. Then alone canst thou by worthy to be called a Muhammadan. Otherwise by the practice of falsehood and deceit, only false things can be had and not the true religion." (*Var Majh, Shlok* 7(3))

The Effects of His Words

The admonition went home. They all realized the truth of the Guru's words. They recollected how the Muhammadans had everywhere forcibly snatched away other people's goods and were even then doing so all around them. They realized that, with most of them, religion had come to mean a mere mechanical repetition of little understood Arabic text, the observance of certain forms and ceremonies, fasting during the prescribed month, and hating their Hindu neighbours; that religion had ceased to inspired goodly, human virtues in the Muhammadans, was engendering inhuman and irreligious vices, sins, and crimes, and was inciting them to the murder and oppression of the Hindus. Those who heard the Guru's narration of the qualities which should distinguish a true Muhammadan felt all this and more. They were struck at the daring of the Guru in having uttered these truths at the court of a Muhammadan ruler and in the presence of a large gathering of fanatic Muslim of those dark days. But the sweet humility of the Guru had disarmed all opposition. There was a force in the look of his eyes that overcame and suppressed all words of protest as they took shape in the hearts of the Muslim hearers. All of them bowed in deep reverence.

In the Mosque to Pray

I was the time for the afternoon prayer. As the company was about to proceed to the mosque, the Qazi said to the Guru, "You have instructed us what we should do to become true Muhammadans. You have told us how we should pray. We are now going to say our prayers. Will you go with us and join us?"

"By all means", said the Guru. All went to the mosque. The Qazi stood at the head of the gathering and began to repeat the Arabic text and perform the prescribed bodily movements. Others imitated him in these latter. The Guru looked at the Qazi, who appeared to be devoulty engaged in prayer and laughted. Another act of great daring—to laugh at a Qazi at prayers in a mosque. The Qazi's face changed not a little. When the prayer was over, he complained to the Nawab that Guru Nanak had insulted the whole assembly, nay the Muhammadan religion, to boot. The Nawab was of a generous temperament. He approached the Guru and said, "Good Sir, you promised to join us in prayers, but instead, you laughted at the Qazi as he was engaged in them."

The Qazi Confounded

"Yes", replied Guru Nanak, "I did promise to join him at prayers. But he was not praying at all. While with his tongue he was repeating the text and with his body was performing the prescribed movements, he himself was chasing his new born colt which he had left untethered at home and was trying to save it from falling in the deep pit in his courtyard. I could not join him at that. It was amusing to see him thus, his body at prayers and he at home running after the colt. So I laughed. How we deceive ourselves and the world, and try to deceive God Himself!"

The Qazi lowered his head. Guru Nanak had read his mind. But then taking courage, he said, "But here was the Nawab than whom no devouter Muhammadan exists hereabouts. You could have joined him."

The Nawab Enters the Path

"No doubt," replied the Guru," the Nawab is a good man; but he, too, was not engaged in prayers. He was purchasing horses at Kabul. All others who imitated your movements were, likewise, not here at prayers. They were far off, each attending to his own affairs. Such prayers are worse than useless. They engender pride, vanity and intolerance. I could not have joined you at such prayers."*

Saying this the Guru rose to go away. The Nawab reverently touched his feet and said, "O true faqir, accepted of God, stay here. All this authority, and all this estate, I lay at your feet. Accept them. Be my Master, let me be the slave for ever. Don't go away."

"No friend", replied the Guru with half-shut eyes," The Great Commander calls me. I must go forth and engage in His service. Duty calls me to distant lands. Keep thy authority and estate; but also keep the love of God and man in thy breast. Then shalt thou be surely saved."

The Nawab bent his head in reverence and said, As your please. But do kindly accept for the use of your family the sum that has been found due to you from the *Modikhana*?"

The Guru desired him to distribute the amount among the poor. "As for my family and myself, the Sustainer of all will provide for us."

Renunciation

Saying this, the Guru rose and repaired to the same secluded place from where he had come to the court when entreated in the name of God. Many holy men of both communities followed him there and stayed with him. Every day people gathered round him to obtain light and instruction. Many were blessed by the Master with the priceless gift of the True Name, of a life of love and service practised in the name of God.

It was during this period, when the Guru had given up his home and work, and was staying outside Sultanpur, that his second son, Lakhmi Das, was born.

His Relative's Protest

The news of Guru Nanak having renounced the world reached his and his wife's parents. They were greatly perturbed. They came to Sultanpur. A learned Pandit was with them. He tried to dissuade Guru Nanak from the path of renunciation which he had entered upon. He advised him, on the authority of the *Vedas* and *Shastras*, to worship God in the usual Hindu way and to look after his family. His father Mehta Kalu said, "We are old now. It is your duty to serve us in our old age." His father-in-law, Baba Mul Chand, said, "You are a husband and father. It is your duty to look after your family, to bring up and educate your sons, to do for them what your father did for you. If you were thrust to desert your wife and children, you should not have married." His wife clasped his feet, washed them with tears, and said, "Who is mine in the world but thee, O Lord of Life? In whose care dost thou leave me and these thy sons? Have pity on them if not on me."

His sister, Bebe Nanki, stood quiet. In her eyes were tears of sorrow at the imminent separation from her beloved brother and Guru, and on her face was a deep calm, born of a willing resignation to the will of the Master. She liked him to stay, but she would not stand in the way of his resolve.

His Reply to His Parents

The Guru heard all that his friends and relatives had to say, He then looked up and said, "Sir, I admit that my duty is to serve my father. But there is the Father above you is the father of all. He bids me go abroad and cool and scoothe the flaming, distressed world. The Divine call is too strong and urgent for me to resist. He who sends me thus on His own mission will be your stay in your old age. Rely on Him, permit me to go, and blessed me with your prayers that I may prosper in my undertaking."

The words of the Guru and the look of his eyes had their effect. His parents, under some mysterious influence, and even against their deep desires, said "All right" and stepped back.

To His Father-in-Law

The Guru then turned to Baba Mul Chand, his father-in-law, and said, "It is not man that brings forth children into the world. They are sent hither by the Creator and Sustainer of the world. We are here to carry out his divine plan. Have no anxiety for thy daughter and thy grand-children. God, whose children they are, will take care of them. I am called forth to serve and save God's children in other places. The whole wide world, the offspring of my Father above, is henceforth my family. I must do my duty that way now. Don't grieve, but extend thy blessings to me."

Baba Mul Chand and his wife, Mata Chando Rani, were reconciled to the will of their son-in-law.

To His Wife

The Guru then turned to his wife, and said, "Take heart, O favoured daughter to the Eternal Father. My duty here is ended. He who bids me leaves thee and my dear sons will look after you all. Great is thy love, great has been thy devotion, and great is to be thy sacrifice, but be sure that greater still will be the reward which the Lord will bestow on thee. May He ever abide with thee and thy sons. I must go to save my Father's sons and daughters from sin and sufferings. Bid me a cheerful adieu."

She felt resigned to her lord's will. Her head bent low and the Master's hand blessed it.

To His Sister

The Guru then turned to his sister and said, "My respected sister, the love is different from that of all others. It is a higher type. I read thy mind in thy looks. Have no anxiety. God will be every with thee. I, too, shall be ever with thee. Whenever thy love for me rouses in thee an unsuppressible longing to see me, I shall hear thy unuttered summons and shall come to three.* But, all the same, try to alm thy beating, loveful heart. Think of the Lord alone. I know my duty towards thee. But innumerable sisters in woe and agony are crying to be comforted. I must go."

The Guru then look up his son in his arms, in turn, pressed them to his breast and lips, smiled on them his gracious smile, and then handed them back to their mother. He then lovingly passed his hand over their heads and faces and blessed them. After that a bade farewell to all his relatives. They went away.

The news that Guru Nanak was about to set on travels soon spread in the city. All his disciples and admirers came to take his blessings. The Nawab also came among them. The Guru blessed them all with the gift of True Name, instructed them in the fundamentals of his faith, and bade them return to their places and lead virtuous, useful lives.

Prophecy about Goindwal

A little time after, the Guru resolved to go n his extensive tours. He finally took leave of his sister, wife, and sons, and set out with Mardana as his companion. Crossing the river Beas, he came to the place where now stands the town of Goindwal. It was a wide wildness then. Sitting on the river's bank, the Guru meditated on Nature and her indwelling Lord. His soul was attuned to the celestial music that was, inaudibly to the ears, filling the earth and the sky. Beside him Mardana was playing his rebeck and singing the Master's songs in marvellous modulation. On light, strong wings the Guru's soul rose to the feet of the Blissful Lord and held them fast. For two days the Guru sat thus with his eyes closed, and his countenance glowing with a calm, radiant glory.

Mardana sat near him. He was feeling hungry. He laid aside his rebeck. He looked all round for any sign of a habitation nearby or of a chance traveller. None was there. He was getting impatient. When the Guru came to himself, Mardana said to him, "Master, either bless me with a little of they power of enjoying the Lord's company in complete disregard of the bodily needs, or please to choose thy was through inhabited zones; otherwise this poor *Mirasi*, whom thou hast taken out of the very dregs of society and made a *Bhai* or brother of thine, will some day lie a corpse in some jungle. Who will then sing to thee thy ambrosial, delicious songs? What attraction dost thou find in this wilderness that thou has sat here for the last two days, unmindful of the needs of the body, and of the cravings of the weak companion?"

Guru Nanak smiled and said, "This place had been blessed by the Lord. A great one will erect here a Temple whence he will bestow on all at all hours food for both the body and the spirit. As for thee and me let us learn to look to God."

At this time a Zamindar came, 'by chane' as some will say; persuaded by the Provident Lord as Guru Nanak said; under subtle influence of the thought waves sent forth by the Guru as the modernists would assert. The Zimindar gave them food for the body. In exchange he got the priceless food for the soul—a food which could never surfeit or exhaust.

Visits the Present Site of Amritsar

From there the two started on their way. What way? That which the Guru's feet took under the Lord's direction. At all places that they visited the Guru weaned people from irreligion or Godless religion and put them on to the right path. The next day they reached a pool of clear eater in the vicinity of Sultanwind. Here, sitting on its bank, under a shady *Ber* tree the Guru sang the Lord's praises. When re-starting, the Guru said, "Here shall another great one build a Temple of Hari whence divine, nourishing food of the spirit will be distributed freely at all hours." That pool is the site of the sacred tank of Amritsar—the Lake of Nectar—in the midst of which stands the Golden Temple. One the bank of the Lake the old *Ber* tree under which the Guru sat still exists. It is called the *Dukhbhanjani Ber* or the Tree that Destoryeth all sorrow and suffering.

Reaches Syedpur

Travelling in this way, halting in several places as his mood directed him, and everywhere knitting people to the feet of the Almightly Father, and laying in every place, the foundation of the Holy Fellowship which he had come to found, the Guru reached Lahore. During his stay there he continued delivering to all, in his own swept, friendly way, his divine message of Love and Service. People in large numbers heard him and became his disciples. After a few weeks' stay at Lahore the Guru started from there and reached Syedpur, now called Eminabed, in the district of Gujranwala. He went to the house of a low caste artisan, Lalo by name. The Lalo was a God-fearing man who lived by the sweat of his brow. Such people were dear to Guru Nanak. He would go miles and miles to see such a one.

Welcomed by Bhai Lalo

Bhai Lalo joyfully received the holy guest. One took on the countenance of Guru Nanak radiant with divine glory was enough to convince Bhai Lalo that the devotion to the Lord was about to bear fruit. The saviour had come who would rekindle his soul with a divine spark, make him reborn into a life of the spirit, bestow on him the gift of true Devotion, and ultimately make him one with the Lord. At the approach of the guests, Bhai Lalo left his tools and rose to welcome them. He took them into his humble cottage, seated the Guru on a little cot—the only one that he had—, and began to cook food in a regular cooking square. Mardana was surprised at the Guru's choice of a host. There were in the city several men of wealth and position who would have gladly welcomed him and feasted him in grand mansions. He had halted at the hut of a poor man who had only one cot and had no wife or cook. What sort of food could the artisan prepare?

The Guru read Bahi Mardana's thoughts. He was amused. With his face beaming with a smile of love, the Guru said, "Brother, don't he puzzled. I have chosen a holy one as my host. Holy is the man who loved the Lord and earns is food by honest labour. This place is holy and far more comfortable than the spacious abodes of the rich parasites who live on other people's earnings."

The Cooking Square

Bhai Lalo had, by then, cooked the food—simple, coarse bread and *sag*, or green pot-herbs boiled and salted. He begged the Guru to step into the *Chauka* or the cooking square and partake of the humble fare. The Guru replied, "Brother, the whole earth is as good as a cooking square, True and devoted servants of the Lord need not brother about ceremonial purity; for they are even pure and undefiled. Bring the food here." At the sight of this simple coarse bread Mardana became a little uneasy at first. He thought he would not be able to chew and swallow it. He saw that the Guru was eating it with a cheerful countenance. Mardana also reluctantly put a morsel in the mouth. Lo! the wonder of it! He found that he had tasted nothing so delicious as this coarse bread. As Guru Nanak said, love, truth, and honest labour formed the ingredient of the coarse fare. It could not but be delicious.

After a few days' halt the Guru made ready to go. But Bhai Lalo fell at his feet and prayed him to stay a little longer. Such a loving request the Guru had not the heart to refuse. He agreed to stay. Bhai Mardana begged permission to go and see his people at Talwandi. He was allowed to go.

Opposition and Appreciation

During his stay at Bhai Lalo's the Guru used to repair to a secluded place where, sitting or lying on a bed of pebbles or sand, he meditated on the Lord.* At nightfall he returned on the house of Bhai Lalo. By and by, the news spread in the city that a Bedi Khatri of Talwandi, who had turned a *Sadhu*, was putting up at the house of a *sudra* and was eating the food cooked by that low-caste man. The high-caste people, Brahmins and Kashattriyas, were scandalized. They named him *Kurahia* or a man who had abandoned the right path and taken to the wrong one. Some learned Brahmins came to counsel him. They hoped to bring him back to the path prescribed in the *Vedas* and *Shastras*. But they had to go back in utter confusion. Their own old faith got a shaking, but they would not give it up. They were making a living by it means. Still, several Hindus and Muhammadans, who heard his divine songs and looked on his gracious, glorious countenance, owned him as their spiritual guide and become his Sikhs. The Hindus began to call him 'Nanak Tapa or Nanak the Hermit'. The Muhammadans called him 'Nanak Shah' or 'Nanak the Divine Faqir.'.

Conspiracy of Mullas and Pandits

In a short time the Guru came to be visited by people from the neighbouring villages. The Guru's message of liberation from all the snares of superstitions, forms, and ceremonies encouraged and enforced by *Pandits* and *Mullas* was heartily welcomed by the people, Hindus and Muslims alike. This perturbed these persons who lived on the religious offerings of the populace. They felt that the Guru was undermining their position as custodians and dispensers of religion and religious knowledge, for he was teaching that everybody could be his own priest and worship God without the intercession of *Pandits* and *Mullas.* They were afraid that their means of livelihood, comfortable and plenteous, would be destroyed. So they jointly conspired to force the Guru to leave the place. They began to poison the ears of Malik Bhago, who was a Khatri by caste and a servile and corrupt official of the local Muhammadan ruler. The Nawab, too, was approached.

Malik Bhago

However, for a time the Guru was not molestead. More and more people were coming to listen to his sacred songs and divine, soul-inspiring discourses. At last, something occurred which gave Malik Bhago an excuse to molest the Guru. On account of some happy event in the family, the Malik gave a *Brahmbhoj* or feast in the name of God. The custom was to invite to it all Brahmins and Sadhus who were near-abouts. Guru Nanak was also invited. The Guru declined the invitation. He had no taste, said he, for the sumptuous but blood-tainted articles of diet that which be served at Bhago's.

The Brahmins found their opportunity. They said to the proud and haughty Malik, "So you see! This person, whom people call a hermit and who belongs to a high caste, is really a heretic of the worst type. He ignores the *Varnd Dharma.* He dines with a Sudra. He has scornfully declined your invitation. He was scoffed at your. He has said that your dainties are interfused with blood. This is a grave insult, black infamy, and dark heresy. This is too much. He deserves chastisement."

Malik Bhago's pride was hurt. A 'homeless, wandering sadhu' has slighted him. He sent a Brahmin to call the Guru. But the Guru again refused to see the proud official, saying, "What has a faqir to do at the court of an official? We do not know each other. I see no reason why I should go to him." The Brahmin returned and repeated, in an exaggerated form, what the Guru had said. The Malik's wrath was excited. He sent a batch of footmen to bring the Guru into his presence, using force, if necessary. When they disclosed their errand to the Guru, he smiled and said, "All right friends. The Lord's work has to be done, the sooner the better. Go and tell your master that I am coming to do my duty."

The Guru meets Malik Bhagi

The Malik was waiting for him with impatience. The Guru went and stood calm and quiet. Bhago had been resolving to pounce upon the Guru in wrath. But a look at the Master's countenance sent a strange quiver through his body. The fire in his soul got cooled. He addressed the Guru respectfully. He remonstrated with him for his lodging and dining with low-caste people and his refusing an invitation to a *Brahmbhoj* or a feast given in the name of God by a high-caste Hindu. Above all, he resented the Guru's remarks that the Malik's dainties were interfused with blood.

The Guru heard him out calmly. Then he said, "Misguided brother, to invite all to your feast was certainly your duty and you did that; but to enforce acceptance of the invitation does not become you. We *Sadhus* eschew delicacies. We eat what the Bounteous Lord sends us in His mercy. As for my remarks about the nature of the food served at your feast, I said what I felt. For fear of no man shall I bet kept from speaking out the truth. Dainties and comforts which are had by tyrannizing over the labouring poor are verily interfused with the blood of the unfortunate victims. All your wealth has been extorted mercilessly from the poor toilers of your *Ilaqa*. Enjoyment of this ill-gotten wealth cannot but engender low passions and evil tendencies in the heart and mind, and produce pain and disease in the body. Hence I shunned your feast."

Malik Bhago felt the justice of the Guru's remarks. But his attendants, dependents, and friends were all gathered there. He would not own defeat so easily. So he said, "If the food served by a high-caste man like me you deem to be unfit for you, how can you go on taking every day the food prepared by that Sundra, whose very touch defiles the Twice-born? His coarse bread doesn't contain milk, does it?"

The Pride of Caste Denounced

Guru Nanak replied, "O yes, it is interfused with milk and honey. The earnings of a pious man, obtained by the sweat of the brow, are pure; they are sweet and nourishing like milk and honey. They sustained the body and lift the soul. As for thy vaunted high caste, remember:

"Truly low-caste men are they
Who forget the Lord;
Without meditation on the Supreme Lord, O Nanak,
Man becomes low and despicable, a mean outcast. *(Rag Asa)*

"Recognise the Divine Spart which illumines every human form.
Raise no question of caste or tribe;
For, in the Holy court of the Father above
Exist no distinctions of caste or creed. *(Rag-Asa)*

"Caste and distinctions based on them
Are but the idle inventions of evil brains.
All men, all creatures, are under the protecting shade of Supreme Lord.
All who deem and call themselves to be great and pure
Will be really so if, in the Court of God, they are found to be worthy of honour.

(Var Sri Rag)

"My misguided brother, do not pride thyself on thy high caste. Despite no man. God dwells in every heart. The Divine spark, the immortal soul, inspires every human form. All are equally the sons of the Father above. Birth in this or that family cannot exalt or degrade a man. It is actions that do so. A good pious man of humble birth is far more dear a God and men of God than a high-born tyrant or evil doer. Service of mankind, honest labour for the body, does not degrade a man. It elevates him. As for me,

"People who are lowliest among the lowly,
Of a caste that is deemed the lowest of all low castes—
All such are the friends and brothers of Nanak.
What has he to do with the high and great?
Where the lowly are treated with a loving care.
There do rain Thy Mercy and Grace, O Lord." *(Sri Rag)*

The Malik Becomes a Disciple

The discourse of the Master interspersed with his matchless divine songs went straight to the heart of the hearers. Malik Bhago was subdued, Scales fell off his eyes and he fell at the Master's feet. A strange thrill entered at his forehead, which touched the feet of the Master, and passed through his whole body. He begged to be forgiven his hideous past. He prayed for life and light. The Guru bade him rise and sin no more. Malik Bhago rose a changed man. There was a new light in his eyes; a joy unknown ever before filled his heart and thrilled his soul. The Guru blessed him with the priceless gift of the Name and a life of love and service. The Malik went home, light in body and heart. He distributed all his wealth among the poor. He vowed, thenceforth, to live a life of love, devotion and service. Bhai Lalo, whom erstwhile despised as a low-caste man he began to deem his elder brother and dearest friend.

Thus did the Guru lift the lowly into eminence. Thus did he destroy the pride of caste which was degrading and demoralizing the people. Thus did he lay the foundation of his Holy Fellowship where 'the lowest is equal with the highest in race as in creed, in political rights as in religious hopes.'

A few days after, Mardana returned from Talwandi. He delivered to the guru the humble request of his old disciple, Rai Bular, that the Guru Might be pleased to visit him. "I am old," he had said, "and took weak to go to him. He is kind and gracious. I would I could see him with these eyes; for soon they will close for ever." Other disciples of Talwandi had also sent their entreaties. So, after a short further stay at Syedpur the Guru stated towards the place of his birth.

CONVERTS A THUG INTO A MISSIONARY

At Talwandi

On reaching Talwandi, he took his seat outside the village. His parents heard of the arrival. They went to see him. His uncle, Mehta Lalu, also accompanied them. They once again tried to persuade him to give up the life of renunciation that he had chosen and take to family life and some profitable occupation. The Guru listened to all that they said and then replied, "The whole world is my family now. I have not renounced the world. I have given myself to it. I have chosen a really profitable calling, one which gives me untold riches of peace and happiness both here and hereafter. More, it will be the means of bringing the misguided. impoverished humanity to a realization and enjoyment of the infinite treasures which it can make its own but which it has lost and forgotten. I am an agriculturist as well. The human heart is my field. The Eternal Name and Infinite Love are the seeds that I sow. I am a trader, too. I deal in the souls of men. Procuring the precious commodities of Truth, Love, and the Name, from the Bounteous Lord of treasures, I deal them out to those who need them. But I don't throw away my precious goods. I sell them very dear indeed. Those who would have these must hand over their own selves to me. I then knit them on to the feet of the Lord. So try not to dissuade me from such a useful and profitable calling. Rather, bid me proper in my business.

"Desirest thou to play the game of love with me?
Then, come but thy head on thy palm must be?
If choosest thou to tread this path, be ready O friend,
To part with thy head, to lay down thy life, in perfect joy and peace."

Words as these made his parents and relatives hold their peace and let Guru Nanak his own course. The Guru then got up and went to the house of Rai Bular. The Rai was an old man by then. He rose and was about to fall on the Guru's feet, when the letter held him in his loving arms. The Rai hugged the Guru lovingly to his breast. In that embrace of love the Rai tasted true, lasting joy. He felt himself to be light as air and happy as the bride that has found her lord after a long separation.

The Guru stayed a few days at Talwandi. Disciples and friends of his childhood and youth gathered round him. He enkindled their souls. He awakened them from dreamy sleep of greedy, tenacious worldly life and made them taste the pleasures of an active, wakeful life of the spirit. During daytime he remained with his relatives and friends, chiefly with Rai Bular. At night he would retire into the solitude of the forest where his collected soul enjoyed an unbroken communion with the Lord.

Tour in Southern Punjab

After a few days he got ready to depart. The divine call, which had lured him four Sultanpur, was urging him on to give up the restful life. He started. Crossing the river Ravi, he travelled southwards through forests and little inhabited tracts. Mardana was with him. Neither hunger nor fatigue seemed to affect the Guru. He seemed to be possessed and drawn by some invisible, irresistible force. He seemed to be in a hurry. Some good bargain was up again. Mardana felt the pangs of hunger and fatigue. He bravely bore them for sometime. The fruits that could be picked up or plucked from here and there on the way were not enough to satisfy his body's craving for food. He wanted bread and milk.

By then they had reached the neighbourhood of Harappa. The Guru permitted Mardana to go into the village, assuring him of a hospitable reception. Mardana went. People treated him with kindness and charity. They feasted him on dainties. They made him offerings of money and clothes. Towards evening, Mardana gathered up the offerings into a bundle and took them to the Guru. When the Guru saw Mardana, with the bundle on his head, he laughed loud and long. "What is it, Mardana?" asked he. "Clothes and money, Master", replied Mardana. "The good people offered them, to me and I have brought them for you."

The Guru replied, "But these things are of no use to us. We have renounced all worldly wealth and taken to this life. Shall we let ourselves be encumbered again? Throw them away. Let the poor and needy have these things. He, in whose service we are, will look to our needs. Lovers of God have relish for naught but the True Name. They want nothing else. They feel a constant craving for singing the praises of the Bounteous Lord. His thought sustains them ever. Let faith in Him grow in thy heart. Throw these things away." Mardana obeyed.

At the House of the Thug

The two started again and soon reached near Talamba in the modern district of Multan. About five or six furlongs from the present railway station of Mukhdumpur on the Khanewal—Shorekot line, there was the habitation of a notorious *thug* named Sajjan. It was a spacious building. On one side of it was a mosque and on the other was a Hindu temple. At the gate stood two servants ever on the look out for guests and wayfarers. They welcomed the Guru and his companion. The radiance born of spiritual grandeur that lit the Guru's countenance was taken by them to be due to a consciousness of great worldly wealth. The two were seated in a cosy, well-furnished room. Sajjan also came there. Greatly imposing were the dress and mien of this imposter. In his left hand he had a rosary like a Hindu Hermit and in his right a staff like a Muslim faqir. He was glad for he believed that the Guru had with him some priceless gems. All that wealth would be his before daybreak.

With ostensible humility, Sajjan seated himself at the Guru's feet. He tried to fish out information about the sort of wealth that the Guru had with him. When asked his name, he replied, "I am a friend and humble servant of all. Hindus call me Sajjan Mall and Muslims call me Sheikh Sajjan. But I am neither a Hindu nor a Muhammadan Rather, I am both."

Servants brought food and drink for the two. The Guru declined to have anything. Sajjan and his accomplices tried all their arts but failed to persuade the Guru to take either food or drink. Mardana, of course, could not eat or drink without his Master's permission. Sajjan then took them to a room where cosy beds were prepared for them. The Guru sat on the floor. Sajjan begged him with folded bands to lie on the bed and take rest for the night. The Guru smiled and said, "No friend, cosy, soft beds are not for us faqirs. I am all right where I am. Duty has to be done. Time for rest is not yet. Go and rest, if you may."

Divine Music

Sajjan bowed and went away. He assembled his confederates. All thought out ways and means of plundering the Guru's wealth. They did not know that the Guru had come to give armloads of his really precious, peerless wealth to them who were really paupers possessing thousands. It was decided to strange the two in the small hours of the morning. Sajjan retired to his bedroom. He was yet lying awake, immersed in thought, when he heard sweet music coming from the Guru's room. It charmed him out of his bed. He quietly stole to the door of the Guru's rcom. He saw that the Guru was sitting with his eyes closed. There was a 'sparkle of innumerable gems on his forehead'. Strange quieting, attracting emanations seemed to be radiating from his person. Mardana was playing the reback and singing one of the Master's songs. The music and the song and the look on the Guru's face drew him in as if with strong invisible chains. He went quietly in. An atmosphere of soothing calm and attunement filled the room. He bowed partly as a matter of show that was in his nature and partly on account of a mysterious force which he could as little resist as explain or understand.

After a time Mardana stopped singing. The music on the rebeck continued. The Guru then lifted his sweet melodious voice and sang a song which described the characteristics of imposters and criminals like Sajjan. It denounced all show of false piety and skin-deep devoutness us utterly useless, may as highly baneful. If the heart was impure and given to sin and vice, to evil and corruption, all wealth, all practices, all forms and observances, all worship and charity, proved only as so many snares for the soul. Mansions and balances, heaps of wealth and riches, were but heavy loads which the soul, maimed and blind, had to carry over steep, horny, endless paths. People who, forgetful of the life to some, lived on the life-blood of others cruelly sucked, and received the world with their hypocrisy, had yet to render an account of all their doings. There, all deeds, committed under the cover of the darkest night or in depths of the deepest dens, would stand before man and arraign him with thousand tongues. The false friends of the world who helped him in his dark deeds, egged him on, and shared with him the short-lived pleasures gained thereby, would desert him then. He alone would suffer for all his deeds. True friends would be those who could be of help and assistance on that occasion, who could lift, in howsoever little a part, the pressing and crushing burden from the tortured soul. Such friends should a man seek and make his own. False relations of this world, with all their longings, needs, and allurements simply helped to tighten the strings that bound a man. Constant mediation on God and His attributes, a steady sincere exertion in the path of Love and Service, association with those who had found their souls, could alone loosen the strings and free the captive soul.*

The Thug Reclaimed

As the deep-penetrating notes of the moving, divine some followed other in a sweet cadence, the heart of Sajjan, which had been callous and cruel and devoid of all softer feelings, beggar to melt in a deep anguish of the soul, throb in anxiety, to flutter in fear. All his dark deeds stood stark before him. He tightly shut his eyes but they still stared him in the face. A heavy burden as of big countless loads seemed to be pressing on him and crushing his soul. A deep dark abyss appeared to be yawning before him ready to swallow and efface him. He was convinced that the Guru had read, like an open book, his ugly soul and vicious heart. He stood up. With a faltering, unsteady step, an moist, downcast eyes, he approached the Guru and clung his feet. A thrill passed through his whole frame. A current as of electricity seemed to have entered at this hands and forehead. The burden of his heart and soul was becoming lighter and lighter. He washed the Guru's feet with his tea of repentance and sorrow.

He remained long in that posture. Then the Guru smiled passed his hand over the back and shoulders of Sajjan, anbade him rise. The touch of the Guru's hand sent another thrill through his body. He had no heart to rise. He wanted to lie for ever at the blissful feet of the Master, he tarried. The Guru held him by the hand—the hand which had administered cups of poison to and cut the throats of innumerable unsuspecting wayfarers lured to this den by the prospect of a night's rest and lodging. Sajjan let go the Guru's feet and sat up with folded hands and streaming eyes. The Guru's song had washed him clean. He was filled with remorse. He begged the Guru to forgive him, to save him, to deliver him from the consequence of his sins. The Guru asked him to confess his past crimes and sins, and vow to abstain from them in future. Sajjan did as bidden. He confessed all the evil deeds that he had done. He vowed to live a virtuous life. He felt relieved. Of his own accord he realized that as long he bad with him the wealth procured by murder and deceit, he could not taste true calm or joy. So he distributed all that he had to the needy and the poor. His spacious mansion, where thousands of murders had been committed, with all its dens and snares, he razed to the ground. For himself he built a simple, little hut.

The First Sikh Missionary

The Guru blessed him with the Name of the Lord. He bade him made his house a *dharmsal*, or a house of worship and devotion, of open-handed charity and active, all-embracing love and service. He instructed him in the undamentals of his Faith and charged him with the duty of reclaiming others. He bade him earn his living by honest labour, meditate on the Lord every moment of his life, and share his earnings with the needy and poor. Thus would he a true *sajjan* or friend not only of himself but of all mankind. From a thug or a robber Sajjan became a holy, active servant of God and man, the first Sikh missionary appointed by the Guru for the propagation of his religion. It was thus that Guru Nanak made converts to his faith.

2

Travels of Guru Nanak

Having realised that the age of ignorance and strife requires the message of truth and peace, Nanak took the momentous decision of spreading it. To do so, he undertook arduous and extensive tours in the North, South, East and West and visited the important centres of the Hindus, Muslims, Buddhists and Jains, Sufis, Jogis etc. and met people of different races, different tribes, diverse culture-patterns. His travels covered a period of nearly thirty years.

In his first udasi, he traversed in terms of the modern political geography of India and Pakistan, Haryana, Delhi, Utter Pradesh, Bihar, Bengal, Orissa, Madras, Kerala, Mysore, Andhra Pradesh, Maharashtra, Gujarat, Madhya Pradesh, Rajasthan and West Pakistan. He also visited Ceylon. He went there from Nagapathinam, and returned via Rameshwaram. The second udasi (tour) took the Guru into the interior of the Himalayan region where he visited the Kangra valley, the Spiti table land, Western Tibet, Ladakh, Kashmir and Punjab (Pakistan).

After this, the Guru undertook his third missionary journey to the muslim countries of West Africa wearing the dress of a muslim devotee. Some prominent places connected with this tour of the Guru were Multan, Uch, Lakhpat, Hinglaj, Mecca, Medina, Baghdad, Mashad, Herat, Kandhar, Kabul, Para Chinnar and Gorakh-Hatri (Peshawar).

Besides the place of the visit of the Guru recorded by Janamsakhis or other sources, there may be many more which bear the Guru's association for the reasons that Guru made frequent tours, short and long, through the length and breadth of the area. Even when the settled at Kartarpur, occasional tours were undertaken. In the course of these tours, the Guru generally followed the village routes and thus passed through numerous placed which have not been recorded anywhere.

His first udasi was eastward. According to Meharban the Guru immediately turned east and proceeded to Delhi wherefrom he went to Hardwar. According to the Puratam Janamsakhi before turning east, the Guru went to Tolumba (modern Makhdumpur-West Pakistan) where he met the Sajjan Thug. It was after this that he went to Panipat and Delhi. Bhai Gurdas gives no specific information about it. The Bala Janamsakhi informs us that before leaving the central Punjab the Guru first went to Eminabad and then to Talwandi. Following the general trend of writers, we may accept the view that the Guru, when he left Sultanpur, straightway marched eastward and Guru's visits to Eminabad and Tolumba came off much later.

After starting from Sultanpur the first important places visited by Guru Nanak were Korra, Pehoa and Kurukshetra. All these places have old historical gurdwaras keeping green the memory of the Guru's visit to the places.

When the Guru visited Kurikshetra, occasion was that of solar eclipse when hordes of people and a large number of Brahmans and saints had gathered there. The object of Nanak's visit was to draw the attention of erring humanity from the unreal, and from external ceremonies to inner purification. The Guru took his seat near the sacred tank and began to cook deer which was presented by a prince (Raj Singh). A great crowd gathered round him, for to them it was a sacrilege which had never been committed before and on such day when Sun God was harassed by his enemies. The Brahmins led by Nanu besseiged him and were ready to club him to death. But the Guru stood up and spoke. His words worked like a magic. The crowd stood spell-bound. The Guru expressed:

"Fools wrangle about eating meat
They know not the true nor the way of right action Or the difference between
meat and vegetables and acts that are sinful and those that are sinless.
They, in ancient days, killed rhinoceros.
Hold their noses and forswear flesh and offered its flesh.
In oblation at the sacrificial fire.
They, the man eaters, pitiless and cruel.
It is any good telling the blind who cannot seen or act upon what is right".

(Slok Moh I)

The next place visited was Panipat where the Guru had a meeting with Sheikh Edul Kabir (d. 1450) a successor of Sheikh Sharaf-ud-din Bin Ali Qalandar (d. A.D.1325), a renowned Sufi of his days. Sheiks Edul Kabir was also known as Sheikh Tahir or Tatihar as the Puratan Janamsakhi has put in.

After Panipat the Guru visited 'Delhi and stayed at a place called 'Majnu da Tilla'. This Majnu was pious faquir and wielded considerable influence. The place is on the right bank of river Jamuna and is now marked by a good gurdwara where thousands of devotees throng every year on a occasion of the Baisakhi.

From Delhi, the Guru proceed to Hardwar. At this place a larger number of Hindus had assembled to wash away their sins by a dip in the sacred water of Ganges. White standing in the river, they were throwing handfuls of water towards East so that it might reach their ancestors. The Guru in order to exhibit the futility of this action entered the water and began to throw water towards the West. This brought about him a crowd of pilgrims who questioned him as to what he was doing. He replied that he was watering his newly-sown fields at Kartarpur, 300 miles away from here. They laughed at him and asked him "How can your handfuls of water reach your fields which are nearly 300 miles away?" The Guru replied, "If his water cannot reach his fields which are 300 miles away on this planet, how would your water reach your ancestors in the world beyond?"

After staying for sometime at Hardwar, the Guru proceed to Kotdar and from there onward to Pauri (Srinagar, District Tehri Garhwal). Then the Guru reached Joshi Math via Badri Nath and Kedar Nath. The Guru took the well-known pilgrims route which were perhaps the only link then available between the districts of Tehri-Garhwal and Almora, considering the Guru Nanak's visits to Hardwar Kotdar, Pauri on the one side and Retha Sahib and Gorakhmata on the other, it seems both natural and logical and that the Guru would have made his journey by this very difficult but well-known old route.

From Joshi Math, the route lay through the Antra and Sepula passes to the Kali river, also called the Sarda and then proceeded along the river towards Almora. The Guru probably followed this route and reached a center of Jogies situated thirty-three miles east of Haldwani. It is said that a wall-nut tree was made to bear sweet wall-nuts by the supernatural power of the Guru. The Gurdwara marking the sacred spot is reverentially called the Retha Sahib.

From this place, the Guru reached a place, then called Gorakhmata via Deohaj stream. As its name indicates the place was a seat of Sidh Jogis. Here the Guru had a long discourse with the Jogis on matters of religion and metaphysics. The Guru explicitly told the Jogis that religion did not consist in wearing parched coat or in the blowing of horns. They should live in the world and assume the role of the true guardian of inner values. He message was 'Abid pure in the midst of impurities of the world'. The Jogies were much impressed with the sincerity and description of the 'World'. Gorakhmata, out of veneration for the Guru is called Nanak Mata now a days.

From Gorakh Mata, the Guru took a southerly route which brought him to Tanda Vanjara From there, travelling in south-easter direction, the Guru reached a place of the Hindus in the modern *Lakhimpur* Kheri district.

Having covered a short distance from Gola, the Guru reached Ayudhya,[10] a very old pilgrimage centre of the Hindus being the birth place of Rama.

From Ayudhya, the Guru visited Tanda, Singh holi and Nizamabad (district Azamgarh). From Nizamabad the Guru proceeded to Prayag (Allahabad). Puratan Janamasakhi does not refer to it; only Meharban makes a definite mention of it. In our opinion, Meharban is right because his view is supported by the internal evidence of one of Guru's own hymns. Moreover, the Purani Ghusi, a place near the Tribaini Sangam of Prayag has a long-standing local tradition connected with the Guru's stay there. From Chusi, he proceeded to Benaras by a road which lay along the left bank of the Ganges.

From there, Nanak went to Benaras which was said to be the seat of learning and the abode of Shiva. The Guru sat near a famous ghat. His garments were neither of a house-holder nor of a Sanyasi. His Hindu and Muslim companions attracted attention. Janamsakhis state that he had to indulge in long discussions with Pandits and Sanyasis. The Guru brought home ot the Pandits that the knowledge of Vedas or of Shastras is useless if what they teach is not practised by them. Would it help a man who has lost his way to gaze at the light without taking the road which the light is destined to show? To the Sanyasis, Nanak said

"In ignorance they leave their house and then visit the house of others. Having run away from the duties of a house-holder they are lost in the whirlpool of desire. Without meeting a teacher, they wander about and read books whetting the edge of desire."

One of the leading most Pandits Chatur Das held a long talk with the Guru on the question of idol worship and symbolism. Most of these talks were verified in 'Omkar' a composition in 'Adi Granth'. "The Pandit who was made to realise that God resided in every human heart and could be adored in the form of the body Name. Chatur Das alongwith others became a Sikh and did much to spread Sikhism in the locality. The Press is now marked with a Gurdwara called Guru ka Bagh.

From Benaras the Guru took up the route to Hajipur Patna. On the way, he visited Gaya associated with the name of Lord Buddha, but a strong-hold of Hindu priest who declared that any offerings made at a particular place on the river secured salvation for seven generations for those who had departed from earth. The simple-minded people made huge offerings and the priests used to feed pitries (ancestors) by offering rice balls, lighted up little lamps to illuminate their path in the high heavens. The Guru standing on the banks of the river Sarju suddenly burst into loud laughter. The priests engaged in ceremonies were surprised and angered. They asked him what he was laughing at. Then Guru told them that the futility of the ceremonies and wrong faith are evoking his laughter. The Guru addressed them that who had left this body did not need food nor a glow lamp to see, because when a materials body was no more it could not require material things. If this body could not go to the other side, obviously it was not possible for any materials thing of this earth to reach the other side.

From Gaya, the Guru reached Hajipur and passed through where later on the modern city of Patna grew-up. When the Guru went there, where were only ruins of the ancient city of Patliputra except Hajipur situated at the confidence of the Gandak. A Gurdwara now stands to commercial the Memory of the Guru's visit.

From Hajipur, the Guru reached Kantnagar and from this place to the town of the Malda, situated at the confluence of the Ganga and Mahanadi. According to the prevalent tradition a local merchant of Malda did a great service to the Guru for which he received the Guru's blessings.

The next important place of visit was Dhubri in Assam. Some scholars say that the Guru took the road subsequently known as the Sher Shah Suri's road which led to Sunargaon and reached Dacca. He however do not agree with him. In our view 'From the place (Malda) onwards there are two possible routes he could take (i) He could take the road, subsequently called after Sher Shah Suri, leading to Sunargaon, via Murshadabad and reached Dacca, (ii) He could travel north and passing through what we today call North Bihar and North West Bengal and reached the Kamrup town of Dhurbri. In all probability, it was the second route which was followed by Guru Nanak. "We have our reasons to hold our views. Dhubri where subsequently Guru Tegh Bahadur raised a platform in the hallowed memory of the Guru Nanak's visit was in Assam. The first important place which was visited by Guru Nanak. As this place is and was situated on the right bank of the Brahamputra River, the likelihood is that the Guru arrived there from the west and not from the south, i.e. the say from the side of Dacca. Secondly, for a traveller desiring to tour the region of Assam, as the Guru was, the Dacca route was much longer, circuitous and unnatural. Thirdly, the northerly route is marked by many old historical gurdwaras bearing association with Guru Nanak and Guru Teg Bahadur. Fourthly, when later on Guru Teg Bahadur proceeded to Assam, he too followed the northerly route.

After Dhubri, the Guru proceeded along the Brahamputra river on to Kamrup, a place near the modern town of Gauhati. Janamsakhis say that it was here that the Guru met Nura, head of conjurers by her usual alluring gestures and extraordinary display of empting charms who tried to cast spell on him. But the Guru, to bring home to her the futility of these things, sang a hymn which had a magical effect on her. She became a changed woman and fell down at the Guru's feet.

The story reads more a fable than a reality. Janamsakhis set this story in *Istri Desh* (country of women). Nura has been mentioned as a chieftain or as a ruler of some area in Kamrup. But according to McLeod, in the contemporary history of Assam or Kamrup, there is no mention of this name.

But this does not mean that the Guru did not pay visit at Kamrup. The Guru visited Dhanpur in Kamrup and met Vaishnava Saint Shankerdev. A muslim chroniclar Mohammad Kazim who has left a detailed description of Assam testifies this account to the existence of the tribe known by the name of Nanak.

After passing through Kamrup, the land of Tantrism which then it was, the Guru entered Asa Desh, which was at that time being ruled by Raja Swarg Narain (A.D. 1497-1593), a descendant of Samundar, the first known ancestor of the Ahoms.

Continuing his journey upto river Brahmputra, the Guru reached the place called Gola Ghat Nagar, wherefrom he entered Dhanasri valley. In this valley the Guru had to confront with cannibals who inhabited it in a large number. The story that the Guru met Koda Rakshash is true only to the extent that the Guru met the people of Kodan tribe in this area. Puratan Janamsakhi seems to place Dhanasri valley in Central India and regards the visit of the Guru to it in his second missionary tour to the south; but this does not seem to be correct because there is no Dhansari valley in Central India.

From Dhansari valley, the Guru went back to Gauhati by the river route as he had followed during his upward journey. At Gauhati, the Guru changed his route and went to Shillong and what place to Silhet where an old Gurdwara stands to token of the memory of the Guru.

In the Silhet area, the Guru travelled by boat and come down to Dacca first by Surma and they by Barak River. Dacca, at the time did no enjoy the political importance as it enjoyed later or now. Neither it was capital of the province, not was it any trade-centre. It was famous for temple of the Dakeshwari Goddess to whom did it owe its name. The Guru stayed here for sometime, and the site which he hallowed is the present day Razabazaar. An old local will is also associated with Guru Nanak.

From Dacca, the Guru marched to Puri. On the way, he passed through Calcutta and Cuttock. From Cuttock the Guru took the pilgrim's route to reach Puri.

Jagan Nath Puri where the temple of Jagan Nath, the Lord of the East, stood one of the four most revered temples—other being Som Nath, Badri Nath, Vishva Nath. The Guru visited the temple, not to adore the Lord but to teach the people that the worship of Nam was superior to the worship of the deity. At the appointed time, the priest began to perform *Arti* (sort of Hindu prayer). The Guru did not join the service, which enraged the priests. On being asked the reasons, the Guru sang a hymn of his own, in which he told the people that "a wonderful serenade was being sung by nature before the invisible alter of God. The sun and the moon were the lamps, placed in the slaver of the firmament and the fragrance wafted from the Malayan mountains was serving as incense." There is no need of offering artificial worship to Him.

According to Biman Behari Majumdar who bases his conclusion on Chaitanya Bhagwat, Guru Nanak also met the Great Vaishnavite Saint Krishna-Chaitanya in 1510 popularly known as Chaitanya Prabhu. "The two saints seem to have spent sometime together, and enjoyed the divine music, Kirtan, in which both of them found special pleasure." The other persons who joined the Kiran (Recitation of Word) were Mardana and Ruh, Sanatan (Two brothers) Jagai and Madhai Nagar Purshotam Jangali Nandini, Gopal Guru and Nityananda Prabhu. The presence of a small Gurdwara at this place commemorating the Guru's visit is another supporting evidence.

According to Puratan Janamsakhi, the Guru ended his first udasi with the visit to Puri and returned to the Punjab. It was only after some time he set out on the second udasi. The Meharban version does not accept the view and treats the eastern and souther journcys as the constituents of a single udasi. In our opinion, Meharban's version is more plausible. The reason are not far to seek. In the first place, it the Guru returned from Puri he must have visited some important places on the way back, but surprisingly, the Puratan Janamsakhi does not make any mention of it. Secondly, the geographical location of Puri is such that a visitor planning to visit south India would not come to the Punjab first and then start for the southward journey. Since Guru Nanak had a definite plan to visit the south, he must have preferred to start his journey from Puri rather than come back all the way to the Punjab and then start from here.

The Guru, after a short stay at Puri returned to Cuttock and took the route heading towards Kanchpuram. Enroute, he visited Guntur of the present Andhra State. From here he reached Kanchi Puram a famous Hindu pilgrimage centre, noted for his temples of Shiva and Vishnu.

After this, the Guru reached Tiruvannamalai (Distt. South Arcot). From here, the Guru proceeded the Tiruchirupalli and paid a visit to the historic temple of Sri Rangami built on the island formed by the Daveri and Coleroon rivers.

All these places, Guntur, Kanchipuram, Tiruvannamalai, Tiruchchrupalli have Gurdwaras to mark the visit of the Guru.

From Tiruchchirupalli, the Guru sailed down the Kaveri river and reached Nagapatnam a very old port of south India. From this port, the Guru proceeded to Ceylon and Betticola was the first important place of his stay in the island. Twelve miles south of Betticola, the Guru reached Kurukal Madah which to date, enshrines the memory of the visit of Sikh Baba from northern India.

After staying there for sometime the Guru started in the southerly direction and reached Katargama, a Hindu Tirath having many sacred traditions associated with Shiva's son, Katargama. Herefrom, the Guru proceeded to Sitawaka (Avisvella of the present day). The latter place is also called Sita Eliya from the tradition of Sita having spent her period of captivity here. At the time of Guru Nanak's visit, this place was in the Kotte kingdom of Raja Dharma Prakarma. The inscription discovered by Dr. Karuna Ratna and Parana Vitana in the famous museum of Anurodh Pura furnishes a brief account of the encounter of Jananakacharya (Nanak) with the Buddhist Bhikshu, Dharma Kirtsthavira. This inscription also informs that the Raja Dharma Prkramabahu had promised to embrace Nanak's creed if he won in the debate. Nanak won. But before he should embrace Nanak's creed. The Brahmins very cleverly got arranged another public debate, this time between Nanak and Dharma Dvajapandita and maneouvered the result in favour of the latter. In this way, they did not allow the ruler to fall under the influence of Nanak.

Starting from Kotte, the Guru reached Anurdhapura a capital town of Ceylon in olden times. Continuing his journey he reached the part of Manner near the modern town of Talaimanner. At Mannar, the Guru left Ceylon and sailed for Rameshwaram wherefrom he proceeded to Trivandrum where there was a famous Hindu Temple of Anantapuram. After this, the Guru visited Palam and Kottayam where according to Sikh tradition used to be a Gurdwara marking the visit of the Guru. The shrine was situated midway between the two places and was called after both the places by the name of Palam Kottayam Gurdwara.

Then the Guru reached Bidar by taking a northerly route passing through Nilgiri Hills. A historical Gurdwara stands at the place of the Guru's sojourn. From Bidar, the Guru reached Nader. After this the Guru's important sojourn was Baroach were a Gurdwara named Nanakwara reminds us of the Guru's visit. According to Dr. Fauja Singh this Gurdwara enjoys an old annual jagir of Rs. 75 and this thing undoubtedly points to its historic city. "In the light of the Baroach tradition and in view of the wide travels in the land of Saurashtra, we are of the opinion that from Baroach the Guru journeyed to the area of Gujarat Kathiawar where he visited the temples of Som Nath and Dwarka. After this he marched to the Girnar Rocks and visited places around it. Meharban's Janamsakhi makes mention of these tribes. A local tradition also preserves memory of the Guru's visit to this place. Junagarh, 10 miles from the Girnar Rocks, was also visited by the Guru. According to a local tradition, there used to be a Gurdwara in the name of Guru Nanak. This Gurdwara does not exist now."

From the Girnar Rocks, the Guru reached Ujjain. On the way, he probably passed through Ahmedabad. At Ujjain, the Guru stayed near the famous Bharthari cave of Ujjain and to all probability, must have discussed issues relating to the Jogies and his own point-of-view. From Ujjain, the Guru reached Ajmer via Chittorgarh. The city was famous for the Dargah of the renowned Chisti Saint Muin-ud-din and for the Pushkar Lake considered to be sacred by the Hindus. From Ajmer, the Guru reached Mathura via Ambar. The city, at the time of Guru Nanak's visit, was a great pilgrimage centre of the Vaishnavite Hindus. According to the Meharban's Janamsakhi, the Guru visited the Keshva temple of Mathura which later on was destroyed by Emperor Aurangzeb as a part of his campaign against the Hindus.

From Mathura, the Guru set out for the Punjab.

The Guru's homeward journey from Mathura is not very clear because neither any written record nor any local tradition enlightens us about the route by which the Guru reached the Punjab. The possibility, however, is that the Guru took a slightly southerly route and reached Sirsa. At Sirsa, he stayed with a Muslim faqir outside the town and one of the walls of a house near it still bears the inscription bearing Chillia Baba Nanak. Recently a place has been discovered indicating the Guru's visit to this place.

From Sirsa, the Guru reached Pak Pattan, renowned for the Dargah of the Chisti Saint Farid Ganji Shakar. At the time of the visit of Guru Nanak, Sheikh Brahma (Ibrahim) was on the *gaddi* of Baba Farid. Guru Nanak discussed with him matters relating to his faith. Both of them developed respect for each other. From Pak Pattan the Guru reached Talwandi via Dipalpur.

Northern Udasi (Second Udasi)

After a brief say at Talwandi the Guru set out on his second udasi. The first important place he visited was Lahore. All the Janamsakhis make mention of this visit. From Lahore, the Guru proceeded to Sultanpur to see his sister Nanki visiting Ghawindi, Khalra and Patti on the way.

After short stay at Sultanpur, the Guru passed through the areas of Jullundur and Hoshiarpur and reached the abode of Pir Budhan Shah. At the place where he stayed, Guru Hargobind founded the city of Kirtarpur.

At Kirtarpur, the Guru entered the hilly region and proceeded to Bilaspur, the headquarters of Kahlur Raja. Besides this, the Guru visited Mandi, Rawalsar, Jawalaji and Kangra. From Kangra he marched to Baijnath which was then called Kirgram. Kir was after the name of the tribe 'Kir' that had established its ascendancy in this area. From Baijnath, the Guru, after crossing through Dulchi Pass reached Kulu. From Kulu to route led the Guru into Spiti valley, through Hamtu Pass. The Guru stayed in an old village called Mulani. Local tradition confirms this fact. Some relics of the Guru are also reported to have been preserved and worshipped by the people of the village.

Passing through the sprang or Prang Passes, the Guru was able to enter into Tibet and then proceeded on to the Mansarovar Lake and the Kailash Parbat (Sumer Parbat). While moving through the area, the Guru met some Jogi hermits living in caves. They were astonished to find him there and asked him how things were going in the plains below. In reply to them Nanak said that the moon of truth was completely enshrouded in the darkness of ignorance. Sin had devoured the world such was crying in distress. Jogis have retired to the mountains, and know nothing and were busy in besmearing their bodies with ashes. Who should save the world? Without a true Guru, it was sunk in ignorance. The Guru tried to convince them that instead of wearing empty forms and doing hard penances, they should exert themselves in the service of mankind.

Images of Guru Nanak are said to be present in some of the temples of this area. There is a class of people living in this area who have substituted or added the mantra Om Aham, Bhadra Guru Parm Sidhi Ham for or to the usual Buddhist Mantra, Om Manj Padmi Hami and it is these men in whose temple the image of Nanak is given a permanent place.

From the area of the Sumer Parbat the Guru turned north-west and after passing through Gartok and Rudok entered into Ladakh through the Chasul Pass.

From the Chasul Pass the Guru came to Upshi and from the place to Karunagar. "A remarkable point about this place is that in its neighbourhood, there are a few villages where none except Guru Nanak is worshipped." At a short distance from Karunagar, there is an old place called *Gumpha Hemus* which keeps the memory of the Guru's visit alive. The people here have preserved a stone on which the Guru is believe to have seated himself during the visit. From this, the Guru took the route going along the Indus and reached Skardu. This place has a Gurdwara named after Guru Nanak, a fact which testifies the Guru's visit.

From Skardu, the Guru reached Kargal wherefrom after passing through Joshila Pass and Baltan Nagar reached the famous Hindu Tirath Amarnath famous for a temple of Lord Shiva.

From Amarnath, the Guru reached Pehlgam and then to Matan the site of ruins of the historic temple of Martand. Here a Kashmiri Pandit Brahm Das had a religious discussion with the Guru. The Guru convinced him of the importance of Nam Marg and the futility of the knowledge having no connection with actions.

From Matam, Guru Nanak visited Anantnag, Srinagar and Baramula. All these places have Gurdwaras to mark the visit of the Guru.

From Baramula the Guru wended his way to Hasan Abdal, popularly known as Panja Sahib. It is said that here the Guru had to encounter a faqir, Wali Qandhari who in a fit of anger rolled down a heavy piece of rock on the head of the Guru which the Guru stopped with the outstretched palm of his hand. It is said that the impression of the Guru's palm was embedded in the stone which can still be seen. The story is not found in any early account and is probably a later addition.

At Hasan Abdal Guru Nanak decided to go to Talwandi to meet his people. On his home-ward journey he reached Tilla Bal Gudai, a major centre of Sidhi Naths. The Guru met an assembly of Sidhs here and had a long religious deputation with them. After this the Guru's important sojourn was Sialkot where a big Gurdwara stands in the honour.

From Sialkot, the Guru having halted at many places on the way reached Talwandi, the most important places of his stay were Pasrur and Saidpur (modern Eminabad in Gujranwala district, Pakistan).

Western Udasi (Third Udasi)

After staying for sometime at Talwandi, the Guru came to Sultanpur and from there started his journey to the west. During this udasi, the Guru like a Muslim pilgrim, carried a pot for his ablutions, a carpet under one arm and a book under the other. He was also accompanied by his devoted rebeck-player, Mardana.

From Sultanpur, the Guru visited Pak Pattan for the second time and met Sheikh Ibrahim Farid II in whose company he always felt great pleasure.

Therefrom he reached Multan, an ancient town of the Punjab. On the way, he passed through Tolumba (modern Makhdumpur), where he came across a notorious thief named Sajjan. He always dressed himself in pure white; wore the Hindu mark of sanctity on his forehead and displayed a Muslim rosary round his neck. He had built a Hindu temple and Muslim mosque at his gate. He invited way-farers to his residence and then robbed them. He was always in the watch for travellers and when he saw the Guru and his follower, he rejoiced for his victims. He invited them to his house. The Guru accepted the invitation with a sparkle of amusement in his eyes. When night fell the Guru asked Mardana to play the *Rabab* (a musical instrument) and invited Sajjan to come and listen to his hymns. Sajjan agreed. The Guru sang a hymn. The heart-searching voices of the Guru struck the tender chords of the Sajjan's otherwise stony heart, and no wonder, he was a changed man. 'The criminals' den became a temple for God's worship. It is said that he was the first to build Dharmshala for the spiritual and temporal attainment of all those who sought shelter and Sajjan was entrusted the job of disseminating the Guru's Gospel.

While at Multan the Guru had a meeting with Baha-ud-Din, a descendant and successor of the famous Sheikh Baha-ud-Din Zakaria, the founder of Suharwardy Sufi Silsilah in India. This Silsilah was not as liberal as that of Chisti.

From Multan, the Guru reached Uch and had discussion with Sheikh Haji Abdullah Bukhari (d. 1526 A.D.) a successor of Jala-ud-Din Bukhari who set up a center of Sufi faith before the 13th century.

From Uch, the Guru visited Sakhar. From there he travelled to Lakhpat by boat down the Kori stream which is now not extent. A Gurdwara stands at this place marking the visit of the Guru to this place. From Lakhpat, the Guru proceeded to the sea-shore where at Kuriani, he visited the old temples of Koteshwar and Narayanan Swami. A tank at Kuriani is called after the Guru's name marking the memory of his visit.

From Kuriani, the Guru reached Son Miani or simply Miani, fifty miles west of modern port of Karachi. At a few miles distance to the south of Miani was the famous temple of goddess called Kali Mata by the Hindus and Nana Devi by the Muslims at Hinglaj. According to Meharban's account the Guru paid a visit to this temple. Not far from Hinglaj, there is a Dharmsala preserving the memory of the Guru's visit to this place.

From Hinglaj, the Guru came back to the part of Miani and boarded ship for Arabia. Obviously, the Guru was not alone in the ship but in the company of a group of Muslim pilgrims bound for the same destination. At the coastal town of Alaswad the Guru landed. This place was a famous port for passengers from the east intending to go to Mecca which was not far off from here.

On reaching Mecca, he quietly lay down in the mosque and fell asleep with his feet stretched towards the Kaaba. The high priest (Rukun-ud-Din) admonished him for committing an act of sacrilege and said, "Why should you be so rude as to turn over your feet towards the House of God?" The Guru replied, "Pray be not so furious. Turn my feet to the direction where God is not." The Kazi saw reason in his statement because the prophet himself had said in Quran, "Allah is in the east and west. So wherever your turn there is cace of Allah". After this the Guru was asked whether he was a Muslim or a Hindu. He said, "I am neither of the two." Next they asked him as to who was superior of the two. "Neither as such" said he, "would be loved by God." "Both would weep if they had no good actions to recommend them."

Dr. W.H. McLeod, however, raises an objection to the authenticity of the Guru's visit to Mecca. He bases his conclusion on the ground that no non-Muslim could be allowed to enter even the precincts of the city of Mecca, not to speak of holy Kaaba, and hence the Guru did not stand any chance to visit this place. But this conclusion is incorrect because of the three reasons: firstly in the 16th century there was no strict restrictions on the visit to Mecca and it was possible for even a non-Muslim to make a visits to the place and secondly, the Guru was in the garb of a Muslim and was travelling in the company of a large number of pilgrims bound for the place. Thirdly, all the Janamsakhis make mention of the Guru's visit to the place and their evidence cannot be brushed aside without some really solid evidence to the contrary.

From Mecca the Guru proceeded to Medina, another holy city of the Muslims where the Prophet Mohammad had lived for so many years and died. The Guru reached there about nightfall and stopped outside the town. It happened to be a place where lepers were segregated and no provision was made for their comfort or treatment. The tradition goes that the Guru healed them all and as a result, the people came in crowds to see the Guru.

From Medina a common route led to the north through Palestine, Syrai and Turkey. It connected the various parts on the eastern coast of the mediteranian sea, with constantinople on the strains of Dardanelles. Both the Meharban and Bhai Mani Singh accounts say that the Guru visited Sham (Syria) and Rome (Turkey). This possibility is not altogether ruled out because Bhai Gurdas also throws a general hint of Guru Nanak's wide travels in this region. In case, we accept this view the journey of the Guru to Baghdad would have to be routed differently possibly through Damascus, the capital city of Syria.

The Puratan and Bala Janamsakhis make no mention of this visit, Meharban version only suggest it by implication. Janamsakhis record that Guru Nanak on being asked the source of light replied in the darkness itself. The dawn of morning is hidden in the gloom of the night. There is none but darkness in light and light in darkness. Self-assertion freezes the self into darkness. The fire of love melts the self into light. The historic city of the Guru's visit to Baghdad is established by the discovery of an inscription by one S.D.O. Kartar Singh during the days of the First World War. The place of discovery was outside the city where now a platform is raised. A significant point is that the visit is confirmed by the statement of Bhai Gurdas that the Guru on reaching Baghdad fixed up his place of stay outside the town. The English translation of the inscription is as under :

> "In memory of the Guru, that is the Divine Master, Baba Nanak, Faqir Aulia, this building has been raised with the help of seven Saints, and the chronogram reads. The blessed disciple has produced a spring of Grace year 917."

Swami Anand Acharya mentions in his book 'Snow Bird' that during the his visit to Baghdad, he found there another inscription, dated 917 Hijri which corresponds to A.D. 1511. The inscription reads:

> "Here spoke the Hindu Guru Nanak to Faqir Bahlol, and for these sixty years since the Guru left Iraq, the soul of Bahlol has rested on the master's world like a bee poised on a dawn-lit honey rose."

McLeod however, holds that Guru's visit to Baghdad is an un-substantiated possibility—a remote possibility not a strong one. He does not believe in the statement of Bhai Gurdas that Guru visited Baghdad. Moreover, he discredits the pertinent evidence of Baghdad inscription, referred to earlier. A careful analysis of the arguments advanced by him in support ofhis thesis shows that this was a hastly inference. Bhai Gurdas was no ordinary person, unconnected, unconcerned or uneducated. Moreover, he belonged to the family of the Gurus, being related to both Angad Dev and to Guru Arjan Dev. Obviously it is not easy to brush aside what he says.

There is another shrine built by Sherif Hussain in memory of Guru Nanak and situated at a distance of 12 miles outside the city of Baghdad to which Pakistan Diarist and writer, Zafar Pyami had made a reference in one of his books.

Resuming his journey from Baghdad, Guru Nanak set out on the caravan route to Tehran, the present capital of Iran. From Tehran, he followed the same route for Kandhar and Kabul. On the way he passed through Meshd. Bhai Mani Singh's Janamsakhi makes a reference to the visit.

From Meshd the Guru proceeded towards Kandhar and from there journeyed to Kabul alongwith the popular route. This city, at the time of the Guru Nanak's visit was the seat of Babur's government. Here existed a Gurdwara in memory of Guru Nanak in the Pan Chowk Jubba (now called god-i-Mehmand) of the old city upto the forties of the present century when the Government purchased the buildings of that area for their expansion and reconstruction plan for the city.

Since the visit of Guru Nanak, the Sikh contact had been carefully maintained. Sikh preachers were stationed there to disseminate the teachings of the Guru. At one time Bhai Gurdas also served as one of the Sikh-missionaries at Kabul. The Sikh sangat of Kabul was one of the most distinguished ones as grew up outside the Punjab.

Still another view, sometimes, offered is that the Guru while coming back, travelling in what we now call the central Asian Republic of the U.S.S.R. In support of this, the arguments given are (i) the existence of Dharmshala having udasi, Suthra or Sikh priests, (ii)Gyan Singh in his Panth Prakash and Twarikh Guru Khalsa makes mention of these places.

The view, however, in unacceptable, being somewhat far-fetched. The Dharamshalas which have been mentioned in this connection were built by Sindhi and Multani traders who carried on their trade in these areas and who were the followers and admirers of Guru Nanak.

From Kabul, the Guru took up the road which led through Jalalabad and the Khyber. At Jalalabad there is a historical Gurdwara marking the Guru's visit. Another place, Sultanpur, eight miles to the north west of Jalalabad also has a gurdwara in memory of the Guru, besides certain springs of water associated with the visit. Every year the Sikhs of Afghanisatan assemble there to celebrate the Baisakhi Festival. The astonishing feature of the celebrations is the procession marching from Jalalabad to Sultanpur. All this evidence indicates that the Guru proceeded by the Jalalabad route and passed through the Khyber Pass to reach Peshawar, the Peshawar of Tazik-i-Baburi.

In Peshawar, the Guru paid a visit to the Gorakh Hatri and had a long discourse with the Jogies impressing upon them the importance of the path chosen by him for the regeneration of the people and the individuals. This visit is mentioned in both the Puratan and Meharban Janaṃsakhis.

From Peshawar, the Guru travelled homeward by the road which passed through Hassan Abdal, Tilla Bal Godai, Gujarat (Pakistan) etc. and reached Lahore. On the way, he passed through Saidpur. Babur, at this time, invaded the Punjab for the third time in A.D. 1520-21) and inflicted horrible atrocities on the people.

According to the memoirs of Babar, "The inhabitants of Saidpur were put to the sword, their wives and children carried into captivity and all their property plundered." At this, the Guru's heart bled and moved to the core and he composed one of the finest compositions found in any language. Collectively, the hymns composed at this occasion are called `Babar vani.' The composition is an epitome of Guru Nanak's humanism and ethico-political philosophy. The deep anguish felt by the Guru is well-represented in the following lines:

"Thou ruled over Khurasan.
Now Thou terrifiest Hindustan.
He has sent you the mughal as a messenger of death.
Has slaughter and lamentations
Awakened no compassion in Thee?
The creator is the supreme Lord.
If a strong man beats a strong man
No feelings of resentment arise
But if a revenous line falleth on a herd of sheep.
The Shephert is expected to show his manlines."

It is said that the Guru was so much pained at the sight of loot, sack and rape that he fell down in anguish and went into a trance. "He had no nation at his back. He and his successor were yet to create one. Still he did not sit down in important range and uttered idle jeremiads. He did whatever he could be put heart into demoralised herd. It is said that the Guru was taken to concentration camp along with other prisoner and was given grinding mill to grind the corn, but the mill worked automatically. People observed the strange phenomenon and carried the news to one another. Babar saw the things for himself and was greatly moved by the scene. He begged the Guru to accompany him to his tent. The Guru agreed. When they were seated, a servant, at the gesture from the King brought two cups of wine and the King offered one to the Guru. The Guru smiled and said, "I take no intoxicants that cloud the mind. Their effect passes off. I have taken the intoxicant of love of my Lord, which fills me all times. Babar was greatly impressed and ordered all to be set at liberty.

From Saidpur the Guru proceeded to Talwandi and from there to Sultanpur. On the way, he came to the spot on the bank of the Ravi where he founded a new Basti named Kartarpur (city of the creator) where he lived a normal householders' life between 18 to 20 years. Even now he undertook short tours in the Punjab. One of them according to Bhai Gurdas, was to Achal Vatala and Multan. He cast off his udasi's garb and putting on the dress of a normal householder, began to lead a settled life.

The Chronology of Guru Nanak's Travels

Different Janamsakhis give different dates regarding the travels of the Guru. There is general agreement for the period upon Guru Nanak's departure from Sultanpur, but for the years which follow this event the Meharban, Puratan and Gyan-Ratanavali accounts all give different chronologies. The Bala version also leads us nowhere in matters of chronology.

We, however, can fix the probable dates of two fixed points, the departure. And the sack of Saidpur after which we understand that the Guru did not undertaken long tours. The first may be located about the year A.D. 1500. An association with Daulat KhanLodi has been acknowledged as likely and from this is follows that Guru Nanak probably began his travels in or about that year. The actual date may have been a few years earlier, but is unlikely to have been much later as it must have been in or soon after A.D. 1500 that Daulat Kahn received his appointment to Lahore. The second point which we are probably entitled to regard as fixed is 1520, the year in which Babar sacked Saidpur.

Guru Nanak's Activities at Kartarpur

Guru Nanak's life-period can be divided into three sub-periods on the basis of his activities. The first sub-period which was a period of three decades covered his childhood and early manhood; the second period which covered two decades was spent in travelling, and the last period whose span was two decades was that of relatively settled life at Kartarpur.

This last period is very important because the Guru gave expression to his own ideals in the context of normal family life. Besides, the Guru found time to concretise his plans and to evolve patterns to be followed by his followers. After a persual of a different Sakhis and vars of Bhai Gurdas we come across the following features of the Guru's activities:

Foundation of the Sikh Church

Guru Nanak toured all over the world to communicate his programme of awakening the people to realise truth. So that his work should endure, he established a network of centres which he called *manjis* side by side with the centres of all other faiths. In this way, he founded, in a well-planned way, a community of his new faith, and this community of inspired disciples became the body of Sikh Church which he called *sangat.* There was a Sikh Church now all over India and outside India, in Ceylon, Tibet and Middle East. No founder of any religion had built such a vast organisation, breaking all provincial, national and cultural barriers during his own life time. Guru Nanak knew that unless it was centralized he could not expect his noble faith to survive.

To this purpose, he addressed himself vigorously. He made it clear to every one that his church was to be embedded in secular society. When Guru Nanak went on his missionary tours he put on the robes of religious orders of the holy places he was visiting. Holiness in these centres was inseparable from the holy garb. Now when 'Baba came to Khartarpur he laid aside the pilgrims apparel, and put on ordinary worldly dress of the Panjabis of those days' He sat on cot and strove hard to dispel the darkness of ignorance in the mind of the people.

Disciplined Devotion

The second feature which we come across was the Guru's added emphasis in the religious and social discipline. The *Japji,* the *Rahiras*, the *Kirtan Sohila* were fixed as morning, evening and night prayers. In the day time, discussions were held, and the Master delivered sermons on the basis of questions put to him. Kirtan was held both in the early morning, following individual meditation, and also in the evening following the conclusion of the day's work. No one was expected to take the programme lightly. Guru himself observed the discipline very strictly.

Regular Instruction

The next feature of the Kartarpur pattern was the regular instrtuctions imparted by the Guru. Such instructions could be given to individual followers as also to the regular gatherings of his disciples although the latter was more probable. The content was, however, the same. "In both cases there would be the same emphasis upon the greatness of the God, upon his gracious self-revelation, upon the perils of human condition, and upon and paramount necessity of meditation on the Divine Name. Trust in conventional external forms would be exposed as essentially futile sometimes by means of gentle irony and at other times by direct denial of their efficacy. Those who placed their confidence in status conferred by caste or by health would be sternly admonished, and any one who depended on religious hypocrisy would be soundly condemned. His teachings had very deep effect on the people, many of whom embraced his religion. Bhai Budha, Lehna (later Guru Angad). Taru Poput, Prithi, Kheda, Ajita Randhava, Shdikh Mallo and Ubae Khan are some of the examples of conversions at first sight to the faith of the Guru.

Emphasis on Honest Labour

The fourth feature of the Kartarpur activities was regular daily labour. In the works of Guru Nanak asceticism in explicit rejected and in its place a disciplined worldliness is set forth as the proper path for the believer. The Guru himself worked in his fields and did all odd jobs which a peasant had to do. His concept of a disciplined worldliness also injoined a continuation of normal relationships and no wounded that his wife and sons lived with him at Kartarpur. After the fall of Sultanpur under the sway of Babur, Bibi Nanki and Jai Ram are also said to have shifted to Kartarpur.

Common Free Kitchen—*Langar*

The next thing of the Kartarpur pattern of activities which strikes is the foundation of regular free kitchen. Every one worked for his living and gave a part of his earning for the free community kitchen. All the people, the Brahmins and the Parihia, the king and the pauper, the Muslim and the Hindus had to sit together and eat their meals to their satisfaction. Free kitchens were attached to the *Khanqahs* of various sufi orders but they were never regarded either as the internal part of the Church or the social institution to serve as an instrument to evolve a society, free from caste-prejudices and wealth prejudices etc.

Collection of Compositions

The next important aspect of the Kartarpur activities of the Guru was the committing of his sacred words to writing. These were the years when Guru Nanak was surrounded by disciples who received instruction from him and who presumably recorded what they have received. According to Dr. Trilochan Singh "The scribes wrote down the compositions of the Guru and many devotees copied the daily prayers and hymns. These collections were called Bani Pothies (books of hymns). Some scholars suggest that *Japji* was composed at Kartarpur. This contention is unfounded. The *Japji* was composed at different periods. The first verse, according to all records, was composed when he received the all at Sultanpur Lodi. There is a story in old Manuscripts of Balas Janamsakhis in which Guru Nanak is said to have exited it and rearranged the verses in the present final orders. *Asa di var,* another composition was composed by Nanak at Pak Pattan at the request of Sheikh Ibrahim before he set out for his eastern and southern Journeys. Similar *O In Kar* was composed on the return from the South Pothi has been accepted as his maiden composition written during his early years. In this way, all the major compositions were completed before he settled down at Kartarpur. Out of the smaller compositions *Bara Maha,* seems to have been composed at Kartarpur. The Bani Pothis or the Book of his sacred hymns, compiled during his life time, became the spiritual regalia which passed on from him to Angad and from Angad to the third Guru. Out of the three or four Pothis brought by Guru Arjan from Goindrical one was Pothi which Guru Nanak got compiled and edited under the supervision of Angad during the last few years of his life.

Punjab Tour

No doubt, the Guru led a settled life at Kartarpur but he stole some time to go out of the place to enlighten the Yogis of Achal Batala which was one of their important centres. The occasion was the Shivratri festival. Guru Nanak acquainted them with his own philosophy. The Yogis who were at first furious at the sight of Namak calmed down and their leader Bhangar Nath expressed "Your are

Nanak, the greatest living enlightened of the dark age. In this iron age of ignorance and moral degradation you have shown to the people the path of sight and truth." Guru Nanak also met Bhai Lalo at Gujranwala where he had shifted from Eminabad after its sack by Babur. The Guru also went to Multan. Maqdoom Baha-ud-din accorded him hearty welcome. Jalal-ud-din of Uch also received him warmly. After meeting his friend Sheikh Ibrahim at Pak Pattan, Guru Nanak came back to Kartarpur. On September 22, 1539 A.D., Nanak passed away. According to Puratan Janamsakhi "Before Nanak's death, a quarrel arose between his Hindu and Mohammadan followers as to the disposal of his corpse. The former wished to burn, the latter to bury it. Nanak was asked to decide it. He said, 'Let the Hindus place flowers on my right and the Musalmans on my left in their natural state; one should not cut one's hair, dye one's clothes, nor change one's mind. It true that most Tibetan monks wear yellow, and shave their heads; these are practices that come from India, and symbolise humility and detachment from worldly things, Outside the more organised monastic tradition, however, the emphasis is that the natural goodness and power of growth within should be allowed to develop freely without interference from outside.

VISIT TO TIBET

From the accounts of a travaloque of a military officer, we come to know that Guru Nanak visited Tibet. The details of the travaloque is detailed here. After de-training at Siliguri in West Bengal, nearly 70 miles of rather tiring and nerve-breaking twists and turns is Gangtok, the capital of Sikkim State. Here the road bifurcates. The eastern section heads for the majestic and once most treated pass between India and Tibet—Natu La. The other track continued in northernly direction Pegong. The Pegong feature in the welcome rays of winter morning sun which had turned the countryside into a golden landscape. From the forward ledge of this feature the first glimpse of Lachen Chu and Lachung Chu marrying up and resulting into the mighty restless Tista river. The scenic beauty of the valley of river tri-junction is one that it shall probably ever remain beyond the descriptive power of any pen. It is a flat stretch about one mile long and nearly half a mile wide accommodating the small hamlet of Chunthang dotted with fluttering prayers flags and colourful lively people. Here are the gates of greater Himalayas.

The winter of North Sikkim is long and rigorous. Snow covers the ground for over half the year. The loneliness of its vast solitudes appals the heart and naught living meet the eye. The rocky wastes of the elevated regions with the scanty acres, where the stars can be discerned at mid-day and the thin air scarcely bears the sound of thunder to the ear, yields unequalled crops of simplicity and truth through the ages old influence of Lord Buddha's ancient World. Chunthang too has its heritage and richness, being in this part of the world. We had seen abundance of maize and potato crop is the surrounding areas. At places barely and millet were also grown. The fruit trees were loaded with peaches, plums, pears, appricots and other hill fruits. About half a century ago some Christian missionary had penetrated this virgin soil and introduced apples and cross. Only apply survived the rigours of climate, and it was also blossoming.

We descended to the river bed and crossed Lachen Chu over a shaky cane bridge, swinging and bumping at each step. Village Chunthang had not seen any strangers in the recent past, hence the whole population welcomed us by beating the drums and chanting prayers. The throngs appeared jubilant and bubbling with gaiety and high spirits. We entered the village with a trail of ever increasing multitudes. At one time there seemed to be no end to the stream of humanity. Was this influx for courtesy of custom or curiosity? The language barrier barred the discovery. Here only, for the first time I saw a Khampa, towering over crowds, nearly six and half feet tall, solidly built, tough and hardy with thick plaits of long hair. Although homeless and destitude but patient and resigned to fate. They are victims of Mao's elder-brotherly admonish of Tibet about a decade ago and now are a wandering tribe as we were in 1947 days.

At last we were lucky to discover a local volunteer guide who spoke five languages, Gorkhali, Lapcha, Bhutia, Tibetian and Hindi. The irony was that he spoke all of them simultaneously. Although we never agreed about the ratio of mixture but we were unanimous about. Hindi, the only language we understood, being only 10 per cent or less. However, he worked with zeal and utmost devotion and kept on giving running commentary without carrying whether we understand or not. We did not care either.

We were looking for some spot to open our pack lunch for a quick early munch before setting on the rest of day's journey. As if in answer to this demand we saw the accent appear. Around a glittering Chorten a red robed Lama came out briskly into the sun shine. He had a bell in his hand and he rang it with a wide sweep of vigour. The sound went up the surrounding hills, clear and full and echoes resounding much after he had retired from the scene. Can it be noon already? If it was mid-day, then we had let the morning pass without any work done. I looked up through the leafy green above me. The sun was poised at the zenith above the top of the trees, and moreover, we were hungry. The morning was over. Behind the Chorten where Lama had appeared was a mound of solid black rocks about 30 feet high and over 100 yards in diameter located in the centre of the meadow at the back of the village. Surprisingly it supported two huge trees at the top to give a deep cool shade and a trickling spring at its base was oozing cold refreshing drink. Was not it a traveller's abode? Is the nature not strange considerate? The mound was littered with hundreds of strands of multi-coloured flags fluttering in the unceasing gush of northly wind, conveying the gospel of Truth preached by Lord Buddha in the sultry and humiud Gangetic delta over 25 centuries ago. From the top of this mound, where we had settled down for our lunch we could see over the village roofs and tree tops and panoramic beauty of tri-river embrace. The flow of Tista's molten silver between the lush green mountains took the eye beyond the limits of perception.

During his apostolic sermons the guide uttered 'Nanak' which pricked our ears. We were now alert and all composed to de-cipher each world. He told us that a great personality called 'Rimpoche Nanak Guru' while on his way to Tibet had rested on that mound. The Guru had brought his rice-meal packed in banana leaves, as is the custom even today in banaan growing areas. The two commodities were unknown to hill folks. Guru having noticed their inquisitiveness bestowed them with a share of this strange cereal. This displayed fore-thought and instead of eating it away sprinkled the rice all over the meadow and buried the banana packing in a corner. Today the village harvests a rich crop of rice and bunches of delicious banana. As it was crop season, we had the unique opportunity the privilege of seeing Nanak's gift to the inhabitants of that unknown and Godforsaken part of the world, sprouting golden yellow paddy. We also saw clusters of banana trees but no fruits, probably we were off banana season. We were wonder-struck to see this strange phenomenon of rice and banana in the land of maize and apple. Is it not a miracle?

Nearly a year prior to this I was confronted with an identical issue. I had gone to Jelap La, a historic pass to the south-east of Natu La, which connects Tibet with West Bengal, skirting around eastern boundary of Sikkim and through Kalimpong. This was the pass traversed by Younghusband's Tibet expedition, and it is through this pass that the first telegraph link with Tibet was established. I was basking in the October sun right in the mouth of the pass, taking cover under a rock from a perpetual 30 miles-an-hour gale. I was lost in my imaginations of Jelap La's ocean of history. How many millions from times immemorial must have trodden this pass each one adding a pebble to its glory and enchanting *Om mani, padma e hum.* Will the day every revive itself? My thoughts were broken when startled by the soft steps of an approaching Lama. He had defied all artificial barriers and in the quest of the solace and tresspassed into India to unite with Buddha through the grace of His Holiness the Dalai Lama. His interrogation was not possible as we did not understand each other, however, a search produced few idols of certain deities which always formed part of every Lama's prayer kit. As customary with all religious devotees and more so with Mahayana Buddhist monks, without any provocation, this intruder got into a fit of exhortation explaining in his own lingua about the images he carried. He was unconcerned about my ignorance and blank looks. What he said I shall never know, but his devotion to his religion and sincerity of purpose was such that even from a communist with least conscience, he would have earned admiration and appreciation. One of the statue was miniature of 'Guru Nanak of Amritsar'. This was the only part of his lengthy speech which I had understood. I had ruled it out as a trained agent's good deception plan. A year later at Chunthang this fact was taking shape. A new light had dawned casting off the shadows of doubt which I had entertained against innocent refugee.

I was eager to find out the facts about Nanak's visit to Chunthang hence after lunch we climbed to a monastery located at the top of hill behind the village. We wanted to contact the in-mates of this Gumpa on the subject. We found that the Lamas there were on a 6-months praying spell with *'Man Varat'* and no one was allowed to see them. In utter disappointment we walked back to Chunthang and spent the night dog-tired but full of suspense and speculation.

Next morning we left for Lachung. Though the distance was not much but it turned out to be a real tough march. The attitude was telling on us and carriage of one's own limbs looked heavy and exhausting. The village Lachung is situated on the eastern bank of the river. The western bank is a precipice hundreds of feet towering above the water surface. Numerous streamlets converge on to this cliff and nearly half a dozen falls are formed vomitting milky streaks of vapourised discharge against the background of sky high black rock walls. Up hill and away from the village is an attractive Gumpa, which maintains record of all visitors. I saw an entry in the name of a French couple who visited the place in year 1910. Is this venture on part of these foreigners no as striking as the surroundings?

I was rather impatient. The moment Head Lama Sri Gelong Chang Chube at Lachung Gumpa finished with the introductory talk about the monastery, I dragged him on to the subject of 'mound in Chunthang village.' He spoke fairly good Hindi, hence there was no room for conjectures. He gave the name of the saint who visited that area as 'Rimpoche Nanak Guru of Punjab'. He also conformed the legend of rice and banana plantation. He confused that he was unaware of any written record of Nanak's visit, but he confirmed that this myth was a firm belief amongst the locals. He gave further details of Guru's journey. According to him Guru went to Tibet by that route. From there a track leads to Khora La which connects North Sikkim with Pahari in Chumbi Valley of Tibet. He also told us that on the out-skirts of Payako Chin village, which is at the base of Khora La ridge, there is a stone with inscriptions in a non-local language, probably in Hindi or Gurmukhi and it is a common notion that it is an allegory giving details of Guru's journey through that point. This 'udasi' or Guru Nanak has not appeared in any history so far as it yet remains to be discovered. Therefore, the very idea of visiting the spot where this rock was indicated was exciting. I was wanting to photograph the inscription and approach the archaeological department for its interpretation if in an unintelligible script. The village Payako Chin was another 3 to 4 days march, and with our will and determination the objective seemed to be well within our reach, but unfortunately the weather betrayed us and for the next 4 days we had a literal cloud-burst. Movement became impossible for quite sometime to come due to the rivers being in spate. We were dwindling on our provisions, hence very reluctantly we had to take most unwelcome decision to abandon the proposed venture and retire.

Many a time the fascinating idea of another attempt intoxicates me, but it seems that for the time being it shall remain only a question with me, "Did Nanak visit Tibet?"

(Will some adventurous explorer undertake the journey to this part of the country and find out if there is any document or inscriptional record of the visit of Guru Nanak to Tibet? Traditions and legends are seldom without historical truth and are, therefore, worth collecting. Who knows some one may get at some tradition based on unalloyed truth on the subject.—GS)

GURU NANAK AT PURI
with
Sri Chaitanya and his followers
(Ganda Singh)

According to the Sikh accounts Guru Nanak visited Puri in the year 1566 Bikrami, corresponding to April 1509-March 1510 *(Gurusabda-ratnakar Mahankosh*, new edition, p. 375). The shrine of Jagannath here is of particular attraction for the Vaishnavite Hindus who gather here in large numbers for the *Rath Yatra*, or Chariot festival, held on Asarh Sudi 2, in June or July. At the time of the after-dusk *arati*, performed in the temple with a large number of lamps lighted for the purpose, and flowers and censors placed on salvers, the Guru was invited to participate in it. He was, however, not interested in this type of artificial worship, "while the expanse of the firmament, the sun and the moon, the procession of stars, the natural incense of the sandal, the winds and forests, were the fitting accessories of Nanak's purer worship of the God of creation." He then recited there his well-known hymn on the real *arati* of God beginning with '*Gagan mai thal' (Dhanasri, Arati)*. This bewildered both the priests and the worshippers present there.

Here he also exposed a Brahman who used to tell the people that with his eyes closed he could see the secrets of the world with his mental eyes. And, when he had closed his eyes, the Guru quietly hid his water-jug which he was unable to find (Macauliffe, *Sikh Religion*, i. 81-83).

Dr. Bimanbehari Majumdar tells us in his *Chaitanya-chariter Upadan*, on the authority of Ishwardas's Uriya *Chaitanya Bhagawat*, that at Puri Guru Nanak also met the great Vaishnava saint Krishna-Chaitanya, popularly known as Chaitanya *Prabhu*. The two saints seem to have spent sometime together and enjoyed the divine music, *Kirtan*, in which both of them found special pleasure.

The *Chaitanya Chariter Upadan* (Calcutta University, 1939, 1959) has quoted, on page 500, the following two passages wherein Guru Nanak is mentioned as participating in *Kirtan* with Chaitanya *Prabhu* and his disciples and devotees. These passages have been transliterated into Devnagri, Gurmukhi and Roman scripts, and translated into English for the benefit of our readers.

Gurmukhi Transliteration

Transliteration in Roman

Srinivasa ye Vishvambhara
Kirtana Madhya bihara,
Nanak Saranga e dui
Rupa Sanatana dui bhai,
Jagai Madhai ekatra
Kirtana Karanti e nritya,

(Chapter 61)

Nagar Purushottama Dasa
Jangali Nandini ta pash
Nanak sahite gahana
Gopala guru Sanga tena
Sangeta matta Balarama
Bihara Nilagiri Dhama

(Chapter 61)

Translation in English

Visvambhara (Chaitanya), the resort of the world, takes delight in the *Kirtan* song with Nanak and Saranga, the two brothers Rupa and Sanatana, Jagai and Madhai. All of them dance while participating in the *kirtan.*

At Puri Chaitanya roams about with Nagara Purushottam Dasa, who was accompanied by Jangali and Nandini on his side. He also took along with him Nanak, Gopala guru and *Matta* Balarama.

There is a difference of opinion about the date of the *Chaitanya Bhagawat* from which the above quotations have been taken. There is no mention of the date in the manuscripts preserved in the Prachi Samiti at Cuttock. There are two of them there. According to Dr. Prabhat Mukhopadhyay, Reader in History, Utkal University, in his article in Bengali in the *Sahitya Parisat Patrika* (Calcutta), in 1343 B.S./1936 A.D., part II, page 76), the book was written towards the end of the sixteenth century, Dr. Bimanbehari Majumdar, the greatest living authority on Chaitanya studies, and the author of the *Chaitanya-Chariter Upadan,* however, is of the opinion that "it could not have been written before the seventeenth century." Even in the latter case, the *Chaitanya Bhagwat* is a very reliable source of the life the great saint and may be said to have been based on contemporary or semi-contemporary material which would then have been readily available to its author, Ishwardas.

The two references quoted from *Chaitanya Bhagwat* leave us in no doubt about Guru Nanak having met Chaitanya Prabhu and most of his disciples and admirers at Puri and participating in *Kirtan* with them. For Guru Nanak, *Kirtan* was, in fact, the most effective method of preaching and spreading his message. On the other hand, Chaitanya was also enamoured of the divine music and dance in praise and honour of Radha and Krishna.

The other persons, who, according to Ishwardas joined the *kirtan* of the two saints were Sarang, the companion of Guru Nanak, the two brothers Rup and Sanatan and Jagai and Madhai, as also Nagar Purushottam Das, accompanied by Jangali and Nandini and Gopal Guru and *Matta* Balram.

About Sarang, the companion of Guru Nanak at Puri, I have no doubt about his being the Guru's *Sarangi-wala* or *Sarangid—Sarangi* or rebeck-player—Bhai Mardana, who might have been called so by those who did not know his real name. Mardana *Sarangi* or *Rubabi*, as we know, was an inseparable companion of the Guru during his travels.

The two brothers Rup and Santan were high class Brahmans, having descended from a prince of Karnat, Rupesvara, who had settled in Bengal and whose descendants Padamnabha, Mukand and Kumar had become completely Bengalized. Kumar's sons Rup and Sanatan were ministers of Allauddin Husain Shah (1483-1519). They left the royal service and became followers of Chaitanya.

Rup met Chaitanya at Prayag (Allahabad) and received his lessons in *Krishna-bhakti* and was sent to Vrindaban to revive there the places sacred to the memory of Lord Krishna. Sanatan Goswami followed Chaitanya to Varanasi where he was initiated into the Vaishnavite cult. Krishnadas Kaviraj Goswami, the author of the *Chaitanya Charitamrit*, gives us the details of Chaitanya's teachings to the two brothers, with particular reference to Sanatan. Both of them, according to Sir Jadunath Sarkar, died in 1554. They were both poets and philosophers. Rup wrote three dramas and numerous hymns, lyrics and theological works.

Their nephew Jiva Goswami (1511-1596), like his uncle, was a scholar of considerable merit and his invaluable work the *Sat-Sandharbha*, contains the essence of the philosophy of the Bengal School of Vaisnavism, known as *Achintya-Cheda bheda vada* (Inexplicable Monism in Dualism). He was also a poet and a grammarian.

Jagai and Madhai were two drunken ruffians of Navadwip who had been reclaimed by Chaitanya, and thenceforward they 'lived in Nadia as very pious men.' They occasionally visited their teacher at Puri.

In the second quotation from the *Chaitanya Bhagawat* (chapter 64), there are the names of Jangali and Nandini, two male Vaishnavites who went about dressed as women or Lord Krishna's *Gopis* to worship their deity. In *An Account of the District of Purena in 1809-10* by Francis Buchanan, edited from the Buchanan MSS, by V.H. Jackson, published at Patna in 1928, it is mentioned under 'Sects of Mithila Hindus', on page 273, that :

> In the territory of Gaur, at a place called Jangallitola, mentioned in my account of the topography of Kaliyachak, is the chief seat of the Sakhibhav Vaishnavas,

who dress like girls, assume female names, dance in honour of God, and act as religious guides fro some of the impure tribes. The order is said to have been established by Sita Thakurani, wife of Adwaita, but so far as I can learn has not spread to any distance, nor to any considerable number of people. The two first persons who assumed the order of Sakhibhav were Janggali, a Brahman, and Nandini, a Kayastha. Janggali, was never married, and it is only his pupils that remain in this district, and these are all Vaishnavas who reject marriage. Nandini was married, but deserted his wife to live with the pious Sita. He settled in Nator, where his disciples still remains.

Nagar Purushottam-das, whom Janggali and Nandini accompanied to Puri, was the son of Sadasiva Kaviraja and an intimate disciple of Nityananda.

Gopal Guru was a prominent disciple of Chaitanya. He prescribed rules of meditation for the followers of the Prabhu. He is a different person from Gopal Bhatta, the nephew of the celebrated Vedantist Prakashananda, who were latterly converted to Bhakti by Chaitanya and changed his name to Prabodhananda.

Matta (or Mast, God-intoxicated) Balram was the popular name of Nityananda who was one of the earliest disciples and companions of Chaitanya Prabhu and was like a brother to him as was Balaram to Lord Krishna. He was verily Chaitanya's twin-self. It was he who was mishandled by the drunken *badmash* Madhai and was rescued from his hands by Jagai. And this incident was responsible for their reclamation by Chaitanya. There was also a famous Uriya Poet by the name of Balaram, one of the renowned 'Pancha Sakhas'. But *Matta* Balram, mentioned as a close partner of Chaitanya Prabhu in music and dance, could not be other than Nityananda. Vrindabandas, the author of the Bengali *Chaitanya Bhagavata,* was a disciple of Nityananda.

Now about the date of the historic meeting of Guru Nanak and Chaitanya Prabhu at Puri. According to Kahan Singh's *Gursabdaratnakar Mahan-kosh,* second edition, p. 375, Guru Nanak visited Jagannath Puri in Sambat 1566 Bikrami, corresponding to March 27, 1509, to March 27, 1510 AD.

In his introductory chapter on 'A short life of Chaitanya' of *Chaitanya's Life and Teachings* (third edition, 1932, p.10), Sir Jadunath Sarkar tells us that Vishwambhar—that was the original name of Chaitanya—son of Jagannath Mishra, a Brahman of the Vaidik subcaste, was initiated as a *Sanyasi,* with the name of Krishna-Chaitanya, in January 1510 by Keshav Baharati of the village of Katwa. Born at Navdwip on February 4, 1486 Chaitanya was then 24 years of age, with the 25th year beginning on February 4, 1510. Having taken to the life of *Sanyas,* he set out on a pilgrimage in the month of June 1510.

The distance from Navdwip to Calcutta is 75 miles, and from Calcutta to Puri in 250 miles, making the total distance from Navdwip to Puri, which was Chaitanya's main destination in the first instance, to about 325 miles. There was then no other place of any great religious importance, from Chaitanya's point of view, to have detained him unnecessarily on the way. He must have, therefore, arrived at Puri in about three weeks, towards the end of June or in the beginning of July 1510. This can coincide with Guru Nanak's visit to Puri in the Bikrami year 1566 (mentioned in the *Mahan-kosh*), which ended on March 27, 1510. Presumably, the Guru was already there, having arrived at Puri in March 1510, and had been either staying on there or visiting the surrounding areas.

All things considered, therefore, it may be reasonably inferred that Guru Nanak arrived at Puri towards the end of 1566 Bikrami (March 1510) and met Chaitanya Prabhu and his followers there is July 1510.

GURU NANAK AT BAGHDAD

Sewaran Singh

At Baghdad, the Master (Guru Nanak) stayed at the graveyard outside the town, and Mardana as usual was with him early in the morning before dawn, Mordana, as usual, played upon the *Rabab*, and the Master sang his song about the infiniteness of God and His Creation wherein occurred the expression: "There are numerous *patals*, earths, and innumerable *akashs*, skies," when some Muhammadan who was listening to it and understood its purport went and reported the blasphemy of the utterance, inasmuch as the Koran had mentioned seven earths and seven skies only, to the *Sajj ıdanashin* of the shrine of Peer Dastgir Abdul Qadir Jilani. The Dastgir Pir directed the offender to be stoned to death, and numerous people of the town immediately armed themselves with stones and rushed out. In the meanwhile the Master's morning prayers had concluded, and at the end the Master shouted out his greetings of *Sat Kartar*, in a voice full of Divine Electricity, which immediately disarmed the people. On this, one of the Peers, Bahlol by name, came forward and had a discourse with the Master on the subject of the Morning Song. The Peer was accompanied by his son, and such was the effect of the Master's answers, which it may be mentioned were never argumentative, that first the son and then the father confessed their conversion and admitted the truth of the maxim that Almighty God' creation was not confined to seven earths and seven skies, but was composed of millions and millions of planets and universes. The Master stayed in Baghdad for four months and held many conversations with the Peers and other holy men of the place. Before his departure from there he was presented with a robe as a token of respect and submission, on which some verses in Arabic characters were inscribed. This *Chola* or Robe is still preserved at Dera Baba Nanak. Bhai Santokh Singh mentions a similar Robe, with inscription on it in five different characters, having descended on the Master from the Heavens in Abbysinia.

Swami Anandacharya, now said to be settled in Norway, in his work, entitled *Snow Birds*, records that, during his travels, he found an inscription, dated the year 912 *hejri*, in the outskirts of Baghdad, in the Arabic language, which, translated, read thus:

> Here spake the Hindu Guru Nanak to Faqir Bahlol; and for these sixty winters, since the Guru left Iran, the soul of Bahlol has rested on the Master's word,

like a bee poised on a dawnlit honey-rose.

It has been suggested that Bahlol, referred to in it, was probably the *sajjadanashin* of Bahlol Dana, who was a Faqir of considerable renown. The matter certainly to worthy of further investigation.

During the recent Great War, when the British and Indian armies conquered Baghdad, they discovered this place where the Master had his Discourse with Bahlol. It lies to the west of the town and between the old graveyard to the north and the present Baghdad-Samara railway line to the south. The present writer's brother, Dr. Kirpal Singh, then a Captain in the Indian Medical Service, also saw it during the War, and he, in his letter to the present writer, dated the 15th October, 1918, described it as follows :

> It is really a very humble looking building and know to very few people except the local Sikhs. To some Arabs it is known as well by the name of tomb of Bahlol. You enter the building by a small door, on which something is written in Arabic, not visible to a casual visitor. Even with attention it is difficult to read. I could not read it and hence could not copy it. I have taken a photograph of the outside which I shall forward to you in due course. Entering the building, you come to a brick paved passage going to your right straight into the room (with a *verandah*) wherein you find the tomb and the Raised Platform. In the courtyard there are a few trees, mostly pomegranates. The room in which there are the platform and the tomb, has two doors, one of which is open whilst the other is barred. As you enter the room, you come face to face with the platform which roughly is about 2 to $2^{1}/_{2}$ ft. high, and about 3' by 4' in dimensions. It is now covered with handkerchiefs of various colours presented by the Sikhs. In the centre close to the wall you find a picture of Sri Guru Nanak, presented by some energetic Sikh, above which you find the slab with the writing which I reproduced in this letter for you. The name of the man is charge is Sayad Yusuf."

The site plan of the Memorial is given below:

Note: No. 1 is the Master's platform. No. 2 is Bahlol's Tomb and No. 3 is the tomb said to be of Muhammad Pasha Arnaoot.

A free translation of this inscription, which is in the Turkish language, is as follows :

> Murad saw the demolished building of Hazrat Rab-i-Majid, Baba Nanak, Fakir Aulia, and rebuilt it with his own hands, so that historic memorial may continue from generation to generation, and His *Murid-i-sa'eed* (the blessed disciple) may obtain heavenly bliss.—Year 917 H.

It is obvious that this inscription is not the same which Swami Anand Acharya saw and translated in his *Snow Birds*, and it is possible that the inscription deciphered by the Swami is the old and ancient Arabic inscription which the writer's brother noticed outside the outdoor of the building, but which he found no longer decipherable. The inscription of which the photograph is reproduced seems to be a later one which some descendant in faith of Bahlol seems to have put up on reconstructing the building, but he has not mentioned the year of the reconstruction.

The year under this inscription may be 917, or it may, it is said by one who is competent to read it and has given the above translation, be also read as 927. The latter reading seems to coincide with the chronology adopted in this biography. In this light, the Master visited Baghdad in the year 1520-21 of the Christian era. The reading of the year by Swami Anandacharya, in the old inscription, which is either now lost or become undecipherable, seems erroneous.

From Baghdad, the Master seems to have returned, through Baku (where some Gurmukhi inscriptions on old delapidated temples, obviously giving the pedigrees of certain udasi Sikh priests of the Temples, have been discovered, and formed the subject of a paper by Lala Parma Nand before the Punjab Historical Society, some years ago), Persia, Turkestan, Kabul and Peshawar. A Gurdwara in Kabul, and another at the Water Springs at Askara, nine miles from Kabul, towards Jallalabad, are still associated with the Master's name.

ON READING AN ARABIC INSCRIPTION
In a Shrine Outside the Town of Baghdad
Dated 912 Hejira

Shri Ananda Acharya

182 Upon this simple slab of granite didst thou sit, discoursing of fraternal love and holy light, O Guru Nanak, Prince among India's holy sons!

What song from the source of the Seven Waters thou didst sing to charm the soul of Iran!

What peace from Himalaya's lonely caves and forests thou didst cary to the vine-groves and rose-gardens of Baghdad!

183 What light from Badarinath's snowy peak thou didst bear to illumine the heart of Bahlol, thy saintly Persian disciple!

Eight fortnights Bahlol hearkened to thy words on Life and the Path and Spring Eternal, while the moon waxed and waned in the pomegranate grove beside the grassy desert of the dead.

And after thou hadst left him to return to thy beloved Bharata's land, the fakir, it is, said, would speak to none nor listen to the voice of man or angel;

His fame spread far and wide and the Shah came to pay him homage—but the holy man would take no earthly treasures nor hear the praise of kings and courtiers.

Thus lived he—lonely, devoted, thoughtful—for sixty winters, sitting before the stone whereon thy sacred feet had rested;

184 And ere he left this house of Ignorance he wrote these words upon the stone: "Here spake the Hindu Guru Nanak to Fakir Bahlol, and for these sixty winters, since the Guru left Iran, the soul of Bahlol has rested on the Master's word—like a bee poised on a dawn-lit honeyrose."

3

His Teachings

Guru Nanak's teachings may be evaluaged in the context of the contemporary socio-political and religious condition and his vision vis-a-vis the people. Politically, the Punjab was not well. Undoubtedly, it experienced peace during the Lodi rule, yet it could not escape the strain to which it was put on account of the political intrigues at Delhi. Its administrative apparatus had to be overhauled to meet the new challenges; but it was not possible for Daulat Khan to do on account of his own uncertain future and the danger of the Mughals hovering on the periphery of the Punjab. Besides this, the corruption, the absence of the Political will to uplift the masses and growth of feudalistic tendencies—all these things had made the political scene unpleasant—rather irritating. Socially, the people were lacking in dynamism, so essential for the progress of a nation. Still the society based on caste-system was the norm for the Hindus. Muslims too, had lost their initial robustness and the will to go ahead. They too had developed classes which believed in exclusiveness. Moral corruption, voluptuousness, hypocrisy had stalked both the Hindus and Muslims. Besides the religious groups, there were tribal, regional, local and social groups—each having air of superiority to the other and reposing faith in social exclusiveness. Religiously too, the contemporary society presented a somber picture. It was marked by so many religious sects—each affirming faith in its own indispensability and finality.

Shaivites, Vaishnavites, Siddacharyas, Jogies were the cases in point. So far as the Jogies were concerned, they were quite strongly entrenched in the minds of the people and were a factor to be reckoned with. Neo-Brahmins was also making headway. It was helped by the Hindu Zamindars who were able to acquire some political powers during the last days of the rule of the Sultans. All these sects and certain good principles; but certainly none put forward a programme suitable for the general uplift of the people.

Islam which, during the initial stages of the Muslim rule, the vitality which could initiate social processes for general good of the people, also failed to do the needful because firstly it became the religion of conquerors instead of remaining the religion of the people and secondly many empty rituals and ceremonies crept into it.

Guru Nanak observed all this. Obviously his task was extremely difficult. Social groups having religious sanction die hard. Similarly religious faiths and ideas, regional and local affinities also required strong bettering. Caste barriers also were not easy to demolish. Punjab was the welter of semitic civilization and Aryan civilization opposed to each other. Guru Nanak was to prepare a programme in a way acceptable to all types of people.

He, notwithstanding the hurdles, framed his teachings which epitomised the Guru's vision and also the due consideration which he gave to different psychic, psychological, sociological and social facets of the people. His concept of God, his theories of Karma, Hukam, Shabd, Guru, his social and economic ideas, his emphasis on ethics-based political and social actions—all these things aimed at the liberation of men from parochialism of all kinds and lending him necessary dynamism to enable him to shed off his characteristic inertia and to work for the betterment of the people as a whole.

NATURE OF GOD OF GURU NANAK

Concept of God—Monotheism

The Unity of God-Head

'Mul-Mantra' starts with figure 1 and sikh tradition is unanimous in accepting this as a declaration of the Unity of God. There is no other than the One. Guru nanak himself says : The Lord is manifest in the three worlds. He is eternal, Giver and there is no other.

God is for him simply Ek, the one, "There are six systems of philosophy, six Gurus and six patterns of instructions but the Guru of these Gurus is one though his manifestations be many."

The affirmation of unity raises an obvious question : Is this the one of monotheism or is it the one of monism? If the thought is t be designated monotheistic, we must be clear that the monotheism of Nanak was quite different from that of Islam or other semitic religions. In Islam, God is unity and the sole cause of creation and is beyond it, but in Nanak's thought, stress has been laid on divine immanence whose revelation is of fundamental importance in the quest for salvation. The express it in simple words, Guru Nanak's concept of God is monotheistic in the sense that He is unity and the created universe is also the expression of the oneness of God. Guru Nanak's monotheism is also different from that of neo-Brahamanism. In the latter's case implicit Monotheism is expressed through a plurality of deities. Guru Nanak, no doubt, occasionally makes use of the deities of Hindu Mythology, but he uses them only as symbols to represent particular aspects of the divine activity.

God is Transcendent and Immanent

To Nanak God is both transcendent and Immanent. Trascendence has been expressed in term of distance as well as authority. He is apram-par—further and farther. He is Baikunth-ke-wasi—resident of Heaven and Ucho-Ucha—higher than the high. At places, the Guru names Him Malik, Sahib—Master, Jagan Nath, the Lord of the world; Nar-Pati—the Lord of Man, Jagdish and Tribhawan Dhani. Closely connected with it, God is transcendental in the sense that it is His will which is responsible for all creations and he is not subject to material limitations. God is immanent as well. Guru Nanak did not believe in an absentee God sitting idle outside the universe and watching it. He sees the Supreme Being, within the world-process as well as outside it. Out of his own, Absolute Being, God created nature, the indwelling spirit of the creation :

> God created Ḥimself
> And assumed a Name
> Second besides Himself
> He created Nature
> Seated in Nature He watches
> With delight what he creates.

Guru Nanak himself says :

> The one Omkar, wholly apart, immortal
> Unborn, without caste, wholly free
> Ineffable, without form or visible sign
> But scorching I perceived him in every heart

By making it express that He resides in every heart, the Guru established communications between God and Man. Failure to grasp this is regarded and immense loss. The immanent spirit of God is continuously present in nature and within the human heart and nature which are dependent on His Will. God Himself transcends the worlds of things and selves. He is beyond the creation in the sense while nature depends on Him. He acts through it. Similarly He does not depend on man but acts through him.

Nirguna and Sarguna

God is both Nirguna and Sarguna, both absolute and conditioned, both unmanifest and manifest. For Nanak's God, in his primal aspect, is absolute, unconditioned for attributeless (without Tamas, Rajas, Satwik).

He was unfolded the three gunas has made His abode in the fourth, i.e. to say beyond three gunas. In this absolute aspect God is beyond the scope of human comprehension.

But in order that he should be within the range of human perception, He endows Himself with attributes. He the nirguna of His own volition became sarguna in order that man might know Him enter into a unitive relationship with Him.

From His absolute condition He, the Pure One became manifest; from Nirguna He became Sarguna.

It is in this Sarguna aspect that man can know God and accordingly it is this aspect which is the object of Guru Nanak's meditation and of his expository utterances. This Nirguna nature of God, for all its fundamental quality received little attention, for beyond the mere affirmation there is nothing man can say of it. In the ultimate condition of union man does indeed participate in this absolute quality and so in experience it can be ultimately known out the way to God, the Sadhna must be conceived with the Sarguna expression.

The term Sarguna is Vaishnavistic and implies belief in Avtars, the divine incarnates; but in Guru Nanak's usage, this is certainly not the meaning of the term. Nanak uses this term to denote divine immanence and certainly not something resembling antropomorphic God.

Creator, Sustainer and Destroyer

There are a number of references in Nanak's compositions which pertain to the creative activity of God. He affirms "For countless aeons there was undivided darkness. There was neither earth nor heavens; but only the infinite order of God (Humak)." Then is the order of God that was responsible for the creation of the universe. Guru Nanak uttered:

> "His will is that creates the universe through will one cannot tell
> Through Will the stream of life both flow
> Through Will is greatness won." *(Jap)*

> "The Lord of Himself created himself, and
> Assumed He Himself the Name
> And then He created Nature and abiding with it
> He revealed in His wonder." *(Asm* M.1) 463

Sustainer

God not only creates world but also loves it and in doing so sustains it.

> "He who created the world watches over it
> Appointing all to their various task."

And in another passage, both his creative and sustaining activities are affirmed.

He being sustainer participates in the life of the universe which he has established but from this it may not be inferred the God was not self-existent, it only means—

God, the one is creator and sustainer and so too He is destroyer:

"He who created also destroys; apart from His there is no other.......Having destroyed, He builds and having built He destroys. Casting down He raises up and raising up he casts down. Having filled the sea He causes it to dry up and then fills it again for He, the one beyond care and anxiety has the power to do it.

God is Omnipotent and Omniscient

He is very powerful. According to Nanak, God is the sovereign Lord, the wielder of absolute authority, the possessor of unqualified power. Guru Nanak is his composition 'Jap' says:

"Whatever is, is by His will, nothing is outside His sway."

After the manner of a King, He works His will be simple order 'God said, let there be light and there was light'. Such is power of God that he can make hills disappear and rivers flow in their place and seas to emerge in place of sandy deserts (Var Majh ki Slok Mohalla 1). He is the Lord of Sur (gods) and Asur (demons). He is Asur Sangar and Sarb Kala Samrath. He has immeasurable power.

God is accordingly Anath, Omnipotent. He is also Omniscient; He is Dana, Bina and Prabin (Knower, Seer & Wise) and Antaryami (knower of the innermost things). Guru Nanak utters:

> The Sovereign Lord created and visible world
> He sees all, comprehends all and knows all
> (creation) both within and without.

God is Ternal. God is Satya—Permanent

Guru Nanak is 'Jap' says that God is that—permanent. He is 'abnasi'—eternal, 'anandi'—without beginning, 'akal'—beyond time. He is Ajuni—unborn, non-incarnated. He is Achal—constant. He is Amar—deathless, Achut—incorruptible. Since God is unborn and, self-existent; he cannot come as incarnate; because to be incarnated would mean caught up in the cycle of death and birth, the characteristic quality of the unstable world and the ultimate anti-thesis of God's own Eternal being. But the world which he has been created is unstable and unpermament subject to flux, decay and dissolution. God is, therefore, detached from his own creation which is maya; He is *Niranajan, Atit Nirmal* and *Nirlep.* Nor can he be represented in idols because idols can never be beyond time and can perish any moment. In this way the doctrines of Avtars and idols worship have no place in Nanak's theistic thought.

Formless

As a complementary to the absolute nature of God, He has been regarded as formless because to give form to God would mean circumscribing the absoluteness of Him. In token of the affirmation of this belief, Nanak rejects not merely idols and avtars but also authromorphic language. He is Arup—Nirankar—the formless one. Nirankar is in fact the oft-used epithet of Guru Nanak to express this particular concept. Nanak utters 'You do not have any form nor any material sign; you are above all this."

"The absolute nature and the eternal being of God are metaphysical qualities and there now arises the question of whether for Guru Nanak the human understanding of God can proceed from the strictly metaphysical or something more concrete. The answer is a firm negative and a negative which in its firmness rejects nor merely idols and Avtars but also authomorphic language." He is arup—

formless, nirankar—the formless one. Guru Nanak says :

Thou the eternally unchanging formless one.

(Nirankar)

Ineffable

God who is absolute, eternal, Akal and formless cannot be grasped by human understanding which is strictly limited and any effort to define Him would circumscribe the infinite to bring within narrow bounds the one who is boundless. God is ineffable and man's proper and inevitable response to any authentic glimpse of the Being of God can only be that of me (*vissed*), of fear and wonder before him Who is beyond comprehension. 'He is *agam, agochar*—inscrutable beyond the reach of intellect. He is Alakh—ineffable.

As God is beyond expression so is His Hukam, the Divine Order of creation.

"No one has comprehended Thy Hukam and one can describe it. Were a hundred poets to gather together their singing could not even approach a description of it. No one has grasped its worth; all but repeat what they have heard."

Critical Appraisal of the Concept of God

Guru Nanak's concept of God should be understood and appraised against the background of the experiences, he gathered. The Guru travelled far and wide. He came across different people with different religious faiths. He met Shaivites Vaishnavites, Neo-Vaishnavites, Naths, Sidds, Sunnies, Shias, Sufis, the Muslim divines of Mecca, Medina and Baghdad, Lamas and the multitudes having faiths in local of regional deities as well as totems, magical and esoteric practices. People of different races inhabiting India and Central Asia also came in his contact. He also saw the operation of different culture-patterns and political set-ups. It can also be surmised that the Renaissance Movement which opened new vistas in the domain of the ideas on the position, role and dignity of man had its effect on the ultra-sensitive mind of the Guru. Likewise, the Guru could have not escaped the effect of the Reformation which greatly weakened the authority of the Roman Catholic Church and its Pope of Rome, thereby opening the way for rational thinking in matters of religion and morality. Being extremely inquisitive, he discussed his points with people of variegated shades of opinion. His 'Vani' is replete with examples elucidating his anguish and dissatisfaction at the meaningless wranglings of the people on religious and social matters. The crafts of priests of different religious communities were perhaps the most dangerous obstacles which is not removed would spoil all the chances of Global Society to materialise. At the same time, he perceived that the basic urge of the people was to coalesce together and live peacefully.

In this context he propounded his concept of God. His God is not national because it would strengthen the national groups and encourage national partiularism. Not is He communal or of any religious group. Frederic Pincott rightly says 'For Nanak there was no such thing as a God for the Hindus, a God for Mohammadans and God or Gods for the outer heavens.' Nor did he believe in any anthropomaphic God of Raanand etc. He loftily invokes the Lord as the one, the sole, the timeless being, the creator, the self-existent, the Incomprhensible and the Everlasting. He likens the deity to Truth which was before the world began which is and which shall endure for ever, as the ultimate idea or cause of all we know or behold. Besides this, the Guru did not recognise any deity of the Hindu Pantheon. Dr. Trumpp however views that the Guru did not forbid the worship of other Gods on ground of the unity of the Supreme. The view stands contradicted on account of the two reasons; firstly Guru Nanak at one place says : "A hundred thousand of Muhammads, a million of Brahmas, Vishnus and a hundred thousand Ramas stand at the gate of the most High" Implying that he did not have faith in Gods and secondly no verse of Nanak conveys that the Gods should be worshipped. The misunderstanding developed because at one place in 'Japji' the Guru spoke of "Three approved disciples—one the creator of the world, one the sustainer and the one who exercises the authority of death." These three approved disciples apparently corresponded to the Hindus Trinity: Brahma, Vishnu and Shiva. But the Guru did not recognise any difference between them on the basis of their function and considered them as the three aspects of His functional activity.

"He the one, is Himself Brahma, Vishnu and Shiva and He Himself performs all."

As a matter of fact by recommending belief in some deity or deities, his spirits-social purpose might have been defeated; the same old manifold socio-religious groups clinging to their respective gods must have subsisted. Even monotheistic God of Islam or other semitic religions did not serve his purpose because He was all powerful and beyond creations, thereby making the creations something of inferior stuff. Had Guru Nanak accepted this notion, the already depressed people of India might have not been able to get rid of the depression and demoralisation. Hence Guru Nanak's concept of God was the result of his creative response to the environment and its needs. People of all claims, races, countries and faiths could worship Him because no trace of particularism could be found in Him. He was creator, self-existent, permanent, merciful, deathless, timeless, formless, unfathomable and uncomprehensible. Moreover, Guru's concept was in tune with the expanding political and social visions. The needs of expanding states encompassing different people professing different faiths was to prepare such a psyche that might help the cohesion of the people. Admittedly the Gurus' concept of God did much in this direction. Polytheism, as experience has shown, has always divided the society into a number of groups with propensities to be fanatically exclusive. Sociologically, it has always been the cause of division of society. The Guru's emphasis on monotheism of its own type initiated the process of the unification of the mankind in general and the Indian in particular.

How should man Obtain God or feel Union with God?

This will involveus in an other vital problem i.e. to say that how the nature of the man is who wants to seek union with God. Man's nature is dependent upon affiliation: if his affiliation is to the world, he suffers from pride, self-centredness, sin, death and transmigration. This condition which must be transcended if man is to attain release from transmigration and seek union with God. But how to do so; The key to the problem is the cleansing of mind and developing it spiritually so that it becomes the fitting abode for the Name, but how to achieve this?

The greatest fault of a unregenerate man is that his mind is a victim of Haumai (self-centredness) which involves man in worldly attachments and does not allow him to see truth.

"The man victim of Haumai is unsteady. He does not know the way. He does not recognise the word (Shab.)

It is not to be crushed but restrained, for the same 'man' is something priceless. In unregenerateman, the Man (mind) is impure and unrestrained. Its evil properties are permitted to assert themselves and in consequenceman remains a slave of his passions. In unregenerate 'Man' (Mind) the dominant impulse is that of Haumai or self-centredness. Guru Nanak in one of his hymns described the operation of self-centredness on man :

> "In Haumai he comes and in Haumai he goes;
> In Haumai he is born and in Haumai he dies;
> In Haumai he gives and in Haumai he takes;
> In Haumai he acquires and in Haumai he casts away
> In Haumai he is truthful and in Haumai he lies
> In Haumai he pays regard sometimes to virtue and similarly to evil."

All the activities of a unregenerate man are guided by Haumai. Even that which man call right or good is done only if it accords with the individual's haumai, and if it is not keeping with it it is rejected—might be in favour of the evil. Without getting rid of Haumai the path to Sehaj Avastha cannot be recognised.

Evil Impulses

The mind of the unregenerate man expresses itself in the evil impulses which are five Haumai dominant forms: Kam (lust); Karodh (anger); Lobh (greed); Moh (attachment to worldly things) and Hankar (Pride). Experience shows that these five basic impulses, responsible for the deeds of violence and falsehood which earn adverse Karma and

> "My adversaries are five and I am but one.
> How shall I defend my house, O Man!
> Daily they attack me and plunder me
> To whom shall I cry?"

Maya

A man caught up by Haumai inevitably means involvement in Maya. "The Maya in thought of Nanak, is not the illusion of classical Vadanta. The world is indeed Maya, but it is not unreal. It is an illusion only in the sense that it is accepted for what it is not. Delusion is a more appropriate word. The essence of the world is its impermanence. It is real, but it is impermanent, both in the sense that it is itself perishable and in the sense that its attributes cannot follow a man after his physical death." "Maya is basically untruth as opposed to Truth and the expression of this untruth is the world. It is in worldly affection, in the desire to appropriate the thing of this world, that man's great temptation lies and acceding to this temptation means involvement in untruth. The result can only be separation from God and continued transmigration."

Maya is, of course, the work of God, for it consist in the creation and is inseparable from it. According to McLeod "The creation is both a revelation of God and a snare. What matter is a man's response to it. If he perceives the revelation, he is on the way to a Sehaj Avastha (Equipoise). If, one the other hand, he regards it as a means of indulging in Haumai, he is one the road to his ruin. It can be either his ally or his enemy, an opportunity or a trap, a firm path or a quicksand. Even evil is from God and is to be regarded as an aspect of man's opportunity. Everything depends upon the response which a man makes, and unregenerate man makes the wrong response.

But how to transform the fate of unregenerate man? The transformation of the fate of the unregenerate an cannot be assured by blind adherence to sacred texts. "The Pandits might say that by reading of Vedas simple inclinations are destroyed, but the reading of Vedas is a secular profession. Without understanding this, every one shall be disgraced." Indeed God's secrets are not found in Vedas or books of the Muslims. Though the thousands of Purans and Mohammadan Books tell that in reality there is one principle, none has discovered Him. There are some scholars who assert that Guru Nanak rejected the sacred Hindu books; but this seems to be a hasty conclusion. The fact seems to be that the Guru neither rejected nor accepted the sacred Hindu books. In fact, the issue of acceptance or rejection of them was irrelevant from the view-point. He simply wished his followers to discern the all pervading principles underlying the whole creation.

Now are Pilgrimages of any Value

Going on pilgrimages to obtain Him is also of no value. Guru Nanak writes:

> "Ganga, the Jumma, the meeting of these rivers at Tribeni, Prayag, the seven oceans.
>
> Alms, Charity, and worship are all contained in God's name.
>
> I recognise Him the one God in every age.
>
> Nanak, in the month of Magh, if I repeat God's name with great delight, I bathe at the
>
> sixty-eight places of pilgrimages."

Idol Worship also is Irrelevant

The idol-worship was also rejected as a means of regeneration of un-regenerate man. Firstly, God being formless and Omnipotent can't be represented in idols and secondly, it would mean God dwells only in temples and outside them, any crime can be committed. Thirdly, in no case, the idols can be the ultimate aim, though in a very narrow sense these might help man to acquire the quality of the concentration of mind. On idolatory the Guru commented:

> "Blind and dumb (They i.e. the Hindus, walk) pitch darkness worshipping this ridiculous stone which they have set up. It sinks, so how can it carry you across (the ocean of existence)."

Ascetic Practices are also Futile

The belief that ascestic practice would help an un-regenerate man is also a mistake. The Guru is one of his hymns dwells at length in the futility of the current ascetic practices.

> "He who sings songs about God without understanding them; who converts his house into a mosque in order to satisfy his hunger; one being unemployed, has his ears pierced (so that he can beg as yogi); who becomes a faqir and abandons his caste; who is called a giver or pir but who goes around begging—never fall at the feet of such persons."

Conventions and Rituals would not Avail

Guru Nanak's condemnation of the traditional rituals was practically unequivocal. To him, the far better method of washing off impurity was to hear, obey and love God.

The regeneration of the unregenerate man can only be achieved through treading the path of 'Nam', Hukam and Shabd. He is advised to seek the help of Guru. But then the questions arises: What is 'Nam'? What is Hukam? and what is Shabad? and who is 'Guru'? Now we endeavour to explain all these concepts.

The Guru

Sikhism assigns a significant place to Guru. Guru was held equally important in Bhakti movement. Nath tradition and Budhist Tantric Tradition, Sant Tradition also inherited the traditional esteem for the Guru; but in this tradition a major modification was effected in the traditional doctrine of the Guru. Kabir, the greatest representative of Sant tradition did not believe in any human Guru, for him the Guru or Sat Guru represented the inner voice. No doubt he regarded the Guru as an essential mediator of Divine Truth but certainly the Guru was not human link. Guru Nanak, by and large, follows Kabir, although imparts clarity and tensenses to the conception. Guru Nanak lays emphasis on the absolute necessity of the Guru. According to Nanak.

"The Guru is the ladder, the small ship, the raft by means of which reaches God.

The Guru is the lake, the ocean, the boat, the river, the sacred place of pilgrimage.

If it pleases Thee I am cleansed by bathing in the lake of truth."

But who is Guru ? The term Guru is used in three senses: (1) The Guru is God, (2) The Guru is the voice of God, (3) The Guru is the word, the truth of God. The Guru is God is clear from the following verses in the Guru Nanak's composition:

> The Guru is God ineffable, unsearchable.
> He who follows the Guru commands the nature of the Universe.

Similarly the following passage proves that the Guru is the voice of God:

> 'The Master is near at hand and yet,
> O my wretched soul, you do not perceive Him.
> It is the True Guru who reveals Him..

Yet there is another piece of composition of Guru Nanak which goes to prove that Guru is the word. In the Sidh Gosht the Siddhs asked the Question :

Who is your Guru, of whom are your disciple?

Guru in his reply uttered :

"The 'Word' is the Guru," and the mind (which is focussed on it) is the disciple. By dwelling on the ineffable one, on Him the eternal Guru Gopal, I remain detached. It is only through the 'word' that I dwell on Him and so through the Guru the fire of Hauman is extinguished.

How to reconcile these three senses of the term, Guru? Apparently these terms do not reflect any identify; but no probing deep into the matter one would find one of the basic identity which these three senses possess. In the words of McLeod, the passage quoted above from Siddh Gosht brings our this identity not just with the announcement that the word is the Guru, but also with the reference to the Guru Gopal. God Himself is Truth. In order to accommodate this fundamental belief to the limitations both of language and of the human understanding, distinctions, if not absolutely essential, are at least very convenient.

This definition of Guru poses a problem. "Where the Ten Gurus not Gurus of the Sikhs?" The human forms of the Guru were not Guru, but the essence, the spirit and the Divine Light they embodied. This can be amply proved by quoting an example. It is stated in the old Janamsakhi that when Guru Nanak finally resolved to make Lehna his successor he put five paise before Guru Angad and fell down before his feet. In the Takki-di-Var or the coronation ode we are told that Guru Nanak in having the Guru Angad reversed the order of things. If this was really so, if Guru Nanak had actually bowed down before Guru Angad, it must be regarded as a very significant fact. It shows that from the very beginning the impersonal character of the Guruship was recorded. The personality of the Guru was detached from the spirit of the Guruship, which was to be regarded as the one indivisible and continous.

Guru Gobind Singh himself writes in Bachitar Natak:

> "Nanak assumed the body of Angad and made his religious current in the world.
> Afterwards Nanak was called Amar Das
> And One lamp is lit from another
> The holy Nanak was revered as Angad
> Angad was recognised as Amar Das
> And Amar Das became Ram Das
> The Pious saw this, but not the fools
> Who thought them all distinct;
> But some rare person recognised that they were all one."

Mohsan Fani writes at one place that in a letter to him, Guru Hargobind actually signed as 'Nanak' and according to Bannerjee, in private correspondence all the Gurus followed this practice.

'NAM' (Name of God)

Name has been assigned a very important place in the process of the regeneration of man. "Without Name one has no honour and lives his life in shame and is in the tight rip of Maya and is totally robbed by it."

The Guru regards 'Nam' as the remedy for a diseased world. Again the Guru says "without the Name of God births into this world is fruitless. Without the Name one eats poison, speaks evil, dies without merit and so transmigrates. Without the Name, there is no salvation. At another places it is said there is nothing but 'Name' in the house of the Guru." Then what is the Name? Does the Name mean names of God. The names such as Khuda, Allah, Sahib, Prabhu, Jagdish, Ram, Hari, Keso, Gopal, Parmeshwar all but names and are non-essential. There are, however, some names as for instance 'Nirankar' and 'Niranjan' but they express aspects of 'Nam' and not 'Nam'.

The Nam is the total expression of all that God is. In fact, whatever he has made is an expression of His Nam. There is no part of creation which is not such an expression. It is also the pervading spirit the bright essence which informs all life and all creation. It treasures within itself all that God is and is not. In the Nam, the Lord's spirit resides. May the 'Nam' in me be dwelling. Without the Guru we would be in darkness. Without the Word we understand not life. The word of the Guru is light. His word's light leads to Truth.

Since creation is expression of creator and so as manifestation of His birth, we herein find the answer to the question as to how the individual is to perceive his truth. Let anyone look within him, around him and in all that he has created, he will understand the nature of what he sees and thus ultimately understand God and the way to Him.

To realise Nam one should prepare oneself by following eight fold path; Santokh; contentment; Saram; Jugat (self-cultivatism); Jamati (faith); Ai Panthi, Sagal Jamati (Respect for all faith); Man Jite Jagjit (Kindness and courtesy to others); Daya (Compassion) and Gian (Knowledge).

The Nam is a realisation, the coming of God's grace within oneself which obliterates the sense of the other and makes one not only Be Himself, but be a portion and link of God. Like the Vedantist, however, the sikh does not believe that he ever becomes He. Nor does he become a seer, or a witness, into the play of life thereafter, he plunges himself into that activity, believing all the write that he is acting only as the will of the Lord.

Discipline of 'Nam'

In order to realise the name; one must observe the discipline of Name. The practice of Name is mechanical to start with and has its dynamic adjuncts, without which it cannot go together.

The first adjunct is ethical life. Unless a man leads an ethical life he cannot come near God, but Sikhism does not confuse the ethical values with the religious experience.

One must rely on prayer and the company of holy men (Sangat) to support and sustain him in his life of ethical restitude.

The second adjunct of the practice of Name is 'Sewa' (self-service) i.e. to say that he should endeavour to the best of his capacity and ability to help others to trend the path of seva through socio-political activity.

The third adjunct is that the discipline of Name must be constantly vitalised by Bhakti, devotion to God. The word Bhakti has the literal meaning of 'well-joined'. Since Bhakti is 'joining with' or participation in the God's, it pre-supposes an object distinct from subject. The object in the case of Sikhism is not avtar as it is in Vaishnavism but Bhakti in its positive sense of canalising and sublimating and whole motive energy of the individual to sustain the continuous yearning for a vision of God. The Guru says :

"Guru Man Mario Kar Sajog, Ahinis Ravio Jog"

The last adjunct of the discipline of Name in the intuitive understanding of the philosophical truths which underlie the world of phenomena. This is called true knowledge or Gyan. The Sikh scriptures commend that a Sikh must always strive to have intuitive understanding of scientific and philosophical truths through discussion or meditation etc.

"This is short outline is the discipline of Name. It consists of the synthesis of the three well-known paths recognised in the religious of mankind naming the path of disinterested action, the path of devotion and the path of knowledge. The modern Hindu thinker Aurovindo Ghosh in his own way, has tried to express something similar under the title of 'Integral Yoga', though it is definitely something less but expressed in a more sophisticated and modern literacy style.

Meaning of the Realisation of Nam

Even after realisation, 'Nam' cannot be defined, it can only be imperfectly described. One who has realised 'Nam' feels that it is aesthetical insight leading man through appearance to reality, through world of God. In that state the whole, the experience, the experience and experienced is one linked unity. People denying the existence of God do not and cannot deny the existence of God, transcendental aesthetic experience and some power which is the source of such an experience. Thus, for instance, Huxley once wrote, "There are certain experiences which transcend ordinary experience make the individual feel enlarged and have a quality of absoluteness and perfection which is absent in the human affairs of everyday."

In communion with the 'Nam', one enters into a state of wismadi—and cannot but express wonder and joy at the indescribel immensity, infinite of God and His Divine manifestation.

Name should be practised while living in the world, since in the eyes of a wismadi—who is the aesthetic union with 'Nam', there is no duality between the individual and the universal, he is the right type of person (Gurmukh) who can do good to humanity. Hence he should not absjure world—rather live in it but live like a lotus in water. He is a Panch, Plato's Philosopher King-Brahm Gyani—one who has realised God and has acquired Divine knowledge. "Such a man does not fear any body or does he forget anybody. The Panch is the ideal man of the Guru. His qualities have been described by Nanak in his Japji. His is saint in religion, a true statesman in political assembles—all his actions are guided by *Bibek Budhi.* He is Jiwan-Mukt—enjoying perfect release while living in the world. He attains perfection in virtue and happiness. Although the limitation of body and the world are there, yet they do not restrict his perfection which is more of the soul than of the body. Perfection does not come after death. It is attained while the Panch is alive. He overcomes the idea of Haumani and feels one with the universal in nature.

Shabd (Word)

Closely connected with Nam is the term Shabd. Guru Nanak's concept of Shabd is different from that of the Naths. In the context of Nath theory, the term is used in conjunction with Shabd which denotes mystical sound which can be heard only to the persons who, through Hath Yoga, succeed in making the Kundalini awake and cause Ida and Pingla flow in Susumana. The Guru's concept of Shabd recognises no Ida no Pingla, no chakra, no sasumana, and no dasam dura. Shabd in Guru Nanak's connotation is revelation as also the vehicle of revelation of God and is regarded by the Guru as the only proper object of man's contemplation. By doing so and by the total conforming one's life to its spirit, man passes into a condition of union with God. He has neither form, colour, nor material sign, but he is revealed through the true world (Shabd).

By the Guru's leading he obtains salvation and is no longer bound to the wheel of transmigration. Meditating on the word (Shabd), repeating the name of God, he is released.

"Without the word (Shabd) one is condemned to wonder. Worldly affection, cause way to sink (in the ocean of existence).

O man, apply your understanding to the word (Shabd) and cross over. He who has not followed the Guru and has not understood the divine Name (such a person) continues to transmigrate"

> 'Nanak, the true creator and the Lord is
> comprehended through word.'

A close examination of the different connotation of Name and Shabd would show that Nam is synonymous with the word (Shabd). The functions which have been assigned to Nam can without exception be found in word. Nam is the expression of His total personality, manifest or unmanifest, conditioned or unconditioned, the word is also the expression of the same. Nam is revelation as also the word (Shabd). Nam and shabd both are objects of contemplation. The standard to which the lures of the individuals must confirm. There are many passages in the composition of Guru Nanak where the identity of these two terms is obvious.

There are however, some extracts in the compositions of the Guru which bring out implied distinction. "In such cases the word appears as the medium of communication and the Name as the object of communication. Both remain, however, expression of God's truth."

Hukam

'Hukam' is one of the fundamental concept of Sikhism. In 'Jap' the Guru puts a question of himself 'How is truth to be comprehended by man?' And then he answers 'Truth is to be found by submission to Hukam'. Now what is the Guru Nanak's concept of Hukam?

The concept of Hukam a propounded by Guru Nanak implies in it the Giver of the order and the order itself. This being so, its form depends upon the concept of the order-giver. Rigvedic religion was polytheistic and only in its later phase, the idea of supreme God began to be hinted. In Upanishads, the idea of Par-Brahm was undoubtedly emphasised but because of the differences on this point of various Upanishads, it could not be put forth with clarity. As a result of these differences six schools of philosophic thought came into being but the differences could not be ironed out.

Sankhya does not believe in the existence of God. Yogeshastra believed in God, but does not believe in his power creating Prakriti and Jiva. According to it, both these things are self-existent just as God. Jaimani has not even mentioned Ishawar.

In the 8th century Shankar Acharya propounded the concept of monistic God but he too regarded Parkirti and Jiva as separate entities. Ramanuj and other Hindu religious thinkers with a little difference here and there, preached such like ideas of Parbraham.

In view of this, it can be safely inferred that God of the Hindus cannot be equated with God of the Sikhs. In the latter case He is considered all powerful, sole creator, timeless, deathless and so on.

So the other of such God is obviously different in nature and form than that of the God or Gods of the Hindus. According to Dr. Fauja Singh, there is no doubt that there are some stray hints in Upanishads but vague hints do not portray the details of the concept. Buddhism and Jainism were not in a position to express themselves on Hukam, because of their non-belief in the existence of God.

The concept of Hukam is very near the Muslim traditions. In Islam, as in other semitic religions, Hukam of God is sole creator of the whole creation. Guru Nanak affirms his faith in this. According to him it determines the regular cycle of human existence, all are under it. In accordance with the 'Hukam' we are born and we die. Ahead and behind the Hukam pervades all.

From all this, it can easily be surmised that the basis of Sikh concept of Hukam is Islam, but the concept in its totality is quite different from that of Islam. Karma and Grace are necessary adjuncts of Hukam. It is closely connected with the Karm theory and also with the concept of Grace. Hukam, Karm theory and concept of Grace are so much intermixed that each is affected by the other and aquires new significance.

The operation of the law of Karma, according to which man has to reap the reward of his own actions is a must in Buddhisms, Jainism and Brahmainism. It smacked of determinism in our fate and gives impression to the persons concerned that there is no way out to salvation, thereby making them pessimistic. The concept of Hukam emphasises that if he can order any thing to happen, he can also order that this thing should not happen. In view of this the mechanical operation of the law of Karma can be stopped. By striking this note, the Guru opened gates, flood-gates of optimism and hope, because there was scope for the people to strive for salvation. From this viewpoint; Guru's concept of Hukam proved to be lever to optimise the people.

The Guru uttered :

> "As the Hukam, soon too the deed."

When one meet the True Guru and understands the Hukam, one attains to Truth. Salvation is not wrought through one's own efforts. "Nanak, such a claim would bring destruction." Again at one place, the Guru says :

"Their deeds follow them, and they reap that they sow. But the Guru's word erases the blot of thousands of evil deeds of the past and the greatest sinner can become the greatest saint."

Grace is also the quality of Hukam (the Divine Order Giver). In fact, the grace is also a sort of Hukam. Grace is that aspect of divine order whereby there is imparted internal and pre-requisite illumination. Grace can obliterate sins of many births instananeously.

When the balance of deeds is struck the Yama striketh us in our head. Then we have to render the account when he asketh for it.

It is on the meditation of True one that we are saved and the Lord forgiveth us.

But should it be understood that Guru Nanak by propounding the concept of Grace, denied the relevance of Karma. But it is certainly implied that Karma theory was not to be preferred to His Grace or His Hukam. Karma determines the nature of birth but it is through Grace that the door of salvation is opened.

Some scholars have defined Hukam a cosmic order but is does not sound correct. In fact, this order is tridimensional: Nadar, Karm and Human are its three dimensions.

Ultimate Object

The ultimate object of man is not to be God but to be God-like. He must enjoy Absolute into himself in the fulness of its self-consciousness. Many in this stage is the union with God and he becomes Supra-soul. This union means an end for ever to the trans-migratory process with all its attendant sufferings and instead an eternal, changeless tranquibility. The exact description of this stage is by silence. But this does not mean that the Absolute is mere blank any more than the apparent sleep of a spinning top going round at full speed means absence of motion. Human understanding like the human eyes can operate only within certain limits and certain conditions when the speed of a spinning top goes beyond a certain limits, the eyes cannot see the revolutions that are being made. But that does not mean that the top has come to standstill. Similarly, when the very excess of this stage in the Absolute makes us unable to understand it we cannot say that it is a mere negation.

Rebirth and Transmigration

By transmigration, we mean that after the death of the individual of souls shuffles off to another body. Through all the ages since the creation millions of souls have passed from one specie to the other. Thus there is a chain of life.

According to Dr. Trilochan Singh "There is a difference between re-birth and transmigration. A man may be reborn as a man to continue his spiritual journey. Enlightened souls are reborn to redeed the world of sin. They are sent by God as his messengers and they go back when their mission is complete. Souls condemned for their wickedness suffer transmigration through a cycle of rebirths and deaths in lower animals which is Sikh theology is termed as Hell."

Every man can cut as under the bounds of birth and death during human life, and attain perfection. This hope is extended by the Sikh Gurus to the lowliest of the low the every human being living on the planet, no matter, what is status colour of the skin or nationality and race.

> The bonds are cut asunder,
> Rebirth his ended.
> The mind is conquered and victory achieved.

Hence wanton defacement of this temple of God, the both is considered scrilege. Man should eat, drink and live cheerfully enlightened and decent life. But from it, it should not be surmised that preservation and beautification of flesh is the ideal. Sikhism does not encourage man to look on the flesh with cynical contempt but enjoins them to control it. Sikhism is basically different, so far the attitude towards man is concerned, from Hinduism, Buddhism and Jainism, because while they lament the misery of the body, the Sikh Guru Sing the nobility of the body. The Jain Monk is particular feels ashamed that his soul has been housed in this repulsive physical structure of flesh, blood and bones of nine opertures each of which ceaselessly secrets filthy substances.

Creation—a Sagun aspect not a Veritable Hell

Unlike semitic religions, which regard creation as the result of first sin, and the Aryan religions which being essentially metaphysical regard creations as a mere illusion, Nanak considers creation as an emanation from God. Out of His one Absolute Being (Ekam-Kar); emanated through his creative Will Kavao; emanation, on aflux of His spirit and all-pervasive sight (Im-Kar). Out of this will there emerged the five existential elements air, water, fire, earth, either which were antogonistic in spirit but were created through the sixty principle, the unseen life-spirit (Parana Shakti); life owner. It is the all-pervasive spirit of God, the eternal Omkar. Guru Nanak says :

> Through countless ages
> Complete darkness brooded
> Over utter gloom and void
> There were no worlds, no firmaments
> There was neither night nor day; nor the sun nor the moon.
> But only God existed in ceaseless trance.
> There had not been inscribed in the Vedas
> Nor the scriptures of the semitic
> Nor read a gospel at down, an epistle at sun-set.
> Only the unspeakable spoke of Himself to Himself
> Only the unknowable of Himself had His knowledge

When he so willed, He shaped the universe
The permanent He spread without roof to support it
He made the planets, the suns and stars.
Over universe in endless space
Above, below the around it
Out of the unmanifested, unmovable ground of being
To us and in us, He made Himself manifest.

(Nanak : *Rag Maru* p. 1035)

The creation, thus, is a sagun aspect of God. It is not a veritable hell or something to be scorned and condemned as semitic or Aryan religious world have us believe; it is the dwelling place of God as Guru Angad would have us believe. According to Guru Nanak:

"True are His regions
True are His universes
True are His worlds
True are His forms"

(Jap ji)

Social Ideas

The objective of Guru Nanak's teachings is to achieve Sahej, or Parmatmik Anand of Jiwan Mukti or Maham Skuh. Most of the hymns exemplify this aim and enjoin upon the devotees to exert to their best to achieve and said goal; but while doing to the Guru in so many verses, exhorts the people to do all this in the context of the world around. In Pauri 16 of Japji, the Guru asks the people to be 'panch' in the right sense. The Guru himself led a householder's life and impressed upon the people to emulate him because this life is not an obstacle on path-way to Bliss, thus bringing out clearly the importance of living life in the world. This being so, the Guru was interested in society and the people constituting it. 'Asa Di Var' is replete with vitriolic criticism of the meaningless superstitions, Brahmanical rituals, caste exclusiveness, caste spirit, untouchability and the exploitation in the name of religion or deity, which were obviously social evils. Some scholars aver that the Guru's references to social affairs are merely social comments and do not dwell on any form of society. We feel that the even social comments simply some form of society. Whatever picture of society emerges having persued the impositions of the Guru, we give hereunder.

Guru Nanak preached social egalitarianism. He roundly condemned caste-system, untouchability and other differences based on birth, wealth, locality, climes and creeds. Guru Nanak emphasised 'understand people by the light, ask not their caste'.

"In the presence of God, no one is differentiated by caste. Ask not about the birth and lineage of a person. The social world which Guru Nanak was seeking to create was a world of complete understanding between man and man. Guru Nanak also condemned the attitude of regarding woman as inferior to man. He seems to have admonished the people for denying due respect and status to them because in Guru's views woman is as much part of God as man and is the progenitor of even the greatest of men in the world. According to Prof. Puran Singh "the whole of Guru Granth is the voice of a wedded woman pining in love for the Beautiful. Her nobleness in Guru Granth is infinite, her freedom is of the highest. Both man and woman as sexes are forgotten in her voice. She becomes the supreme reality and a freed soul. In the freed soul alone is the subordination of one to the other effectively abolished and all disputes hushed."

He strongly protested against considering woman as something inferior to man. Similarly untouchability has been strongly denounced. Vaishnavites' reposing faith in observing pantry at cooking places finds no recognition in the Guru's teachings. Nor do the external practices, rituals, practice.

Penances, and pilgrimages have any value in the society as postulated by Guru Nanak.

Kirt Karo and Wand Chakko

The Puratan Janamsakhi, the earliest written records has the following triple precept as the basis of an ideal society:

(a) Kirt Karo
(b) Wand Chhako
(c) Nam Japo.

By Kirat Karo, it means that thou shall earn thy livelihood by honest creative labour, thou shall share the fruits of thy labour with the fellow-beings and thou shalt practise the discipline of Name. By Kirt Karo, it is means every individual must engage himself in honest creative work. One might adopt any profession—farming, trading or so-called menial professions; but one must be honest and truthful. In Nanak's views, it is tantamount to committing sins if we look down upon these persons who have adopted the professions of sweepers and scavengers. Guru Nanak says "There is no instrinsic merit in professions. All are alike." Parasitism in any form or shape is anti-social and anti-religious as well. This precept also ensures that there shall be no exploitation of man by man with capital, that is, the accumulated wealth shall not be employed as an instrument of exploitation.

By 'wand chhako' it was implied that one must share the fruits of one's labour with one's fellow-creatures. By doing so, the spirit of selfness of sacrifice is inculcated and self-expands. Giving is the quality of God and in 'Japji' Nanak considers God the eternal Giver. From it follows, Sikhism regards a cooperative society as the only true society. "The basic element which distinguishes a Sikh co-operative society from all those modern socialistic concepts is grounded in the Sikh concept of the world as the very form of God—Hari-ka-rup, and the status of the individual as the very microcasm of God, Joti Sarup and an individual, therefore, must never be imposed upon or coerced. 'It therefore follows that while Sikhism seeks to establish a socialistic pattern and eventually a global society in which the socialist ideas of individual welfare, equality and freedom shall have full application, it is opposed to any development, which, in practice and reality seeks to destroy the worth and inner autonomy of the individual. It is for this reason that Sikhism conceives of the religious evolution of man as a necessary and integral pre-requisite and condition of its march towards the ideal society.'

The Sikh Society should not be taken as a church society or a theocratic organisation. A religious state is based on the assumption that unity of religion, more or less, is essential. This attitude on the part of the state has resulted many a life and death struggle in world. The wars of religion which have disfigures the history of Europe for hundreds of years speak eloquent testimony to the fact. Similarly, a theocratic state is based on the presumption that the rulers are answerable not for the welfare of their subjects but for the salvation of their souls and the end of all political endeavour is not this world but the next. Sikhism considers these assumptions based on falsity and it believes that there lies a fundamental unity in all human beings and that unity is constitutes by the thread of divine love for one-another which is embedded in every heart. For achieving agreement and unity, the order of the Khalsa relies on the methods of enlightenment and persuasion, recognising all the time that the heart of so great a mystery cannot every be reached by following one road only.

Mediation of Nam

By this precept, it is meant that people should meditate on 'Nam' i.e. to say that they should never lose sight of the cosmic process and the divine will permeating every thing of the world. This would ensure them mental acquipoise and the large vision without which people are likely to fall victim to parochialism. Moreover, by imbibing Nam-culture, one does not fall victim to Haumain which cause many evil impulses to emerge in the man. The person imbibing Nam culture should not worship gods and goddesses. The Guru categorically states :-

> "My brethrens, you worship goddesses and gods
> What can you ask them, and what can they give you.
> Even it as stone be washed with water it will again sink in it."

The Guru views that no stable and healthy society can be built without ethics. Moreover, he roundly condemned the unethical attitude of the people. But the ethics as preached by Nanak is life-offering while Hindu and Budhist ethics are life-negatism because they are dominated by the ethical idealism of the Monk and the recluse. Dr. Tirlochan Singh calls the ethics of the Sikhs as that of "created enlightenment and activitism," because the Sikhs are supposed to seek enlightenment and not salvation, and even this he did not want to achieve for his personal benefit—rather it should inspire people to dedicate their lives to the service of community. In view of all this, Guru Nanak considered the following cardinal virtues to be essential for the member of the society to imbibe:

(1) Truth, Contentment and Reflection.
(2) Compassion, Righteousness and Charity
(3) Faith, Tolerance and Restraint.
(4) Forgiveness, Humility and Service.
(5) Love, Knowledge and Work.

The acquiring of these virtues would bring about harmony and purity in social relations of the people.

GURU NANAK ON OTHER RELIGIONS AND SECTS

1. Vaishnavism and Guru Nanak

The cult whose influence was predominant in India as also in the Punjab was that of the Sahajiya Vaishnavism. The final aim of the votaries of this cult was the 'Sahaj'. By it is meant not the liberation either in any sense of negation or in the merging of the individual self in the absolute but the supreme state which is a positive state though of supernatural nature of the enternal flow of divine love—like the smooth and incessant flow of oil. Obviously the character of Sahaj is beyond any consideration o good or bad, sin or merit, birth and death and hence waveless. But how to achieve this state? The reply to this question is intimately connected with the philosophy of Radha-Krishna as conceived by the Vaishnavism. According to the philosophical and theological works of Vaishnavism, Radha is nothing but transfiguration of the infinite potency of love contained in the very nature of Krishan. The ultimate being may be conceived in three of its states, either as the unqualified Brahmin or as the Paramatman, the indwelling principle of all beings or as the Bhagwan, the active and qualified God.

Krishna as Bhagwan possesses three powers, viz. *Svarupa Sakti* i.e. the power which he possess by virtue of His ultimate nature, *Jivan Sakti* or the power through which all the beings are produced, *Maya Shakti* (also known as the Tatastha Shakti through which evolves the material world and its three attributes, Sat (existence), Chit (Pure consciousness) and Ananda (Bliss)). The potency of the three attributes act like three powers, in the nature of God, which are known as Sandhini (the power of existence), Samrat (the power of consciousness) and Haldini (the power of Bliss). The transfiguration of this power of bliss or love is Radha, and as such the very being of Radha is already involved in the very nature of Krishna and the two are one and the same principle. Why then the apparent separation of Radha from Krishna? It is for want of the self-realization of Krishna.

God has with His nature two aspects, the enjoyer and the enjoyed. He cannot even realise His own nature as the enjoyer. Radha represents the eternal enjoyed while Krishna is the eternal enjoyer and the enjoyed and the enjoyer being co-relative, the reality of the one involves the reality of the other, or in other words, Radha as the eternal enjoyed is as much real as Krishna the ternal enjoyer. The inseparable relation between the two is the eternal love-alliance of Krishna and Radha—and as Radha is eternally realising the value of her whole being with reference to her relation to the eternal enjoyer Krishna, Krishna is ternally enjoying

Radha to realise the infinite potency of love and bliss that is in Him. The objective of the Vaishnavism is that everyone should place themselves in the position of Radha and long for the union with the beloved Krishna or to express it in simple words, every one should develop Radha Bhava or Sakhi Bhava. This relation of eternal love between Radha Krishna has been conceived and expressed in Vaishnava theology anthropomorphically through analogies of human love that exists between man and a woman who become bound together by the ideal of love for love's sake.

In fact terrestial love between man and woman proceeds towards their divine love. The path was open to any body irrespective of caste and in this way, Vaishnavism did not assign any importance to caste.

Vaishnavism does not repudiate the authority of Vedas and faith in Hindus mythology: so far as the practical side is concerned, Vaishnavism recommends the adoring of the personal God in idols.

The Guru's teachings are marked by considerable difference from the tenets of Vaishnavism. The ultimate aim of the human endeavour in Nankism was the same as that of the Vaishnava. However, the Guru does not believe in developing Radha Bhava or Sakhi Bhava nor in the Radha-Krishan Philosophy. In Nanakism the state of Sahaj can be achieved by merging oneself in the Absolute God. In Vaishnavism, the incarnations are sometimes enumerated as six, ten or twenty in number but the most important are Krishna and Rama but Nanakism does not believe in Avtarvad. The Vaishnavites have faith in worship of idols symbolising different incarnations of God, Hindu mythology rituals and emotional worship.

The Guru does not response faith in any of them. Guru was most intolerantly opposed to the use of idols symobilising God. Mohsan Fani, in the days of the sixth Guru wrote that 'Sikhs have neither idols nor temples for idols'. Similarly the ritual side of Vaishnavism brewed a sharp reaction in the mind of the Guru. Guru Nanak found ritualism and formalism in every religion and no wonder he attacked every kind of formatlism. Plato went too far when he said that God is not to be cajoled by rites or by prayer or sacrifice. The Guru believed in prayer but he condemned the belief that God could be pleased by rituals and mechanical worship. The Guru did make use of Hindu mythology but in a different sense. Our study shows that the Guru had no faith in mythology. It entered the Guru's hymns either as survival element in his religion for purpose or illustration. The Granthic allusions to Vaishnava mythology are not to be taken as a part of Guru's teachings much less as an element of Sikh religion. The same is true of Vaishnava incarnations. The Guru instead of accepting these Avtars as Gods on earth used the same names for the High and formless God. So far as utterance of 'Nam' is concerned the Guru connoted it differently. In Guru's system, it stood for totality of God's creation or the spirit that sustains the totality but in Vaishnavism it meant only God's name, or muttering of God's name.

Thus from the above discussion it becomes clear that Guru's religious system cannot be equated with Vaishnavism.

II. Guru Nanak and Nathism

In the sixteenth century, Nathism was very popular in the whole northern India. The Guru, during his travels, met them at least three times and shared his views with them. All the janmsakhis undoubtedly are of the view that the Guru brought home to the Naths the superiority of his message; but the fact that the Guru made copious use of the Yogis terms in his compositions leads one to thing that the Guru borrowed his religious precepts from them. It is in this context that the comparison between Nanakism and Nathism or Jogism is warranted.

Nathism traces its origin from Sew who is regarded by them as the Adi Nath or original Master. There were also nine human naths, great like, Mina Nath, Malsyendra Nath and Gorakh Nath who had attained immortality and became objects of worship. In addition to them the Jogies held in high esteem, the Sidhs who had attained the stage of perfection through the discipline and practice of Yog.

The ultimate aim of the Naths, Sidhs or Jogis was the attainment of Jiwan Mukti or liberation while living. This state of liberation is what is meant by immortality in Nath literature. While the other schools of thought regard the final dissolution of the body or its final dissociation from the spirit indispensable for liberation; the Siddhs seek liberation in a transformed or trans-materialised body, which is the perfect body i.e. to say the body that cannot be defiled and is associated with principles of Visuddha Maya which prevents it from becoming absolutely static and acts as the absolutely purified dynamic principles for its further evolution through subtler stages to lead it to the final state para-mukti. The Yogies in their perfect body are prompted by the principles of the Visuddha Maya to benevolent activities rendering spiritual guidance to the aspirants.

But, how to attain this state? The Yogic text 'Yog-Vijay' states that it can be done by observing *Ulta Sadhana.* which involves *Kaya Sadhna.* By this term is meant a slow and gradual process of continual purification, rejuventation and then trans-substantiation of the body through various Yogic processes. It is believed that though the fire of Yoga (the purifying processes of Yoga) the ordinary body of change and decay is burnt away and from the process of purification and rejuvenation results a new immutable divine body as a transformation of the old. But how to do so. Various processes have been suggested but a particular form that has been most emphasised is as under :

In the yogic texts in general, the moon and the sun represent the two elements underlying physical existence viz., the element of creation and preservation and the element of change and distribution. These two principles have been identified with Sakti and Siva on one hand, and with woman and man on the other. The moon situated just below the sahassare or the lotus of thousand petals in the cerebrum region—it is facing downwards and the sun is situated in the region of the naval or in the lowest plexus (*Muladhara*) falling upwards. It is held that bindhu which is the quintessence of the body is of two kinds viz., the yellowish white bindu and the red bindu (Lehita Bindu)—the former is of the nature of semen (sakra) while the latter is of the nature of ovum (*maharajas*). The *Bindus* is contained in the moon in the upper region while the ovum is contained in the sun in the navel; this bindu is Siva and ovum is *Sakti.* Since it is held that the *Amrit* or *bindu* is always to be consumed by sakti, the nath Yogin's aim is to save Amrita from being consumed by the sun.

This aim in itself involves principle of eternal conservation effecting the perfect commingling of the principle of destruction and creation. But how to do so? This implies many things in Yoga. It implies the practice of purifying the nerves like Ida and Pingla by controlling *Prana* and *Apana* through processes of Pranayam. The three important nerves Ida, Pingla, and Susumana in the left, right and the middle are frequently described in the yogic texts as of the nature of the moon, the sun and fire respectively.

Since in the Nath cult, the commingling of sun and the moon has the deeper significance of transforming the material body into an immutable body (Div-Deh) along with the perfect control over the destructive force of the sun and then rejuvenating the whole body with the nectar oozing from the moon is suggested, this can be done by shutting the Dasam Dura (Tenth door) or placing sentinels on it. If Yogin drinks this nectar by following the practice by *Khichari Mudra*, he will undoubtedly become immortal.

Since the sun was equated with sakti, woman who was always eager to consume the Amrita of the moon, the Nath Yogis tried to keep away from woman as far as possible. They regarded woman as the enchantress of the day and tigress of the night. The face of Mina Nath in the company of women of Kadoli and his rescue by Gorakh Nath seems to be a popular poetical version of the general attitude of the Naths towards women, although in some of the yogic practices, they used women but only as mere instruments.

Differences between man and man on the basis of caste, creed and climate were irrelevant to their system. Any one could have Div-Kaya and attain liberation in life. Traditional Karma theory and its concommitant, the theory of transmigration also found no accretion in Nathism. To this extent this system was heterodox, non-conformist and protestant.

Guru Nanak's system as delineate in the foregoing pages in similar to Nathism in so far as their attitude towards caste, rituals and other formalities and concerned. But this resemblance does not go beyond. Guru Nanak's final aim was *Sehaj* or *Mahasukh* or *Jivan Mukti.* Jogies also used this term but the meaning was different. While Guru Nanak meant by it realisation of the ultimate nature of self-incomprehensible Beloved, the Naths meant by it the attainment of immortality and Mahasvarehood: moreover, the methods employed in both the systems are altogether different. While Nathism suggests employing of the means of Ultra Sadhna (Regressive process) and Kayasadhna to achieve the goal, the Guru enjoined upon his disciles to follow 'Nam Marg'. The place assigned to woman in an equal partner of a man in the drama of life. The followers of Nanak, unlike Yogies, lived in the world and still could get the ultimate objective.

The Guru, like Naths, did not reject Karm theory but had his own views about it. In Nanakism, the Karmic law is not immutable and thus its cycle can be ended by the Grace or Hukan (Divine Order) of Gold. In its social reflection, Nanakism was a religion of householders and hence it was interested in social, political actions of the people on the whole. While Nathism reduced itself into an order, or at best a sect, committed more to the esoteric and ascetic practices than in the social well being of the people in general. Nathism, in the course of time, incorporated occultism as one of its essential features, wile Nanakism regards all these things as hurdles on the path to Bliss.

Some scholars, on finding a few terms such as Angad Shabd, Amrit Samana, Dasam Duar in the compositions of Guru Nanak have jumped to the conclusion that the Guru incorporated the principle of Nathism. McLeod at one place says "the roots of Nanakism lies in Nathism."

Certainly there is no substance in the above statement. Naths used Amrit in the sense of 'Bindu' or Semen (maharas). But the Gurus uses it in the sense of Nectar of immortality. Nowhere the Guru uses the images of moon and sun in connection with the Amrit. Rather, he uses it in association with Nam. Dasam Duar in Nathism has been used in a technical sense as the mouth of Sankhini through which the Amrit pours down, Guru Nanak never uses the term in this sense. So is the case with Angad Shabd. In Nathismit means mysterious sound, audible only when one attains the state of Sahaj, but the Guru always uses it in the sense of Shabd which the Guru equates with God a Truth and which has the power to destroy ego—Haumai.

Thus it is clear that the Guru's approach to the problem was different as also his final aim. Even a cursory glance at both Nathism and Nanakism would convince one that Nanakism is a system distinct in itself.

From the above, it is clear that the Guru's approach and outlook was radically different, and Guru Nanak did not incorporate anything of Nathism as such. Even the roots of Sikhism do not lie in Nathism because the Guru did not base his system on any of the fundamentals of Nathism. No wonder, the Guru felt irritated at the behavioural pattern which Nathism inspired or recommended.

Guru Nanak and Brahmanism

The Guru agrees with Brahmanism so far as the precept 'God creates the universe by transforming Himself into it and He alone is real is conceived'; but as a religious system the following animal which are considered to be the six main planks of the Brahmanical faith have been rejected by the Guru :

(a) The Guru asked his followers not to believe that the truth revealed in the Vedas is absolute.
(b) Yajna or Yagya, Havan and sacrifice were discarded.
(c) As a necessary corollary of the above, the priestly class was not recognised.
(d) The Ashram Dharma Theory of dividing man's life into four stages was rejected by Guru Nanak and in its place a healthy psychological re-

adjustment with man's environments within the household life was preached and emphasised by the Guru.

(e) The Varn-Ashram-based society was not given any credence.

(f) In the Guru's system, Sanskrit ceased to be the only vehicle of expression of divine knowledge. According to the Guru, no language was sacrosanct. God understands our feelings and intentions—even without their being clothed in words.

(g) The Guru does not believe that matter exists independently of God or creation remains independent of God. He, on the other hand, believes that creation is emanation of God Himself.

(h) The Karma and Re-birth are accepted by the Guru; but they have undergone a change on account of his, what we may call, the religion of grace. The nature of release or Moksha has also been conceived differently on account of the same element of grace in his system.

The teaching of the Gita have been interpreted in three different ways. One believes in Advaitism, absorption of individual souls with God with Gyan (knowledge) through sanyas (renunciation). The other is Dvaitism (dualism), soul when becomes perfect does not merge into God but reached His presence with Gyan through Bhakti (mystic devotion); the third which has been more clearly expounded by late B.G. Tilak, is what is known as Energism—Karma Marga, is derived from the practical dilemma in which Arjun was placed. This agrees with the first school except that the path in the case of the latter is renunciation and in the case of the former, it is Karma (action). The Guru makes a new synthesis. He takes up Advaitism as philosophy with Gyan in practical life. The approach to it lies not exclusively in any part of three traditional paths but in aesthetic appreciation of the working of God in every minute detail of our worldly life.

There are some other points of difference too. Gita accepts Avtara Theory which the Guru rejects. The Gita and the Vedanta goal of Mukt—the released person—is essentially individualistic. It is true that he achieves the goal through community, but on its achievement he does not live for the community. Moreover, when a men gets release by Gyan in his own life, he continues to live because of the *Paurabadh* commenced Karma. This of course dissuades him from committing suicide. But, what if he dies by accident? The Guru says that all Karma is lost as soon as the Sikh reaches the stage of Jiwan Mukt. Afterwards, he gives under the will of God, not aimlessly but to help others to attain release. He swims across the worldly (Sansarik) ocean and also makes others swim. He lives to help others. He dies not when the already commenced Karma comes to an end but when God wills him to die.

The difference becomes more poignant when we took at the effort for the attainment of Mukti. The Hindu concept of Mukti is more egoistic. The Guru preaches it through Grace, combined with the humility of efforts.

Guru Nanak and Advaitism

It is true that Sankara has influenced every philosophy and religion in India, but if closely examined the Guru inspite of subscribing to many views held by Sankara differs from him on many important points. The concept of ultimate reality is almost the same in both the systems. Both Sankara and the Guru are monistic idealists. The soul, the world and the Brahma are not conceived by the Sikh Gurus as three distinct realities like the Sankhya. According to Sankara all the three are one, the Brahma being the only single reality. The apparent multiplicity of men and things is due to Maya or Avidya—illusion and ignorance. The unity can be achieved through the acquirement of knowledge—Gyan—with which he separateness between Jiva—soul, Jagat—world, but the similarity ends here, Sankara's system gives no place to 'Bhakti' when the Guru regards it as one of the most important adjunct of Nam philosophy.

The Guru does not regard the world as simply an illusion in the sense Sankara does. The Guru's cry, opines Carpenter, "Rid Thyself of Duality" has no metaphysical significance. It summons to the exclusive worship of the only True. God is universal Father, who abides in every heart and makes all partners in His infinite activity. For the Guru, the reality of the world and the souls is not an illusion but they are real only in a relative sense. Nothing is real in the sense in which God is real. On the practical plane too, the Guru differed from Sankara. The Guru preached Pavriti in Naviritic spirit living in the world with a detached frame of mind, while Sankara preached Naviritic spirit.

GURU NANAK AND KABIR

Sant Tradition and Guru Nanak

It is said that Kabir had profound influence on Guru Nanak's thought, and as a corollary to it many a strand of Nanakism can be discerned as borrowings from the thought-pattern of Kabir, the greatest exponent of Sant tradition in India. The protagonists of this view reinforce their point of view by stating that the Guru had a meeting with Kabir.

On analysis and scrutiny, the above view does not sound correct. Even if the two saints had a meeting and a discussion, it does not follow that one must have borrowed from the other. In certain matters such as caste, idolatry, formalism, faith in monotheistic God both the teachers resemble in their approach; so are they in agreement regarding the final objective i.e. say Sahaj. Both emphasise the need of a Guru but not as human link. Both understand by Shabd, the same meaning, although Guru Nanak is clearer in his expression. But similarities do not go far.

On issues like rejection of the authority of the Vedas and disapproval of ascetism, Kabir was inclined towards compromise, while the Guru did not mince words while rejecting them. Both looked at life from fundamentally different points of view. Guru Nanak was not a visionary like Kabir; he was far too deeply interested in the fate of his fellow beings upon earth than to linger upon in the rare mystic regions. Furthermore, Kabir was deeply impressed by the futility and misery of life and sought as much isolation from life as possible instead of framing a constructive programme of reconciliation of man's spiritual and material needs.

Guru Nanak regards life a beautiful thing to be enjoyed in fulness. Kabir does not distinguish between the psychological notion of mind and metaphysical idea of soul because for him mind undergoes the process of transmigration of souls, but for the Guru mind is gross in the sense that it is attached with the body and is the outcome or five element (Ih man panch tat te janma).

Kabir's teachings bear an imprint of Tarik beliefs and faiths, handed over to him probably through Nath tradition. He uses the imagery of Ganga and Yamuna to mean the right and left nerve channels, the Triveni to mean the middle channel and the hundred-petal lotus the sun and the moon etc. and expresses his intense dislike of women. Guru Nanak does not make use of such words, phrases and images nor does he harbourhatred for woman. Nanak, in fact, considers woman as man's equal.

Guru Nanak and Islam

Islam had brought to India concept of strict monotheism which not only affirmed that there is one God and none other, but rejected the belief that there can be any incarnation or Avtars of the supreme Being. The Islamic monotheism rejected even the installation of imges of God as being contrary to the ideal belief in the unity of God—hend. The concept of monotheism was not totally absent in India and could be and has been traced back to the Rig Veda and the Upanishads. But the Hindu concept possessed such a great measure of elasticity that there was practically little differentiation discernible between monotheism and polytheism.

Unlike the Hindus again, the Muslims, viewed God as the sole creator of all living and non-living things. According to them, nothing is eternal or exists independently of Him. Similarly He is the sole Sustainer and the sole destroyer of all. He is transcendent and He is also here, there and everywhere, but Islam has nothing of the type of the Hindu belief in immanence. As such, though man is wonderful and also the premier creation of God, the soul within him, is not a spark of divinity as the holder of the Hindu belief of immanence would have us believe. The immance as created by God, according to Islam, is not limitless but consists of seven upper and seven nether regions—the Imperial throne of the Almighty having seated atop the uppermost region, called Arsh-i-Barin. The founder of Islam. Muhammad was accepted as the special messenger of God and Muslim scripture, the Quran, was recognised as the revealed word of God. For the worship of God, the votaries were enjoined to offer daily prayers of Namaz (each at an appointed time) to observe fasts every where for the full month of Ramzan and to give in charity 10% of the income (zakat). The human mind is concerned by Islam as an inter-play of angelic and demonic forces. As such, the believers are expected to be beware of machinations of the Devil in them and to lead to Godly and noble lives. Islam shows deep concern with the mode of living in this world. The actions of all human beings are held subject to divine judgement and they are told that they will reap rich rewards (seat in Paradise) or punishment (seat in Hell) in accordance with the way they acquit themselves during their stay in the world. As the universe has a beginning, it must also have an end and the end will come with the Day of Judgement. Another important principle of Islam is the equality of all human beings, which in fact is a necessary corollary from its doctrine of strict monotheism.

The idea of Guru Nanak about the unity of God-head had Islamic emphasis. He recognised the one God alone and even regarded the ideas of incarnations and images as a negation of His One-ness. But the total view of Supreme Being was not identical with the Islamic concept of the same. Guru Nanak's God was both transcendent and immanent. He dwells in everything living and non-living and this being so, they were all believed to contain within them a spark of divinity a belief not shared by Islam. The difference in approach was responsible for the differing views in the two cases regarding the ultimate destiny of man, reunion with the Lord according to Guru Nanak and admission into paradise according to Islam. Difference of outlook is also to be seen in regard to the root of evil. Whereas Islam attributes it to the Devil or Satan in many as its primary cause, the Guru regards Haumai as the source of five evil impulses (lust, anger, greed, worldly affection and pride) as also the mother of three Gunas (Satawik, Rajas, Tamas). The differing approaches were reflected in the respective views of Islam and Guru Nanak on the nature of worldly life. Both took a positive view of the matter and attached great importance to the living in the midst of society without shirking the consequent responsibilities. Yet a great divergence marked the view-points. Islam accepted the world as such and did not look upon it as a place to run away from. If due attention was paid to the morality of conduct, the life on earth could be envisaged as an opportunity for elevation. According to Guru Nanak, though the world was not a place to run away from, the element of Maya (attachment) found in abundance in it was certainly something from which one must abstain.

There were also a few other points distinguishing the thinking of the Guru from Islam. He was a believer in the Law of Karma and transmigration of soul. Islam attaches great importance to the need of good deeds but does not view it as a determinant of any cycle of birth and death. Guru Nanak recognised God and His creation both as infinite, but Islam makes a distinction accepting God alone as such. Guru Nanak does not recognise the concept of Prophethood enabling Mohammad as the soul channel of communication between God and man rather he believes in bringing man face to face with God without rejoining the help of any mediator.

Regarding the mode of worship, Guru Nanak did not care for the observance of a formal religious discipline, as he did for the actual conduct based on the cultivation of such virtues as love, devotion, purity etc. But both attached great value to collective worship, though the modes of this were not identical. Guru Nanak was very close to Islam when he emphasised that all people are equal in the eyes of God. On the whole, we can say that the approach of Guru Nanak was more spiritual than moral, whereas that of Islam was more moral than spiritual.

But no account of Islam can be complete without taking into consideration the thinking of the Muslim Sufis. Since the advent of the Muslim Turks in the beginning of the eleventh century, several Sufi Silsilas had come into bring. Guru Nanak had meetings and discussions with may eminent Sufi Leaders of his time and with some of them he had even intimate friendship. This fact has led certain writers to see in such of Guru's institutions as Sangat Pangat and Kirtan a measure of influence of the Sufi Khanquah, particularly the Chisti one at Pakpattan. The suffis were great spiritualists. At their hands and spiritual side of Islam was immensely enriched. They accepted God as transcendental and immanent reality. The creed of the sufis laid down a path of spiritual progress marked by Shariat, Tariqat, Marafit and Haqiqat. A parallel is sometimes drawn between these Sufi stages of spiritual development, and Guru Nanak's fives stages of Dharm Khand, Gian Khand, Saram Khand, Karam Khand and Sach Khand given in the 'Japji'.

But on close examination it will be seen that the similarity between the two is only of the limited character. They both relate to the domain of spiritual development and thus a measure of similarity between them is inevitable, but on the whole the two conceptions are not identical and differ in so far as they spring from different assumptions as far instance, in the Khands of Guru Nanak, there is nothing corresponding to the Sufi Muqaims such as Shariat (observance of the five fundamentals of Islam namely Kalma, Nimaz, Roza, Zakat and Haj) tariqat which is also related to Shariat Nasut (sensuality) etc. The Janamsakhi accounts of Guru Nanak agree that the Guru had respect for high moral and spiritual character of the Sufis. They led married lives like ordinary people and yet were able to live piously. All this was in line with the thinking of the Guru who compared the ideal life to a lotus flower which while growing in water remains unaffected by it. He, however, showed much greater sense of social commitment than was to be found in the Sufis.

The view lately made much of, that the Guru's vision was entirely Hindu and that there was no Islamic influence in him, fails to explain why it was absent when Islam had existed in India for the past several centuries and held a position of great power and prestige and when the Guru had personal meetings and discourses with so many Muslims and travelled so widely in Muslim countries.

Another view, that Guru Nanak owed some of his beliefs to Islam and some to Hinduism, errs in the assumption that his thought had no real originality about it and was a collection or borrowings from different sources, mainly Hinduism and Islam, intelligently pieced together and presented in the easily understood language of the people; so that whatever newness it possessed was here on account of the new synthesis that was evolved out of the welding together of the diverse borrowed elements. If the former view is unhistorical, the latter view is too facile to be accepted in the use of a mystic and religious thinker of the caliber of Guru Nanak. At the same time, it would be incorrect to rule out entirely Hindu and Islamic influences on the Guru. If we study his works, one thing which strikes us the most, is the divine inspiration underlying all his writings. His authority is neither the Hindu nor the Muslim scriptures, but the divine light enshrined deep within him. The chief source of knowledge for him was his intuition. Thus the truth imparted by him was the truth as perceived by Him, or as he often puts it, revealed to Him by God Himself. But while disseminating that truth, he moved among people both Hindus and Muslims, read their books closely, exchanged his ideals with their leaders of thought and could not be unaware of insensitive to the conditions prevailing around him. It was in the way that the Hindu, Muslim and several other influences worked on him.

A critical appraisal of the relations of Nanakism vis-a-vis different religions in India of Guru Nanak's time leaves no doubt that Guru Nanak's religion is a distinct one. It is certainly wrong to say that the Guru attempted to establish a religion commingling the higher elements of Hinduism and Islam. The foregoing discussion has made it amply clear that Guru Nanak's approach and ideas were set in different frame-work. Nor is the statement of Toynbce that Sikhism was the work of ex-Hindu religious inquiror who adopted monotheism and rejected caste-system under the inspiration of Islam appropriate. That Guru Nanak rejected caste-system under the inspiration of Islam does not seem to be correct particularly in the context of the Sant tradition and Nath tradition whose central theme who also this. Similarly, the Guru's thought-pattern was quite different from Nath tradition and Sant tradition, as also from important Brahmanical or non-Brahmanical cults.

We, however, do not deny that different religious sects were important environmental factors but other factors, such as sociological, political and even economic too went a long way in shaping the Guru's views. Even their impact was not direct. The Guru, like a true artist, perceived them and correlating them to his own vision, gave his programme. Thus Nanakism was creative origination, the scientific approach to the basic problems of mankind, the rationale of life, the certainly it did not involve any synthesization.

Was Guru Nanak a Revolutionary or a Reformer?

As a reply to this question, different opinions have been expressed. I.B. Bannerji is the chief protagonist of this view that Guru Nanak was a reformer. According to him Guru Nanak did not attack the fundaments of the Hindu society—rather in the fundamentals of his teachings, he differed very little. He did not reject or abolish caste-system. "He simply warned his listeners that exclusive reliance on caste was absolute foolishness". If we want to understand the attitude of Guru Nanak is seems essential that we should recognise a distinction which is very easily lost sight of the distinction between caste and caste pride." As best the used his lash vigorously on the pride of caste and the pride of name but his remarks hardly entitle as to conclude that he wanted a total destruction of the entire social system. In fervour of proving his contention, I.B. Bannerji under-rates that "Gurdas remarks that Guru Nanak had reduced the four castes into one", and held that "all that to all the four castes under the protection of the same true God and the name."

Similarly I.B. Bannerjee opines that "Nanak's denunciation of sacred thread, pilgrimages, fasts and penances, is not directed against the customs and the basic beliefs of the Hindus but against the perversions that these things produced in proud and hypocrital minds. In fact Mohsan Fani speaks of a disciple of Guru

Hargobind, Sadha who gave his sacred thread to serve him as a belt."

Similarly the attitude of Guru Nanak towards pilgrimages, fasts, and penances was condemnatory only in the limited sense, that is to say he did not plead the rejection of these things—rather he laid emphasis on the purity of mind while undertaking these practices. He did not enjoin upon his followers that they should not fast or go on pilgrimages. What he really wanted them to understand was, that as compared to devotion and love for God, these practices renunciation, rites, and formalities had little value.

Likewise when Guru Nanak challenged the sacred position of the Hindu divinities and avtars, he did not mean any disrespect of them. In fact Guru Nanak does not deny the missions of prophets and holy persons. On one occasion we are told that many such came into the world, started many religions, served the one Lord who is the God of all and departed after playing their respective parts. And as regards divinities we should not forget that Guru Nanak does not reject them altogether. 'It thus appears that what Guru Nanak did not deny the place to the divinities themselves but rather to those who allowed them to obscure the vision of the Lord and worshipped them exclusively in utter ignorance or disregard of true one Himself."

Similarly in his attacks on Vedas or Puranas or Kuran, Guru Nanak did not question the wisdom contained therein. "Nanak had no mercy for men who had no real devotion and piety but still prided on their knowledge of the sacred texts, for those who considered reading of those texts by itself a greatly meritorious act." Such persons were told plainly that the reading of Vedas was secular occupation of, and not a religious practice. According to I.B. Bannerjee "the apparent inconsistencies would automatically disappear if we could once realise the difference between an attack on scriptualism and one on the scriptures themselves." In the opinion of Dr. Bannerjee Guru Nanak attacked scriptualism and not scriptures.

Besides, the protagonists and this view plead that some of the great tenets of Nanak's creed were identical with those of Bhakta. The idea of supreme God—His Immanence and transcendence, on which Guru laid great emphasis was not new to the Hindu world of his time. According to Dr. Radha Krishan, even Ramanuj believed that God is both transcendent and immanent. Similarly the surrender of human will to the Divine Will was simply the repetition of the old doctrine of 'Prapti'. Belief in Karma, Transmigration of soul, Guru-Bhagti, emotional worship and service of God had all been emphasised earlier by the Hindu saints. Moreover, the inclusion of the compositions of Bhaktas in Adi Granth also leads to the conclusion that close kinship exists between the teachings of Nanak and those of Bhaktas.

Thus, in the words of Payne whose views have been elaborated by I.B. Bannerjee Guru Nanak's aim was not to sweep away Hinduism but to restore it to its ancient purity. Like Luther, he came to protest—to protest against idolatory, the blind superstitions and the empty rituals which had so long estranged vision from morality and the hearts of men from their creator. I.B. Bannerjee says "Sikhism no doubt, had its start in a protest but it was a protest against conventionalism and not against Hinduism. In Nanak, perhaps, the reaction reached its limits and thus gave a poignant tone to many of his utterances which at first sight gave the impression that his was a destructive and revolutionary ideal. But there is no satisfactory evidence to show that he intended to over-turn the social order. He had realised that ignorance and strife from which his contemporaries suffered was due primarily to the fact that from had supplanted spirit. The Guru was out not to kill but to heal, not to destroy but to conserve."

Our study of Guru Nanak leads us to the conclusion that he was a revolutionary. By 'Revolution is meant great reversal of conditions or turning over in mind', Webster New Dictionary also says like that. According to Encyclopaedia of the Social Sciences Revolution was a sudden and far reaching change, a major break in the continuity of development.

Nanakism as it has been seen in the foregoing section was a distinct religious ideology, a creative origination. Nathism, Brahmanism, Vaishnavism, Islam, all these religions had their own ethics, and it would be absolutely incorrect to regard Nanakism either as a copy of any of the faith, or an attempt to make a few reforms in Hinduism. Guru Nanak nowhere states that his mission is to reform Hindu Society alone.. Had it been so, the Guru would have not held discourses with the Sufis or gone to Muslim Central Asiatic countries to disseminate his message or made comments on Muslim precepts and practices. In fact, the Guru had its own vision. His connotation of Shabd, Guru and Name had distinct character. His concept of Hukam was neither semitic nor that of Bhakta; it had three adjuncts, namely Name, Grace and Karm and in its effect, it lent dynamism to the society.

Guru Nanak condemned caste-system because it served as the backbone of the Hindu religion and Hindu society. The Guru's condemnation was unequivocal. Dr. I.B. Bannerjee's contention that the Guru was against caste pride and not against caste-system is, at best, an exercise in the art of hair-splitting on this point; because the Guru's views vis-a-vis castes leave no doubt regarding the position of caste on his scheme of things. In fact, caste system is anti-thesis of a monotheistic religion.

So was the Guru's attitude towards pilgrimages, fasts and penances. These were rejected and condemned because they had negative value and unneccessary hurdles on the pathway to Bliss.

Similarly the Avtars and divinities were not given any place by the Guru. We fail to understand what the learned Dr. Bannerjee meant while saying that the 'Guru did not mean any disrespect to them.' Obviously the 'Guru bring a man of culture did not show any disrespect; but he showed no respect other. Nor a few verses in Guru Nanak's compositions show that the Guru did not recognise them at all, so far his own religious ideology was concerned. In fact the Guru had its own vision of monotheism. His connotation of Shabd, Guru and Nam had distinct character. His concept of Hukam was neither semitic, nor that of Bhakta (Divine

Will), it had three adjuncts; Nam, Grace, and Karm and in its effect it lent dynamism to the society.

Dr. Banerjee's assertion that the tends of the Guru's creed were identical with those of Bhaktas is untenable. Guru Nanak's monotheism was pronounced and marked involving total elimination of incarnations and subordinate deities. The Bhaktas, in general, were far less insistent in this regard. The Bhaktas copious use of mythology and tradition kept the door open for many gods and observance of idolatrous rituals. Karma theory and the concept of Divine Will were also subjected to new connotation by the Guru. Bhaktas did not repudiate asceticism while the Guru was uncompromising in its opposition to it. Caste system, no doubt, was attacked by the Bhaktas but it was left to the Guru to found a casteless society. The Guru rejected vedic authority of Vedas, while the Bhaktas did not. Even Sant tradition which was the latest development of Indian religious tradition differed from Guru's views in more than one respect.

In the same way the Guru did not recognise the authority of any sacred text. He repudiated Veda as also Koran. He regarded self-revelation as the sole inspire. This being so, I.B. Bannerjee's opinion that the Guru condemned scriptualism and not scriptures has no alibi.

Guru Nanak's religion had definite and positive points which emphasise its revolutionary character.

On socio-economic place Nanak had a clear picture of society in his mind. Nanakism, unlike other prevalent Indian religions, had positive social content, which did not exclude even the political aspect of the society. Nanakism was not a protest but a revolutionary retort against the enormity of spiritual obscuratism, superstition-ridden, caste-riven society debased by meaningless rituals totems and esoteric practices. He was a society which was egalitarian and based on three postulates viz., Meditation on Nam, sharing of wealth with the needy and doing honest creative labour. The political framework of such a society was the rule wedded to Truth which in Guru Nanak's connotation was an integrating or a progressive force. The aim of the society was to bring about a metamorphosis of a man so that he might grow to be a model man or a true Sikh or Gurmukh.

Caste system did not find place in Guru's concept of society. In this society, sex differences can find no niche. Indu-Bhushan's assertion "that Guru Nanak was against caste-pride and not against caste-system as such is, at best, an exercise in speculation because Guru Nanak's point of view pertaining to caste becomes crystal clear if we caste but only a cursory glance on his verses."

The Guru did not regard world as veritable hell or life, as something futile or the effect of the first sin. The people are enjoined upon by Nanak to lead their lives in fulness and not in parts. Each one is advised to abide pure amid the impurities of the world. But never renounce the world. Body was considered to be temple of flesh to house mind or to express it otherwise, body was regarded as microcosm of macrocosm. Guru Nanak's renunciation of asceticism was a significance breach with Indian religious tradition. Religion for house-holders had, of course, been distinguished from religion for sanyasis from times immemorial; but religious teachers always played the role of ascetic guiding their followers from a distance. It was not recognised that the Guru and the Chelas could form an integrated community.

Guru Nanak's preference for householder's life was indicated by his settling down at Kartarpur and also by his choice of Angad, a house-holder with wife and children as his successor in preference to his own eldest son, Sri Chand whose character was marked by the other-worldliness. It was a revolutionary as also a decisive step. By having shut the door to ascetics the Guru made Sikhism a householder's religion in a special sense. The Guru lived the same life as their disciples did; they shared their joys and sorrows. The human side of their character gave a new tone and intensity to their spiritual solidarity within the community.

The Guru recommended a particular set of attitudes for a member of his society. Apart from effecting self-purification, one should develop certain social attitudes i.e. to say that one should not consider oneself as a puppet in the hands of God, one of the other hand, one should consider oneself as microcasm of macrocasm and do one's best to improve the Garden of the world or the dwelling place of God as Guru Angad would have as believe. Even to attain salvation out of the context of the world is of no service to the development of universal brotherhood. One should resist all types of exploitation—political, social, economic and intellectual. The Guru condemned in unequivocal terms the hoarding or accumulation of wealth because it cannot be done without ceasing to be virtuous or without committing sins and social evils. Even the hoarding on the part of state is a sin if the people do not get all the amenities of life they have a claim to. Whatever the profession—farming, shopkeeping, service—on must not ignore the need for pure mind and good actions.

In the society as envisaged by the Guru, sex prejudices or difference on this account were not recognised. The woman has the soul as the man and thus she has an equal right with man to grow spiritually, politically and socially. In this respect it will be quite fair to say that Guru Nanak conceived a picture of New type of Ladyhood wherein Woman would be co-partners in building new social edifice.

What should be social attitude to sufferings—individual as well as social? What should one do while coming face to face with sufferings? The Indian attitude before the Nanak was of gross in difference or of escapism or of withdrawing from the world and passings one's days in some cave or cell in some lone area. The Guru does not like this type of attitude.

There is no doubt that the annulment of suffering and the attainment of bliss or supreme joy in the goal of human endeavour but one should not be indifferent to the sufferings of the world and of the suffering which tyrants and evil-minded parsons inflict on humanity. The Guru himself was deeply sensitive to the sufferings of men, of a colossal tragedy which has gripped our nation. But such suffering instead of remaining merely individual and meaningless must by the man of God, be made meaningful and creative in the sense that by owning suffering, the man of God must help the Good to prevail, must put up resistance to evil and induce in others the attitude of mind to do likewise.

Gurbachan Singh Talib beautifully elaborates this idea. He says "herein we are on a ground familiar to the modern man, though not to the medieval man in India. The saints and sages of India held better the purely individualistic attitude of gaining personal merit, or thought only in terms of ritual actions of approved character. Political and such issues had never been throught of; resistance to tyrants was a concept which simply did not exist except perhaps on individualistic basis as the wreaking of personal vengeance. The attitude of mind which counts martyrdom was not quite familiar in those times. As a matter of fact, the term so far as the Indian people are concerned, gained currency only in the wake of martyrdom suffered by the fifth and ninth Gurus of the Sikhs—Arjan Dev and Tegh Bahadur and later by large number of those who followed Guru Gobind Singh. As a matter of fact, it was the Sikh teaching stemming from the vision of Guru Nanak which extended the meaning of morality so as to take it out of merely personal piety and intimate relationships to embrace the operation of the conscience in relation to matters touching the widest social relationships."

Apart from the radical differences between Nanakism and Hinduism or other religious faiths, there are significant facts which go to show how serious the Guru was in giving shape to his views and getting them perpetuated.

The first fact was the establishing of Langar. Apart from its religious importance it strengthened the trends towards the development of new social structure. What we call dignity of labour was promoted and individual's responsibility for contributing to social welfare was emphasised. All those who come to take their food in the Langer had to take it together irrespective of caste or creed. It was a direct blow at the caste system. It was also a direct incentive to the promotion of fraternity and social solidarity.

The second fact was the establishment of the institutions of Sangat and Guruship. Both these institutions epitomised the Guru's intention of giving his followers an organisational solidarity and educating them in respect of Nanakism—which could not but draw a line of clear distinction between them and other creeds. There was no analogous development in any of the sects founded by Bhaktas or within the fold of orthodox Hinduism. Similarly with the nomination of the successor to the Guruship, the Guru assured the continuity of centralised spiritual leadership, which contributed a lot towards the moulding of the Sikhs into an integrated community. This was certainly a revolutionary step which was neither anticipated nor followed by any other medieval reformer.

The foregoing discussing makes it clear that the Guru Nanak's message was not only new but also contained progressive content. It started not as a protest but as a revolutionary retort and till todate its tenor is the same. No wonder those persons who have come under its impact are dynamic and sensitive to the progressive calls.

Place of Guru Nanak in History

Writing about the person as Guru Nanak was, Macleod says "The impression which emerges is that of a deep devout believer absorbed in mediation and rejoicing in the manifestations of the divine presence, but refusing to renounce his family or his worldly occupation. Discipline there certainly was but not renunciation and total withdrawal. The impression is also that of a revered teacher giving expression to his experience in simple direct hymns of superb poetic quality. Around him would be gathered a group of regular disciples, and many more would come for occasional darshan, or audience, with the master. And the impression is that of a man, gentle and yet capable of sterness, a man of humour and mild irony who could nevertheless reprimand and if necessary denounce, a man who experienced the unexpressible and who yet maintained an essentially practical participation in the every day affairs of his community and of the world beyond it." From the account narrated in the foregoing pages we gain impression that Guru Nanak had a mission and the necessary determination to see that the mission was put into practice. This being so, he was bound to play his role in his history of mankind much more in the history of the region where he grew up and where he finally settled.

Guru Nanak's vision was as vast as the whole humanity. He saw for himself humanity strife-riven and divided into different social and religious compartments on the frivolous bases of caste, creed, clime, colour and coat. The idea of the brotherhood of mankind did not claim any respect from the people. Moreover, the people were steeped deep in superstitions empty rituals and unmeaning ceremonies. Minds of the people by and large were fettered. This being so, the people were not in a position to make onward march in their evolution. The Guru's message in this context was unique; it was comprehensive and all embracing. It gave new message to the people, the message of brotherhood of man, that of their capability to realise this thing in their work-a-day like. To achieve this aim, he evolved suitable strategy. He established requisite institutions to give local habitation to his ideas as also to preserve them. The institutions of *langar* and *pangat* are cases in point. Thus the Guru's role, in this respect, was that of a creative genius who by his example and preachings, articulated the masses to awaken to new realities and new heights.

Religion by definition, is a programme to integrated the people in the bonds of harmony, love and respect for one another. When religion declines, it has always become an aggregate of superstitions, rituals and ceremonies. It ceases to be an integrating force; rather it hampers and hinders the progress and extinguishes the spark of social dynamism without which no nation, much less individuals, can progress. Guru Nanak seemed to comprehend the importance of religion both as a lever of progress and when degenerated as a means of impeding the progress. He, therefore, advised the people to shed off the useless accretion to their religions and to understand their true messages. He denounced all those people who upheld, in religions, the unneccessary and useless precepts and practices. He himself declared, he is neither Musalman nor a Hindu. He is a man committed to truth. He admonished the Hindus as also the Muslims who were engrossed in mud-slinging on each other's religion. He ridiculed and exposed the hypocrisy of the priestly classes of both the main religious groups of the country—Hindus and Muslims—and underlined the need of that social order wherein truly religious things should enjoy the respect of the people as a whole. In a way the Guru gave a new social philosophy of evolving a multi-national society. This idea was certainly a revolutionary one in the context of the contemporary society—even in reference to the modern society.

The Guru was not a political leader in the sense we understand today or in the sense people understood then; but he was certainly not insensitive to the political happenings around him. He writhed with pain at the unjust and foolish acts of the contemporary kings. He did not relish and foreign invasions and the cowardice shown by the people in submitting to them. He was deeply moved at the tyrannus march of the Mughals and the havoc they wrought upon the Punjab, especially upon the city named Sayyad Pur (Eminabad) and expressed his agony in his composition entitled 'Babar Vani' which is in fact a soulful lament of the Guru at the cruelties perpetrated by Babur.

That shows with what intensity and concern. The Guru witnessed the political vents being enacted on the stage of contemporary India. In view of this, he can be ranked among the greatest of patriots of this country; but his patriotism flowed from his world vision and not vice-versa. It is, therefore, in the fitness of things to assume that he was the first revered leader who put premium always on the moral content and would advise his followers to assess everything in terms of moral values. Thus if he commented on the sad political affairs and did not forbid his disciples taking part in political affairs, it does not mean that he permitted political permissiveness—rather he tethered the politics of his disciples to the pegs of morality. In this way he propounded a relatively new doctrine that politics should be based on morality and it should not be only a handmaid of Satan or degenerate persons. Against this background, the Guru favoured the extirpation of the evil-minded persons (Asursanghar).

The Guru's teachings, gave birth to Punjabi Nationalism. The Hindus, the Muslims and other social groups, under the impact of the Guru, began to realise that the truth belonged to all and it was not the monopoly of any one religion or social group. This awareness brought many of them near to one another, thereby causing Punjabi nationalism to take birth. This is why that most of the scholars think that the history of the Punjab began to take shape only after the advent of the Guru Nanak. But certainly the Guru's aim was not circumscribed to the emergence of Punjabi Nationalism. He had a wider aim of uniting the people of the whole world on the basis of his programme. This Panjabi Nationalism was the expression of Guru Nanak's impact on a regional level.

Guru Nanak's work was so significant that it did not leave the march of civilization, a social phenomenon bigger than that of nationalism or regionalism—untouched. Civilization declines if the institutions upholding it go insert and cease to be tractable. Hindu civilization which determined to a large extent the social and religious patterns in this sub-continent was heading fast towards it decline and fall because of it rotten institutions and the absence of any creative genius to revitalise them or to give new directions to them. Similarly Islamic civilization upto Guru Nanak's times had fallen to the evils which often sap the vitality of any civilization. The humanizing effect of this civilization had vanished and it had assumed the function of Islamic Imperialism. Guru Nanak did his best to remove the clogs from the wheels of the aforesaid two civilizations by establishing new institutions and performing himself the duties of a creative genius. Sikhism was certainly an attempt to ensure the onward search of the civilization and there is no wonder, the Sikhs, even today, are exerting their utmost to contribute their mite to this sphere. In this context, Guru Nanak ushered an ocumenical epoch with the whole world as its base. He showed us how the churches of East and West could not only come close to each other, but could unit and co-operate in the spirit of justice and truth and thus create unity in diversity. He could sit with a Muslim and pray with him. He could sit with a Vaishnava Hindu and could sing with him. Wherever he went, he meet people of all shades and all types. He oriented human passion with tender kindness.

The Punjab like the rest of India was in the throes of frustration which was caused partly owing to here defeats at the hands of the foreigner partly because of the rude shock they had met in the wake of the inability of their ancestral faith, to stem the tide of Islam and Islamic culture and partly by the impact of Samkhya philosophy. Guru Nanak understood the crisises gripping Indian mind. He, accordingly, strived to bring about change in their attitude. He rejected other-worldliness and asceticism as the basis of life and also as the true path to Bliss. He regarded life as the top creation of God and the world the nicest place to live in. He called this world as 'Great Garden of God' and the man as microcosm of Macrocosm. Activities of the world were regarded as 'must' by him. Activities would not cause degeneration of man only if they were done honesty without exploiting anyone and with full faith in God and God's scheme. He fixed new goal before the people, the goal of establishing global society on the basis of social equality, honest creative labour and faith in oneness of God. The precepts of social equality and honest creative labour naturally evoked new aspirations and hopes among the majority of the people, and they began to view the future with hope, confidence and optimism.

Resultantly, pessimism began to give way to robustness and the spirit to do and dare. The fruition of this type of teaching took place in the time of Guru Gobind Singh when the confectioneries, washermen and other who had never touched the hilt of the sword became doughty warriors. In the same way, the creation of the Khalsa, the vanguard of the humanity committed to establish brotherhood of mankind, marked the culmination of the philosophy of Idealism-energism as preached by Guru Nanak.

Nanak, as a force or spirit, has always been playing its part in history. During the later Mughal period, when Banda Bahadur ousted the Mughal Government from Sirhind, he struck a coin which bore and invocation to God and statement expressing that "the sword of Nanak guarantees boons of every kind and to everybody." His seal also bore the impact of the Guru.

In the life and death struggles of the Sikhs against the Mughals, the sacred name of Nanak was frequently referred to for inspiration and by way of the determination of the Sikhs to put the ideas of the Guru into practice. The Sikhs in their prayer, the second part of which, is, to all probability, a composition of the later Mughal period, invoked the name of Guru Nanak for optimism and for guaranteeing welfare for all.

4

Contemporary Events

It was an epoch-making period during which Guru Nanak was born and lived (1469-1539). Events of great significance took place then both in Europe and India.

The establishment of Tudor rule in England in 1485 heralded the Modern Age, not only in England but also in Europe generally. It was an age of renaissance, adventure and discovery and of religious reformation. In India too there was religious renaissance. The *Bhakti* movement was at its height. Prominent leaders had done commendable work in various parts of the country—Ramanand and Kabir in Uttar Pradesh; Namdev and Eknath in Maharashtra, who had given to the people their message of the Unity of God, Love and Peace.

Among Nanak's contemporaries may be mentioned (1) Vallabhacharya, born in 1449, with a large following in Gujarat and Rajasthan; (2) Chaitanya Maha Prabhu, who flourished in Bengal from 1486 to 1533. He was a great saint of Bengal and a great devotee of Krishna. Through his faith and devotion to God, he inspired among the people a great religious fervour. Through songs and *Kirtan* accompanied by dance his followers went into ecstasy to see the vision of God; (3) Mira Bai—a Rajput Princess born in Jodhpur in 1449—became a devotee of Lord Krishna and a great saint, composer and singer of devotional songs, which are popular till today and are sung in all parts of the country; and (4) the poet Tulsidas who was born in 1532 and was a great exponent of the Rama cult—the author of the immoral *Ramacharitmanas*—a book read and listened to by the largest number of persons in the world till the present day.

Conditions in Pre-Mughal India

When Guru Nanak was born in 1469, Bahlol Lodi (1451-1489) was ruling Northern India. His successor was Sikandar Lodi who ruled from 1489 to 1517. He was succeeded by Ibrahim Lodi (1517-1526). Guru Nanak saw the foundation of the Mughal Empire laid by Babar, who was succeeded by his son, Hamayun, during the life-time of the Guru.

From the tenth century onwards, successive hordes of Muslim invaders had poured in from Central Asia. As the high way to Delhi lay through the Punjab the great suffering had been caused to the people of this province. The Afghans and Turks established their rule and various Muslim dynasties ruled Northern India. Foreign rulers and their foreign functionaries ruled through their military strength. They exploited the people are fleeced them. They committed untold atrocities, imposed *Jazia* (a personal tax of all non-Muslims) and otherwise taxed them heavily. All avenues to higher service were closed to the Hindus, who could not get employment except to the lowest posts. Hindu temples were razed to the ground and a large number of Muslim mosques was erected. Hindu schools were closed and every effort was made to crush Hindu culture and civilization. A great many Hindus were converted to Islam on the point of the sword and the spirit of the people was crushed. There was a wide gulf created between the rulers and the ruled and between the Hindus and the Muslim population—so much so that Hindu *Fakirs* were subjected to all types of humiliations and were made to dress differently from the Muslim *Fakirs*. There are complete segregation between the Hindus and the Muslims—their rites, customs and ceremonies and their way of living. The masses were greatly demoralised and emasculated. Not a single leader of note was produced by the Hindus during the past five centuries. All this time a very low status was assigned to the Hindus. They were required to put marks on their forehead or attach other distinguishing marks to their dress. They were forbidden to eat grain of a superior quality, to wear rich apparel or to ride good horses, or in palanquins and carriages. In Dera Ghazi Khan district a Hindu could ride only on a donkey. The law of blasphemy was strictly enforced and capital punishment was inflicted for any criticism of Islam. Bodhan Brahmin was executed by Sikandar Lodi (1485-1517) for saying that Hinduism was as good a religion as Islam. Conversion of Hindus was a frequent occurrence and it was done on a mass scale on occasions and in certain parts of the country.

As stated by Prof. Arnold Toynbee in *The Sacred Writings of the Sikhs*, p. 10 (a UNESCO Publication), "their India, where Islam has impinged on Hinduism violently. On the whole, the story of the relations between these two great religions on Indian ground has been an unhappy tale of mutual misunderstanding and hostility."

Guru Nanak was 20 years old when Sikandar Lodi ascended the throne. Even as a Prince, he had been a bigoted Muslim—and wanted to kill all the Hindus who had assembled at Thanesar for a bath in the sacred tank. Praising of him Abdulla, the author of *Tarikh-e-Daudi*, writes: "He was so zealous a Musalman that he utterly destroyed diverse places of the infidels, and left not a vestige remaining of them. He entirely ruined the shrines of Mathura, the mines of heathenism and turned their principal places of worship into caravan sarais and colleges. Their stone images were given to butchers for using as weights for weighing meat and all the Hindus were strictly prohibited from shaving their heads and beards and performing their ablutions. He thus put an end to all idolatrous rites of the infidels there; and, no Hindus, if he wished to have his heard or beard shaved, cold get a barber to do it. Every city thus conformed as he desired to the custom of Islam." The famous idols of Nagarkot and Jwalamukhi were broken to pieces, which were given to butchers.

Religion in Decline

At the time of Guru Nanak's advent, both the prevailing religions—Hinduism and Islam—had become corrupt and degraded. They had lost their pristine purity and glory. The *Vedas* were unintelligible to the people and had been replaced by Tantric literature. Castes had grown rigid and had split into numerous sub-castes. The true spirit of Hinduism had disappeared and what went by the name had been reduced to a mockery. Only forms and rituals which benefitted the Brahmans personally prevailed. Similar was the state of affairs in Islam .

The Political Conditions

Political conditions were much worse. As pointed out by Guru Nanak :

"This age is like a dragon sword—the Kings are butchers; Goodness had taken wings and flown."

He adds :

"There is no one who receiveth or giveth not bribes,
The king administers justice only when his palm has been greased (filled)."

Guru Nanak was also an eye-witness to the treatment meted out to the people by the Mughal invaders in 1521. He was one his way back after touring the Muslim countries. He must have had some idea of the preparations Babar had been making in Afghanistan for invading the Punjab, which he had twice in 1505 and in 1519. On both these occasions Nanak was not in the Punjab. He was returning from his tour on foot not far behind the invaders who came on Irani and Iraqi horses. Before reaching his home town, he stayed at Sayyidpur (now known as Eminabad) with his favourite disciple, Lalo, about 50 miles from Lahore in Gujranwal district. When Lalo spoke of the atrocities practised by Afghan officers and soldiers, Guru Nanak replied :

"As the world of the Lord descendeth upon me,
So I make it known, friend Lallo;
With evil as his best man,
Bringing a crowd of sins as his bridal procession,
Like a bridegroom Babar has hastened from Kabul,
To seize by force as his bride, O Lallo,
The wealth of Hindustan.
Modesty and righteousness both have vanished,
Falsehood leading the Van, holds the field, O Lallo;
Both the Qazi and the Brahmin are out of the work;
The devil reads the marriage service.
Muslim women, who read the *Koran*,
In their agony will cry on God, O Lallo;
Hindu women of high caste or low caste
Will meet with the same dire fate.
Men will sing hymns in praise of Murder, O Nanak;
And instead of saffron smear themselves with blood.
....

Bodies of men shall be rent like shreads of the cloth;
And let Hindustan remember what I now say :
The arrival of the Mughals shall be in '78',
Their departure in '97'.

And then again shall arise the disciple of a hero.
Nanak hath spoken the word of the True Lord now.
And will proclaim the Truth
At the True Lord's appointed hour."

Babar arrived at Sayyidpur shortly afterwards. Nanak was then still there. The town was mostly inhabited by rich Hindu traders and zamindars. They offered considerable resistance in order to save themselves from surrendering their wealth and women. The infuriated Babar, and he ordered a general massacre of the people. All the young women were reduced slavery. Others were forced to grind corn and cook food for the troops. The town was looted and then destroyed by fire. Nanak and Lalo were forced to carry heavy loads of looted property on their heads to the camp and then compelled to grind corn.

The barbarous treatment of prisoners in the camp, particularly of women, broke the tender heart of Nanak. The shock and pain were too acute for him to bear. In his agony he took even God severely to ask. He said :

"Though Khurasan has been shielded by Thee,
Though terror has struck at the heart of Hindustan,
Thou, O Creator of all things,
Takest to Thyself no blame;
Thou hath sent *Yama* disguised as the great Moghal, Babar.
Terrible was the slaughter,
Loud were the cries of the lamenters.
Did this not awaken pity in Thee, O Lord?

Thou art part and parcel of all things equally, O Creator;
Thou must feel for all men and all nations.
If a strong man attacketh another who is equally strong;
Where is the grief in this, or whose is the grievance?
But when a fierce tiger preys on the helpless cattle,
The Herdsman must answer for it.

A Kingdom that was a Jewel,
Was wasted by the dogs,
No one will mourn their passing.
Praise, praise be to God
Who bringeth the people together and *divideth* them also.

The man who thinks himself great,
And enjoys himself to the height of his heart's desire,
In the Lord's eyes is no more than an insect
Nibbling an ear of corn.
The true profit of life is learning to die,
And repeating His Name, saith Nanak."

The pitiable condition of captive women is thus described by Nanak:

"The tresses that adorned these lovely heads,
And were parted with vermilion,
Have been shorn with cruel shears:
Dust has been thrown on their shaven heads.
They lived in ease in palaces,
Now they must beg by the road side,
Having no place for their shelter.
Glory unto Thee, O Lord of Glory,
Who can understand Thy ways, O God?
Surely Thy ways are strange and Thy dispensation!

When these whose heads are shorn were married,
Fair indeed seemed their bridegrooms besides them.
They were brought home in palanquins carved within ivory.
Pitchers of water were waved over their heads
In ceremonial welcome.
Ornate fans, glittered waving above them.
At the first entry into the new home,
Each bride was offered a gift of a lakh of rupees;
Another lakh when each stood up to take her post in her new home;
Coconut shredding and raisins were among the delicious fruits,
Served to them at their tables.
These beauties lent charm to the couches they reclined on,
Now they are dragged away, with ropes round their necks;
Their necklaces are snapped and their pearls scattered.
Their beauty and wealth are their greatest enemies now;
Barbarous soldiers have taken them prisoners and disgraced them.
God casts down, God *exalteth* whomsoever He wills.

....

Few, some very few,
From this havoc return home,
And others enquire of them
About their lost dear ones;

Many are lost for ever
And weeping and anguish are the lot of those who survive.
Ah, Nanak, how completely helpless men are,
It is God's Will that is done, for ever and ever."

Reformer of the Bhakti School

It was under these circumstances that Indian reformers of the *Bhakti* school began their movement to remove the bitterness then prevailing between the followers of Hinduism and Islam. As Muslims persecuted the Hindus because they practised idolatry and caste distinctions, the saints of the Bhakti School preached against both these institutions. They laid stress upon the Fatherhood of God and the Brotherhood of Man. They declared that it did not matter if God was called by the Muslim as *Allah or Khuda* and by the Hindus as *Parmeshwar* and *Ram*. The real test was not in what a person believed but in the actions he performed. Both *Koran* and *Puran* taught love of humanity. They emphasized that there was no person high or low, superior or inferior, big or small, rich or poor in the eyes of God. Muslim Sufi saints preached similar doctrines and also peace among the people and through their message of love and equality converted a large number of Hindus to Islam. The main Sufi centres were at Multan, Pakpattan and Sarhind in the Punjab. The *Bhakatas* preached in the language of the common people in witty prose and pithy poetry so that their teachings could influence the hearts of their listeners. They spoke to the people at the village well, under a banyan tree where men rested in the afternoon, at fairs and festivals, and on occasions of marriages and mornings. They were often on the move, going from place to place, spreading their message of love of God.

Nanak's Achievements

Indian Society was in Nanak's time divided by caste into water-tight compartments and birth determined the status of the individual and not his deeds or merits. The concept of equality was inconceivable and there did not exist any spirit of oneness or of human fellowship. Woman was regarded inferior to man and was looked down upon. Guru Nanak gave her a status of equality—nay, of superiority—and she was freely admitted to his congregation. He condemned the practice of *Sati* or the custom of self-immolation of widows on the pyres of their dead husbands. Says Nanak :

"It is by woman, the condemned one, that we are conceived, and from her that we are born; it is with her that we are betrothed and married.
It is woman are befriend, and it is she who keeps the race going.
When one woman dies, another is sought for; and it is with her that we get established in society.
Why should we call her evil from whom great man are born?
It is also from women that women are born; there is nobody who is not born of woman.
Nanak, only the one true God is independent of woman.

> They who ever praise God with their mouths are full of fortune and beauty:
> And, Nanak, they alone will appear with bright faces in the court of True One."

Guru Nanak endeavoured to create a casteless and classless society—in which there was no exploitation and all were regarded as equal. By his own personal example he taught the people to live together as brothers. He himself dined with peoples of all castes and classes, high or low. In his *langar* all sat together and dined of the same food. Nanak insisted that every Sikh house should serve as a place of service and devotion (*Dharmsala*). Bhai Gurdas says : "Wherever the holy feet of Guru Nanak touched, *Dharmsalas* sprang into existence."

Guru Nanak gave the people of the Punjab an ideal, which was ultimately to mould his followers into a well-knit community. For this guidance was essential. This was provided by Guru Nanak by establishing the institution of Guruship. According to Nanak's teaching, a true Guru was essential for leading the people on the path of deliverance.

Conclusion

Was Guru Nanak a reformer or a revolutionary? Some writers, like Macauliffe and Bhai Kahan Singh, for instance, have described Nanak as a revolutionary—because he had strongly condemned the then existing religious and social institutions and the superstitious practices prevailing among both the Hindus and the Muslims. Guru Nanak had also laid the foundations of a new "casteless and classless society". However, Guru Nanak never used violence and believed in peaceful persuasion to achieve his objectives. And he did not condemn either Hinduism or Islam or their institutions in their original or pure form. What Guru Nanak denounced was the corrupt and evil practices which had prevailed in his time and the exploitation of the ignorant masses by the clever and greedy *Brahmins* or *Mullahs*. He, along with Kabir, believed that the *Vedas* and the *Kitebas* were not false—it were those persons who were false or misguided, who did not supply and comprehend their teachings:

> *"Ved, Kateb Kaho mat Juthe;*
> *Jutha so jo na vichare:*

It is the people who do not follow the instructions contained in the *Vedas* and *Puranas* who are unable to take advantage of their teachings. It is like loading a donkey with sandalwood who cannot avail himself of its perfume. That is why Bhai Gurdas attributed the supersitious practices prevailing among the people in his time to their ignorance of the Vedas.

Secondly, the bitterest attacks of Guru Nanak were directed against the caste system and the hierarchical character of Hindu society. He also denounced strongly the prevailing rites and rituals which were being observed without realising their true meaning. Guru Nanak had no desire to destroy the older institutions but wanted to reform them in a peaceful and not in a violent or revolutionary manner.

Thirdly, the institution of the *Sangat* was after all not a new or a revolutionary innovation. It had its fore-runners in the Buddhist *Sangita* and in the holy congregations of Christians and the Muslims. Nonetheless, I cannot be denied that *Sangat* and *Langar* are the two institutions which have worked regularly since their foundation by Guru Nanak and are responsible for keeping the Sikh society both demonstration and equalitratian.

Lastly, it has been claimed by several Sikh writers that the foundation of the system of *Guruship* by Guru Nanak was a revolutionary step, which resulted in the gradual building up of the Sikh community and the establishment of the *Khalsa Panth*. However, the institution of *Guruship* was not unknown before Guru Nanak and even since his times. But it is also a fact that the institution of the ten Sikh Gurus has been unqiue and it resulted in the building up of the national and heroic spirit for which the Sikh community has become famous.

It is thus clear that Guru Nanak did not believe in violence or in enmity towards others. Like Buddha, Nanak wished to live in peace, amity, goodwill and unity with persons of all faiths. His main emphasis was on the removal of superstitious practices and evils from which humanity was suffering; and that, too, not on the point of the sword or by the use of violence, but by methods entirely peaceful and noble. It can, therefore, be safety concluded that Guru Nanak was a reformer and not a revolutionary.

5

Guru Nanak According to Janam-Sakhis

The ideal method of relating the janam-sakhi testimony to the life of Guru Nanak would be to provide a connected account which harmonized in a single narrative the accounts given in our three principal sources. This, however, is impossible. The selection of incidents offered by Bhai Gurdas can, by reason of its brevity, be assimilated with either of the two janam-sakhi narratives, but apart from the period covering the Guru's childhood and early manhood it is not possible to fuse the accounts recorded in the *Miharban* and *Puratan* traditions. Up to the point where Guru Nanak sets out from Sultanpur on his travels there is relatively close correspondence and a harmony of the two versions could, if necessary, be provided. Following his departure from Sultanpur, however, the two narratives diverge so radically that reconciliation is out of the question. For the period of the Guru's eastern and southern travels there is no correspondence at all. In the case of his northern and western journeys there are a number of incidents in common, but there remain crucial differences in sequence. It is accordingly necessary to set out the testimonies of our three principal sources as three separate accounts. Having done this we shall seek to analyse the material which they provide.

The Life of Guru Nanak according to Bhai Gurdas

Bahi Gurdas's account of the life of Guru Nanak is to be found in stanzas 23-45 of his first *var,* and in stanzas 13-14 of his eleventh *var* he gives a list of the Guru's more important followers. Stanzas 23 and 24 of the first var provide little more than eloquent panegyric, but stanza 25 begins with the line:

Baba (Nanak) visited the places of pilgrimage; he went round seeing them all on festival days.

None of these centres are named, but it is clear from the description which follows that the line is meant to indicate a journey of considerable length.

The first reference to a particular event comes in stanza 28 where it is related that the Guru ascended Monument Sumeru and there held discourse with Gorakhnath and the other eighty-three Siddhs. The Siddhs questioned Guru Nanak concerning the condition of the world below and received in reply a report of darkness, sin and corruption. They then sought to persuade him to enter their sect and sent him to a nearby lakeside in order that he might be tempted by the masses of jewels which he would find in the lake. Their efforts failed, however, and the Guru emerged victorious from the debate.

Next he proceeded to mecca and there went to sleep with his feet pointing towards the *mibarab.* Observing this evident blasphemy a Muslim named Jivan kicked him and dragged his feet away from the direction of the *mibarab.* When he did this, however, the whole of Mecca miraculously moved in the same direction as his feet. A discourse followed in which Guru Nanak emphasized that Ram and Rahim, Hindu and Muslim names for God, designate one and the same God.

Having left his sandals in Mecca as a relic, the Guru proceeded on to medina, and from there to Baghdad where, with Mardana the Bard, he camped outside the city. From there he uttered the call to prayer whereupon the city at once became silent. A *pir* named Dastgir went out to investigate the newcomer's credentials and entered into a debate with him. In response to Dastgir's request for englightenment the Guru took the *pir's* son, ascended with him into the air, and in the twinkling of an eye revealed to him the multitude of heavens and underworlds. The two then descended into the regions below the earth and from there brought a bowl of *karah prasad,* the sacramental food of the Sikhs.

Having returned to the Panjab Guru Nanak proceeded to Kartarpur and there began to lead a settled life, surrounded by his followers. His sons proved rebellious and the seal of succession was accordingly set upon Angad.

On one occasion Guru Nanak travelled from Kartarpur to the village of Achal Batala were many yogis had gathered for the annual Sivratri fair. In the debate which ensued the yogis sought to overwhelm him with an impressive display of miracles. Disdaining to use the same methods, the Guru eventually overcame them with his insistence upon the Name of God as the true source of power.

From Achal Batala he travelled south to Multan, but before he could enter the city some *pirs* came out to him bearing a cup filled with milk. Guru Nanak responded by plucking a jasmine flower and laying it on the surface of the milk.

Following the Multan visit the Guru returned to Kartarpur and settled down once again. There has glory daily increased and his fame spread throughout the world. Before he died he appointed his disciple Lahina to succeed him as Guru Angad and then, merging his spirit in the spirit of his successor, he passed away.

The Life of Guru Nanak according to the Puratan Janam-Sakhis

Baba Nanak was born in the month of Vaisakh, S. 1526 (A.D. 1469). The date is given as the third day of the light half of the month, and the birth is said to have taken place during the last watch before dawn. His father, Kalu, was a Khatri of the Bedi sub-caste who lived in the village of Rai Bhoi di Talvandi and it was there that Nanak was born. His mother's name is not given. During his infancy he played with other children, but unlike them he had a concern for spiritual things and from the age of five began to utter mysterious sayings. The local Hindus declared that a god had been incarnated in human form, and the Muslims that a true follower of God had been born.

When he turned seven years old, Nanak was taken to a Pandit to learn how to read. After only one day he gave up reading and when the Pandit asked him why he had lapsed into silence Nanak instructed him at length in the vanity of worldly learning and the contrasting value of the divine Name of God. The Pandit was greatly impressed and permitted him to return home.

The child now began to manifest disturbing signs of withdrawal from the world. He was set to learning 'Turki' at the age of nine, but returned home and continued to sit in silence. The local people suggested to Kalu that he should have Nanak married. Kalu took their advice, a betrothal was arranged at the house of Mula, a Khatri of the Chona sub-caste, and at the age of twelve Baba Nanak was duly married. No reference is made to where Mula lived or to where the marriage took place, and nor is the bride's name given. Nanak now took up a worldly occupation, but his heart was not in it and he spent his time consorting with faqirs.

Two miracles are related of this period. On one occasion he went to sleep while grazing the family buffaloes and the unattended animals ruined a field of standing wheat. The aggrieved owner of the field haled the negligent Nanak before Rai Bular, the landlord of the village. Guru Nanak insisted, however, that no damage had been done, and a messenger dispatched by Rai Bular found that the ruined crop had been miraculously restored. On another occasion Rai Bular happened upon Nanak sleeping in the shadow of a tree and was greatly impressed to observe that the shadow did not move with the declining sun. The same *sakhi* also records the birth of Guru Nanak's two sons, Lakhsmi Das and Siri Chand.

Nanak's habitual withdrawal from the world continued to cause grave concern and both his parents remonstrated with him successfully. Some of the Bedis suggested consulting a physician, but this merely prompted utterances concerning the nature of what the Guru regarded as the real illness afflicting mankind. The family problem was eventually solved by Nanak's brother-in-law, Jai Ram, who was the steward of Nawab Daulat Khan of Sultanpur. Jai Ram sent a letter inviting Nanak to Sultanpur. The invitation was accepted and Guru Nanak departed, comforting his forlorn wife with a promise that he would call her as soon as his work in Sultanpur prospered.

As soon as Nanak arrived in Sultanpur Jai Ram petitioned Daulat Khan to grant his brother-in-law an audience. The request was granted and as a result of the interview Daulat Khan formed a very favourable impression of Nanak. He presented him with a robe of honour and issued instructions that he should be given employment. The nature of the employment is not specified beyond the fact that it was evidently understood to be clerical work. The *sakhi* records that each morning the Guru would first take his orders from the court and then would 'sit down to write'. In the following *sakhi* Daulat Khan refers to him as 'a good vazir' and uses the same word to describe him to *sakhi.*

During this period Guru Nanak lived a very simple life, keeping only enough of his food allowance to meet his own limited needs and devoting the remainder to God's work. Mardana the Dum came from Talvandi to join him and was followed by others. All were commended to Daulat Khan by Nanak and received employment as a result. The group regularly sang the praises of God until late into the night, and during the last watch of the night the Guru would go to the river and bathe.

One day Nanak went to the river and removing his clothes left them in the care of a servant. While he was bathing messengers of God came and he was transported by them to the divine court. There he was given a cup of nectar *(amrit)* and with it came the command, 'Nanak, this is the cup of My Name *(Nam)*. Drink it." This he did and was charged to go into the world and preach the divine Name.

In the meantime the servant had come anxious at his master's failure to emerge from the water. He returned to the town and informed Daulat Khan of the apparent tragedy. Daulat Khan rode out at once and had the river dragged, but Nanak's body was not to be found. Three days later, however, the missing Nanak suddenly reappeared at the point which he had entered the river. Daulat Khan joined the crowd which gathered, but Guru Nanak evidently remained silent, for the people explained to the Nawab that he had sustained injury in the river. Hearing this Daulat Khan departed with a heavy heart and Nanak, wearing only a lion-cloth, went with Mardana to live with some faqirs.

For One day Guru Nanak maintained his silence and then one the following day he spoke, saying : 'There is neither Hindu or Mussulman'. This was reported to Daulat Khan, but dismissed as the sort of utterance one might expect to hear from a faqir. His qazi, however, took a more serious view of what appeared to be a clear rejection of Islam's claims to superiority. Daulat Khan agreed to question Nanak on the subject, but found nothing offensive in the reply which he received.

It so happened that the appointment time for the second daily prayer came while Guru Nanak was being examined. Everyone present arose and went to the mosque, and Nanak went with them. There he caused even greater offence to the qazi by laughing out loud during the reading of *namaz*. The qazi protested angrily to Daulat Khan, but Nanak explained that he had done so because the qazi has been thinking, not of the prayer he was uttering, but of a new-born filly he had left in the compound, dangerously near a well. The qazi was now convinced of Nanak's powers and made his submission. The people all followed his example and Daulat Khan was so impressed that he offered to surrender his entire authority and all his property to the Guru. When he returned home he found that his treasury had been miraculously filled. Guru Nanak then left Sultanpur, taking with him Mardana the Bard.

After leaving the town the Guru and Mardana first proceeded to a wilderness and for sometime deliberately avoided all inhabited places. One one occasion Mardana became hungry and was sent ahead to a village of Uppal Khatris to receive the generous offerings they would make. On another occasion Mardana entered to town where reverence, clothing, and money were lavished upon him. He returned laden to the Guru, but was told to throw the offerings away as they were unneccessary encumbrances.

Journeying on they came to the house of a certain Sheikh Sajjan. The house was situated out in the country and its owner had built both a temple and a mosque. These were ostensibly for the convenience of Hindu and Muslim travellers, but Sajjan was a *thag* and his real purpose was to lure travellers into his house in order that he might murder them and so acquire their wealth. His method of dispatching his guests was to throw them into a well. Baba Nanak was Mardana were welcomed in the usual way and when night came they were invited to take rest. Before doing so the Guru sang a hymn. The words which he sant convicted Sajjan of his sin and falling at the Guru's feet he implored forgiveness. This was granted on condition that he made restitution for all he had stolen. The *Hafizabad* manuscript adds that the first *dharmsala* was built there.

After leaving Sajjan they travelled to Panipat where Guru Nanak held a successful discourse with Sheikh Sharaf, the *Pir* of Panipat. The name of the *Pir's* disciple is given as Sheikh Tatihar. From Panipat the proceeded on to Delhi where they encountered some mahouts employed by Sultan Ibraham Beg. The mahouts were bewailing the death of the elephant which had provided their employment. At the Guru's bidding they stroked the dead animal's face and uttered, 'Vahiguru!' The elephant was instantly restored to life and the sultan, hearing of the miracle, asked for a repetition of it. The elephant duly died again, but Guru Nanak made no effort to revive it. His cryptic explanation was, however, understood by the Sultan and accepted as a thoroughly laudable one.

These early incidents were evidently a part of the Guru's first journey (*udasi*), but this is not explicit declared to have begun until after the Delhi visit. *Sakhi* 16 records that the first journey was to the east and that on this occasion the Guru's companion was Mardana. It also details the bizarre dress which he adopted for this journey. It is given as an ochre garment and a white one, a slipper on one foot and a wooden sandal on the other, a faqir's *kafni* and a necklace of bones around his heck, a *qalandar's* hat on his head, and a saffron mark (*tilak*) on his forehead. His food is said to have consisted of air. The same *sakhi* also refers to a certain Sheikh Bajid whom they happened to observe being transported in a litter and then being massaged and fanned by servants. In response to Mardana's inquiry concerning the inequalities of the human condition Baba Nanak replied, 'Joy and pain come in accordance with the deeds of one's previous existence.'

Travelling on they reached Banaras where they sat down in a public square. A Pandit named Chatur Das, who happened to pass, observed with surprise that Guru Nanak had neither *salgram, tulsi-mala*, rosary, non-sectarian mark. A discourse ensued, ending with a complete recitation of the lengthy work titled *Oankaru* and was the conversion of Chatur Das.

The next incident is set in place which the *Puratan* Janam-sakhis refer to simply as Nanakmata. It was evidently a Nath centre and the Siddhs who were there at the time observed that a banyan tree which had stood withered for many years suddenly became green when the Guru sat beneath it. They sought to persuade him to join order, but ended by hailing him as one exalted.

The next hour *sakhis* are given on explicit geographical location. The first concerns a community of traders who were busy celebrating the birth of a son to their leading merchant and who ignored Mardana in spite of his obvious hunger. Guru Nanak is said to have smiled when Mardana reported their ungracious behaviour and to have informed him that the new arrival would depart next morning. The prophecy proved to be correct, for the next day the community was lamenting the death of the infant.

The second unlocated *sakhi* briefly describes a watchman who, because he sought to give the visitors the best food he had available, received an underfined 'royal authority."

The third is the story of a disciple whom the Guru won while staying in a village during a rainy season. One day the new disciple's neighbour accompanied him to meet the Guru, but on the way stopped instead at a prostitute's house. Thereafter the two would go out together, one to the Guru and the other to his mistress, until one day they decided to test the merits of the radically different habits they were following. That same day the neighbour discovered a pot filled with coal, but containing also a gold coin, whereas the disciple had the misfortune to pierce his foot with a thorn. Guru Nanak explained to them that the neighbour's gift of a gold coin to a sadhu in his previous existence had earned him a pot of gold coins. The disciple, on the other hand, had performed deeds meriting an impaling stake. The neighbour's subsequent immorality had, however, converted all but the original gold coin to coal, the disciple's piety had reduced the impaling stake to a thorn.

The fourth of the unlocated *sakhis* describes an encounter with some *thags.* Like Sajjan the *Thag* (in the *Puratan* version) these *thags* decided that the evident brightness of the Guru's face must surely mean the possession of much concealed wealth on his person. Before killing the travellers, however, the *thags* were persuaded to send two of their number to a funeral pyre which could be seen burning in the distance. There they observed angels of Ram snatch a body from messengers of Yam. One of the angels explained that the man had been a monstrous sinner, and that accordingly he should really have been the rightful property of Yam. 'The smoke of his funeral pyre has, however, been seen by that divine *guru* whom you come to kill, and as a result he has gained access to Paradise.' The *thags* were appalled to think that they had been about to kill one who imparted salvation simply by seeing smoke. They made their submission and were prodoned on condition that they took up honest agriculture and devoted any surplus they might have to renunciate *bhagats.*

Sakhi 23 is set in a land called Kauru, or Kavaru, a land ruled by female magicians. The queen's name is given as Nur Shah. Mardana went ahead to beg for food and was turned into a lamb by one of the enchantresses. Guru Nanak, following him, caused a pot to adhere to the woman's head, and told Mardana to restore himself by saying 'Vahiguru' and bowing down. The female magicians all converged on Guru Nanak when they heard what he had done, some riding on trees, some on deerskins, some on the moon, several on a wall, and some on a whole grove of trees. When their efforts to enchant him failed Nur Shah herself came and tried magic and various sensual temptations. All failed and the women finally submitted.

Next the Guru and Mardana come to a wilderness where they rested. At God's command Kaliyug came to try and deceive the Guru. To Mardana's inexpressible terror a great darkness fell and trees were swept away. Next there appeared fire, with smoke ascending on all sides from four abysses of fire. Black clouds than gathered and rain began to fall. Finally, Kaliyug appeared in the form of a demon giant so tall that the top of its head reached to the havens It advanced towards them, but the nearer it came the smaller it grew, until eventually it assumed the form of a man and Kaliyug stood before Guru Nanak in a posture of respect. In the discourse which followed he sought to tempt him with offers of a beautiful place, of jewels, of women, of the power to work miracles, and finally of temporal sovereignty. All were rejected by the Guru, and Kaliyug finally made his submission and asked for salvation.

Having left Kaliyug, the travellers came next to a city of insects. Wherever, they looked everything was black and Mardana was once again in the extremities of terror. Guru Nanak related to him a macabre story of how a raja had once shown disrespect to the insects, and of how they had first destroyed his army with poison and then revivified in with nectar.

Sakhis 26 and 27 obviously constitute a single story. The first concerns a village which refused hospitality, and the second a village which gave it liberally. After leaving the second village Guru Nanak uttered the pronouncement: 'May this town he uprooted and its inhabitants scattered.' When Mardana observed that this was strange justice indeed, he explained that the inhabitants of the first village would, if dispersed, corrupt others, whereas those of the second would spread true beliefs.

After this they reached the land of Asa and there found the famous Sufi Sheikh Farid sitting in a jungle. Three incidents are recorded of the period which they spent with Sheikh Farid. In the first a devout person offered the two holy men a cup of milk, having surreptitiously dropped four gold coins into it. When he returned later he discovered a gold cup filled with gold coins and realized that by offering worldly things instead of an open heart he had received a worldly reward and so had missed a great opportunity. The second describes a problem which was bothering the people of Asa. The Raja of Asa, Syam Sundar, had recently died, but in spite of persistent efforts his skull would not burn. The astrologers had been consulted and had declared that he was in affliction as a result of once having told a lie, and that his salvation could not be effected until a sadhu set foot in the kingdom. For this reason Farid and the Guru were welcomed when they arrived. Farid declined the honour and insisted that Guru Nanak should be the one to pass through the gate which had been erected at the point of entry into the kingdom. The Guru did so, the raja's skull duly burst, and his soul went free. The third incident describes how Sheikh Farid threw away a wooden *chapati* which he had previously kept in order to have an excuse for refusing food. The raja's unfortunate experience had shown him what would happen if he were to persist with this falsehood. The *sakhi* concludes with the statement that there is a *manji* in the land of Asa.

Much of *sakhi* 29 is incoherent, and the *Colebrooke* and *Hafizabad* versions differ considerably. It concerns a visit to a land called Bisiar where everyone refused hospitality except a carpenter named Jhanda. Sitting on 'an island in the ocean', Guru Nanak composed a work called the *jugavali* which he delivered to Jhanda. There is an obscure reference to a city called Chhuthaghataka, and there is said to be a *maji* in Bisiar.

During these travels hunger was never a problem for the Guru, who could subsist on air alone, but for Mardana it was different. After leaving Bisiar they entered a great desert and here Mardana's hunger became so extreme that he could proceed no further. Guru Nanak showed him a tree which would provide him with fruit, but strictly enjoined him to take none with him when they proceeded on. Mardana disobeyed the command and later ate some of what he had brought with him. He at once collapsed and Guru Nanak explained that it was poisonous fruit which had turned to nectar because of the word he had spoken. He then cured him by placing his foot on his forehead.

After twelve years of wandering they eventually arrived back at Talvandi and stopped in the jungle at a distance of two *kos* from the village. Mardana was given permission to enter the village, and was instructed to go to Kalu's house as well as his own. He was, however, to refrain from mentioning Nanak's name. In the village he received a reverent yet warm welcome. When asked where Nanak was the replied, 'Brethren, when the Baba was in Sultanpur I was with him, but since then I have had no news of him.' The Guru's mother refused to believe this and when he left the village she followed him at a distance. A touching reunion with her son followed. Kalu galloped after her as soon as he received the news and did his best to persuade Nanak to remain in Talvandi. The Guru insisted, however, that they had renounced the world and that the settled life was not their calling.

Leaving Talvandi, Guru Nanak and Mardana visited the Ravi and Chenab rivers, and then proceeded south towards Pak Pattan. In a jungle, three *kos* outside the town, they encountered Sheikh Kamal, a disciple of Sheikh Braham who was the contemporary successor of the famous Sufi Sheikh Farid. Kamal informed his master and Sheikh Braham went out to converse at length with the Guru.

From Pak Pattan the two travellers moved north-east and passing through Dipalpur, Kanganpur, Kasur, and Patti, entered Goindval. There no one would give them shelter except a faqir who was a leper and who, as a result of the meeting, was healed. They then travelled on though Sultanpur, Vairoval, and Jalalabad, and entered a village called Kirtan Prathanan where the Guru made more disciples.

From there they moved north through Batala to Saidpur, or Sayyidpur, the modern Eminabad in Gujaranwala District. By this time they had been joined by some faqirs and all were hungry. Guru Nanak himself asked the townfolk for food, but the Pathans who lived there were all busy celebrating marriages and paid no heed to his requests. This lack of response made him exceedingly angry and in his wrath he uttered the verse which begins, *jaisi mai avai khasam ki bani.*

A brahman who had evidently heard the verse, and who had recognized it as a summons to Babur the Mughal to punish the town, brought an offering of fruit and asked the Guru to retract his curse. Guru Nanak replied that what has been uttered could not be recalled, but assured the brahman that if he were to remove his family to a pool twelve *kos* away they would all be saved. The following day Babur arrived and fell upon Saidpur. Everyone it it, Muslim as well as Hindu, was slaughtered, house were looted and then razed to the ground, and the surrounding countryside was devastated.

At some stage the Guru and Mardana were seized and committed to the Saidpur prison under the supervision of a certain Mir Khan. Both were made to do forced labour, Guru Nanak as a coolie and Mardana as a horse attendant. Mir Khan, when he came to watch the prisoners, was startled to observe that the Guru's load remained suspended a full cubit above his head and that the horse followed Mardana without a halter. This information was conveyed to Babur who declared, 'Had I known there were such faqirs here I should not have destroyed the town.' He accompanied Mir Khan to where the prisoners were working and observed that a hand-mill which had been issued to Guru Nanak turned without any assistance.

Babur then approached the Guru who uttered two verses. Hearing these the Mughal fell and kissed his feet, and offered him a favour. Guru Nanak asked for all the prisoners to be released, and Babu at once issued orders to free them and restore their property. The prisoners, however, refused to go unless Guru Nanak accompanied them. Mardana subsequently asked why so many had suffered for the sins of one and was told that he would be given his reply after he had slept under a nearby tree. While he was sleeping ants were attracted by a drop of grease which had fallen on his chest. One of the ants bit him and, without awaking, Mardana brushed them away, killing them all as he did so. This, Guru Nanak subsequently informed him, was his answer.

To this the *Hafizabad* manuscript adds a lengthy account of the manner in which Babur, who was really a clandestine *qalandar*, was impressed by the Guru. When asked to free the prisoners he agreed to do so on condition that his throne should endure for ever. Guru Nanak would promise only that the Kingdom would endure 'for a time'. This was accepted as sufficient and the prisoners were all released.

Leaving Saidpur, Guru Nanak and Mardana passed through Pasrur and came to the small fortress of a local celebrity named Mia Mitha. They stopped in a grove at a distance of one *kos* and when Mia Mitha was informed of the Guru's arrival he boasted that he would skim him as cream is skimmed off milk. Guru Nanak replied that he would squeeze Mia Mitha as he squeezed juice from a lemon. A debate followed and Mia Mitha finally made his submission.

Next Guru Nanak proceeded to Lahore where his coming was brought to the notice of a wealthy Dhuppar Khatri named Duni Chand who happened to be celebrating his father's *sraddh*. In response to Duni Chand's invitation Guru Nanak came and, upon arrival, asked him what point there was in feeding brahmans when his father, in whose memory the *sraddh* was being held, had not eaten for three days. Duni Chand at once asked where his father was to be found, and was informed that he had been born as a wolf and was lying under a certain bush five *kos* away. Taking some food he went in search of his reincarnated father and was told by the wolf that the unfortunate rebirth was the result of having coveted some boiling fish when at the point of death.

Duni Chand subsequently took Guru Nanak to his house. Over the door were seven flags, each representing a *lakh* of rupees. The Guru made no comment, but gave his host a needle with the request that he return it in the hereafter. 'Good God!' exclaimed his wife when he told her what the Guru had said. 'Will this needle accompany you to the hereafter?' Appreciating the force of her rhetorical question Duni Chand took the needle back to Guru Nanak, who asked him, 'If a needle cannot go there, how can these flags get there?'

Sakhi 38 provides the setting for a denunciation of unneccessary ceremonial purity. An excessively scrupulous brahman refused Guru Nanak's food and tried to dig a cooking-square which would satisfy his own notions of purity. After digging all day and everywhere turning up bones he finally made his submission.

The next incident evidently belongs to a later period, for it describes Guru Nanak's practise of daily communal *kirtan*. The Guru happened to observe that a boy aged seven had become a regular attainder at *kirtan* and one day asked him why he engaged in such serious practices at such an early age. In reply the boy related that the necessity of doing so had been impressed upon him as a result of his having observed how when he kindled a fire the small sticks were consumed first. The boy's name is not given.

The two *sakhis* which conclude the *Puratan* account of the first journey are recorded in the *Hafizabad* manuscript, but not the *Colebrooke*. According to the first of them, Guru Nanak took up residence on the banks of a river near Talvandi where crowds of people flocked to see him. A local official (*karoria*) who lived in a neighbouring village concluded that Nanak was taking advantage of this popularity to corrupt both Hindus and Muslims, and that accordingly he should be imprisoned. He set out to make the arrest, but on the way was struck blind. This convinced him that Nanak must indeed be a great *pir* and, greatly chastened, he remounted his horse, only to fall off again. The people who had observed these misfortunes assured him that the only proper way to approach a great *pir* was on foot. This he did and was so impressed by the Guru that he decided to build for him a village which was to be called Kartarpur.

The second of the *Hafizabad sakhis* relates the story of Bhagirath and an unnamed shopkeeper. A poor Sikh once came to the Guru asking for financial assistance in order that he might his daughter married. Guru Nanak acceded to the request and dispatched another Sikh, Bhagirath, to Lahore with instructions to purchase everything that would be required, and to return at all costs that same day. Failure to do so would mean forfeiting his opportunity of salvation.

The shopkeeper to whom he went for his purchase provided him with everything except a set of bangles, informing him that these could not possibly be ready until the next day. When Bhagirath insisted that delay was more than his salvation was worth the shopkeeper became curious and decided to visit the guru who could evidently give or withhold salvation as he pleased. He provided a set one bangles from his own house and set off with Bhagirath. While they were still on the way the Guru's voice came to them. The shopkeeper was instantly convinced and spent three years with Guru Nanak before returning to Lahore.

When he eventually did return it was to entrust his property to other shopkeepers. He then embraked on a shop, sailed to the city where Raja Sivanabh lived, and there established a trading business. He lived a life of great piety there, but it was not one which accorded with the superstitious practices of the local people. There people were not Hindus and they made a point of defiling any Hindus who went there. The shopkeeper did not observe local practices, but nor did he follow Hindus customs and so eventually he was reported to the raja. Sivanabh summoned him, demanded an explanation, and was given a description of Guru Nanak. This aroused a great longing in him for an opportunity to meet the Guru. The shopkeeper replied that the proper place to meet him was in his own heart, but before leaving he comforted the raja with the assurance that the Guru would one day come to him in person. He warned him, however, that there could be no knowing the guise in which he would come.

After the shopkeeper had sailed away Raja Sivanabh devised a method of testing all visiting faqirs. Summoning a number of alluring women he instructed them to exercise their charms on any faqirs or sadhus who might arrive, knowing full well that in this degenerate age only the perfect Guru would be able to resist such advances.

Sakhi 42 opens with the announcement that Guru Nanak's second journey was to the south. The *Puratan* janam-sakhis are confused concerning the number and names of his companions on this journey. The *Hafizabad* manuscript usually gives their number as two and their names as Saido and Gheho, both jats, but in one place it refers to three companions named Saido, Gheho, and Siho, again all Jats, in another simply to Saido and Siho, and in yet another it adds the name of Mardana. The *Colebrooke* manuscript usually names them Saido a Jat and Siho a Gheho, but in one place refers to them as Saido and Gheho.

The first visit was to a country called Dhanasari where the Guru's companions encountered Khwaja Khizar. They had previously come to the conclusion the Guru Nanak's frequent visits to the river were for the purpose of worshipping this deity, and had themselves begun worshipping him. One night, however, they met Khwaja Khizar himself taking an offering to the Guru whom he worshipped daily. While in Dhanasari Guru Nanak conducted a successful discourse with Anabhi, the superior of a very influential Jain monastery. He then completed *Majh ki Var* and proceeded on.

The next recorded incident is set on 'an island in the ocean, in foreign parts, where a savage man exercised tyrannical rule'. The savage seized the Guru and set about cooking him in a cauldron. Instead of becoming hot, however, the cauldron become cooler. Perceiving this the cannibal fell at the Guru's feet and asked for salvation. Siho administered baptism and so he became a Sikh. The sevage's name is not given.

The *sakhi* which follows is both confused and fantastic. It concerns a meeting with Makdhum Bahauddin whom Guru Nanak encountered sporting in the sea on his prayer-mat. After this Guru Nanak is said to have travelled out into the ocean to converse with Machhendranath and Gorakhnath.

Sakhi 47 records another crossing of the ocean, this time to the kingdom of Sivanabh in Singhaladip. When Guru Nanak arrived there Sivanabh's garden, which had remained withered for years, suddenly blossomed. The gardener reported this to the raja who at once sent his alluring women to test the new arrival. Later Sivanabh came himself and after questioning the Guru invited him to his palace. Babu Nanak replied that he did not travel on foot, but that he required as his mount one who was of royal blood and ruler of a city. Sivanabh at once afford himself and the Guru proceeded to the palace on the raja's back.

At the palace Sivanabh and his wife, Chandarakala, asked him what he wished to eat. In reply the Guru asked for human flesh and specified that it was to be that of 'a son who is of royal parentage and twelve years old'. Sivanabh consulted his own son's horoscope and discovered that he was, as required, twelve years of age. Both the boy and his wife agreed that the Guru's wish should be met, and while the mother held his arms and the wife his feet Sivanabh proceeded to cut his son's throat. The boy's body was then stewed and placed before the Guru who instructed them to shut their eyes, utter 'Vahiguru', and begin to eat. This they did and when they opened their eyes again the Guru had disappeared. As a result of this experience the raja became insane, but twelve months later was vouchsafed a *darisan* and became a Sikh.

They party incoherent conclusion of the *sakhi* records that while in Singhaladip Guru Nanak composed a work entitled the *Pran Sangali.* A group of believes met regularly in the *dharmsala* and there secret teaching were revealed. Raja Sivanabh received a *manji* and Guru Nanak departed.

The final *sakhi* of the second journey describes how Guru Nanak wrecked the hut of an hospitable carpenter. The reason for this seemingly ungrategul action was revealed when the carpenter discovered under the remains of his broken bed four pots of gold.

The third journey was to the north and Guru Nanak's companions this time were Hassu, blacksmith, and Sihan, a calico-printer. On his head and feet he wore leather and round his whole body he bound rope. The small groups first travelled to Kashmir where a Pandit named Braham Das came to meet them wearing an idol round his neck and bringing with him two camels loaded with Puranas. The discourse which followed converted him and he threw away his idol.

His conversion was, however, incomplete and one day Baba Nanak told him to take a *guru.* For this purpose he directed Braham Das to some faqirs out in a tract of waste land, and they in turn sent him on to a nearby temple. There a woman in crimson beat him severely with a shoe and the wailing Pandit returned to the faqirs to be informed that he had just met *Maya*, the *guru* he had hitherto served. The completed Braham Das's conversion. He threw away his books and became a humble servant of the pious.

After leaving Kashmir, Guru Nanak traversed many mountains and eventually ascended Mount Sameru where he conversed with Siva, Gorakhnath, Bharathari, Gopichand and Charapat. The Siddhs sent him to fill a pot with water, but when it kept filling with jewels the Guru broke it, repaired it, exercised the spell with a *slok*, and then filled it with water.

A lengthy discourse followed, at the end of which the Siddhs suggested the Nanak should proceed to the village of Achal where many Siddhs would be gathered for a fair. The journey, they informed him, would take them three days as they travelled on the wind. They then departed, obviously expecting to arrive well before him. The Guru, however, was transported there in an instant and at their arrival the Siddhs from Mount Sumeru were amazed to hear from others at the fair that Nanak had appeared three days previously. A brief discourse followed.

The fourth journey took Guru Nanak westwards to Mecca, evidently without a regular companion. For this journey he wore leather shoes, pajama, a blue garment, and a necklace of bones. Having reached his destination he went to sleep with his feet in the direction of Mecca and a qazi named Rukandin, who happened to observe him in this position, rebuked him severely. The Guru suggested that the qazi should drag his feet round and leave them pointing in a direction away from God and the *Ka'bah.* Rukandin complied and was amazed to discover that as he moved the Guru's feet the *mibarab* moved with them. He summoned Pir Patalia and the three engaged in discourse. At its conclusion Guru Nanak uttered 'Vahiguru' and water appeared in the wells, thus fulfilling a prophecy contained in the Muslim scriptures that Nanak, a *darves*, would come and cause water to spring in the wells of Mecca.

The fifth journey was a much shorter one than any of the previous four. On this occasion the Guru travelled to Gorakh-hatari where he met Siddhs and held the discourse which is recorded in the work entitled *Siddh Gost.* The Siddhs sought to impress him with displays of their magical power, but without success.

Sakhi 53 describes the conversion of Lahina who was subsequently to become Guru Angad. Lahina lived in Khadur where he was the priest of the Tehana (Trehan) Khatris. In the same town there lived a Bhalla khatri who was a Sikh, the only person there who did not worship the goddess Durga. One day Lahina happened to overhear him reciting the *Japji* and this so impressed him that, having learnt the identity of the author, he went at once and became a disciple. The service which he rendered to his master was particularly devoted. He regularly sourced the Guru's pots and waved the fan, and on one occasion willingly ruined a new suit of clothes in order to obey a command to bring in some wet grass. The *sakhi* also refers to Durga's practice of coming every eighth day to serve the Guru, and terminates with an incoherent story concerning a maid-servant who once sought to waken the Guru by licking his feet.

Gorakhnath once visited Guru Nanak and the Guru devised a test to show how many true followers he had. The two set out walking, followed by the Sikhs. At the Guru's command copper coins appeared on the ground, and many of his followers picked them up and departed. Next silver coins appeared and then gold coins. Each time he lost more Sikhs and after the appearance of the gold coins only two remained. Further on they came to burning funeral pyre. Over the corpse there was a sheet and from it there issued a foul smell. The Guru asked if there was anyone prepared to eat the corpse and at this one of the two remaining Sikhs fled, leaving only Lahina to obey the command. Lahina asked which end he should begin to eat and was instructed to start at the feet. Raising the sheet he found Guru Nanak lying there. Gorakhnath, impressed by this display of loyal obedience, declared, 'He who is born from a part (*ang*) of you will be your Guru', and the name Angad was accordingly bestowed upon Lahina.

In *sakhi* 55 Makhdum Bahauddin reappears, this time as the *Pir* of Multan and as one near death. Realizing that his end was near he sent a *slok* to Guru Nanak in Talvandi, informing him of the fact, and received in reply another *slok* with this comment, 'You go and I shall follow after forty days'. Loudly lamenting the prospect of forty days of darkness Makhdum Bahauddin passed away.

Guru Nanak was also aware of approaching death. Before it took place he appointed Angad as his successor by laying five copper coins in front of him and prostrating himself before him. The news at once spread that he was about to die, and Hindus and Muslims flocked for a last audience. He then went and sat under a withered acacia, which at once blossomed, and his family gathered around him seeping. His sons asked what would become of them and were assured that they would be cared for. A dispute then arose between the Muslims and the Hindus, the former claiming that they would bury the Guru's body and the latter that they would cremate it. The Guru himself settled the argument by instructing the Hindus to lay flowers on his right and the Muslims to place them at his left. Whichever side's flowers were still fresh on the following day would have his body to dispose of as they wished. The assembled followers then sang *Kirtan Sohila* and *Arati*, and the concluding *slok* of the *Japji*. Guru Nanak covered himself with a sheet and went to sleep. when the sheet was raised the body had gone and the flowers on both sides were still fresh. The Hindus took their share away and the Muslims did likewise. The data was the tenth day of the light half of Asu, S. 1595, and it was at Kartarpur that Guru Nanak passed away.

The Life of Guru Nanak according to the Miharban Janam-Sakhi (Pothi Sach-Khand)

The *Puratan Janam-sakhi* contains only fifty-seven *sakhis* and accordingly it has been possible to include them all in the outline given above. In the case of Miharban's *Pothi Sach-khand* this is not possible, but the exclusion of some individual *gosts* need not involve any significant omissions as far as the biography of Guru Nanak is concerned. Several of the *gosts* offer no biographical details and frequently a single episode is spread over more than one *gost.*

The first three *gosts* of the *Miharban Janam-sakhi* recount the greatness of the first Raja Janak and describe an interview with God wherein Janak is informed that he is to return to the world once again. His name is to be Nanak and his task is to be the salvation of the world from the evils and degeneracy into which it has fallen.

The details of Guru Nanak's birth are given in the fourth *gost.* His father was Kalu, a Bedi Khatri, and his mother's name is given as Tipara. The Damdama Sahib manuscript gives the village of Chahalavale as the place where the birth took place, but the second Khalsa College manuscript omits this details and is *gost* 17 the Damdama Sahib manuscript gives "Talvandi Rai Bhoe ki' as the birthplace. The date given in the Damdama Sahib manuscript is a moonlit night in the month of Vaisakh, S. 1526, and the second manuscript adds that it was the third day. The hour is said to have been the last watch of the night. There was great celebration both in heaven and in the village, and Hindus and Muslims of all tribes and ranks came to offer their congratulations. On the ninth day after his birth he was given his name. Various faculties are recorded as having developed with consecutive months during the first year, at eighteen months, and with each year up to the age of five when he began to give utterance to spiritual wisdom. Hindus declared that he was the image of God, the Muslims that truly he was a godly child.

At the age of seven Nanak was taken to a Pandit to learn how to read. The Pandit wrote out the alphabet for him, but the child kept silent and refused to repeat it. A discourse followed based, as in the *Puratan* account, on the verse *Siri Ragu* 6, and at its conclusion the Pandit acknowledged that one so wise should certainly be permitted to decide what was best for himself.

When he was eight years old Nanak would play with ground of other children and give them instruction in the things of God. During this period Kalu decided that he should learn "Turki" and summoned a mullah for this purpose. This time Nanak applied himself to his studies and started both the mullah and the village with his incredible progress. Within a matter of days he had mastered not only Persian but also Hindvi, Arabic, and accounting. After this he became silent and refused to communicate with anyone. The mullah was called again and with some difficulty managed to persuade Nanak to speak. When he did eventually speak it was to utter a verse empounding the transient nature of man's worldly abode. Hearing it the mullah saluted him as a blessed child.

When he reached the age of nine arrangements were made for him to be invested with the sacred threat (*janeu*). It appears that he did not actually refuse it, as *gost* 11 makes reference to his wearing it, but the occasion provided him with an opportunity to criticize external ritual, and to affirm inward acceptance of the divine Name and praises offered to God as the only true *janeu.*

The next recorded incident is the restoration of the crop ruined by Nanak's buffaloes. This is said to have occurred at the age of about ten or twelve and is substantially the same as in the *Puratan* account. One significant difference is that the landlord's name is given as Rai Bhoa, not Rai Bular. Two minor differences are that the field in said to have contained paddy, nor wheat, and that the reason given for Nanak's negligence is meditation, not sleep. *Gost* 9 relates the story of the tree's stationary shadow and in *gost* 10 Rai Bhoa discusses with Kalu the significance of this incident and that of the restored field. The owner of the field is summoned to ascertain that he had told the truth and Rai Bhoa assures Kalu that Nanak is obviously no ordinary son. Nanak's age at the time when Rai Bhoa observed the stationary shadow is given as thirteen or fourteen.

About the time of his sixteenth birthday Guru Nanak was betrothed to the daughter of Mula, a Chona (khatri) of Batala. The betrothal ceremony is said to have been held on the first day of the dark half of Vaisakh, S. 1542. The wedding took place in Batala soon afterwards and when it was over Nanak returned with his family to Talvandi. In *gost* 22 his wife's name is given as Chumi.

At the age of went Guru Nanak lapsed into silence and inactivity, and his mother's efforts to rouse him were unavailing. In the following *gost* he explains that his silence is the result of having no godly people to converse with. *Gost* 15 records that he neither ate, drank, nor spoke for four or five days and that eventually the anxious townfold persuaded Kalu to summon a physician. The physician duly came and feeling the patient's pulse pronounced it a case of madness. Nanak's reply was essentially the same as that given in the *Puratan* version, and the physician acknowledged him as Guru.

Next family pressure was tried. Guru Nanak was summoned before a family conclave and the Bedis remonstrated with him, seeking to persuade him to take up agriculture. The effort was unsuccessful and so too was another which the family made when he was twenty-two.

When Guru Nanak was twenty-seven or twenty-eight his two sons, Lakhmi Das and Siri Chand were born. At the age of thirty his renunciate tendencies became even more pronounced and he abandoned all other activity in favour of discussions with yogis and sanñyasis. Efforts made by both his father and mother to persuade him to take up agriculture, shopkeeping, trade, or civil service employment met with the usual negative response.

Eventually Jai Ram, his brother-in-law, came to the rescue with his suggestion that Nanak should join him in Sultanpur. The invitation was accepted and Guru Nanak departed, leaving his wife in the meantime but taking Mardana the Dum him with. Jai Ram is described as an Uppal Khatri and as Daulat Khan Lodi's steward. The Damdama Sahib manuscript gives his home as Khanpur and the second manuscript as Sultanpur. The name of the wife, Guru Nanak's sister, is not recorded. Guru Nanak's age at the time is given as thirty-five years, six and half months.

His meeting with Jai Ram and his interview with Daulat Ram are described in some detail. At the interview he presented to the Nawab a fine Iraqi horse and an offering of money, and in return received a robe of honour. Daulat Khan pronounced himself highly pleased with the new arrival and commanded that all authority over his province and property be entrusted to Nanak. This was evidently to be understood as complimentary hyperbole as the employment to which he was actually assigned was in Daulat Khan's commissariat. His daily life, combining pious exercises with proper fulfilment of his secular duties, is also described.

It was not long, however, before doubts began to arise in the Guru's mind. He continued to fulfil his responsibilities in the commissariat, but his mind turned increasingly to spiritual things, even while he was engaged in his quartermaster duties. In a discourse with his cook he expressed his concern at his involvement in worldly affairs. Eventually the climax of his developing spiritual crisis came with the summons to the court of God, received while he was taking his regular early-morning bathe in the river.

As in the *Puratan* account the river is not named, but the author indicates that it was in the direction of Goindval. One morning Nanak plunged in as usual, but did not reappear, having been transported to the divine court. Miharban's version is characteristically diffuse, occupying four times the space of the *Puratan* account without making any significant additions to it. The river was dragged without success and on the third day Nanak emerged to the acclamation of the crowd, gave away his belongings, and joined a group of faqirs. The people were perplexed and many concluded that he must be possessed. Some of the common folk, observing that he appeared to be conforming to neither Hindu or Muslim practice, asked him what path he was now following. He replied, "There is neither Hindu nor Mussulman so whose path shall I follow? I shall follow God's path. God is neither Hindu nor Mussulman and the path which I follow is God's.

This comment was communicated to the local qazi and at his request Nanak was summoned before Daulat Khan to answer for it. Once again Miharban provides an account which is appreciably longer than that of the *Puratan* janam-sakhis, but which adds nothing except extra quotations from Guru Nanak's works, protracted expositions, and incidental details of no importance. The Guru successfully answered the qazi's charge, humbled him by reading his thoughts during *namaz*, and expounded to him and to Daulat Khan the meaning of true *namaz.* At the conclusion of the exposition Daulat Khan prostrated himself adoringly and Guru Nanak assured him that he had attained salvation. Taking the dust of the Guru's feet Daulat Khan returned home. No reference is made to his treasury having been miraculously filled.

Baba Nanak and Mardana then set out on the first journey *(udast)*, having spent two years in Sultanpur. As in the *Puratan* janam-sakhis the account of this journey begins with a description of how Mardana would enter a village to ask for food whenever necessary, and of how the Guru commanded him to throw away the money and clothing which a generous village had bestowed upon him as offerings. Following the experience they entered a wilderness devoid of human habitation. Mardana became apprehensive, but the Guru calmed his fears by assuring him that no place where the divine Name was repeated could be uninhabited. Some days later there occurred the incident of the forbidden fruit.

After a conversation with some herons Guru Nanak and Mardana reached Delhi where they observed food being distributed to mendicants on behalf of the king, whose name is given as Salem Shah Pahan. The guru preached to the people on the necessity of the divine. Name and the entire population became his Sikhs. There is no mention of a resurrected elephant.

Leaving Delhi they proceeded on to the Ganges where, as it happened to be a festival day, they observed thousands of people bathing in the river. The festival which was being celebrated was that of Baisakhi and the pilgrims were throwing water in the direction of the rising sun. Guru Nanak also entered the river and began splashing water in the opposite direction. This provoked offended demands for an explanation. The Guru responded by asking his questioners to whom they thought they were conveying water and they replied that they were sending it to their ancestors in heaven. Guru Nanak then informed them that he was, in the same manner, watering his fields near Lahore. When his brought a scornful rejoinder he answered that if their water could travel as far as heaven his could certainly reach Lahore. This silenced them for they now realized that they were conversing with a person of exalted spiritual insight. Continuing the discourse on the banks of the river he emphasized the futility of *mantras* and cooking-squares. Two more discourses follow. The first of these, another discourse on cooking-squares, provides a setting for the verse *Basant* 3, which in the *Puratan* janam-sakhis is set in an entirely different incident. The second refers to Hardwar as the location of these discussions.

From Hardwar Guru Nanak and Mardana moved on to Prayag (Allahabad) where the Guru's fame had preceded him and a large crowd had gathered to pay their respects. After a discourse with some devout people they proceeded on to Banaras where the Guru engaged in several discourses with Pandits and groups of devout believers. The first of these was with a single Pandit, but he is not named. On another occasion the entire population of Banaras, and specifically all of the Pandits in the city, are said to have been present at a discourse held on the Bisarati (Visranti) Ghat, and at the conclusion of the discourse all of the Pandits became Sikhs.

After leaving Banaras they came to the city of Raja Harinath in 'the east country' where, to begin with, Guru Nanak observed silence and was consequently mistaken for a *moni*. Hearing of his arrival the raja himself went on foot to meet him, listened to his instruction, and asked if he might accompany him as a disciple. He was, however, told to practise piety while yet remaining a raja.

From Raja Harinath's unnamed city they proceeded 'to where Gusai Kambir's house was'. Kabir went out to meet Baba Nanak and in the discourse which followed acknowledged him as the supreme Guru. In reply Guru Nanak uttered his *Gauri Astapadi* 8, a composition which if it were to be applied to Kabir would imply very high praise of him.

Travelling eastwards from where Kabir lived they came next to Hajipur Patna where the Guru discoursed with and converted a group of Vaisnavas. Continuing to the east they entered an unnamed city where Guru Nanak observed his common practice of initial silence and subsequently instructured the members of the town council in the nature of 'the true food', namely God Himself.

From that city they turned south and, entering a wilderness, met and conversed with an unidentified raja. Next they arrived at another unnamed city where Guru Nanak's presence exercised an attraction so compulsive that eventually the whole city gathered to pay him homage and declared him to be an incarnation of God. In the following *gost* they are back in 'the east country.' There they visited Ayodhya where, after the Guru had conducted two discourses, 'all the *bhagats* gathered at God's command and came to meet him—Namdev, Jaidev, Kabir, Trilochan, Ravidas, Sain, Sadhna, Dhanna, Beni'. A lengthy discourse followed, based on *Siri Ragu* 10-12, at the end of which the *bhagats* hailed him and departed for heaven. There they reported their experience to God who, well pleased to hear their praises, summoned Nanak to an interview.

Leaving Ayodhya they travelled down to Jagannath where they met Raja Bharathari, the famous yogi. *Gost* 62 records that they spent three years in 'the east country' and that having seen it all they turned south. Jagannath Puri in accordingly the eastern terminus in Miharban's account and after this visit we find Guru Nanak travelling south, presumably down the east coat of India.

From Jagannath Puri the Guru and Mardana travelled a considerable distance and eventually came to a temple surrounded by a desert. There a piece of brick happened to fall on Guru Nanak after he had been meditating and the consequent pain greatly distressed him as he had believed his meditation would free him from such suffering. Which he was lamenting this the voice of God was heard assuring him that all who live in the world must experience pain of this kind.

Two strange incidents follow. The first relates how the thirsty travellers were led to water by a jackal, and how Guru Nanak, entering the water, travelled thence to the court of God and returned with food. In the second story Guru Nanak cures a fit of depression in Mardana by revealing to him that the stars are worlds in which dwell those *bhagats* who have served God faithfully.

Their journey southwards finally brought them to Rameswaram where Guru Nanak recited the hymn in the *Dhanasari* metre entiteld *Arati* and held discourse with the worshipers of the idol installed there. Proceeding on from Rameswaram beyond Setu-bandha ('Adam's Bridge') they entered a foreign country in which an unknown language was spoken. There they passed through a series of regions in all of which the one God was worshipped. The first two of these were human kingdoms, but the remainder were areas inhabited only by either spirits or animals. In all of them they found the one God worshipped and Guru Nanak gave praise accordingly.

Next they met Kaliyug who appeared to them as a man carrying fire in his hand and raw meat in his mouth. He is an altogether milder being than the *Puratan* version and explains his coming as simply the result of is desire to see a great *bhagat.* A more fearsome monster is encountered in the next *gost* where a high mountain turns out to be a massive creature. Guru Nanak distended himself to the equivalent size, seized the creature, and was about to eat in when Mardana intervened and begged him to free it. His request was granted, but he was greatly upset to learn that he had been instrumental in freeing Kal (Death). Guru Nanak assured him, however, that it was really God who had spoken through him.

Their next experience was the encounter with the cannibals who were unable to heat their cauldron. In Miharban's account it is Mardana whom the savages try to boil. Following this the Guru turned a deceitful people to righteousness by causing a harvest to grow without moisture after local *sakti* practices had failed to produce the necessary rain. Guru Nanak renamed the country Sadiq and the people, following their raja's example, all became Sikhs. A *dharmsala* was built and the Sikh devotional discipline was adopted.

Next, still in 'the south country', they met Sajjan the *thag.* After his exposure and confession his *dharmsala* of blood was destroyed and a new one built in its place. This is followed by a series of unimportant discourses, most of which are held in wildernesses or various unidentified cities of he south and none of which add any significant details. *Gost,* a discourse with God, is said to have taken place 'in a city of *thags* in the south country. *Gost* 75 purports to be a discourse held in a desert with a certain Raja Mitr Sain, and *gost* 78 concerns a Raja Jagannath. In *gost* 83 a storm which kills all the birds in a grove where Guru Nanak happened to be sitting prompts a soliloquy on death. The birds are revived in the following *gost.*

This groups of south country *gosts* is followed by another groups which are said to have taken place in the city of Ujjain or the area to the south covered by the modern Indore District. This is still regarded as 'the south country'. In the second of these Mardana's name reappears, having been absent since gost 72. The first of the Ujjain *gosts* records a meeting with Bharathari, but the discourse is with God. Guru Nanak was Mardana then left the city and came to 'Vijhni where there are elephants'. From there they continued on to the Narabad river where Guru Nanak conversed with a converted and earnest sanyasi named Chiti Giri.

After leaving the Narabad they turned north again and on the way back to Ujjain fell among *thags* who surmised that the Guru must be a person of much wealth who had disguised himself as a faqir in order to conceal the fact. The *thags* of the *Puratan's sakhi* 22 based alike conclusion upon their conviction that a bright face much indicate a full pocket. This appears, however, to be an entirely different story. There is no struggle on a funeral pyre as in the *Puratan* incident and the customary quotations differ. In Miharban's account all that is required to effect the *thags* conversion is the recitation of an appropriate hymn.

Gost 91 contains in its alleged meeting with Bharathari a common kind of anachronism and it also provides some unusually specific details concerning the location of the meeting. The discourse on this occasion is said to have been held with celibate sadhus, but Bharathari is referred to in the introductory portion and appears as a participant during the latter part of the conversation. Two more discourses with Bharathari follow, then one with God, and finally one with a groups of Sikhs.

Leaving Ujjain, Guru Nanak and Mardana continued their travels in'the south country' and eventually, after a number of discourses with sundry people in various unnamed places, reached 'the Bikaner country in Rajputan'. Here they moved around for sometime, holding discourses with people both in Bikaner city and in the surrounding countryside. After leaving Bikaner they entered 'the land of Sorathi'. Mardana asked the Guru if this meant they were in the land of the Sorathi who was associated with Bije and received anaffiarmative reply. This indicates Saurashtra and means that Miharban has taken them in a southerly direction once again.

Eventually, after spending five years in 'the south country', the travellers moved on to the north and come to Mathura. There they visited the Keso Rai temple, bathed in the Yamuna, and then proceeded to the eastern part of the town where a large convocation of sadhus had gathered. After the usual discourse the sadhus all became Sikhs.

From Mathura they moved on to Kurukshetra where a festival was in progress in and many people were bathing. Guru Nanak's arrival there brought a large crowd, and a discourse on the ineffectiveness of their bathing. Finally, they arrived back in Sultanpur where they received an affectionate welcome from Daulat Khan Lodi. Three discourses followed, in the second of which Daulat Khan declared that although God was 'the Master of hearts' no one had ever seen Him and that here on earth the title belonged to Guru Nanak. The Guru also conversed with some pious people and was acclaimed a pir by both Hindus and Muslims.

After the interlude in Sultanpur Guru Nanak set out through 'the north country' to Mount Sumery, evidently travelling alone. The only place named on his journey there is a temple of Durga. Climbing Mount Sameru, Guru Nanak found all nine Siddhs seated there—Gorakhnath, Machendranath, Isarnath, Charapatnath, Barangnath, Ghoracholi, Balgundai, Bharathari and, Gopichand. When Gorakhnath asked the identity of the visitor his disciples replied, "This is Nanak Bedi, a *pir* and a *bhagat* who is a householder. Nanak Bedi is a great *bhagat.*' Gorakhnath then addressed Guru Nanak, asking him from where he had come. The Guru replied that he had come from *Ass-andesa* ('Hope and Fear') and that he dwelt there asa water fowl floats on water. Gorakhnath commented that a water-fowl knows all that is taking place along the river and asked him to tell them what was happening in the present evil age (*Kaliyug*). Guru Nanak responded with three *sloks*, all of them describing a condition of degeneracy.

There is a famine of truth, falsehood prevails, and in the darkness of *Kaliyug* men have become ghouls...

The *Kaliyug* is a knife, kings are butchers, *dharma* had taken wings and flown....

Men given a charity the money they have acquired by sinful means...

The discourse then takes up *Var Ramakali, sloks* 2-7 of *pauri* 12, and in the succession of *gosts* which follows there are quoted other *sabads* and *sloks* which imply an audience of Naths.

The series concluded with a discourse in God's court, after which Guru Nanak descended to 'this world' again and journeyed to Gorakh-hatari. He arrived there during a fair, conversed with 'the yogis' *guru*', and continued on. No reference is made to any attempt by the yogis to overawe him with magic.

Leaving 'the north country', where he had spent one year. Guru Nanak entered 'the west country' and proceeded towards Multan. Mardana reappears in the janam-sakhi at this point and a group of Multan *gosts* follows. One of these was with a descendant of Pir Bahauddin, and in the next *gost* it is recorded that the Guru visited the Pir's tomb where, according to the people's report, he paid homage.

From Multan Guru Nanak set out on a pilgrimage to Mecca. On the way he came to a village which belonged to a mullah and entering the village mosque without removing his shoes he lay down with his feet in the direction of the *Ka'bah.* When the mullah and his congregation entered the mosque for the *pesi,* the second prayer, they discovered him lying in this sacrilegious position. The mullah demanded an explanation and the Guru replied, 'Baba Sahib, turn my shoes in that direction where the house of God will not go. Place my shoes in that direction where the *Ka'bah* is not.' The mullah did not accept the challenge. He first performed the office and then gave orders for the Guru to be thrown into prison. Guru Nanak asked for permission to make a single comment and when it was granted declared that God alone and not his accuser was the true Mullah. He then recited *Sri Ragu* 28:

He is the true Mullah who has caused the world to blossom and be verdant....'

The Mullah, evidently acknowledging defeat, retired to the graveyard and there expired.

Proceeding on from the mullah's village he met two faqirs who were going to Mecca and who suggested that they should all travel together. Further on, when they reached a village, the Guru asked them their names. They informed him that they were called Rahim and Karim, and inquired what his name was. When he told them it was Nanak they commented with evident surprise that it sounded like a Hindu name. The Guru replied that he was indeed a Hindu, and when he added that he was a Khatri and a Bedi they at last recognized him as the renowned faqir of Sultanpur fame and became very respectful. When he refused food which the Muslim villagers brought, excusing himself on the grounds that he was fasting, world quickly spread that a great *darves* had arrived and he was acclaimed by the village.

Next morning they all set out again and on the road the two faqirs asked him how be, a Hindu, could hope to visit Mecca. He replied that if God so willed then it would come to pass. The faqirs were carrying paper, pen, and ink, and at this point they wrote down the date. Guru Nanak was then transported to Mecca in an instant. His two companions arrived on foot some months later and discovered the Guru already there. When they asked the local people his date of arrival they were given the very date they had written down and as a result word soon spread in Mecca that a great *darves* had arrived. Guru Nanak remained there for twelve months.

After having visited mecca and seen 'the west country' Guru Nanak travelled eastwards to Hinglaj. There the pilgrims were unable to recognize his religion or his caste. They also observed that he seemed to neither sleep, walk, eat nor drink.

Continuing on to the east he arrived back in the Panjab and passing through Gorakh-hatari came to Saidpur. He had spent three years in 'the west country' and had seen all of it, including Rome, Syria, Kabul and Peshawar. When he reached Saidpur Mardana suggested that they should enter the town to seek alms. This they did and discovered the weddings were being celebrated everywhere. No one, however, paid any attention to them. No food was offered to them, nor any place to rest, and wherever they asked they were ignored or refused. As punishment for its callousness the Guru called down Babur upon the town, invoking his coming by the utterance of the verse *Tilangs.*

As in the *Puratan* version the ronouncement of the curse came to the knowledge of a certain brahman who was a friend of faqirs. Knowing that God invariably heeds the request of a faqir he hastened to the Guru and, presenting him with a basket of fruit, begged him to be merciful. Guru Nanak reminded him that the town had inflicted harm on faqirs, thereby implying that the imminent punishment was merited. The brahman, however, was told to take his family and go to a pool out in the waste land at a distance of fifteen *kos.* Babur then fell upon the city and all save the brahman and his family were massacred. 'And so Saidpur was devastated in accordance with the utterance given by the Guru.'

Next day Guru Nanak and Mardana returned to Saidpur and the Guru commented, 'Mardana, see what has befallen Saiapur Saloi. Behold the will of God in what has taken place.' They looked upon Saidpur and there was nothing to be seen. From there they travelled to Tilla Balgundai. The following day Babur also arrived there and, in accordance with an implied warning which Guru Nanak had given the arrogant yogis, assaulted the village.

After witnessing the sack of Saidpur and visiting Tilla, Guru Nanak at last turned towards his home in Talvandi. They stopped at a distance of two *kos* from the village and Mardana asked if he might continue on into the village. Permission was granted on condition that he was not to mention the name of Nanak and that if anyone should ask for news of him he was to give the following answer: 'Brother, since the time when Baba Nanak left Sultanpur we, being separated from him, have continually held his name in remembrance. If anyone knows his whereabouts it is God.'

In the village the people showed great respect to him. He went to Kalu's house and prostrated himself before the Guru's mother. When she and others asked where Nanak was he replied that he did not know but was looking for him. After further conversation he departed and the Guru's mother said to himself, 'There is meaning in his having come and then departed again. He has gone to Nanak.' Taking sweets, fruit, and clothing, she followed Mardana out into the jungle called Sandal Bar and there the reunion took place. A series of discourses followed in which both his parents unsuccessfully sought to persuade him to abandon his itinerant way of life and settle in Talvandi.

After leaving Talvandi Guru Nanak moved sought through the Majha to Pak Pattan, passing through a number of villages on the way and stopping two *kos* short of the town. The account of his meeting with Sheikh Kamal, who was out gathering firewood, and of the first discourse with Sheikh Ibrahim is essentially the same as the *Puratan's sakhi* 32, except the Mardana appears to be absent in the Miharban version. Most of the scripture quotations are the same and both put Guru Amar Das's *slok* 104 into Guru Nanak's mouth on this occasion. Miharban extends the meeting with Sheikh Ibrahim over two more *gosts,* but adds only scripture and interpretation.

From Pak Pattan Guru Nanak travelled north to Dipalpur where a pious merchant presented him with some dried fruit and some mangoes. The Guru asked him why he was offering fruit from both Khurasan and Hindustan together. The merchant explained that the mangoes were the first of a consignment which had just arrived from Delhi and in order that his business might prosper he wanted Guru Nanak to be the first to taste them. The raisins had been left by Babur's army, which had been in Dipalpur, and some had been saved for any man of God who might come. Guru Nanak tried a sample from each and then blessed both the donor and the town, reciting a *slok* which is really by Guru Angad. He then proceeded on through the areas of Shergarh, Mustafabad, Chunian, Talvandi, Kanganpur, Hari, Kasur, Roheval, Nanier, Bhikiria, and finally reached Khokhoval.

The following *gost,* which is set in Khokhoval, relates a series of biarre incidents, essentially disconnected but loosely linked by the presence of a brahman boy. The language is later and the collection is evidently a subsequent addition.

Leaving Khokhovali, Guru Nanak moved through Kirtan Pathanan to the village of Pokho. The area so attracted him that he settled there on the banks of the Ravi and soon crowds were coming to pay their respects. The local official, however, was sckeptical and, as in the *Puratan* version, set off to imprison the corrupter of Hindus and Muslims. The results were the same, except that the fall come first and blindness second, and that a third effort to proceed on horseback produced a pain in his stomach. When he continued on foot all was well. After his interview he donated some fertile land for a village and built *dharmsala.* Guru Nanak settled there, naming the new village Kartarpur.

At this point *Pothi Sach-Khand* concludes.

Summaries

The three best available accounts of the life of Guru Nanak have now been set out in some detail. In so far as they include references to specific dates, recognizable places, and people of some significance they may be summarized as follows :

Bhai Gurdas's Var

Guru Nanak's visits to 'all the centres of pilgrimage'.

Mount Sumeru.

Mecca.

Medina.

Baghdad.

Kartarpur, on the right bank of the Ravi, immediately opposite Dehra Baba Nanak.

Guru Angad appointed successor.

Achal Batala, four miles east and Batala.

Multan.

Kartarpur.

The Puratan Janam-sakhis

Guru Nanak was born in the light half of the month of Vaisakh, S. 1526 (A.D. 1469) in the village of Rai Bhoi di Talvandi where his father, Kalu, a Bedi Khatri, lived. The landlord of the village during his childhood was Rai Bular. At the age of twelve he was married to the daughter of Mula, a Chona Khatri.

Two sons, Lakhmi Das and Siri Chand, were subsequently born.

His brother-in-law Jai Ram, the steward of Daulat Khan, invited him to Sultanpur where he was given employment in Daulat Khan's service.

From Sultanpur he left on his first journey accompanied by Mardana, a Dum from Talvandi. This journey was to the eastern parts of India and included, in the following sequence:

Panipat (Sheikh Sharaf)
Delhi (Sultan Ibrahmi Lodi)
Banaras
Nanakmata
Kauru or Kavaru, evidently Kamrup in Assam (Nur Shah)
Talvandi, twelve years after leaving Sultanpur
Pak Pattan (Sheikh Ibrahim)
Goindval
Saidpur, or modern Eminabad (Babur)
Lahore
Kartarpur

His second journey was to the south and his companions are variously given as Saido and Gheho; Saido and Siho, Saido, Gheho, and Siho; or Saido, Siho and Mardana.

Ceylon (Raja Sivanabh)

The third journey was to the north. His companions' names are given as Hassu Lohar and Sihan Chhimba.

Kashmir
Mount Sameru
Achal

The fourth journey was to the west. No regular companions are named.

Mecca (Qazi Rukan-din)

The fifth journey was a brief one to Gorakh-hatari, perhaps the Nath centre in modern Peshawar. No companion is named.

Lahina of Khadur became a disciple, was subsequently renamed Angad, and was eventually designated successor to the office of Guru by Guru Nanak himself.

Guru Nanak died at Kartarpur on the tenth day of the light half of Asu, S. 1595 (A.D. 1538).

The *Puratan* janam-sakhis also indicate that the Guru was acquainted with Pir Bahauddin of Multan. Two prominent omissions from the places named are Baghdad and Jagannath Puri. The only dates of significance which are mentioned are those of his birth and death, and (by obvious implication) that of his marriage which would have been in A.D. 1481 or 1482. Two which may be added are those of the accession of Sultan Ibrahim Lodi in 1517 and Babur's sack of Saidpur in 1520. This at once involves a contradiction, as Guru Nanak is said to have returned to Talvandi twelve years after the journey began, and the journey is said to have begun after the occasion of Guru Nanak's meeting with Ibrahim Lodi in Delhi. One of the dates much be rejected forthwith and of the two incidents the one which had the greater claims to probability to obviously the Saidpur visit. The Delhi *sakhi* can have no claims whatsoever and accordingly the 1517 date may be summarily eliminated.

The Miharban Janam-sakhi

Guru Nanak was born in the light half of the month of Vaisakh, S. 1526 (A.D. 1469), the son of Kalu, a Bedi Khatri and Tipara. The place where the birth took place is variously said to have been the village of Chahalavale and Kalu's village, Rai Bhoe Ki Talvandi. The name of the contemporary landlord of the latter village is given as Rai Bhoa.

At about the time of his sixteenth birthday Guru Nanak was married in Batala to Ghumi, the daughter of Mula, a Chona Khatri of Batala. Two sons, Lakhmi Das and Siri Chand, were born when he was twenty seven or twenty-eight years of age.

At the age of thirty-five years, six and a half months, we went to Sultanpur in response to an invitation from his brother-in-law Jai Ram, an Uppal Khatri and steward of Daulat Khan Lodi. There he was given employment in Dualat Khan's commissariat.

After two years in Sultanpur he left of his first journey, accompanied by Mardana. This journey was to the east of India and then from there to the far south. It included the following places :

Delhi (Salim Shah Pathan)
Hardwar
Allahabad
Banaras
Hajipur Patna
Ayodhya
Jagannath Puri
Rameshwaram
A 'land of darkness' beyond Adam's Bridge (evidently Ceylon)
Ujjain (Raja Bharathari)
Vindhya Mountains
Narabad River
Ujjain
Bikaner
Saurashtra
Mathura
Kurukshetra
Sultanpur (Daulat Khan Lodi)

The second journey was to the north and then to the west.

Mount Sumeru
Gorakh-hatari
Multan (a descendant of Pir Bahauddin)
Mecca
Hinglaj
Gorakh-hatari
Saidpur (Babur)
Tilla Balgundai (Babur)
Talvandi
Pak Pattan (Sheikh Ibrahim)
Dipalpur
Khokhoval
Pokho and Kartarpur

In Miharban's account the notable omissions are Kamrup and Baghdad. Nanakmata is also missing and Ceylon is not mentioned by name. The significant dates, stated or plainly implied, are the Guru's birth in S. 1526 (A.D. 1469), his marriage (A.D. 1485), his move from Talvandi to Sultanpur (A.D. 1504), and his departure from there on his first journey (A.D. 1506). To These may be added the date of the attack on Saidpur (A.D. 1520) which means that according to Miharban's account all of Guru Nanak's travels outside the Panjab took place within the space of fourteen years and between the ages of thirty-seven and fifty-three. The period spent in 'the east country' was three years, in the south five years, in the north one year, and in the west three years, a total twelve years. This leaves a balance of two years to be allocated to the initial journey from Sultanpur to the 'the east country', and the gap between the departure from 'the south country' and the commencement of the second journey. The pattern would then be as follows :

From Sultanpur to 'the east country'	1506-7
Travels in 'the east country'	1507-10
Travels in 'the south country'	1510-15
The Journey from 'the south country' to 'the north country' via Sultanpur	1515-16
Travels in 'the north country'	1516-17
Travels in 'the west country'	1517-20

6

The Panth

Guru Nanak established the *Panth* in the seven years after raising his headquarters at Kartarpur late in 1521. He found the work so absorbing that he did not leave the place for the next seven years. He successfully accomplished three things in this period: lived the life of a householder like his followers, built up Kartarpur as a "community centre" radiating his philosophy, and composed four of his most important *bants*. By successfully doing these three things, he laid the foundation of a new way of life and thereby gave birth to the Sikh *Panth*.

Guru Nanak began his stay at Kartarpur by publicly demonstrating his determination to harmonize the secular life of a householder which complete devotion to the Alimighty. Giving up his "weired costume", he donned the "worldly garment' and within a few months of settling down at Kartarpur, he not only invited a number of admirers to come and make Kartarpur their home but also prevailed upon his ageing parents to shift from Talwandi and live with him. When his devoted wife Sulakhani and their two grown up sons also joined him and began to live in the same house in which he lived, Guru Nanak's *gribasth* was complete. There could be no mistaking now that his opposition to complete renunciation of life was not confined to the airy plane of argument and discussion but meant to be taken seriously.

As if that was not enough, Guru Nanak did not divide the entire land in the village among his followers, but reserved a few acres for himself also to undertake agriculture in the same way as others. He insisted that Sri Chand and Lakshmi Chand should get up early in the morning, yoke the bullocks to their ploughs and till the fields. At times, he would personally go with them in spite of the age. His wife would milk the cows, stir the butter from the *lassi* (butter-milk) and cook for the family. To his old father, Kalu, and his old mother, Tripta, Nanak's transformation must have been complete, setting at rest their apprehension that Nanak would never give up his wandering life.

After some devout followers had come and settled at Kartarpur, Nanak began to hold daily congregations and "teaching all to live in the world and wórk, while at the same time thinking of God always and praying to receive nothing but His grace." Out of those discourses were to be born four long compositions of Guru Nanak. Every *sloka* constituting *Var Malar*, *Var Majh*, *Var Asa*, and the *Japuji* must have been composed, thought over, sung and played on the *rabab* in congregations, before they were set in an artistic literary pattern as we know them today.

Var Malar was the first to have, thus, come to its final form. It started with a description of the descent of man to the earth and then painted him "in nature" before relating his fall under the twin influence of *maya* and *haumai* (egoism). The fallen man, badly misled, became the cause of almost all the conflicts in the world. It was in the world's interest that he should be set on the right path. But that would not happen till a true *guru* taught him the "unity of God-head".

The *Var* took its final form in about six months and when finished became a sublime composition with a "systematic structure of beauty, vastness of imaginative flight and devotional praise of the Lord", besides propounding a theory of virtue to guide the disciples.

The Guru did not wait for long to begin his next composition, *Var Majh*. The new *Var* dilated on the same subject—unit of God-head—but in a different way. The presentation here was less concrete than in the preceding *Var* and spelt out what defects in a man's character misled him. It detailed what happens to one fallen under the influence of *maya*, and how, while behaving as "a self-conceited" and "puffed up man" he would become totally "careless of virtues".

The *Var Majh* in its finished form, as intended by Guru Nanak, was complementary in thought and content to the *Var Malar*. Conflict between the negative and the positive forces in the *Var Malar* became the "play of the Lord" in which truth and falsehood struggled for supremacy over each other. Mankind was shown to suffer in this play for falling a prey to falsehood and continuing to suffer till a *guru* appeared as the hero to liberate it. Guru Nanak made this *Var* an extremely dramatic piece. He made the conflict between good and bad to continue right up to the twelfth *Pauri*.

That the conflict became more and more complicated and reached a climax before the *guru* came into a man's life, guided him out of 'ignorance', underlined the role that the concept of a *guru* began to assume in Nanak's religious through. It was further underlined when the appearance of a *guru* was described in the *Var* dependent on the grace of God.

The Two *Vars* and their *slokas* produced a tremendous impact on Guru Nanak Dev's disciples at Kartarpur and his daily congregations became a favourite features of life there. When the seasoned Mardana would sing them to the tune of the sweet rebeck, the listeners would undergo a soul-elevating experience. After Mardana's deaths, Guru Nanak installed Mardana's son, Shahzada, to undertake the work being done by his father till death.

Soon after installing Shahzada as the minstrel. Guru Nanak Dev Ji started composing the *Var Asa*, his third *Var*, the "the best representative of all aspects of his genius". In This *Var*, he expounded the nature of the Supreme Reality, matter and *Jiva*, and their relationship with the Supreme Being. While doing so, he dilated upon the "Laws of God as they are operative in nature" and emphasised that man must look upon these laws as "justice of the Lord" and bow before them cheerfully.

The *Var* propounded the thesis that when ego guided the activities of men, they became selfish and "ruin the nation" because once the rot begins "the whole nation becomes bankrupt spiritually, morally and politically", the egoistic behaviour of the various classes produced "religious conflicts, class conflicts, economic conflicts and political conflicts" causing tension "between the orthodox and the unorthodox, the strong and the weak, the more advanced section of the society and the less advanced section of the society."

The state of affairs, the *Var* emphasised, could be overcome only by all individuals becoming true *sevaks* imbued with the spirit of service. They must, in fact, develop this spirit to the same extent as the true "servants of God".

Var Asa had, thus discovered not only the laws of "degeneration of a nation" but also showed the path by which a people could "regenerate itself". Little wonder that this *Var* soon became the most popular *Var* at Kartarpur.

From the *Asa di Var* to the *Japujit* was to be only a step but Guru Nanak Dev took sometime in giving it the final form. That was understandable. It was to be the most important composition of his life and the very foundation of the *Panth* that he seemed to be creating at Kartarpur.

Japuji was an "essay on the infinite truth". Guru Nanak Dev Ji believed that men would never be able to comprehend that Truth in its entirely but its physical and moral aspects might be comprehended by them to some extent. The *Japuji* was meant to help them to do so. The *Japuji* emphasised that God's most important aspect was Truth and, therefore, Truth and His Truthfulness became the centre theme of the *Japuji* though His other attributes were not ignored.

The *Japujit* summed up Nanak's religious philosophy that he sought to propagate not only among the residents of Kartarpur but also among his disciples elsewhere. Its key words, *sacch* (truth), *hukam* (command), *gaviai* (singing the Lord's praises), *sunniai* (hearing His praise), *mannai* (meditation), *ponch* (the five), *asankh* (myriads), *anant* (limitless), *amul* (priceless), *khand* (stages of spiritual progress), *surt* (i) (consciousness). *mat* (i) (wisdom), *man* (i) (mind), *budh* (i) (intellect), and *data* (merciful) reflected the fundamentals of Guru Nanak's beliefs.

In composing the *Japujit*, Nanak put in all the artistry that he could gather from his armoury of intellect. His combined most artistically *sutra* brevity, variety of meters, union of music, rhythm and rhyme, expressiveness of plain language and aesthetic taste with his philosophical thoughts to make it, when later incorporated in the *Granth Sahib*, the "epitome of the philosophy and beauty" of that Granth.

The four compositions of Guru Nanak—the *Var Malar*, the *Var Majh*, the *Var Asa* and the *Japujit* combined with his *gribasth* life and his activities as the guru gave a distinct pattern of life to those who has chosen to reside at Kartarpur. By devising this pattern of life at Kartarpur, Guru Nanak Dev Ji laid the foundation of the *panth* albeit in an embryonic form.

It is difficult to correctly gauge the impact that the embryonic *Panth* established by Guru Nanak Dev produced among the Muslim and Hindu thinkers in general. In all probability the Muslim Sufis and Hindu Bhaktas who watched the experiment at Kartarpur, extended to the Guru their general appreciation. Laymen in both the communities began looking upon him as *"Hindu ka Guru"* and *Mussalman ka Pir*."

The ascetic order of *Jogis* however, did not react kindly to Nanak's embryonic *Panth* and that forced Nanak to a spirited debate with them.

Jogis, then, exercised quite an influence in northern India. Deriving their inspiration from the Patanjali School of Philosophy, they were founded into an or by Gorakhnath. They were later consolidated into a well-knit brotherhood by eighty four Siddhas who were supposed to be endowed with supernatural power. In Guru Nanak's times, they were divided into many orders but all acknowledged Gorakhnath and the eighty-four *Siddhas* as their preceptors.

The spiritual exercises of the *Siddhas*, often descending to the propitiation of the 'lower spirit', produced a spectacular effect on the unsophisticated population of medieval India in increasing the number of their followers. Their outer form added to the effect. They had a long cut in each lobe of their ears, in which they wore large thick rings of various materials—wood, glass, silver, gold etc.—which were called *mudra*. They rubbed ashes on their bodies, shaved their heads clean, blew a horn and carried a staff and a begging-bowl, or a begging-pouch, called *jholi*. They greeted all by the salutation of *'ades, ades* to Gorakhnath, *ades* to eighty-four *Siddhas'* and generally lived outside habitations, visited places of pilgrimage, travelled to distant lands, and used all sorts of intoxicants, and smoked opium.

In 1529 when Guru Nanak went to Achal near Batala, there took place an acrimonious debate between him and the leader of the *Jogis*, Bhangar Nath. Bhangar Nath tried to be clever when he chose to attack what he must have believed to be the weakest link in Nanak's system. Referring to Nanak's secular dress, he posed to Guru Nanak the following question :

> Why hast thou mixed acid in milk?
> Milk hath sourced and thou cants now have butter by churning it.
> Why hast thou put off the udasi's garb?
> Why hast thou restarted the life of a layman?

Guru Nanak, knowing the Bhangar Nath was being clever and playing to the gallery, paid the mischievous *Jogi* in the same coin;

> Thy mother, O Bhangar Nath, knew not
> how to clear the vessel.
> Want of knowledge thus led to the putrefaction of thy soul.
> Thou gavest up thy home, and adoptest asceticism

> Why shouldst thou be wandering from door to door at the houses of the lay people to
> beg thy food.

That quietened the bully Bhangar Nath and Guru Nanak utilized the occasion to convince the assembled *Jogis* that their ways would not bring 'emancipation' to them. Apparently addressing Bhangar Nath but as much for the hearing of other *Jogis*, the Guru warmed up and said that 'the only way, by which it could be obtained was to shed off 'the filth of ego'. That was the real aim of asceticism also, but not the type practised by *Jagis*. For *moksha*, Nanak said, he would suggest to the Jogis to give up faith in 'supernatural powers' and remember that one miraculous power which could deliver goods was that of the True Name.

A long discourse followed in which Guru Nanak explained to the *Jogis* the limitations of asceticism in leading a really spiritual life. He also expounded his philosophy to all those who had gathered to see Nanak's encounter with the proud Jogi, Bhangar Nath.

Guru Nanak was very keen on weaning away the superstitious people from the hypnotic spell of the *Jogis*. That on returning from Achal Batala, Guru Nanak composed the *Siddh Gost* is a proof of that keenness. In this composition—rightly regarded as supplementary to the *Japuji*, Guru Nanak described the *Nirgun* God as distinct from His *Sargun* self-described in the *Japuji*.

Guru Nanak's opposition to asceticism was a logical corollary to what he was aiming at as a religious teacher. It was the salvation of the entire community as distinct rom the salvation of individuals. A careful analysis of *Siddh Gost* reveals that he did not think very highly of those who were out for individual salvation. He wanted the spiritual uplift of the entire community and wanted his followers to become *gurmukhs* (guru-oriented) as distinct from *manmukhs* (self-oriented).

In his keenness to include in his *gurmukhs* not only those who come to permanently stay at Kartarpur but also who would come there fitfully and for limited periods, Guru Nanak made a limited institution already in existence at his Kartarpur centre, a regular pattern of Kartarpur life. This was the institution of *langar*. All those who would now come to see him would partake of the food prepared in common kitchen daily as long as they stay at the headquarters. On special occasions, the entire people at Kartarpur would also arrange a big *langar* to emphasize their brotherhood and collective obligation to the Guru.

The success of the *langar* as an institution seemed to have given Guru Nanak Dev great delight and pleasure. That was reflected in the choice of his next composition—the *Oankar*. In this—a 54-stanza poem—Guru Nanak dilated on the "concept of joy", while describing "the nature of God and creation, and their relationship." This poem was full of "pictorial beauty (each stanza is a complete picture) and profound thought". Its "short racy metre and easy language" combined with "its witty lines" to make it a poem "perfect" in its "structure" and the "development of the subject".

No sooner did Guru Nanak finish the *Oankar*, than he started composing the *Patti.* Perhaps what suggested this poem was that for sometime past, he had been busy converting the *Nagari* script into something simple and more in keeping with the vocal sounds of the people of the Punjab who constituted the overwhelming majority of those who attended his congregations. He wove this poem round the alphabet that was to constitute his new script, but it was much more than an exercise in acrostics. In dealt with "Brahma manifested, or God as the Name" and put forth the basic beliefs which later became the fundamentals of the Sikh philosophy.

The two poems—The *Oankar* and the *Patti*—between themselves awakened Guru Nanak's followers to the mystery of nature, the laws of the life of *karma*, as it determined the extent of pain and pleasure experienced by an individual. They also started explaining to the Guru's followers the laws which governed creation, maintenance and final destruction and gave them the ideals which they were to pursue. The two poems also suggested the best way of achieving these ideals.

The two poems also suggested a new attitude towards the almightly. This was to be one of wonder rather than one of awe and as subsequently to distinguish the Sikh view of the Lord from that of others.

From the *Oankar* and the *Patti* to his next composition the *Thiti* was only a step. If the first two were woven around alphabets, the *Thitti* was written around 'numbers'. In this poem, the Guru raised his voice against the "futile method of knowing the reality" and showed "the true method" of doing so. In this poem, according to Guru Nanak, He manifested Himself in various stages and to know. Him, it was indispensable to have a spiritual Guru.

The rapidly with which Guru Nanak Dev had composed the beautiful *banis* in *Siddh Gost, Oankar of Rag Rainkali Dakhani, Asa Patti* between 1529 and 1535 as much as their contents were indicated of the great response that his teachings were evoking among his followers. There was something attractive in his "meditation of the divine presence" while "refusing to renounce his family or worldly occupation". More and more of those interested in spiritual pursuits came and settled at Kartarpur to deplete the ranks of the *Jogis* and other similar denominations within half a decade of his visit to Achal Batala.

During those years, Guru Nanak appeared to his followers "a deeply devout believer absorbed in the manifestation of the divine presence, but refusing to renounce his family or his worldly occupation." This combination of piety and practical activity which Guru Nanak manifested in his own life was transmitted to his followers, and those of them who had chosen to live at the Guru's headquarters bore the Kartarpur discipline with good cheer. To them he appeared as a *guru* of humour and mild irony which would, nevertheless, reprimand and, if necessary, denounce a *guru* who experienced the inexperienced who yet maintained an essential practical participation in the everyday affairs of his community and the world beyond it.

Guru Nanak was now a revered teacher, giving expression to his experiences in simple and direct hymns of superb poetic quality with numerous disciples living with him as his headquarters and many more coming to him for occasional *darshan* or audience with him. Among those who thus arrived were his old admirers like Lalo of Eminabad, Sajjan of Tolumba and many others who had played the host to Nanak during his four *udasis.*

Their visits led to an important consequence: sprouting of the *Panth* in embryonic form established of Guru Nanak Dev in 1521. The Panth had now a headquarter and subordinate branches. Men like Lalo, Sajjan and others had gone back to their habitations and formed *sangats* or holy assemblies on the pattern of Kartarpur. In these *sangats,* the founders propagated Guru Nanak Dev's views, sang his verses and meditated on the Name, besides running free kitchens (*langars*). As was only natural in these *sangats,* the 'founders' enjoyed as honoured place and were distinguished from the others with the epithet of *Bhayi* or the 'Revered Brother', when the others were called the 'Sikh' or the *shishyas.*

Sitting on a cot (*manji*) the Revered *Bhai* (Brother), like the Guru at Kartarpur, would preside over daily congregations and instruct the Sikhs in their spiritual, religious, social and moral duties. And when those Sikhs took to service in the spirit of humble and sincere servants of humanity, they brought honour both to *Bhatji* and the Guru.

By the time, the great Guru chose to leave his mortal remains, the *Panth* had grown to include a highly successful headquarter at Kartarpur, committed to spread the philosophy the Guru Nanak Dev had propagated among this followers ever since establishing the Kartarpur centre. It was a simple and a revolutionary philosophy. It enjoined on his followers to live in the world and earn their livelihood honestly while "thinking of God always and praying for nothing but His Grace." He expected his followers to pursue a life of Truth and "to drop meaningless outer forms and complications." He wanted his followers to give up the pride of caste and seek refuge in Name only.

7

Founder of Sikhism

The limits of Race and Religion are not the same, otherwise the two subjects might have been considered together with advantage. In Ludakh the people and the dependent rulers profess Lamaic Boddhism, which is so widely diffused throughout Central Asia, but the Tibetans of Iskardo, the Durdoos of Ghilghit, and the Kukkas and Bumbas of the rugged mountains, are Mahometans of the Sheea persuasion. The people of Kashmir, of Kishtwar, of Bhimbur, of Pukhlee, and of the hills south and west to the salt range and the Indus, are mostly Soonee Mahomedans, as are likewise the tribes of Peshwar and of the valley of the Indus southward, and also the inhabitants of Mooltan, and of the plains northward as far as Pind-Dadun-Khan, Chuneeot and Depalpoor. The people of the Himalayas, eastward of Kistwar and Bhimbar, are Hindus of the Brahminical faith, with some Buddhist colonies to the north, and some Mahometan families to the south west. The Juts of "Manjha" and "Malwa" are mostly Sikhs, but perhaps not one-third of the whole population between the Jhelum and Jumna has yet embraced the tenets of Nanak and Govind, the other two-third being still equally divided between Islam and Brahminism.

In "Malwa" alone, that is, about Bhutinda and Soonam, can the Sikh population be found unmixed, and there it has passed into a saying, that the priest, the soldier, the mechanic, the shopkeeper, and the ploughman are all equally Sikh.

The observers of the ancient creeds quietly pursue the even tenor of their way, self-satisfied and almost indifferent about others; but the Sikhs are converts to a new religion, the seal of the double dispensation of Brumha and Mahomet; *their* enthusiasm is still fresh, and *their* faith is still an active and a living principle. *They* are persuaded that God himself is present with them, that He supports them in all their endeavours, and that sooner or later He will confound *their* enemies for His own glory. The feeling of the Sikh people deserves the attention of the English, both as a civilized nation and as a paramount government. Those who have heard a follower of Guru Govind (Singh) declaim on the destinies of the race, his eye wild with enthusiasm and every muscle quivering with excitement, can understand *that* spirit which impelled that maked Arab against the mail clad troops of Rome and Persia, and which led our own chivalrous and believing foreathers through Europe to battle for the cross on the shores of Asia. The Sikhas do not form a numerous sect; yet their strength is not to be estimated by tens of thousands, but by the unit and energy of religious fervor and warlike temperament. They will dare much, and they will endure much, for the mystic "Khalsa" or common-wealth; they are not discouraged by defeat, and they ardently look forward to the day when

Indians and Persians and Turks, shall all acknowledge the double mission of Nanak and Govind Singh.

In the beginning of the sixteenth century, the Hindu mind was no longer stagnant or retrogressive; it had been leavened with Mahomedanism, and changed and quickened for a new development. Ramanand and Gorakh had preached religious equality, and Cheitun had repeated that faith levelled caste. Kabir had denounced images, and appealed to the people in their own tongue, and Vallabh had taught that effectual devotion was compatible with the ordinary duties of the world. But these good and able men appear to have been so impressed with nothingness of this life, that they deemed the amelioration of man's social condition as unworthy of thought. They aimed chiefly at emancipation from preistcraft, or from the grossness of idolotry and polytheism. They formed pious associations of contented Quietists, or they gave themselves up to the contemplatation of futurity in the hope of approaching bliss, rather than called upon their fellow creatures to throw aside every social as well as religious trammel, and to arise a new people freed from the debasing corruption of ages.. They perfected forms of dissent rather than planted the germs of nations, and their *sects* remain to this day as they left them. It was reserved for *Nanak* to perceive the true principles of reform, and to lay those broad foundations which enabled his successor *Govind* to fire the minds of his countrymen with a new nationality, and to give practical effect to the doctrine that the lowest is equal with the highest, in race as in creed, in political rights as in religious hopes.

Nanak was born in the year 1469, in the neighbourhood of Lahore. His father, Kalu was a Hindu of the Bedi subdivision of the once warlike Khatrees, and he was, perhaps, like most of his race, a petty trader in his native village. Nanak appears to have been naturally of a pious disposition and of a reflecting mind, and there is reason to believe that in his youth he made himself familiar with the popular creeds both of the Mahometans and Hindus, and that he gained to general knowledge of the Koran and of the Brahminical Shasters. His good sense and fervid temper left him displeased with the corruptions of the vulgar faith, and dissatisfied with the indifference of the learned, or with the refuge which they sought in the specious abstractions of philosophy; nor is it improbable that the homilies of Kabir and Gorukh had fallen upon his susceptible mind with a powerful and enduring effect. In a moment of enthusiasm the ardent inquirer abandoned his home, and strove to attain wisdom by penitent meditation, by study, and by an enlarged intercourse with mankind.

He travelled, perhaps, beyond the limits of India, he prayed in solitude, he reflected on the Vedas and on the mission of Mahomet, and he questioned with equal anxiety the learned priest and the simple devotee about the will of God and the path to happiness. Plato and Bacon, Des Cartes and Alghazali, examined the current philosophic systems of the world, without finding a sure basis of truth for the operations of the intellect; and, similarly, the heart of the pious Nanak sought hopelessly for a resting-place amid the conflicting creeds and practices of men. All was error, he said; he had read Korans and Poorans, but God he had nowhere found. He returned to his native land, he threw aside the habit of an ascetic, he became again the father of his family, and he passed the remainder of his long life in calling upon men to worship the One Invisible God, to live virtuously, and to be tolerant of the failings of others. The mild demeanor, the earnest piety, and persuasive eloquence of Nanak, are ever themes of praise, and he died at the age of seventy, leaving behind him many zealous and admiring disciples.

Nanak combined the excellences of preceding reformers, and he avoided the more grave errors into which they had fallen. Instead of the circumscribed divinity, the anthropomorphous God of Ramanand and Kabir, he loftily invokes the Lord as the one, the sole, the timeless being; the creator, the self-existent, the incomprehensible, and the everlasting. He likens the Deity to Truth, which was before the world began, which is, and which shall endure for ever, as the ultimate idea or cause of all we know or behold. He addresses equally the Molla and the Pandit, the Dervish and the Soonyassee, and tells them to remember *that* Lord of Lords who had seen come and go numberless Mahomets, and Vishnoos and Sivas. He tells them that virtues and charities, heroic acts and gathered wisdom, are naught of themselves, that the only knowledge which availeth is the knowledge of God; and then, as if to rebuke those vain men who saw eternal life in their own act of faith, he declares that they only can find the Lord of whom the Lord looks with favour. Yet the extension of grace is linked with the exercise of our will and the beneficent use of our faculties. God, said Nanak, places salvation in good works and uprightness of conduct: the Lord will ask of man, "What has he done:" and the teacher further required timely repentance of men, saying, "If not until the day of reckoning the sinner abaseth himself, punishment shall overtake him."

Nanak adopted the philosophical system of his countrymen, and regarded bliss as the dwelling of the soul with God after its punitory transmigrations should have ceased. Life, he says is as the shadow of the passing bird, but the soul of man is as the potter's wheel, ever circling on its pivot. He makes the same uses of the current language or notions of the time on other subjects, and thus says, he who remains bright amid darkness *(Unjun),* unmoved amid deceit *(Maya),* that is perfect amid temptation, should attain happiness. But it would be idle to suppose that he speculated upon being, or upon the material world, after the manner of Plato or Vyasa, and it would be unreasonable to condemn his because he preferred the doctrine of a succession of habiliments, and the possible purification of the most sinful soul, to the resurrection of the same body, and the pains of everlasting fire. Nanak also referred to the Arabian prophet, and to the Hindu incarnations, not as impostors and the diffusers of evil, but as having truly been sent by God to instruct mankind, and he lamented that sin should nevertheless prevail. He asserted no special divinity, although he may possibly have considered himself, as he came to be considered by others, the successor of these inspired teachers of his belief, sent to reclaim fallen mortals of all creeds and countries within the limits of his knowledge. He rendered his mission applicable to all times and places, yet he declared himself to be but the slave, the humble messenger of the Almightly, making use of universe truth as his sole instrument. He did not claim for his writings, replete as they were with wisdom and devotion, the merit of a direct transcription of the words of God; nor did he say that his own preaching required or would be sanctioned by miracles. "Fight with no weapon" said he, "save the word of God; a holy teacher hath no means save the purity of his doctrine." He taught that asceticism or abandonment of the world was unneccessary, the pious hermit and the devout householder being equal in the eyes of the Almightly; but he did not, like his contemporary Vallabh, express any individious preference for married teachers, although his own example showed that he considered every one should fulfil the functions of his nature.

In treating the two prominent external observances of Hindus and Mahometans, veneration for the cow and abhorrence of the hog, he was equally wise and conciliatory, yielding perhaps something to the prejudices of the education as well as to the gentleness of his disposition. "The rights of strangers," said he, "are the one the ox, and the other the swine, but 'Peers' and 'Gurus' will praise those who partake not of that which hath enjoyed life."

Thus Nanak extricated his followers from the accumulated errors of ages, and enjoined upon them devotion of thought and excellence of conduct as the first of duties. He left them, erect and free, unbiassed in mind and unfetered by rules, to become an increasing body of truthful worshipers. His reforms was in its immediate effect religious and moral only; believers were regarded as "Sikhs" or disciples, not as subjects ; and it is neither probable, nor is it necessary to suppose, that he possessed and clear and sagacious views of social amelioration or of political advancement. He left the progress of his people to the operation of time : for his congregation was too limited and the state of society too artificial, to render it either requisite or possible for him to become a municipal law-giver, to subvert the legislation of Munno, or to change the immemorial usages of tribes or races. His care was rather to prevent his followers contracting into a sact, and his comprehensive principles narrowing into monastic distinctions. This he effected by excluding his son, a meditative and perhaps bigoted ascetic, from the ministry when he should himself be no more; and, as his end approached, he is stated to have made a trial of the obedience or merits of his chosen disciples, and to have preferred the simple and sincere Lehna. As they journeyed along, the body of a man was seen lying by the way side. Nanak said, "Ye who trust in me, eat of this food." All hesitated save Lehna; he knelt and uncovered the dead, and touched without tasting the flesh of man; but, behold! the corpse had disappeared and Nanak was in its place. The Guru embraced his faithful follower, saying he was as himself, and that his spirit would dwell within him. The name of Lehna was changed to *Ung-i-Khood*, or *Angad*, or own body, and whatever may be the foundation of the story or the truth of the etymology, it is certain that the Sikhs fully believe the spirit of Nanak to have been incarnate in each succeeding Guru. Angad was acknowledged as the teacher of the sikhs, and Sree Chand, the son of Nanak, justified his father's fears, and became the founder of the sect of "Oodassees," a community indifferent to the concerns of this world.

8

The Japji

There is but one God whose name is true, the Creator, devoid of fear and enmity, immortal, unborn, self-existent; by the favour of the Guru.

Repeat His Name

The True One was in the beginning; the True One was in the primal age.

The True One is now also, O Nanak; the True One also shall be.

I

By thinking I cannot obtain a conception of *Him*, even thought I think hundreds of thousands of times.

Even though I be silent and keep my attention firmly fixed on Him, I cannot preserve silence.

The hunger of the hungry *for God* subsideth nor though they obtain the load of the worlds.

If may should have thousands and hundreds of thousands of devices, even one would not assist him in obtaining God.

How shall *man* become true before God? How shall the veil of falsehood he rent?

By walking, O Nanak, according to the will of the Commander as preordained.

II

By His order bodies are produced; His order cannot be described.

By His order souls are infused into them : by His order greatness is obtained.

By His order men are high or low; by His order they obtain preordained pain or pleasure.

By His order some obtain their reward; by His order others must even wander in transmigration.

All are subject to His order; none is exempt from it.

He who *understandeth* God's order, O Nanak, is never guilty of egoism.

III

Who can sing His power? Who hath power to sing it?

Who can sing His gifts or know his sings?

Who can sing His attributes, His greatness, and His deeds?

Who can sing His knowledge whose study in arduous?

Who can sing Him, who fashioneth the boy and *again* destroyeth it?

Who can sing Him, who taketh away life and again restoreth it?

Who can sing Him, who taketh away life and again restoreth it?

Who can sing Him, who appeareth to be far, *but* is known *to be near.*

Who can sing Him, who is all-seeing and omnipresent?

In describing Him there would never be an end.

Millions of men give millions upon millions of descriptions of Him, *but they fail to describe Him.*

The Giver giveth; the receiver growth weary of receiving.

In every age man subsisteth by His *bounty.*

The Commander by His order hath laid out the way of *the world.*

Nanak, God the unconcerned is happy.

IV

True is the Lord, True is His Name; it is uttered with endless love.

People pray and beg, 'Give us, give us'; the Giver *giveth* His gifts;

Then what can we offer Him whereby His court may be seen?

What words shall we utter with our lips, on hearing which He may love us?

At the ambrosial hour of *morning* mediate on the true Name and *God's* greatness.

The Kind One will give us a robe of honour, and by His favour we shall reach the gate of salvation.

Nanak, we shall thus know that God is altogether true.

V

He is not established, not is He created.

The pure one *existeth* by Himself

They who worshipped Him have obtained honour.

Nanak, sing His *paises* who is the Treasury of excellences.

Sing and hear and put His love into your hearts.

Thus shall your sorrows be removed, and you shall be absorbed in Him who is the abode of happiness.

Under the Guru's instruction *God's* word *is heard*; under the Guru's instruction its knowledge is *acquired*; under the Guru's instruction *man learns that God* is everywhere contained.

The Guru is Shiv; the Guru is Vishnu and Brahma; the Guru is Parbati, Lakhmi and Saraswati.

If I knew Him, should I not describe Him? He cannot be described by words.

My Guru hath explained one thing to me—

That there is *but* one bestower on all living beings; may I not forget Him!

VI

If I please Him, that is my place of pilgrimage to bathe in; if I please Him not, what ablutions shall I make?

What can all the created beings I behold obtain without *previous* good acts?

Precious stones, jewels, and gems *shall be treasured up* in thy heart if thou hearken to even one word of the Guru.

The Guru hath explained one thing to me—

That there is *but* one Bestower on all living beings; may I not forget Him!

VII

Were man to live through the four ages, *yea* ten times longer;

Where he to be known on the nine continents, and were everybody to follow in his train;

Were he to obtain a great name and praise and renown in the world;

If God's look of favour fell not on him, no one would notice him.

He would be accounted a worm among worms, and even sinners would impute sin to him.

(a) He is greater than Shiv; greater than Vishnu and Brahma; greater than Parbati, Lakshmi and Saraswati.

(b) For the holy the Guru is Shiv; the Guru is Vishnu and Brahma; the Guru is Parbati, Lakhshmi, and Saraswati.

The tenth Guru says :

Khanda prithme saj ke Jin sab sansar upaiya—

God first created the sword, the emblem of Death, and then the world.

So here Shiv obtains precedence as the agent of destruction. The word uttered by God became the source of knowledge of Him through the Guru in the three forms of Shiv, Vishnu and Brahma.

That is to show him respect.

Nanak, God may bestow virtue on those who are devoid of it, as well as on those who *already* possess it;

But no such person is seen as-can bestow virtue upon Him.

VIII

By hearing *the name of* God men *become* Sikhs, Pirs, Surs and Naths;

By hearing *the Name man understandeth the real nature* of the earth, its supporting bull, and Heaven;

By hearing *the Name man obtaineth a knowledge* of the continents, the worlds, and the nether regions.

By hearing *the Name* death doth not affect one.

Nanak, the saints are ever happy.

By hearing *the Name* sorrow and sin are no more.

IX

By hearing *the Name* man *becometh* as Shiv, Brahma and Indar.

By hearing the Name *even* the low become highly landed.

By hearing the Name the way of Jog and the secrets of the body *are obtained.*

By hearing the Name man *understandeth the real nature* of the Shastars, the Simritis and the Veds.

Nanak, the saints are ever happy.

By hearing the Name sorrow and sin are no more.

X

By hearing the Name truth, contentment, and divine knowledge *are obtained.*

Hearing the Name is equal to bathing at the sixty-eight *places of pilgrimage.*

By hearing the Name and reading it man *obtaineth* honour.

By hearing the Name the mind is composed and fixed on God.

Nanak, the saints are ever happy.

By hearing the Name sorrow and sin are no more.

XI

By hearing the Name, the depth of the sea of virtue is sounded.

By hearing the Name *men become* Shaikhs, Pirs and Emperors.

By hearing the Name a blind man *findeth* his way.

By hearing the Name the unfathomable *becometh* fathomable.

Nanak, the saints are every happy.

By hearing the Name sorrow and sin are no more.

XII

The condition of him who *obeyth* God cannot be described.

Whoever trieth to describe it, shall afterward repent.

There is no paper, or pen, or writer

To describe the *condition* of him who obeyeth God.

So pure in His name—

Whoever obeyeth God knoweth *the pleasure of it* in his own heart.

XIII

By obeying Him wisdom and understanding *enter* the mind;
By obeying Him man *knoweth* all worlds;
By obeying Him man *suffereth* not punishment;
By obeying Him man shall not depart with Jam
So pure is God's name
Whoever obeyeth God *knoweth* the pleasure of it in his own heart.

XIV

By obeying Him man's path is not obstructed;
By obeying Him man *departeth* with honour and distinction;
By obeying Him man *proceedeth* in ecstasy on the way;
By obeying Him man *formeth* an alliance with virtue—
So pure is God's name—
Whoever obeyeth God *knoweth* the pleasure of it in his own heart.

XV

By obeying Him man *attaineth* the gate of salvation;
By obeying Him man is saved with his family;
By obeying Him the Guru is saved, and *saveth* his disciples;
By obeying Him, O Nanak, man *wandereth* not *in quest* of alms
So pure is God's name—
Whoever obeyeth God knoweth the pleasure of it in his own heart.

XVI

The elect are acceptable, the elect are distinguished;
The elect obtain honour in God's court;
The elect shed luster on the courts of kings.
The attention of the elect is bestowed on the one Guru.
If any one say he can form an idea of God, *he may say so*,
But the Creator's works cannot be numbered.
The bull *that is spoken of* is righteousness, the offspring of mercy,
Which supported by patience *maintaineth* the order of nature.
Whoever *understandeth* this is a true man.
What a load there is upon the bull!
Beyond this earth that are more worlds, more and more.
What power can support their weight?
The names of living things, their species, and colours
Have all been written with a flowing pen.

Doth any one know how to write an account of them?
If the account were written, how great it would be!
What power and beautiful form are Thine, O God!
Who hath power to know how great thy gifts are?
By one world Thou didst effect the expansion of the *world*,
Whereby hundreds of thousands of rivers were produced.
What power have I to describe Thee?
So powerless am I, that I cannot even once be a sacrifice unto Thee.
Whatever *pleaseth* Thee is good.
Thou, O Formless One, art ever secure.

XVII

Numberless thy worshippers, and numberless Thy lovers;
Numberless Thine adorers, and numberless thy who perform austerities for thee;
Numberless the reciters of *sacred* books and Veds;
Numberless Thy Jogis whose hearts are indifferent *to the world*;
Numberless the saints who ponder on Thine attributes and divine knowledge;
Numberless Thy true men; numberless Thine almsgivers;
Numberless Thy heroes who face the steel of their enemies;
Numberless Thy silent *worshipers* who lovingly fix their thoughts upon Thee.
What power have I to describe Thee?
So lowly am I, that I cannot even once be a sacrifice unto Thee.
Whatever pleaseth Thee is good.
O Formless One, Thou art ever secure.

XVIII

Numberless are the fools appallingly blind;
Numberless are the thieves and devourers of others' property;
Numberless those who establish their sovereignty by force;
Numberless the cut throats and murderers;
Numberless the sinners *who pride themselves on* committing sin;
Numberless the liars who roam about lying;
Numberless the filthy who enjoy filthy gain;
Numberless the slanderers who carry loads *of calumny* on their heads;
Nanak thus *describeth* the degraded.
So lowly am I, I cannot even once be a sacrifice unto Thee.
Whatever *pleaseth* Thee is good.
Of Formless One, Thou art ever secure.

XIX

Numberless *Thy* names, and numberless *Thy* places.

Completely beyond reach are Thy numberless worlds.

Numberless they who repeat *Thy name* with *all* the strength of their intellects.

By letters *we repeat* Thy name, by letters we praise Thee;

By letters *we acquire* divine knowledge, and sing Thy praises and Thine attributes,

By letters we write and utter the word *of God*;

By the letters *recorded* on man's head his destiny is declared.

He who inscribeth them on others, *beareth* them not on His own head.

As He ordaineth, so shall man obtain.

As great Thy creation, O God, so great is Thy fame

There is no place without *Thy* name.

What power have I to describe Thee?

So lowly am I, that I cannot even once be a sacrifice unto Thee.

Whatever *pleaseth* Thee is good.

O Formless One, Thou art ever secure.

XX

When the hands, feet, and *other members of* the body are covered with filth,

It is removed by washing with water.

When thy clothes are polluted,

Apply soap, and the impurity shall be washed away.

So when the mind is defiled by sin,

It is cleansed by the love of the Name.

Men do not become saints or sinners by merely calling themselves so.

The recording angels take with them a record of *man's* acts.

It is he himself soweth, and he himself eateth.

Nanak, man suffereth transmigration by God's order.

XXI

Pilgrimage, austerities, mercy, and almsgiving on general and special occasions.

Whosoever *performeth, may obtain* some little honour;

But he who hearth and *obeyeth* and loveth *God* in his heart,

Shall wish off his *impurity* in the place of pilgrimage within him.

All virtues are Thine, O Lords; none are mine.

There is no devotion without virtue.

From the Self-existent *proceeded* Maya (athi), whence issued a word which produced Brahma and the rest—

'Thou art true, Thou art beautiful, there is ever pleasure in Thy heart!'

What the time, what the epoch, what the lunar day, and what the week-day.

What the season, and what the month when the world was created,

The Pandits did not discover; had they done so, they would have recorded it in the Purans.

Nor did the Qazis discover it; had they done so, they would have recorded it in the Quran;

Neither the Jogi nor any other *mortal* knows the lunar day, or the week-day, or the season, or the month.

Only the Creator who fashioned the world *knoweth which He did so.*

How shall I address Thee, O God? how shall I praise Thee? How shall I describe Thee? and how shall I know Thee?

Saith Nanak, everybody speketh of Thee, one wiser than another.

Great is the Lord, great is His name; what He doeth *cometh* to pass.

Nanak, he who is proud shall not be honoured on his arrival in the next world.

XXII

There are hundreds of thousands of nether and upper regions.

Men have grown weary at last of searching *for God's* limits; the Veds say one thing, *that God has no limit.*

The thousands of Purans and Muhammadan books tell that in reality there is but one principle.

If God can be described by writing, then describe, Him; *but* such description is impossible.

O Nanak, call Him great; only He Himself knoweth how great He is.

XXIII

Praisers praise God, but have not acquired a knowledge of Him,

As rivers and streams fall into the sea, but know not *its extent.*

Kings and emperors who possess oceans and mountains of property and wealth,

Are not equal to the worm which forgetteth not God in its heart.

XXIII

There is no limit to God's praises; to those who repeat *them* there is no limit.

There is no limit to His mercy, and to His gifts there is no limit.

There is no limit to what God seeth, no limit to what He heareth.

The limit of the secret of His heart cannot be known.

The limit of His creation cannot be known; neither His near nor His far side can be discovered.

To know His limits how many vex their hearts.
His limits cannot be ascertained;
Nobody *knoweth* His limits.
The more we say, the more *there remains* to be said.
Great is the Lord, and exalted is His seat.
His exalted name is higher than the *most* exalted.
Where any one else ever so exalted,
Then he would know that exalted Being:
How great He is He *knoweth* Himself.
Nanak, God bestoweth Gifts *on whom He looketh* with favour and mercy.

XXV

His many bounties cannot be recorded ,
He is a great giver and hath not a particle of covetousness.
How many, yea countless heroes beg of Him!
How many *others* whose number cannot be conceived!
How many pine away in sin!
How many persons receive yet deny God's gifts!
How many fools there are who *merely* eat!
How many are ever dying in distress and hunger!
O Giver, these are also Thy gifts.
Rebirth and deliverance depend on Thy will:
Nobody can interfere with it.
If any fool try to interfere with it
He shall himself know the punishment he shall suffer.
God himself *knoweth to whom He may give*, and He Himself *giveth:*
Very few acknowledge this.
He to whom God hath given the *boon* of praising and lauding Him,
O Nanak, is the King of kings.

XXVI

Priceless are Thine attributes, O God, and priceless Thy dealings;
Priceless Thy dealers, priceless Thy storehouses;
Priceless what *cometh* from Thee, and priceless what is taken away;
Priceless Thy rate and priceless the time for *dealing*;
Priceless Thy justice and priceless Thy court:
Priceless Thy weights and priceless Thy measures;
Priceless Thy gifts and priceless Thy marks;
Priceless Thy mercy and priceless Thine ordinances.

How beyond all price *Thou art* cannot be stated.

Ever speaking of Thee men continue to fix their thoughts on Thee.

They who read the Veds and Purans speak of Thee;

Learned men speak of Thee and deliver discourses on Thee;

Brahmas speak of Thee, and Indars speak of Thee;

The milkmaids and Krishan speak of Thee;

Shivs speak of Thee, the Sidhs speak of Thee;

All the Budhas Thou hast created speak to Thee;

The demons speak of Thee, the gods speak of Thee;

The demigods, men, munis, and servants speak of Thee;

How many speak of Thee or attempt to speak of Thee!

How many depart while speaking of Thee!

If Thou wert to create as many more as Thou hast created,

Even then few of them would be able to speak *adequately of Thee.*

Thou mayest be as great as Thou pleasest.

Nanak, only the True One Himself knoweth how great He is.

If any one were to speak improperly of God,

Write him down as the most ignorant of men.

XXVII

What is that gate, what is that mansion where Thou, *Of God*, sittest and watchest over all things?

How many various and countless instruments are played! How many musicians,

How many musical measures with their consorts, and how many singers ing Thee!

Wind, water, and fire sing Thee; Dharmraj sings at Thy gate.

The recording angels, who know how to write, and on whose record Dharmraj judgeth sing Thee.

Ishar, Brahma, and Devi, ever beautiful as adorned by *Thee*, sing Thee.

Indar seated on his throne with the gods at Thy gate sing Thee.

Sidhs in meditation sing Thee; holy men in contemplation sing Thee.

The continent, the true, and the patient sing Thee; unyielding heroes sing Thee.

The pandits and the supreme Rikhis, reading their Veds, sing Thee in every age.

The lovely *celestial maids* who beguile the heart in the upper, middle, and nether regions sing Thee.

The jewels created by Thee with the sixty-eight places of *Hindu* pilgrimage sing Thee.

Mighty warriors and divine heroes sing Thee; the four sources of life sing Thee.

The continents, the worlds, and the universe made and supported by Thy hands sing Thee.

The saints who please Thee, and who are imbued with Thy love sing Thee.

The many others who sing Thee I cannot remember; how could Nanak recount them?

That God is ever true, He is the true Lord, and the true Name.

He who made this world is and shall be; He shall neither depart, nor he made to depart.

He could created things of different colours, descriptions and species,

Beholdeth His handiwork which attesteth His greatness. He will do what *pleaseth* Himself; no order may be issued to Him.

He is King, the King of kings, O Nanak; *all* remains *subject to* His will.

XXVIII

Make contentment and modesty thine earrings, self-respect thy wallet, meditation the ashes to *smear on the body;*

Make thy body, which is only a morsel for death, thy beggar's coat, and faith thy rule of life and thy staff.

Make association with men thine Ai Panth, and the conquest of thy heart the conquest of the world.

To Thee sing chaste and patient of mankind,
Unyielding heroes of true faith approved.
To Thee sing pandits and the chiefs of saints;
The ages four and Veds to them assigned.
To Thee sing maidens who delight the sense,
This world of ours, high heaven, and hell below.
To Thee sing gems from Vishnu's sea that rose,
And eight and sixty spots of pilgrims' haunt.
To Thee sing heroes and the man of might;
The sources four from which all life doth spring.
To Thee sing regions, orbs and universe,
Created, cherish'd, and upheld by Thee!
To Thee sing those whose deeds delight Thine eye,
The hosts who wear the colours of Thy faith.
All things beside which sing Thy glorious name,
Could ne'er be told by Nanak's lowly song.

Hail ! Hail to Him,

The primal, the pure, without beginning, the indestructible, the same in every age!

XXIX

Make divine knowledge thy food, compassion thy storekeeper, and the voice which is in every heart the pipe to *all to repast*

Make him who hath strung the whole world on *His string* thy spiritual Lord; let wealth and supernatural power by relishes for others.

Union and separation is the law which *regulateth* the world. By destiny we receive our portion.

Hail! Hail to Him,

The primal, the pure, without beginning, the indestructible, the same in every age!

XXX

One Maya in union *with* God gave birth to three acceptable children.

One of them is the creator, the second the provider, the third performeth the function of destroyer.

As it pleaseth God, He *directeth* them by His orders.

He *belholdeth* them, but is not seen by them. This is very marvellous.

Hail ! Hail to Him,

The primal, the pure, without beginning, the indestructible, the same in every age!

XXXI

His seat and His storehouses are in every world.

What was to be put into them was put in at one times.

The Creator beholdeth His creation.

Nanak, true is the work of the True One.

Hail ! Hail to Him,

The primal, the pure, without beginning, the indestructible, the same in every age!

XXXII

Were one tongue to become a hundred thousand, and a hundred thousand to become twenty-fold more,

I would utter the name of the one Lord of the world hundreds of thousands of times *with all my tongues.*

In this way I should ascent the stairs of the Lord, and become one with Him.

One hearing of the exaltation of the religious the vile become jealous.

Nanak, the *former* have found the Kind One, while false is the boasting of the false.

XXXIII

I have no strength to speak and no strength to be silent.
I have no strength to ask and no strength to give;
I have no strength to live, and no strength to die,
I have no strength to acquire empire or wealth which produce a commotion in the heart.
I have no strength to meditate on Thee on ponder on divine knowledge;
I have no strength *to find* the way to escape from the world.
He is whose arm there is strength, may see what he can do.
Nanak, no one is of superior or inferior *strength* before God.

XXXIV

God created nights, seasons, lunar days, and week days,
Wind, water, fire, and the nether regions.
In the midst of these He established the earth as a temple.
In it He *placed* living beings of different habits and kinds.
Their names are various and endless,
And they are judged according to their acts.
Ture is God, and true is His court.
There the elect are accepted and honoured.
The Merciful One *marketh* them according to their acts.
The bad and the good shall there be distinguished.
Nanak, on arrival there, this shall be seen.

XXXV

Such is the practice in the realm of righteousness.
I now describe the condition of the realm of knowledge.
How many winds, waters, and fires! how may Krishans and Shivs!
How many Brahmas who fashioned worlds! *how many* forms, colours and grabs!
How many lands of grace *like this*! now many mountains! how many Dhurs and instructors such as his.
How many Indars, how many moons and suns, how many regions and countries!
How many Sidhs, Budhs, how many Naths! now many goddesses and representations of *them*!

How many demigods and demons! how many saints, how many jewels and seas!

How many sources of life! how many languages! and how many lines of kings!

How many possessors of divine knowledge! how many worshippers! Nanak, there is no end of them.

XXXVI

In the realm of knowledge the light of divine knowledge is resplendent.

There are heard songs from which millions of joys and pleasures *proceed.*

Beauty is the attribute of the realm of happiness.

There things are fashioned in an incomparable manner.

What is done there cannot be described.

Whoever *endeavoureth* to describe it shall afterwards repent.

There are fashioned knowledge, wisdom, intellect and understanding;

And there too is fashioned the skill of demigods and men of supernatural power.

XXXVII

Force is the attribute of the realm of action.

Incomparable are they who dwell therein.

There are very powerful warriors and heroes

They are filled with the *might* of Ram.—

There are many Sitas in the midst of greatness,

There beauty cannot be described—

They die not, neither are they led astray

In whose hearts God dwelleth.

There dwell congregations of saints;

They rejoice; the True One is in their hearts.

God dwelleth in the true realm.

He looketh on its denizens with an eye of favour, and *rendereth* them happy.

There are continents, worlds and universes.

Whoever *thrieth* to describe them shall never arrive at an end.

There are words upon worlds and forms *upon forms.* They *fulfil* their functions according to God's orders: God beholding and contemplating them is pleased.

Nanak, to describe *them* would be impossible.

XXXVIII

Make continence thy furnace, resignation thy goldsmith, Understanding thine anvil, divine knowledge thy tools, The fear *of God* thy bellows, austerities thy fire,

Divine love thy crucible, and melt God's name therein. In such a true mint the Word shall be coined.

This is the practice of those on whom God looketh with an eye of favour.

Nanak, the Kind One by a glance *maketh* them happy.

Slok

The air is the guru, water our father, and the great earth our mother;

Day and night are our two nurses, male and female, who set the whole world a-playing.

Merits and demerits shall be read out in the presence of the Judge.

According to men's acts, some shall be near, and others distant *from God.*

They who pondered one the Name and departed after the completion of their toil,

Shall have their countenances made bright, O Nanak; how many shall be emancipated in company with them!

ASA KI WAR

There is but one God whose name is true, the Creator, devoid of fear and enmity, immortal, unborn, self-existent great and beneficent.

Guru Har Gobind

This *War* includes *sloks.* The *sloks* also were written by the first Guru, and should be sung to the air of 'Tunda As Raja'.

Slok

Guru Nanak

I am a sacrifice to my Guru a hundred times a day,

Who without any delay made demigods out of men.

Guru Angad

Were a hundred moons to rise, and a thousand suns to mount *the sky*;

Even with such light there would be appalling darkness without the Guru.

Guru Nanak

Nanak, they who very clever in their own estimation think not of the Guru,

Shall be left like spurious sesames in a reaped field.

They shall be left in the field, saith Nanak, without an owner :

The wretches may even bear fruit and flower, but they shall be as ashes within their bodies.

Pauri I

God Himself created the world and Himself gave names to *things.*

He made Maya by His power : seated He beheld *His work* with delight.

O Creator, Thou art the Giver; being pleased Thou bestowest and practisest kindness.

Thou knowest all things; Thou givest and takest life with a word.

Seated Thou didst behold *Thy work* with delight.

Slok II

Guru Nanak

True are Thy regions and true Thy universes;
True Thy worlds and true Thy creation;
True Thine acts and all Thy thoughts;
True Thine order and true Thy court;
True Thy command and true Thy behest;
True Thy favour and true *Thy* signs.
Hundreds of thousands and millions declare Thee true;
True is all Thy power, true all Thy strength;
True Thy praises, true *Thy* eulogies;
True Thy might, O true King.
Nanak, true are they who meditate on the True One.
They who are born and die are the alsest of the false.

Guru Nanak

Great is His glory whose name is great;
Great is His glory whose justice is true;
Great is His glory whose seat is immovable;
Great is His glory who *understandeth our* utterances;
Great is His greatness who knoweth all our feelings;
Great is His glory who *giveth* without consulting *others*;
Great is His glory who is all in all Himself;
Nanak, His acts cannot be described.
All that He did and hath to do dependeth on His own will.

Guru Angad

This world is the True One's chamber; The True One's dwelling is therein.

Some by His order He absorbeth in *Himself*; others by His order He destroyeth.

Some at His pleasure He withdraweth from mammon; others *He causeth* to abide therein.

It cannot be even told whom He will regenerate.

Nanak, he to whom God *revealeth* Himself, is known as holy.

Pauri II

Nanak, *God* having created animals recorded their names, and appointed Dharmraj *to judge their acts.*

At His own court the real truth is adjudged; He separateth and removeth those who are attached to mammon.

There the false find no place: they go to hell with blackened faces.

They who are imbued with Thy name win; the deceivers lose.

God recorded names and appointed Dharmraj to record acts.

Slok III

Guru Nanak

Wonderful Thy word, wonderful Thy knowledge;
Wonderful Thy creatures, wonderful their species;
Wonderful their forms, wonderful their colours;
Wonderful the animals which wander naked;
Wonderful Thy wind; wonderful Thy water;
Wonderful Thy fire which *sporteth* wondrously;
Wonderful the earth, wonderful the sources of production;
Wonderful the pleasures to which mortals are attached;
Wonderful the meeting, wonderful parting *from Thee;*
Wonderful is hunger, wonderful repletion;
Wonderful Thy praises, wonderful Thy eulogies;
Wonderful the desert, wonderful the road;
Wonderful Thy nearness, wonderful *Thy* remoteness;
Wonderful to behold Thee present.
Beholding these wonderful things I remain wondering.
Nanak, they who understand them are supremely fortunate.

Guru Nanak

By Thy power we see, by Thy power we hear, by Thy power we fear, *or enjoy* the highest happiness;

By Thy power *were made* the nether regions and the heavens; by Thy power all creation;

By Thy power *were produced* the Veds, the Purans, the *Muhammadan* books, and by Thy power all compositions;

By Thy power we eat, drink, and clothe ourselves; by Thy power *springeth* all affection;

By Thy power are the species, genera, and colours of *creatures;* by Thy power are the animals of the world.

By Thy power are virtues; by Thy power are vices; by Thy power, honour and dishonour;

By Thy power are wind, water, and fire; by Thy power is the earth.

Everything *existeth* by Thy power; Thou art the ominpotent Creator; Thy name is the holiest of the holy.

Saith Nanak, Thou beholdest and pervadest *all things* subject to Thy command; *Thou art* altogether unrivalled.

Pauri III

Man having enjoyed himself becometh ashes, and the soul passeth away.

However great and wealthy a man may be, *the ministers of Death* throw a chain on his neck and take him away.

There an account of his acts is read; *the Judge* on his seat *taketh* the account and passeth sentence.

Such a man shall find no place of *shelter*; when he is beaten, who will hear his cries?

Man, blind that thou art, thou has wasted thy life.

Slok IV

Guru Nanak

In fear the winds and breezes ever blow;

In fear flow hundreds of thousands of rivers;

In fear fire *performeth* its forced labour;

In fear the earth is pressed by its burden;

In fear Indar *moveth* headlong; in fear *sitteth* Dharmraj at *God's* gate.

In fear is the sun, in fear the moon; they travel millions of miles without end;

In fear are the Sidhs, the Budhas, the demigods, and the Naths; in fear are the stars and the firmament;

In fear are wrestlers, very mightly men and divine heroes;

In fear cargoes of men come and go.

God hath destined fear for every one; Nanak, the Formless One, the True, is alone without fear.

Guru Nanak

Nanak, the Formless One is without fear; all the Rams vere dust.

How many stories there are of Krishan! how many Veds and *religious* compositions!

How many beggars dance, and fall, and again beat time!

Actors enter the market-place and draw *forth* their appliances;

Kings and queens sing and utter nonsense;

They wear earrings worth hundreds of thousands, and necklaces worth hundreds of thousands.

The body on which they are worn, O Nanak, shall become ashes.

Divine knowledge is not sought in *mere* words; to speak *concerning it* were as hard as iron;

By God's grace man *obtaineth* it; skill and orders are useless *therefor.*

Pauri IV

If the Kind One look with kindness, then is the true Guru obtained.

The soul halth wandered through many births, and now the true Guru hath communicated the Word.

There is no benefactor so great as the true Guru; hear this, all ye people.

By meeting the true Guru who hath removed pride from his heart, and who *preacheth* the Truest of the true,

The True One is obtained.

Slok V

Let all the gharis be your milkmaids, and the pahars your Krishans and Gopals:

Let wind, water, and five be your jewels; and the moon and sun your avatars;

The whole earth your *stage* properties and vessels, which are all entaglements.

Nanak, they who are devoid of divine knowledge are robbed; the minister of death halth devoured them.

Guru Nanak

The disciples play, the gurus dance,
Shake their feet, and roll their heads
Dust flieth and falleth on their hair;
The audience beholding laugh and go home;
For the sake of food *the performers* beat time,
And dash themselves on the ground.
The milkmaids sing, Krishans sing,
Sitas and royal Rams sing.
Fearless is the Formless One, whose name is true,
And whose creation is the whose world.
The worshippers on whom *God bestoweth* kindness worship Him;
Pleasant is the night for those who long for Him in their hearts.
By the Guru's instruction to his disciples this knowledge *is obtained.*
That the Kind One *saveth those on whom He looketh* with favour.

Oil-presses, spinning-wheels, hand-mills, potters' wheels, Plates, whirlwinds many and endless,

Tops, churning-staves, threshing-frames turn round;
Birds tumble and take no breath.
Men put animals on stakes and whirl them.
O Nanak, the tumblers are innumerable and endless.
In the same way those bound in entaglements are swung round;

Every one *danceth* according to his own acts—

They who dance and laugh shall weep on their departure;

They cannot fly or obtain supernatural power.

Leaping and dancing are human recreations;

Nanak, they who have the fear of God in their hearts have also love.

Pauri V

Thy name is the Formless: by repeating it *man goeth* not to hell.

The would and body are all Thine: what Thou givest man *eateth;* to say *aught else were* waste of words.

O man, if thous desire thine advantage, do good acts and be lowly.

Even though thou stave off old age, it shall come to thee in the disguise of death.

None may remain when his measure is full.

Slok VI

The Musalmans praise the Shariat, read it, and reflect on it;

But God's servants are they who employ themselves in His service in order to behold Him.

The Hindus praise the Praised One whose appearance and from are incomparable.

They bathe in holy streams, *performs* idol-worship and adoration, use copious incense of sandal.

The Jogis meditate on God the Creator, whom they call the Unseen,

Whose form is minute, whose name is the Bright One, and who is the image of their bodies.

In the minds of the generous contentment is produced in their desire to give.

Others give, but ask a thousandfold more, *and still want* the world to honour them.

Why mention thieves, adulterers, perjurers, evil and sinful men?

Many depart from here after eating what they had ammassed *in previous births;* shall they have any business whatever *in the next world*?

The *animals* which live in the water, dry land, the fourteen worlds, and all creation—

What they say Thou alone knowest; for them too Thou carest.

Saith Nanak, the saints hunger to praise Thee; the true Name *is their* support.

In everlasting joy they abide day and night; *may I obtain* the dust of the feet of such virtuous *men*!

Guru Nanak and Shakh Brahm discussed the question of the disposal of the dead. The Shaik maintained that a man who was burned would either go to hell or not rise at the day of judgement.

Guru Nanak

The ashes of the Musalman fall into the potter's clod;

Vessels and bricks are fashioned from them; they cry out as they burn.

The poor ashes burn and weep, and sparks fly from them.

Nanak, the Creator who made the world, knoweth *whether it is better to be burned or buried.*

Pauri VI

Without the true Guru none hath found God: without the true Guru none hath found *God.*

God hath put Himself into the true Guru; he hath made manifest and proclaimed this.

Salvation is ever obtained by meeting the true Guru who hath banished worldly love from within him.

Best are the meditations of him who hath fixed his mind on the True One;

He hath found the Giver of life to the world.

Slok VII

In pride man *cometh,* in pride he *departeth;*
In pride is man born, in pride he *dieth;*
In pride he *giveth,* in pride he *taketh;*
In pride he *earneth,* in pride he *spendeth;*
In pride man becometh true *or* false;
In pride man meditateth evil or good;
In pride he *goeth* to hell *or* heaven;
In pride he *rejoiceth,* in pride he mourneth;
In pride he becometh filthy, in pride he is cleansed;
In pride man loseth his caste and race;
In pride are the ignorant, in pride the clever;
In pride one knoweth not the value of deliverance or salvation;
In pride is mammon and in pride its effect *on the heart;*
In pride are animals created.
When pride is removed, *God's* gate is seen.
Without divine knowledge man worrieth himself by talking.
Nanak, the Commander hath thus ordained it;
As man *regardeth God,* so *God regardeth* him.

Guru Angad

It is the nature of pride that it produceth pride.
This pride is a trammel which subjecteth *man* to repeated transmigration.
What is the origin of pride, and by what device shall it depart?

For pride it is ordained that man wander according to his previous acts.

Pride is a chronic disease, but these is also a medicine for it in the heart.

If God bestow His grace, man shall avail himself of the Guru's instruction;

Saith Nanak, hear, O ye men, in this way trouble shall depart.

Pauri VII

They who have meditated on God as the truest of the true, have done *real* worship and are contented;

They have refrained from evil, done good deeds, and practised honesty;

They have lived on a little corn and weather, and burst the entanglements of the world.

Thou art the great Bestower; ever Thou givest *gifts* which increase a quarterfold.

They who have magnified the great God have found His.

Slok VIII

Men, trees, the banks of sacred streams, clouds, fields, Islands, peoples, countries, continents the universe, The sources of *production* from eggs, wombs, the earth and perspiration,

Lakes, mountains, animals—O Nanak, God *knoweth* their condition.

Nanak, God having created animals *taketh* care of them all.

The Creator who created the world hath to take thought for it also.

It is the same Creator who made the world who *taketh* thought for it.

To Him be obeisance; blessings be on Him! His court is imperishable.

Nanak, without the true Name what is a sacrificial mark? What a sacrificial thread?

Guru Nanak

Man may perform hundreds of thousands of good acts and deeds, hundreds of thousands of approved charities,

Hundreds of thousands of penances at sacred places, sahaj jog in the wilderness,

Hundreds of thousands of braveries, and part with his life in the conflict of battle;

He may study hundreds of thousands of Veds and works of divine knowledge and meditation, and read the Purans—

Nanak, these devices would be of no avail; true is the mark of grace.

The Creator who made the world hath decreed transmigration.

Pauri VIII

Thou alone art the true Lord who hath diffused the real truth.

He to whom Thou givest obtaineth truth, and he then *practiseth* it.

Man *obtaineth* truth on meeting the true Guru in whose heart the truth *dwelleth*.

The fool *knoweth* not truth, and hath wasted his life by obstinacy;

Why hath he come into the world?

Slok IX

Guru Nanak

A man may load carts with books; he may load men with books *to take* with him;

Books may be put on boats; pits may be filled with them.

A man may read books for months; he may read them for years;

He may read them for life; he may read them while he hath breath—

Nanak, only one world, *God's name,* would be of account; all else *would* be the senseless discussion of pride.

Guru Nanak

The more one readeth and writeth, the more is one tormented;

The more one wandereth on pilgrimages, the more one babbleth;

The more religious garbs man weareth, the more discomfort he *causeth* his body.

Bear, O my soul, the *result* of thine own acts.

He who *eateth* not corn hath lost the relish *of life.*

Men suffer much pain through their attachment to mammon.

They who wear not clothes suffer terribly day and night.

Man ruineth himself by *perpetual* silence; how can he who *sleepeth* in ignorance be awakened without a guru.

Even though man *go* barefooted, he must still suffer for his own acts.

If a man eat filth, and put ashes on his head,

The blind food loseth respect; without the Name he *obtaineth* no *abiding* place.

The ignorant man who dwelleth in the wilderness and at burial and cremation-grounds, knoweth not *God* and shall afterwards regret.

He who meeteth the true Guru and fixeth *God's* name in his heart, obtaineth comfort.

Nanak, he on whom *God looketh* with favour obtaineth Him.

He becometh free from hopes and fears, and *destroyeth* his pride by means of the Word.

Pauri IX

The saint, *O Lord,* please Thy heart, adorn Thy gate, and hymn Thy praises.

Nanak, they who are outside the favour, find no entrance and wander *in many births.*

Some know not their origin, and have an excessive opinion of themselves.

I am a singer of low caste; others call themselves of high caste.

I *only* beg of those who meditate on Thee.

Slok X

Guru Nanak

False are kings, false their subjects, false the whole world;

False are mansions, false palaces, false those who dwell therein;

False is gold; false silver; false he who *weareth* them;

False the body; false raiment; false peerless beauty;

False husbands; false wives; they waste away and become dust.

Man who is false loveth what is false, and *forgetteth* the Creator.

With whom contract friendship? The whole world passeth away.

False is sweetness; false honey; in falsehood shiploads are drowned.

Nanak humbly *asserteth*—except Thee, O God, everything is thoroughly false.

Guru Nanak

Man is known as true when truth is in his heart;

When the filth of falsehood departeth, man *washeth* his body clean.

Man is known as true when he beareth love to the True One;

When the mind is enraptured on hearing the Name, man *attaineth* the door of salvation.

Man shall be known as true when he *knoweth* the *true* way;

Having prepared the field of the body, put into it the seed of the Creator.

Man shall be known as true when he *receiveth* true instruction;

Let man show mercy to living things and perform some works of charity.

Man shall be known as true, when he dwelleth in the pilgrimage of his heart.

Let man after inquiry from the true Guru rest and abide *in his own heart*;

Truth is the medicine for all; it *removeth* and washeth away sin.

Nanak maketh supplication to those who are in possession of truth.

Pauri X

Be mine the gift of the dust of the *saints'* feet: if I obtain it, I shall apply it to my forehead.

Forsake false covetousness; concentrate thy mind and meditate on the Unseen One.

Thou salt obtain a reward in proportion to what thou hast done.

It is have been so allotted from the beginning, man shall obtain the dust of the saints's feet.

Ruin not thyself with scant service.

Slok XI

Guru Nanak

There is a dearth of truth; falsehood prevaileth; the blackness of this age *maketh men* demons.

They who have sown the seed of *the Name* have departed with honour; how can half-seed germinate?

If the seed be whole, it will germinate in the proper season.

Nanak, unbleached cloth cannot be dyed without a base.

If the body be put into the vat of fear, modesty be made its base,

And it be dyed with devotion, O Nanak, there will not be a trace of falsehood in it.

Guru Nanak

Greed and sin are ruler and village accountant; falsehood is master of the mint.

Lust, his minister, summoneth and examinent men, and sitteth in judgement on them.

The subjects *are* blind and without divine knowledge, and satisfy the *judge's* greed with bribes.

Priests dance, play musical instruments, disguise, and decorate themselves;

They shout aloud, sing of battles, and heroes' praises.

Fools call *themselves* pandits and with tricks and caviling love to a mass *wealth.*

Pretended religious men spoil their religious acts, *and yet* want the door of salvation;

They call themselves continent, and leave their houses and homes, *yet* they know not the way.

Every one is perfect to himself; no one *admitteth* himself wanting.

If the weight of honour be put into the scale, then, Nanak, man shall appear *properly* weighed.

Guru Nanak

Man's evil becometh known, O Nanak; the True One seethe *all.*

Every one maketh endeavours, *but* it is *only* what the Creator doeth that taketh place.

Caste hath no power in the next world: there is a new *roder* of beings.

They those accounts are honoured are the good.

Pauri XI

They whom Thou didst so destine from the beginning mediate on *Thee,* O Lord.

There is nothing in the power of creatures; *O God,* it is Thou who hast created the different worlds.

Some Thou blendest with Thyself; others Thou leadest astray from Thee.

Thou art known by the favour of the Guru, through whom Thou revealest Thyself.

They who know Thee are easily absorbed in the True One.

Slok XII

Guru Nanak

Pain is medicine, *worldly* pleasure a disease; where there is *such* pleasure, there is no desire *for God.*

Thou art the Doer, I do nothing; if I try to do anything, it *cometh* to nothing.

I *am* a sacrifice *unto Thee*; Thou abidest in Thine omnipotence :

Thine end cannot be seen.

Thy light pervadeth creatures; creatures are contained in Thy light; Thou fillest inanimate and animate creation.

Thou art the true Lord; beautiful is Thy praise; he who uttereth it is saved.

Nanak uttereth the words of the Creator; what is to be done *God continueth* to do.

Guru Angad

The Jogis deem it their duly to acquire divine knowledge, the Brahmans to read the Veds,

The Khatris *to exercise* bravery, the Sudars to work for others;

But the highest duty of all is to repeat the name of the one God.

He who *knoweth* the secret of this

Is a bright God himself, and Nanak is his slave.

Guru Angad

There is one God, the God of all gods, the Supreme God of souls.

He who *knoweth* the secrets of the soul and of God,

Is a bright God himself, and Nanak is his slave.

Guru Nanak

Water *remaineth* if confined in a vessel; but it cannot remain without a vessel.

The mind controlled by divine knowledge is restrained; *but* without a guru there can be no divine knowledge.

Pauri XII

When the literate man is sinful *he deserveth punishment*; but punish not the illiterate saint.

As man *acteth* so shall he be described.

Play not such a game as shall bring thee defeat on arriving at God's court.

The literate and the illiterate shall be judged hereafter;

The headstrong shall be punished in the next world.

Slok XIII

Guru Nanak

Nanak, this body of ours hath one carriage and one driver.

They are both changed in every age; the holy man knoweth this.

In the Sat age contentment was the carriage, piety the driver in front;

In the Treat age continence was the carriage, strength the driver in front;

In the Dwapar age penance was the carriage, truth the driver in front;

In the Kal age passion is the carriage, falsehood the driver in front.

Guru Nanak

The Sam *Ved* saith that the Lord *is* white-robed, that men desired truth, abode in truth, and that all were absorbed in truth.

The Rig saith that God's name is everywhere contained, that it is as the sun in heaven;

That by repeating it sing depart,

And that then, Nanak, man *obtaineth* salvation.

The Yajur *stateth* that Kan Krishan, who was a Yadav, seduced Chandrawal;

That he brought the tree of life for a milkmaid, and amused himself in Bindraban.

The Atharv *belongeth* to the Kal age, when God's name was called Allah.

Men then wore blue clothes, and the Truks and Pathans exercised sway.

The four Veds are true *according to the Hindus;* but if they are read and studied there *are found therein* four *different* doctrines.

When man hath love and devotion and is himself lowly, it is then, O Nanak, he obtaineth salvation.

Pauri XIII

I am a sacrifice to the true Guru by meeting whom the Lord is remembered,

Who gave me the salve of divine instruction; with these eyes I then beheld God in the world.

The dealers who leave the Lord and attach themselves to mammon are wrecked.

The true God is a boat; few there are who consider this,

And those *who do* he mercifully saveth.

Slock XIV

Guru Nanak

The simmal-tree of the desert is very tall and very thick.

Why should the birds which go to it with hopes depart disappointed?

Because its fruit is insipid, its flowers unwholesome, and its leaves useless.

The tree which yieldeth sweet fruit is lowly, O Nanak, but its qualities and virtues are exquisite.

Every one boweth to himself; no one *boweth* to another.

If anything be put into a scale and weighed, the side which *descendeth* is the heavier.

The wicked man like a deer-stalker *boweth* twice *more than any one else;*

But what availeth bowing the head, if the heart be impure?

The following hymn was composed by Guru Nanak at Banaras on the occasion of a discussion with the local *Pandits* who pressed him to dress in the style of the Hindus:

Guru Nanak

You read books, perform your twilight devotions, argue, worship stones, and sit like cranes;

You utter falsehoods as excellent jewels; you meditate on the Gayatri three times a day;

You wear necklaces, put sacrificial marks on your foreheads, *carry* two *dhotis,* and put towels on your heads.

If you knew God's design, you *would know that yours* is verily a vain religion.

Saith Nanak, verily reflect that without the true Guru you shall not find the way.

Some suppose that the following was addressed to Sultan Ibrahim Khan Lodi who it is believed at one time sought to persecute the Guru :

Pauri XIV

Raiment and pleasing beauty man must leave on earth and depart.

Man shall obtain *the fruit* of the bad or good deeds he hath done :

He man have exercised sovereignty to his heart's content, yet must be proceed by the narrow road.

He shall be sent naked to hell, which will then appear very formidable to him;

And he shall regret the sins he committed.

The following slok, addressed by Guru Nanak to pandit Hardial, his family priest, when he came to invest him with a janeu, the sacrificial thread of the upper classes of Hindus, had already been given:

Slok XV

Make mercy thy cotton, contentment thy thread, continence its knot, truth its twist.

That would make a janeu for the soul; if thou have it, O Brahman, then put it on me.

It will not break, or become soiled, or be burned, or lost.

Blest the man, O Nanak, who *goeth* with such a thread on his neck.

Thou qurchasest a janeu for four damris, and seated in a square puttest it on;

Thou whisperest instruction that the Brahman is the guru *of the Hindus*—

Man dieth, the janeu falleth, and *the soul* departeth without it.

Guru Nanak

Though men commit countless thefts, countless adulteries, utter countless falsehoods and countless *words* of abuse;

Though they commit countless robberies and villanies night and day against their *fellow* creatures;

Yet the cotton thread is spun, and the Brahman *cometh* to twist it.

For the ceremony they kill a goat and cook and eat it, and everybody then saith 'Put on the janeu'.

When it becometh old, it is thrown away and another is put on.

Nanak, the string *breaketh* not if it be strong.

Guru Nanak

By adoring and praising the Name honour and a true thread are obtained.

In this way a sacred thread shall be put on, which will not break, and which will be fit for entrance into *God's* court.

Guru Nanak

There is no string for the sexual organs, there is no string for women:

There is no string for the impure acts which cause your beards to be daily apart upon.

There is no string for the tongue, there is no string for the eyes.

Without such strings *the Brahman* wandereth astray,

Twisteth springs *for the neck*, and putteth them on others.

He *taketh* hire for marrying;

He *pulleth* out a paper, and *showeth* the fate *of the wedded pair*.

Hear and see, ye people, it is strange.

That, while mentally blind, man is named wise.

Pauri XV

He to whom the Lord is compassionate the merciful will do the Master's work.

The worshipper whom God *causeth* to abide by His order, will worship Him.

By obeying His order man is acceptable, and shall then reach his Master's court.

He shall act as *pleaseth* his Master, and obtain the fruit his heart *desireth;*

And he shall be clothed with a robe of honour in God's court.

A man at Lahore presented a cow to a brahman. The Brahman took her with him, but had not wherewithal to pay toll at the Sultanpur ferry. He was stopped by the Khatri toll-keeper. The latter collected the cow's dung and at once set about plastering his cooking-place therewith. Mardana went towards him, but was ordered off, lest he should defile the toll-keeper's cooking-place. Upon the Guru Nanak uttered the following:

Slok XVI

Thou takest toll for a cow and a Brahman, the cowdung will not save thee.

Thou wearest a dhoti and a frontal mark, and carriest a rosary, *yet* thou eatest the bread of malechhas.

Thou performest the Hindu worship at home, thou readest the Quran *in public*, and associatest with Muhammadans, O my mother.

Lay aside hypocrisy, repeat God's name, and thou salt be saved.

Guru Nanak

They who have strings on their necks eat men, recite the Muhammadan prayers,

And use knives to *cut men's throats*
Although the Brahmans sound shell in their houses,
And enjoy their viands as they do themselves;
Yet false is their capital and false their dealings.
By uttering falsehood they maintain themselves.
Far from them is the abode of bashfulness and honesty:
Nanak, falsehood everywhere *prevaileth*.
On their foreheads are sacrificial marks; *on their* waists reddish dhotis;
And in their hands knives; they are the world's butchers.
Putting on blue clothes, they are acceptable in the *Muhammadans'* court,
And, while taking bread from the malechhas, worship the Purans.
They eat he goats killed with unspeakable words,
And allow no one to enter their cooking squares.
Having smeared a space they draw lines around it,
And sit within, false that they are,
Saying, 'Touch not! O touch not!
'Or this food of ours will be defiled'.
But their bodies are defiled; what they do is defiled;
Their hearts are false while they perform ablutions *after their meals*
Saith Nanak, meditate on the True One;
If thou art pure, thou shalt obtain Him.

Pauri XVI

All are within Thy ken, O Lord; Thou seet all, and Thou movest them beneath Thy glance.

God himself bestoweth greatness; He Himself *causeth* men to do good works.

He is the greatest of the great; great is His world; He appointeth *all men* to their respective duties.

If He cast a backward glance, He maketh marches as grass;

They may beg from door to door and receive no alms.

Guru Nanak composed the following slok on being invited by a dishonest shopkeeper to attend a *shradh*, or religious service, for his deceased father:

Slok XVII

If a robber break a house and sacrifice the fruits of that robbery to his ancestors,

The sacrifice shall be known in the next world, and make out the ancestors to be thieves.

The hand of the *Brahman* go-between shall be cut off; thus will *God* do justice.

Nanak, it is only the fruit of what man *giveth* from his earnings and toil that shall be obtained in the next world.

Guru Nanak

As a woman hath her recurring courses, so falsehood *dwelleth* in the mouth of the false one, and he is ever despised.

He should not be called pure who sitteth and washeth his body;

Rather is the pure, Nanak, in whose heart God dwelleth.

Pauri XVII

Caparisoned horses fleet as the wind and women adorned with every aid to beauty—

Men fix *their hearts on them*, dwell in mansions, pavilions and palaces, and make display;

They enjoy pleasures to their hearts' content; but they know not God and therefore fail.

They live by their authority, and, beholding their women's chambers, forget death;

But old age shall come and youth fail *them*.

A rich man gave a feast to which Guru Nanak and several Brahmans were invited. During the feast a child was born in the house, whereupon the Brahmans refused food and departed, deeming the house impure. Guru Nanak remonstrated with the following :

Slok XVIII

If the idea of impurity be admitted, there is impurity in everything.

There are worms in cow-dung and in wood;

There is no grain of corn without life.

In the first place, there is life in water by which everything is made green.

How shall we avoid impurity? It *falleth* on our kitchens.

Saith Nanak, impurity is not thus washed away: it is washed away by divine knowledge.

Guru Nanak

Impurity of the heart is greed, impurity of the tongue is falsehood;

Impurity of the eyes is gazing on another's wealth, his wife, and her beauty;

Impurity of the ears is listening to slander.

Nanak, even the *pretended* saint who *practiseth such things,* shall go bound to hell.

All impurity *consisteth* in superstition and attachment to worldly things.

Birth and death are ordained; as it *pleaseth* God, we come and go.

The eating and drinking which God sent as sustenance are pure.

Nanak, the pious persons who know God have no impurity.

Pauri XVIII

Magnify and praise the True Guru in whom there is all greatness.

If the Guru cause us to meet God, we shall behold *His greatness.*

If it please *the Guru,* he will cause *God's praises* to dwell in the heart.

He putteth his hand on our foreheads; and when he giveth the order, removeth evil from within us.

When God is pleased the nine treasures are obtained.

Slok XIX

The Brahman having first purified himself *sitteth* in a purified *square.*

The purified food is placed before him; no one may touch it.

Being thus purified, he *beginneth* to eat and read Sanskrit verses.

If it is thrown into a filthy place; whose fault is that?

The corn was holy, the water was holy, the fire and salt were holy; when the fifth *ingredient, ghi,* was added,

Then the food become holy.

When the food *entereth* a sinful body, it *becometh impure as if* spat upon.

The mouth which uttereth not the Name, and *eateth even* delicacies without the Name,

Consider, O Nanak, as if spat upon.

The following was Guru Nanak's remonstrance to a man who reviled the female sex:

Guru Nanak

In a vessel the man is conceived, from a vessel he is born, with a vessel he is betrothed and married.

With a vessel he *contracteth* friendship; with a vessel he goeth through the world.

When one vessel *dieth,* another is sought for; to a vessel he is bound.

Why call her bad from whom are born kings?

From a vessel a vessel is born; none may exist without a vessel.

Nanak, only the one True God is independent of a vessel.

The mouth which ever *praiseth Him* is fortunate and beautiful.

Nanak, that face shall be bright in the court of the True One.

Pauri XIX

Every one *calleth* Thee his own, O Lord; those who do not so call Thee Thou puttest away.

Every one *must bear the result of his* own acts, and adjust his own account.

Since ye are not to remain in this world, why practise ye pride?

Call no one bad; know this by reading these words.

Dispute not with a fool.

Slok XX

Nanak, the mind and body of him who *talketh* evil are evil :

He is most evil, and most evil is his reputation.

The evil person is rejected in God's court; his face is spat upon.

The evil person is a fool and *receiveth* shoe-beatings as punishment.

Guru Nanak

If a man, foul within and fair without, puff himself up in the world,

His filth will not depart even though the bathe at the sixty-eight places of pilgrimage.

They who wear silk within the rags without, are good in this world.

They have conceived love for God and contemplate beholding Him.

In God's love they weep, in God's love they laugh, or are even silent.

They care not for anything except the true Master.

They beg for food at *God's* door, and *only* eat when He giveth it to them.

For them there is but one court as there is but one pen; we and you shall meet for justice.

The accounts of *the wicked* shall be examined in God's court, and they shall be pressed, O Nanak, like oil in a mill.

Pauri XX

Thou Thyself didst create the world, and Thou Thyself didst infuse power into it.

Thou be holdest Thine own work, the losing and winning dice upon earth.

Whatever hath come shall depart; his turn shall come to every one.

Why forget that Lord who *owenth* life and soul

With thine own hands arrange thine own affairs.

Slok XXI

Guru Angad

What love is that which *attacheth* itself to worldly things?

Nanak, call him a lover who is ever absorbed in God.

He who *deemeth* what is good good, and what is bad bad,

Shall not be called a true love if he proceed in this manner.

Guru Angad

He who *offereth* salutation and *at the same time* criticizeth *God's works,* hath made a mistake from the beginning.

Both *his salutation and criticism* are in vain; Nanak, such a person shall not obtain a place in *God's* court.

Pauri XXI

Ever remember that Lord by worshipping whom thou shalt find happiness.

Why hast thou done such evil deeds, as thou shalt suffer for?

Do absolutely nothing evil, look well before thee;

So throw the dice that thou mayest not lose with the Lord,

Nay, that thou mayest gain some profit.

Slok XXII

Guru Angad

When a servant while performing service is proud and quarrelsome besides,

And talketh too much, he pleaseth not his master.

If the efface himself and perform service, he shall obtain some honour.

Nanak, he who *longeth* for God shall meet Him, and his longing shall be acceptable.

What a man hath in his heart *cometh* forth; lip-worship is of no avail.

Man soweth poison and *expecteth* ambrosia; behold that for justice!

Guru Angad

Contracting friendship with a fool would never be profitable.

He acteth according to his understanding: let any one see and inquire into this.

One thing can be put into a vessel if another be *first* removed.

Commands will not succeed with God; supplications must be addressed to Him.

By practising falsehood falsehood is obtained: Nanak, there is pleasure in praising God.

Guru Angad

Friendship for a fool and love for a great man.

Are like lines drawn on water, which leave neither trace nor mark.

Guru Angad

If a man be a fool and do anything, he cannot do it well;
Even though he do one or two things well, he will spoil the rest.

Pauri XXII

If the servant who is employed in service act according to his master's wishes,
His honour is all the more, and he receiveth double wages.
If he view with his master, he will excite his jealousy,
Lose his large salary, and receive shoe-beating on the mouth.
Thank Him by whose gifts thou liveth,
Nanak, commands will not succeed with Him; the Master must be implored.

Slok XXIII

Guru Angad

What sort of gift is that which we obtain by our own *asking*?
Nanak, wonderful is the gift we obtain when the Lord is pleased.

Guru Angad

What sort of service is that in which the fear of the master departeth not?
Nanak, he is called a servant who is absorbed in the love of his master.

Pauri XXIII

Nanak, God's end is not seen, nor hath He a thither or a hither side.
He Himself createth, and He Himself again destroyeth.
Some have chains on their necks, and some ride on many horses.
It is God who causeth to act and who acteth Himself; to whom else shall be complain?
Nanak, it is for Him who made the world to take care of it.

Slok XXIV

Guru Nanak

It is God Himself who made vessels and He Himself who filleth them.
In some is contained milk; others are put over the fire.
Some sleep on mattresses, and others stand and watch over them.
Nanak, God *regenerateth* those on whom He *looketh* with favour.

Guru Angad

God Himself *arrangeth,* He Himself *putteth* what He hath made into its proper place;
Having in this world created animals, He Himself *beholdeth* their birth and death.
Whom shall we address, O Nanak, since God *doeth* everything Himself?

Pauri XXIV

The greatness of the great God cannot be expressed;

He is the Creator, the Omnipotent, the Bounteous; He provideth His creatures with sustenance,

Man must do the work which God destined for him from the beginning.

Nanak, except in the one God alone there is no *abiding* place.

He *doeth* what He *pleaseth*.

THE RAHIRAS

SODAR

Guru Nanak, Rag Asa

What is that gate, what is that mansion where Thou, O God, sittest and watched over all things?

How many various and countless instruments of Thine are played! How many Thy musicians,

How many Thy musicial measures with their consorts, and how many singers sing Thee!

Wind, water, fire sing Thee; Dharmraj singeth at Thy gate;

The recording angels, who know how to write, and on whose record Dharmraj judgeth, sing Thee;

Ishar, Brahma, and Devi, ever beautiful as adorned by Thee, sing Thee;

Indar seated on his throne and the gods at Thy gate sing Thee;

Sidhs in meditation sing Thee; holy men in contemplation sing Thee;

The continent, the true, and the patient sing Thee; unyielding heroes sing Thee.

The Pandits and the supreme Rikhis, reading their Veds, sing Thee in every age.

The lovely celestial maids who beguile the heart in the upper, middle, and nether regions sing Thee.

The jewels created by Thee with the sixty-eight places of *Hindu* pilgrimage sing Thee.

Mighty warriors and heroes sing Thee; the four sources of life sing Thee.

The contiments, the worlds, and the universe made and supported by Thy hands sing Thee.

O God, the saints who please Thee and who are inbuded with Thy love sing Thee.

The many others who sing Thee I cannot remember; how could Nanak recount them?

That God is ever true, He is the true Lord and the true Name.

He who made this world is, was, and shall be; he shall neither be born nor die.

He who created things of different colours, descriptions, and species.
Beholdeth His handiwork which *attesteth* His greatness.
He will do what *pleaseth* Himself; no order may be issued to Him to the contrary.
He is King, the King of kings, O Nanak; *all* remain *subject to* His will.

Guru Nanak, Rag Asa

As men have heard so all call Thee great;
But hath any one ever seen how great thou art?
Thy worth cannot be estimated or described;
They who seek to describe it are absorbed in Thee
O my great Lord, deep and profound, brimful of excellences,
None knoweth the extent of Thine outline.
Though all meditative men were to meet and meditare upon Thee.
Though all appraisers were to meet and appraise Thee—
They who possess divine and spiritual wisdom, priests and high priests—
Yet they could not describe even a small portion of Thy greatness.
All truth, all fervour, all goodness,
The excellences of perfect men,
Cannot be obtained in their perfection without Thee.
If Thy grace be obtained none can be excluded;
Of what account is the helpless speaker?
Thy storerooms are filled with Thy praises.
Who can prevail against him to whom Thou givest?
Nanak, the True One arrangeth all.

Guru Nanak, Rag Asa

If I repeat the Name, I live; if I forget it, I die;
It is difficult to repeat the true Name.
If man hunger after the true Name,
His pain shall depart when he *satisfieth* himself with it.
Then how could I forget it, O my mother?
True is the Lord, true is His name.
Men have grown weary of uttering
Even on iota of His greatness; His worth they have not discovered.
If all men joined and tried to describe Him,
That would not add to or detract from His greatness.
God dieth not, neither is there any mourning for Him;
He continueth to give us our daily bread which never faileth.
His praise is—that there neither is,
Nor was, nor shall be any one *like unto* Him.

As great as Thou art Thyself, O God, so great are Thy gifts.

Thou who madest the day madest also the night

They who forget their Spouse are evil persons;

Nanak, without His name they are naughty.

Guru Ram Das, Rag Gujari

O servants of God and the true Guru, the true Being, offer this supplication unto Him.

We insects and worms seek thy protection, O true Guru; mercifully englighten us with the Name;

My friend and divine Guru, enlighten me with God's name.

Under the Guru's instruction, the Name is the helper of my soul; singing God's praises is my occupation.

Exceedingly fortunate are the men of God who have faith in Him and thirst for Him;

On obtaining the name of God, they are satisfied; when men meet the company of the saints, God's attributes are known.

They who obtain nor the relish of God's name are unfortunate, and shall go to the god of death.

Curses on the lives, curses on the hopes of living, of those who enter not the true Guru's protection and society!

The saints who have obtained the society of the true Guru are those on whose foreheads it was so written from the beginning.

Blest is that true society, Nanak, by meeting which the relish of God is obtained, and the Name manifested.

Guru Arjan, Rag Gujari

O my soul, why proposest thou exertion when God Himself in engaged in effort for thee?

He even *putteth* their food before the insects which He created in rocks and stones.

O my God, they who meet the society of the saints are saved.

Through the favour of the Guru they obtain the highest rank; though they be as dry wood, they are made green.

No one can rely on mother, father, friends, children, or wives.

God provideth every one with his daily food; why, O man, art thou afraid?

The *kulang* flieth away hundreds of miles, leaving her young behind her.

Who feedeth them? Who *giveth* them *morsels* to peck at?

Have you not considered this?

God holdeth in the palm of His hand all treasures and the eighteen supernatural powers.

Nanak is ever a sacrifice unto Thee; O God, Thou hast no end or bounds.

SO PURUKH

Guru Ram Das, Rag Asa

That Being is pure, God is the pure Being, God is altogether inaccessible and illimitable.

All meditate on Thee; all meditate on thee; O God, Thou art the true Creator.

All creatures are Thine; Thou providest for them all.

O saints, meditate on God who causeth all miserty to be forgotten.

God Himself is the Lord, God Himself is the worshipper; Nanak, what a helpless creature is man!

Thou, O God, the one Supreme Being, art fully contained in every heart and pervadest everything.

Some men are givers, some beggars; all are Thy wondrous sport.

Thou Thyself art the Giver; Thou art the Enjoyer; I know none beside Thee.

Thou art the totally infinite Supreme Being; what attributes of Thine shall I recount?

The slave Nanak is a sacrifice unto those who serve Thee, unto those who serve Thee.

They who meditate on Thee, who meditate on Thee, O God, abode in happiness in this age.

They who meditate on God are emancipated, are emancipated, my friend; for them Death's noose is broken.

All fear hath departed from those who have meditated on the fearless, the fearless God.

They who have worshipped, who have worshipped my God, are absorbed in Him.

Blest, blest are they who have meditated on God; the slave Nanak will become a sacrifice unto them.

O Infinite One, Thine infinite storehouses are filled with Thy worship, Thy worship.

O Infinite One, many are Thy saints, many are Thy saints who praise Thee.

They offer various, various worship to Thee, O God; they practise austerities and repeat Thy name, O endless One.

Various, various *saints* of Thine read many Simritis and Shastars, perform their daily duties and the six acts *prescribed for Brahmans*;

But only they are saints, good saints, saith Nanak, who please God, the Omnipotent.

Thou art the primal Being, the illimitable Creator; there is none so great as Thou.

Thou art the same in every age; Thou art ever and ever the same; Thou art the eternal Creator.

What *pleaseth* Thee *prevaileth;* what Thou doest *cometh* to pass.

Thou Thyself didst fashion the whole creation, yet, being created, it shall disappear.

Nanak *singeth* the praises of the Creator who knoweth all things.

Guru Ram Das, Rag Asa

Thou art the true Creator, my Lord.

What *pleaseth* Thee shall come to pass; what Thou givest I shall receive.

Everything, is Thine : all meditate on Thee.

They to whom Thou shoest kindness, obtain the jewel of Thy name.

The pious have gained, and the perverse have lost it.

Thou Thyself hast separated *these* and blended *those* with Thee.

Thou art an ocean: all are contained in Thee.

There is none beside Thee.

All living creatures are Thy play.

When Thou didst desire separation, they who had met Thee were separated from Thee; when Thou didst desire union, Thou didst blend them with Thyself.

That saint whom Thou causes to know Thee shall know Thee.

And ever dwell on Thy praises.

They who have served God have found happiness,

And have become easily absorbed in His name.

Thou Thyself art the Creator; everything that is made is Thine;

There is none beside Thee;

Thou beholdest and knowest Thy handiwork.

The slave Nanak saith, under the Guru's instruction Thou becomest manifest.

Guru Nanak, Rag Asa

Man bath obtained a dwelling in that tank whose water God hath made as hot as fire.

Man's feet cannot move in the mire of worldly love; we have seen him drowning therein.

O foolish man, thou hast not thought of the one God in thy heart;

Through forgetfulness of Him thy virtues have melted away.

I am ot continent, or true, or learned; I was born a stupid fool.

Nanak *representeth,* he hath sought the shelter of those who forget Thee not, *O God.*

Guru Arjan, Rag Asa

Since thou hast now obtained a human body, *O man,*

It is time for thee to meet God;

All else that thou doest is of no avail;

Join the company of the saints and only repeat God's name:

Apply thyself to preparation for crossing the terrible ocean.

Thy life is vainly passing in worldly love;

Thou hast not repeated God's name, performed penance, austerities, or *other* religious *works;*

Thou hast not served holy men or known God.

Nanak saith, base have been mine acts;

Preserve mine honour who have taken shelter in Thee.

THE SOHILA

Guru Nanak, Rag Gauri Dipaki

In the house in which God's praise is sung and He is ineditated on,

Sing the Sohila and remember the Creator.

Sing the Sohila of my Fearless Lord; I am a sacrifice to that song of joy by which everlasting comfort is obtained.

Ever and ever living things are watched over; the Giver *regardeth their wants*.

When *even* Thy gifts cannot be appraised, who can appraise the Giver?

The year and the auspicious time *for marriage* are recorded *relations* meet and pour oil on me the bride.

O my friends, pray for me that I may meet my Lord.

This message is every sent to every house : such invitations are ever issued.

Remember the Caller; Nanak, the day is approaching.

Guru Nanak, Rag Asa

There are six schools of *philosophy*, six teachers, and six doctrines.

The Guru of gurus is but one, though He hath various forms.

O father, preserve the system

In which the Creator is praised; that will redound to thy glory.

As there is one sun and many seasons,

In which there are wisas, chasans, gharis, pahars, lunar and week days, and months;

So, O Nanak, there is but one God, although His forms are many.

Guru Nanak, Rag Dhanasari

The sun and moon, *O Lord* are, Thy lamps; the firmament Thy salver; the orbs of the stars the pearls *enchased* in it.

The perfume of the sandal is Thine incense, the wind is Thy fan, all the forests are Thy flowers, O Lord of light.

What worship is this, O Thou Destroyer of birth? Unbeaten strains of ecstasy are the trumpets of Thy worship.

Thou hast a thousand eyes and yet not one eye; Thou hast a thousand forms and yet not one form;

Thou hast a thousand stainless feet and yet not one foot; Thou hast a thousand organs of smell and yet not one organ. I am fascinated by this play of Thine.

The light which is in everything in Thine, O Lord of light.

From its brilliancy everything is brilliant;

By the Guru's teaching the light becometh manifest.

What *pleaseth* Thee is the *real* worship.

O God, my mind is fascinated with Thy lotus feet as the bumble-bee with the flower: night and day I thirst for them.

Give the water of Thy favour o the sarang Nanak, so that he may dwell in Thy name.

Guru Ram Das, Rag Gauri Purbi

The city is greatly filled with lust and wrath; but these are destroyed on meeting the saints.

By predestination the Guru is found, and the soul is absorbed in the region of God's love.

Salute the saint with clasped hands—this is a greatly meritorious act.

Prostrate thyself before him—this is a greatly religious act.

The infidel *knoweth* not the taste of God's essence; he *beareth* the thorn of pride in his heart.

The more he *moveth,* the more it *pricketh* him, and the more pain he *feeleth:* his head shall feel death' mace.

9

Hymns of Guru Nanak

Sri Rag

The following was addressed to a man addicted to intoxicants:

The Giver gave man a pill of the intoxicant illusion.

In his intoxication he forget death and enjoyed pleasure for four days.

The abstainers obtained truth to keep them in God's court.

Nanak, know the True One alone as true.

By serving Him man *obtaineth* happiness and *proceedeth* with honour to His court.

The true wine is that which *containeth* the true Name; *it is prepared* without molasses.

I am a sacrifice unto those who hear and explain this. Man is known as properly intoxicated when he *obtaineth* a place in God's court.

Bathe in the water of virtues; apply the perfume of truth to *thy body*;

Then shall thy face become bright, and the One Giver *bestow* hundreds of thousands of gifts *on thee.*

Inform God, with whom resteth happiness, of thine unhappiness.

Why forget Him who *owneth* thy soul and life?

All clothing and food are impure without Him.

All else is false; what *pleaseth* Thee, O God, is acceptable.

A Sikh called Prema asked the Guru where God resided, in what state He dwelt, and how He could be found. The following was the Guru's reply:

The virtues of the virtuous woman and blazoned abroad; she who is not virtuous *regretteth* it.

O woman, if thou desire thy Spouse, *practise truth.* He cannot be obtained by falsehood.

No boat or raft *will take thee* to the distant Beloved.

My Lord is perfect; His throne is secure.

He whom the perfect Guru maketh holy, shall obtain the True and unrivalled One.

God's palace is beautiful; it is *adorned* with bright gems, rubeis,

Pearls, and diamonds; *it is surrounded by a* golden fortress,and is an abode of pleasure.

How shall I scale the fortress without a ladder? By meditating of God *through the* Guru I shall behold Him.

The Guru *giving me* God's name is my ladder, my boat, and my raft;

The Guru is the lake, the sea, and the boat; the Guru is the sacred stream.
If it please God, I shall go to bathe in the true tank and *become* pure.
He is called the most perfect; He reposeth on a perfect throne.
His seat is perfectly beautiful; He fulfilleth the hopes of the hopeless.
Nanak, if man obtain the Perfect One how can his virtues decrease?

A man can only find favour with God by devotion:

Accursed is her life who is separated from her Spouse; she is ruined by mammon.
Like a wall impregnated with kallar she crumbleth down day and night.
She obtaineth no rest without the Word; without her Beloved her grief departeth not.
O woman, what are thine adornments without thy Spouse?
Thou shalt not obtain entrance into God's court; being false thou shalt be despised.
The Lord is wise and forgetteth not : He is true and a great husbandman.
He first prepareth the ground, then soweth the seed of the true Name.
From the name of the one God the nine treasures are produced, and man *obtaineth* the marks of His favour.
What shall be the condition of him who *accepteth* not the Guru's doctrine?
The blind man hath forgotten the Name; the perverse is stone-blind.
His transmigration shall cease not; he shall be ruined by death and birth.
Woman may buy sandal, kungu, and red lead for the partings of her hair,
Distilled aloe wood, sandal, betel, and camphor in great quantities;
Yet, if she please not her Spouse, all her preparations are vain:
All her enjoyments are vain, and all her adornments are useless.
Until she is permeated by the Word, how shall she obtain honour at God's court?
Nanak, blest is the woman who loveth her Spouse.

The Guru's idea of creation :

From the True One *proceedeth* air, from air water,
And from water the three worlds; light was infused into every heart.
The Pure One *becometh* not impure: he who is imbued with the Word *obtaineth* honour.

Guru Nanak composed the following after a conversation with Samangir, a Sanyasi, at Talwandi. The Guru maintained the excellence of his own system and the advantage of repeating God's name obtained from the Guru:

If I turn myself into a woman, the Enjoyer will enjoy me. Love not that which appeareth transient.
The Spouse *enjoyeth* on His couch the pious virtuous wife.
Having under the Guru's instruction obtained God's *name* as the water, quench the four fires.
The lotus of the heart shall then bloom, and thou shalt be completely satiated with nectar.

Nanak, make the true Guru thy friend, and thou shalt obtain happiness in God's court.

The following is a homily addressed to a trader called Ramu whom the Guru met at Kartarpur:

Trade, O trader, and take care of thy merchandise.

But such goods as shall depart with thee.

In the next world is a wise Merchant who will be careful *in selecting* the real article.

O my brother, utter God's name with attention.

Take with thee God's praise as thy merchandise, so that, when the Merchant seeth it, He shall be satisfied.

How shall they whose wares are not genuine, be happy? But trading in counterfeit goods the soul and body become counterfeit.

Like a deer shared in a noose, *such a trader* shall suffer great misery and ever lament.

The counterfeit shall not be received in the great God's treasury, and they shall not behold Him.

The counterfeit have neither caste nor honour; the counterfeit are none of them acceptable.

The counterfeit who do counterfeit work, shall lose their honour in transmigration.

Nanak, instruct thy heart by the Guru's world and advice. They who are imbued with the love of God's name have no load of *sin* and no superstition.

They in whose hearts God dwelleth are without fear, and great shall be their gain by repeating His name.

The omnipresence of God:

He Himself is the Relisher; He Himself is the relish; He Himself is the Enjoyer;
He Himself is the robe; He Himself the couch and the Spouse—
My Lord, who is dyed with love, *pervadeth* everything—
He himself is the fisherman and the fish; He Himself is the water and the net.
He Himself is the lead of the net; He Himself is the bait within it.
O my friends, my Darling is in every way playful.
He ever *enjoyeth* the virtuous wife; see what a state is mine!
Nanak representeth, Thou art the lake, and Thou art the swan;
Thou art the lotus and the water lily, Thou art pleased on beholding them.

The following was a remonstrance to a Mulla and a Qazi who had entered on a discussion with the Guru:

He is the Lord who hath caused *the garden* of the world to flourish and grow green,

And who *restraineth* sea and land; hail to the Creator!

Thou must die, O Mulla, thou must die.

By all means fear and Creator.

Thou art a Mulla or a Qazi only when thou *really* knowest God's name.

Even if thou be very learned *thou must depart*; none may remain when his measure *of life* is full.

He is a Qazi who hath renounced pride, and made the name of God alone his support.

He is, was, and shall be: He was not born, neither shall He die; True is the Creator.

Thou prayest five times a day, and readest thy Quran and holy books.

Nanak saith, when the grave calleth, man shall cease to drink and eat.

Ashtapadi

The following was composed in a devotional paroxysm. Some suppose that it was uttered at Makka in reply to Qazis who had asked the Guru to tell them of the God he adored:

Persuade thy heart to sing *God's name* with every breath thou drawest.

How great is He is whom one playeth and singeth, and where *doth He dwell?*

All Thy eulogists continue to praise Thee with affection.

Father, God is inaccessible and endless.

Pure is the Name; pure is the place of the true Cherisher.

How great Thy sovereignty is cannot be known; not one *knoweth* how to describe it.

If a hundred poets were to be found, they could not describe a particle of it, though they sang their utmost.

Nobody hath found Thy worth; every one as he hath heard *describeth* Thy glory.

Priests, prophets, saints, faithful men, martys,

Saikhs, Strivers, Qazis, Mullas, Darweshes who have arrived *at God's* gate,

Obtain further blessings if they continue to recite God's praises.

He consulteth no one when He createth; He *consulteth* no one when He *destroyeth*; He *consulteth* no one when He *giveth* or *taketh*.

He *knoweth* His own might; He *acteth* and *causeth* others to act.

He *beholdeth* all men with favour, and *bestoweth* on those who please Him.

Neither His place nor His name is known, nor how great His name is among other names.

His great is that place where my Sovereign *dwelleth!*

None can read it; of whom shall I inquire *the way?*

High or low caste *influenceth not God* when He *maketh* any one great.

Greatness is in the hands of the Great One; He *giveth* to whom He *pleaseth*.

He *regenerateth* man by His order without any delay.

Everybody *crieth* 'Give me much, much', in the hope of getting it.

How great shall the Giver be called who *giveth* countless gifts!

Nanak *saith, O God*, Thy storehouses *are full* in every age, and never is there a deficiency.

It is said that a Qazi and a pandit asked the Guru how man could find God and be blended with Him. The following was the reply:

All the wives of the Spouse and adorn themselves *for Him.*

In trumpery red dresses have they come for His inspection.

Love is not obtained by hypocrisy; counterfeit gilding *degradeth.*

In this way God the Spouse shall enjoy the wife.

The good wife is pleasing to Thee, O Lord; of Thy favour Thou decoratest her.

She is decorated with the Guru's word; her body and soul are with her Beloved.

With hands clasped she *standeth* waiting on Him, and *offereth* Him true supplication.

She is imbued with the love of her Darling; she *dwelleth* in fear of the True One; when dyed *with His love,* her colour is the true one.

She is called the handmaiden of the Beloved, and *answereth* to the name of Lali.

Her true affection is not sundered; the True One *blendeth* her with Himself.

Her soul is imbued and saturated with the Word; I am ever a sacrifice unto her.

She who is absorbed in the True Guru, shall not sit down a widow.

Her Beloved is an abode of pleasure ever young and true; He neither death nor is born.

He ever *enjoyeth* His virtuous wife, and *casteth* true glances on her as she *obeyeth* Him.

She *maketh* truth the parting of her hair, and love her dress and ornaments.

She *maketh* the indwelling of God her sandal, and the *tenth* gate her chamber.

She *lighteth* the lamp of the Word, and *weareth* God's name asher necklet.

She *weareth* on her forehead the jewel of love, and she is beautiful among women.

Her beauty and wisdom are charming, and true is her infinite love.

She *knoweth* no man but her Beloved; it is only for the True Guru *she feeleth* love and affection.

But thou who are reckless on a dark night, how shalt thou pass it without the Beloved?

Thy bosom shall burn, thy body shall burn, and thy mind shall burn, O woman.

When women *enjoyeth* not her Husband, her youth passeth in vain.

Her Husband is one the couch; his wife *sleepeth* and *knoweth* not *His presence.*

While I sleep, the Beloved *awaketh;* whom shall I go to consult?

Nanak, the true Guru, having taught me love, hath caused me to meet God, and I abide in His fear.

The mind is impure until it receives instruction from a true religious teacher

When the mind is impure the body is impure, and the tongue impure.

The mouth is impure by uttering impurity; how shall it be made pure?

The heart cannot be cleansed without the Word; from the True One Truth is obtained.

O girl, what happiness is there without virtue?

Brahmans read books aloud, but understand not their meaning.

They give instruction to others as a business matter.

They wander about the world preaching falsehood; while they who abide by the Word are the best.

How many Pandits and astrologers study the Veds!

They glorify battles and enmities, but from quarrels *resulteth* transmigration.

However much they tell and preach what they have heard,man shall not be freed from his sins without the Guru.

All call themselves virtuous, but I possess no virtue.

Beautiful is the woman who hath God for her Spouse; that God *pleaseth* me.

Nanak, she who is united *with God* by the word shall not be separated *from Him.*

The following was addressed to Hindu devotees whom the Guru met in his wanderings in the Himalayas:

Though man perform lip-devotion, penance, and asuterities, dwell at places of pilgrimage,

Bestow alms and perform acts of devotion, what are these without the True One?

As he *soweth* so shall he reap; human life is lost without virtue.

O silly one, happiness is obtained by being a slave to virtue.

She who under the Guru's instruction *abandoneth* evil, shall be absorbed in the Perfect One.

The following is a brief lecture against hypocrisy, with a few precepts to obtain future happiness:

God carefully *draweth* the touchstone over man in order to assay them.

The counterfeit shall not be accepted; the genuine shall be put into His treasury.

Dispel hopes and fears, so shall thy *filth* be washed away.

Everybody *asketh* for happiness; nobody *asketh* for misery.

Great misery *attendeth* on happiness, but the perverse understand it not.

They who consider happiness and misery the same, and *know* the secret of the World shall be happy.

Man may escape from the dangers of this world by accepting the Guru and hearkening to his instructions:

The fearful ocean *of the world* is dangerous and formidable; it hath no shore or limit,

No boat, no raft, no pole, and no boatman;

But the true Guru hath a vessel for the terrible *ocean*, and ferrieth over him on whom he *looketh* with favour.

Love for God is inculcated by familiar Indian examples:

O man, entertain such love for God as the lotus hath for the water.

Such love *doth it bear it,* that it *bloometh* even when dashed down by the waves.

The creatures which God created in water die without it, and *therefore love it.*

O man, how shalt thou be delivered without love?

God pervadeth the hearts of the pious, and *bestoweth* on them a store of devotion.

O man, entertain such love for God as the fish for the water.

The more it hath, the happier it *becometh,* and the greater its peace of mind and body.

Without water it could not live for a moment; God alone *knoweth* the sufferings of its heart.

O man, entertain such love for God as the chatrik for rain:

Though the tanks be full and the earth drenched, it will not drink from either.

If so fated, it shall obtain *the rain-drops, otherwise* it is fated to die.

O man, entertain such love for God as water for milk.

The water alone is consumed in boiling and *alloweth* not the milk to be consumed.

God *uniteth* the separated, and *conferreth* true greatness.

O man, entertain such love for God as the chakwi for the sun.

She *sleepeth* not for a moment, for she *knoweth* that her mate is absent from her.

The perverse she not; to the pious God is ever present. The perverse make calculations, but it is only what the Creator *doeth* that *cometh* to pass.

His worth cannot be ascertained, even though all men desire it;

But it can be ascertained under the Guru's instruction; by meeting the True one happiness is obtained.

If the True Guru be met, true love shall not sunder,

And the wealth of divine knowledge of the three worlds shall be obtained.

If any one acquire virtue, he will not forget the Pure Name.

The birds which peck on sea and land have played and gone away.

Man must depart in a ghari or two; He enjoyment is only for to-day or to-morrow.

He whom Thou blandest with Thyself shall be blended with Thee, and shall take his place in the true arena.

Without the Guru love is not produced, and the filth of pride *departeth* not.

He who *recognizeth* God in himself, and *knoweth* the secret of the Word, shall be satisfied;

But when man *recognizeth* himself through the Guru's instruction, what more *remaineth* for him to do?

Why speak of meeting God? Man hath met Him *already, but it is only* on receiving the Word he iş satisfied.

The preserve obtain not understanding; separated *from God* they suffer punishment.

For Nanak there is but the gate of the one God; there is no other refuge.

It is said the following was addressed by the Guru, during his pilgrimage to the east, to a Raja called Harbans:

Man is led astray by the reading of words; ritualists are very proud.

What *availeth* it to bathe at a place of pilgrimage, if the filth of pride be in the heart?

Who but the Guru can explain that the King and Emperor *dwelleth* in the heart?

All men err; it is only the great Creator who *erreth* not.

He who *admonisheth* his heart under the Guru's instruction shall love the Lord.

Nanak, he whom the incomparable Word hath caused to meet God, shall not forget the True One.

God cannot be deceived and His merits canot be described:

By taking the protection of the Guru man shall be saved; counterfeit is the capital of the perverse.

The eight metals of the King are coined aggreeably to His orders.

The Assayer Himself *assayeth* the coins, and *putteth* the genuine into His treasury.

Thy merits, O Lord, cannot be ascertained; I have seen and tested everything.

Thy merits cannot be expressed by words; if man remain true, he shall obtain honour.

Under the Guru's instruction Thou, O Lord, art praised; otherwise Thy worth cannot be described.

The Guru prefers the repetition of God's name to all other forms of devotion:

My heart is penetrated by God's name; what else shall I reflect upon?

Happiness *cometh* to him who *meditateth* on the Word; perfect happiness to him who is imbued with God.

Preserve me as it *pleaseth* Thee, O God; Thy name is my support.

O man, just is the will of the Master.

Love Him who made and adorned thy body and mind.

Were my body to be cut into pieces and burnt in the fire;

Were I to turn my body and soul into firewood, and burn them night and day;

Were I to perform hundreds of thousands and millions of religious ceremonies, all would not be equal to God's name.

Were a saw to be applied to my head and my body to be cut in twain;

Were my body to be frozen in the Himalayas, even then my mind would not be free from disease—

It would all not be equal to God's name—I have seen and examined everything—

Were I to make offerings of millions of gold, many excellent horses and excellent elephants;

Were I to make large presents of lands and cows, even then pride would remain in my heart.

The Guru hath given me the true gift that my mind is penetrated by God's name.

How many opinions, and how many interpretations of the Veds through obstinacy!

How many entanglements there are for the soul! the gate of deliverance is *only obtained* through the Guru's instruction.

Everything is inferior to truth; the practice of truth is superior *to all else.*

Call every one exalted; let no one appear to thee low. The one God fashioned the vessels, and it is His light *that filleth* the three worlds.

By His favour man *obtaineth* the truth; what He *granteth* in the beginning none can efface.

The holy meet the holy; by love for the Guru man *obtaineth* consolation.

He who is absorbed in the True Guru *pondereth* on the Word of the Ineffable.

He who *drinketh* the nectar of the Name shall be satisfied, and go to God's court with a dress of honour.

The strain of ecstasy *resoundeth* night and day in the hearts of those who bear great love to the Word.

Few there are who obtain understanding by admonishing their hearts through their guru.

Nanak, they who forget not the Name, and who act according to the Word shall be delivered.

The following principally inculcates the inutility of worldly possessions and the superiority of devotion :

We see mansions painted and whitewashed with ornamented doors.

They were constructed to give pleasure to the heart, and through love and regard for worldly things, *but they shall fall to ruin.*

So the body which is empty within and possesseth no love, shall fall and become a heap of dust.

O my brethren, your bodies and wealth shall not accompany you.

God's name is the pure wealth; God *giveth* it through the Guru.

If the Giver give the true wealth of God's name,

The great Creator shall become man's friend, and no inquiry shall be made of him in the next world.

If God deliver man, he shall be delivered; God alone is the Pardoner.

The perverse men deemeth that daughters, sons, and relations are his.

He is pleased on beholding woman, but, as *she bringeth* joy, so she bringeth sorrow.

Holy men are imbued with the Word, and day and night enjoy divine happiness.

The mind of the wavering infidel *wandereth* in quest of transitory wealth.

Men ruin themselves by their search abroad while the Real Thing is in their homes.

The pious obtain It, the perverse miss It through pride.

O vicious infidel, know thine own origin.

Thy body made from blood and semen shall be brought to the fire *at last.*

The body is in the power of the breath according to the true mark on the forehead.

Men pray for a long life; no one *desireth* to die.

He is said to lead a happy life in whose heart God *dwelleth* through the Guru's instruction.

Of what account are they who are without the Name, and who therefore obtain not a sight of the great God?

As a man goeth astray at night in his sleep,

So *doth* he in whose heart there is pride and worldly love, and who is in the power of mammon.

To him who *reflecteth* under the Guru's instruction the world *appeareth* a dream.

As thirst is quenched when one findeth water; as the child *is sustained* by its mother's milk;

As the lotus cannot exist without water, and the fish would die without it,

So, Nanak, may I obtain divine happiness through the Guru's instruction and live singing God's praises!

Without the spiritual condition which is obtained by a repetition of the Name thee is no salvation:

I have become alarmed on seeing a terrible mountain in My Father's house.

Steep is the mountain and difficult to ascent; there is no ladder which will reach it;

But under the Guru's instruction I have found the secret; the Guru hath caused me to meet *God* and I am saved.

O my brethren, the ocean of the world is difficult and formidable.

If I have a satisfactory interview with the perfect true Guru, he will deliver me by *granting me* God's name.

If I say I am perishable, *it will not avail me*; but if I *really* know that I am perishable, *it will.*

Everything that came into this world shall depart; the Creator alone is immortal.

Be sure to praise the True One and love His abode.

Beautiful houses and places and thousands of strong holds,

Elephants, horses with their housing, and hundreds of thousands, yea, countless armed men

Will not depart with any one: *Their masters* pine away and die without gaining any advantage from them.

Thou mayest amass gold and silver, but wealth is an entangling net.

Man's authority may be proclaimed throughout the whole world, but without the Name death standeth over his head.

When the body falleth, the soul fleeth away; what shall be the condition of the evil doers?

The husband is delighted on beholding his sons and his wife on her couch;

He *applieth* distilled aloe wood and sandal; he *weareth fine* clothes and *decorateth* himself;

Yet shall he leave his family and depart; dust shall return to dust.

He may be styled a chief, an emperor, a king, a governor, or a lord;

He may be called the headman of a town or a governor; he may burn with pride;

Yet by perversely forgetting the Name he shall be as a reed burnt in the fire.

Having come into the world, he shall depart however proud he be.

The whole world is a chamber of lampblack; the body and soul which enter it shall be tarnished.

They who are preserved by the Guru are pure; the fire of their desires is extinguished by the Word.

Nanak, man *obtaineth* deliverance by the true name of the King of kings.

May I not forget God's Name! may I purchase it as a jewel!

The perverse man perisheth in the terrible ocean *of the world*; the holy man *crosseth* it, unfathomable *though it be.*

Ghar III

Definitions :

How it Sat Sangat, the *Society of the holy*, known?
The name of the one God is mentioned there.
How are Duhagins—*women separated from their husbands*—known?
They are those who forgetful of their Spouse wander unhonoured.
They who are pleased with God's will,
Remove superstition from their minds.
Nanak, the true Guru, is known by his association with every one.

Sri Rag ki War

Some virtues which contribute to perfection :

Faith and regignation are the characteristics of the holy; patience is the viaticum of angels.

The perfect shall obtain a sight of God; the fool shall find no place will Him.

Caste is vain and contributes not to goodness or holiness:

Castes are folly, names are folly:
All creatures have one shelter, *that of God.*
If a man call himself good,
The truth shall be known, O Nanak, when his account is accepted.

Man, no matter what his caste or social position may be, is exalted by devotion:

What difference is there between a swan and a crane, if God look kindly *on the latter*?

Nanak, if it please Him, He can change a raven into a swan.

Majh ki War

God as the Guru:

The Guru is the Giver, the Guru is the house of snow, the Guru is the lamp of the three worlds

Nanak, the Guru *possesseth* the immortal wealth; by putting faith in Him happiness is obtained.

The ten stages of man:

In man's *first* stage he loveth the milk of his mother's breast;
In his *second* he *recognizeth* his father and mother;
In his *third* his brother, his brother's wife, and his own sister;
In the *fourth* a love of play *ariseth* in him;
In the *fifth* he runneth after food and drink;
In the *sixeth* he *inquireth* not *a woman's* caste in his lust;
In the *seventh* he *colleteth* things for a house to live in;
In the *eighth* his body is wasted by wrath;
In the *ninth* he *groweth* grey and his breathing is difficult;
In the *tenth* he is burnt and *becometh* ashes.
His companions accompany him *to his pyre* with loud lamentations.
The souls flieth away, showing the road *of departure* to others.
He came, he died and departed—*leaving only* a name.
After his death *his relations offer food* on leaves, and call and crows.
Nanak, the perverse love mental darkness.
Without a guru the world is lost.

Other divisions of human life :

At ten a child, at twenty a rake, at thirty man *calleth* himself handsome;
At forty he is in his prime, at fifty his feet halt, at sixty old age *cometh* on;
At seventy he loseth his intellect, at eighty he cannot perform his duties;
At ninety he reclineth on his couch, and feeleth no strength whatever in himself.

I, Nanak, have sought and searched, and seen that the world is a mansion of smoke.

The following is said to have been addressed to a holy man called Thakur Das at Priyag:

Were I to dwell in the cavern of a golden mountain or in a pit of water;
Were I to stand on my head, on earth or in the heavens;
Were I to cover all my body with clothes, and did I nothing but bathe;
Were I to shout aloud the white, the red, the yellow, and the black Veds;
Were I to remain dirty and filthy, all this would be foolish and sinful.
Nanak, since I have pondered on the World, I am not, I was not, I shall not be.

Guru Nanak declared the folly of external purifications :

Man washeth his clothes and his body, and mortifieth himself.

Knowing not of the filth attaching to his heart, he rubbeth and cleanseth himself externally.

Being blind he is led astray, and falleth into Death's noose.

He *deemeth* the property of others as his own, and *suffeereth* for his pride.

Nanak, when pride is dispelled under the Guru's instructions, man *meditateth* on God's name,

Repeateth the Name, adoreth the Name, and though the Name is absorbed in happiness.

Some important subjects are briefly treated as follows :

God hath caused the union of body and soul;
He who created them can separate them.
A fool while enjoying pleasure hath all pain;
Disease proceedeth from sinful pleasure.
From worldly rejoicing *proceedeth* mourning, separation from God, birth and death
The fool while boasting *becometh* involved in disputes;
The decision *resteth* with the True Guru; He *putteth* an end to disputes.
That which the Creator *doeth cometh* to pass; what man hath set in motion must stop.

The following was addressed by the Guru to a Qazi at Sultanpur:

Thou utterest falsehood, eatest carrion,
Yet thou goest to admonish others.
Cheated thyself thou now cheatest thy companions.
Nanak *saith*, that is the sort of guide thou appearest!

As a Qazi beheaded a goat, some drops of blood fell on his garments, which he at once wiped off. He said that he could not join in prayer until the pollution had been removed. The following was uttered by the Guru on the occasion:

If clothes become defiled by blood falling on them,
How can the hearts of those who drink human blood be pure?
Nanak, utter God's name with a pure heart *regardless of thy dress.*
All else is but worldly ostentation; thou, O *Qazi* practisest falsehood.

The Qazi asked Guru Nanak who is was. The latter replied as follows :

Since I am nobody, what shall I say : since I am nothing, what can I be?
As God made me, I act; as He told me, I speak; I am thoroughly defiled *with sin, and desire* to wash it away.
Though I know nothing myself, yet I teach others; such a guide am I.
Nanak, he who being blind *showeth* the road to others and misleadeth all his companions,
Shall he shoe-beaten in the next world, and it will be seen what sort of guide he was.

Everything shall vanish except God:

Of kings, subjects, and rulers none shall remain:
Shops, cities, bazars shall be destroyed by God's order.
Solid and beautiful mansions a fool *deemeth* his own;
Storehouses filled with wealth in a moment become empty.
Steeds, chariots, camels, elephants and their housing, Gardens, properties,

houses and homes,

Tents, comfortables beds, and ornamental pavilions—where shall they be recognized?

The following was delivered to Sikhs who asked the Guru what pleasure God's praises afforded him:

Were rivers to become kine, and springs to become milk and clarified butter;

Were the whole earth to become sugar so that the heart might ever rejoice;

Were the mountains to become gold and silver, and be studded with diamonds and rubies;

I would ever then magnify Thee, and the desire to do so would not cease as I spoke.

Were the eighteen loads of *vegetables of the earth* to become fruit, and grass to become rice;

Could I arrest the moon and sun in their courses, and were my seat to become immovable.

I would even then magnify Thee, and the desire to do so would not cease as I spoke.

Could I inflict pain by means of the two sinful beings Rahu *and Ketu*;

Could I obtain authority over bloodthirsty kings and my glory thus shine forth,

I would even then magnify Thee, and the desire to do so would not cease as I spoke.

Were fire and frost to become my raiment, and the wind my food;

Were all the fascinating women of heaven to become my wives—all pershable—

I would even then magnify Thee, and the desire to do so would not cease as I spoke.

Caste becomes deadly if exclusive reliance be placed on it for salvation:

What power hath caste? It is the reality that is tested. Poison may be held in the hand, but man dieth if he eat it. The sovereignty of the True One is known in every age. He who obeyeth God's order shall become a noble in His court.

The following allegory of mounted cavalry refers to the different stages of asceticism:—

The Master sent obedience to His orders as a steed *into the world*;

Reflection on the instruction which *the Guru* imparteth is its kettle-drums.

Some have mounted their steeds, others have them ready caparisoned;

Some have loaded their baggage *for the march*, and others have set out.

In the following allegory the mill is the world, the corn is the soul, the husk the body, refuge in God the axle:

When *the field* is ripe, it is cut; only the chaff and the hedge remain.

The corn is threshed with the husk, and the chaff is winnowed away.

Men then put together the two mill-stones and sit down to grind corn.

That which *attacheth* to the axle escapeth. Nanak hath seen a wonderful thing.

Good men, like sugar-cane, are subject to torture:

See how sugar-cane is cut down and made into sheaves after the stalks are cleaned.

The labourers put it into a press and squeeze it.

Having expressed the juice, they put it into a pan, and it groaneth as it burneth.

The residue is collected and put into the fire *beneath the pan.*

Nanak, sweet things are thus ill-treated; come and see, O people.

It is useless to endeavour to instruct a fool :

What can deep water do to fish? What can the sky do to a bird?

What can cold do to a stone? What can married life do to a eunuch?

Even though thou apply sandal to a dog, he will still preserve his canine nature:

Even though thou instruct a deaf man, and read for him the Simritis;

Even though thou place a light before a blind man, and burn fifty lamps for him, *all would be of no avail.*

Even though thou put gold before a herd of cattle, they would still pick out the grass to eat.

If a flux be put into iron it will melt, but not become cotton.

Nanak, the peculiarity of a fool is that what is said to him is ever lost.

When his Sikhs inquired how an alliance could be formed with God the Guru composed the following :

When bronzee, gold, and iron break,

The blacksmith *weldeth* them by means of fire.

When a husband *falleth* out with his spouse,

A reconciliation is effected in this world through children.

When the king *asketh* and *his subjects* give, a bond is established between their.

When a hungry man *eateth,* he *establisheth* an alliance *with the world.*

Drought *formeth* a alliance with rivers when they are flooded with rain.

There is an affinity between love and sweet words.

If any one speak the truth, he *formeth* a bond with knowledge.

By goodness and truth the dead establish a bond with the *living.*

Such are the affinities that are established in the world.

The only way to establish friendship with a fool is to smite him on the mouth.

By praising God man *establisheth* an alliance with God's court.

Nanak saith this deliberately.

The following seven sloks form part of the Guru's instruction to Shaikh Brahm, or Farid the second, of Pak Pattan:

The priests, the shaikhs, and the potentates *of the world* are all beneath the earth.

Emperors pass away, but God ever *flourisheth.*

There is only Thou, there is only Thou, O god!

Neither demigods, nor demons, nor men,
Nor Sikhs, nor Strivers, nor this earth *shall abide.*
There is One; is there any other?
There is only Thou, there is only Thou, O God!

Neither the just nor the generous,
Nor the seven regions *beneath* the earth *shall remain.*
There is One : is there any other?
There is only Thou, there is only Thou, O God!

Not the regions of the sun and the moon,
Nor the seven continents, nor the seven seas,
Nor corn, nor wind shall abide.
There is only Thou, There is only Thou, O God!

Our maintenance is in nobody's power *but God's* :
To *all* of us but one hope *abideth*—
There is one : is there any other?
There is only Thou, there is only Thou, O God!

Birds have no money in their possession:
They only depend on trees and water.
God is their Giver.
There is only Thou, There is only Thou, O God!

Nanak, no one can erase
What is written on the forehead.
God it is who *giveth* man power and again *taketh* it away.
There is only Thou, there is only Thou, O God!

Guru Nanak thus discoursed to Prem Chand of Sarhind on the best way of occupying time:

They who in the early morning praise God and meditate on Him with single heart,

Are perfect kings, and die fighting when occasion *ariseth*.

In the second watch there are many says in which the attention of the mind is distracted.

Many persons fall into the fathomless water, and cannot emerge however much they struggle.

In the third watch when hunger and thirst are both barking, food is put into the mouth.

What is eaten *becometh* filth, yet man again *desireth* food.

In the fourth watch drowiness *cometh*, man closeth his eyes and *goeth* into dreamland.

Again rising *in the morning* he *engateth* in turmoil, and yet *maketh* preparations to live a hundreds years.

If man feel love for God every moment during the eight watches of the day,

O Nanak, God will dwell in his heart and true shall be his ablution.

Man's continual thought should be devotion to His Maker:

When Thou art near, what more do I desire? I speak verily.

He who is deceived by false worldly occupations *reacheth* not God's palace:

His heart is hard and he *loseth* his service.

The house which *containeth* not the True One, should be destroyed and rebuilt.

When its owner is weighed, how shall he be found of full weight?

If he lose his pride, no one will say he is of short weight. The genuine shall be assayed, and selected at the gate of the All-seeing.

The true goods are only is one shop: they are obtained from the perfect Guru.

The advantages conferred on men by the True One:

Without the True One all are false and practice falsehood.
Without the True One the false shall be bound and led away;
Without the True One the body is dust and shall be rolled in the dust;
Without the True One dress and food are all hunger;
Without the Time One the false shall not attain God's court.
The false attached to avarice miss God's palace.
The whole world is *deceived,* and cometh and *goeth* in deception.
In the heart is the fire of greed which is quenched by the Guru's instruction.

The adventages of the Guru, who is likened to a life-giving tree:

Nanak, the Guru is the tree of contentment, whose blossom is religion and whose fruit is divine knowledge.

It aboundeth in succulence and is ever green; it *ripeneth* by good works and meditation.

Honour is obtain by partaking of its religh; it is the greatest of gifts.

There is tree of gold; its leaves are corals; its blossoms, jewels and rubies.

It beareth gems for fruit, and the heart of him who *eateth* it *rejoiceth.*

Nanak, it is obtained by him on whose forehead such destiny hath been recorded.

The sixty-eight places of pilgrimage are at the Guru's feet, and ever specially worship them.

Crudty, *worldly* love, avarice, and wrath are four streams of fire:

They who fall into them are burnt O Nanak, but deliverance is obtained by cleaving to good works.

The evil of forgetting god:

In the heart and mouth of the perverse who never remember Thee,

Abide *the bitterness of* the gourd, the colocynth, and the nim, and the poison of the akk and dhatura.

Nanak, to whom shall I tell it? *Whose forget Thee* wander bereft of Thy favour, O God.

The unequal conditions of men:

The bird, man, by his ideas an his acts sometimes flieth high and sometimes low,

He sometimes percheth on a sandal-tree, sometimes on the branch of the akk-shrub, and sometimes again he loveth high flight.

Nanak saith, it is the custom of the Lord to lead all beings by His order.

Women's duty :

If women adorn themselves with love and affection for their Spouse,
They shall not be restrained from their devotion to Him day to night.
They shall abide in His chambers, and the Word shall regenerate them;
They shall humbly supplicate the True One;
And they shall appear beautiful near their Spouse, walking according to His order.
They shall make hearty supplication to the Beloved.
Accursed the homes, wretched the lives of those who possess not the Word.
They whose hopes are fulfilled by the Word quaff nectar.

The Guru was requested to state the extent of his love of devotion:

The desert is not satisfied with rain, and the hunger of fire is not appeased;
Kings are not satisfied with dominion; who hath ever filled the ocean?
How much hath Nanak inquired after the True Name *and not been satisfied*;
Bhai Rama of Sulta pur inquired how God was known. The Guru replied:
He to whom God *giveth* understanding *understandeth;*
He is whom He *giveth* knowledge *knoweth* everything.
Man merely *worrieth* himself when he *preacheth* for the sake of mammon.
The commander, who created all things,
Himself possesseth all knowledge.
He Himself, Nanak, spoke the Word
Doubt shall depart from him to whom He gave it.

The Guru's reward for singing God's praises :

Me, a minstrel out of work, God *applieth* to His work;
He ordered me in the beginning to sing His praises night and day.
The Master summoned the minstrel to His true court,
And put on him a robe of true praise and eulogy:
He then obtained the ambrosial food of the true Name.
They who have eaten under the Guru's instruction are satisfied, and have obtained comfort.
The minstrel uttereth praise and singeth the Word.
Nanak, he who *uttereth* true praise *obtaineth* the Perfect One.

Rag Gauri

The advantages resulting from the fear of God:

The fear of God is very great and very heavy.
Man's wisdom is of little account, and so is his chatter.

Walk with the load *of fear* on thy head;
Meditate on the Guru who is kind and merciful.
No one shall be saved without the fear of God:
His fear hath adorned mean's love.
The fire of the fear of transmigration is burned away by the fear of God.
By fear the Word is fashioned and decorated.

What is fashioned without fear is altogether worthless :

Unless is the mould and useless the stroke thereon.
In the minds of many there is a desire *to fashion the Word without fear*;
But even though they perform a thousand artifices they shall not succeed.
Nanak, the speech of the perverse is nonsense;
What they write is worthless absurdity.

The following was addressed by the Guru to one who had remonstrated with him for having left his relations to lead a wandering life:

Make wisdom thy mother, contentment thy father,
Truth thy brother—this a best.
People talk, but talking is of no avail.
The measure of Thy might, O God, cannot be obtained.
Modesty and attention are my two parents-in-law;
Good works I have accepted as my spouse;
Union *with saints* hath been my auspicious time *for marriage*, and separation *from the* world my wedding.
Saith Nanak, from such a union hath sprung truth as may offspring.

The composition of man's body and the inutility of pilgrimages; the body dies, but not the soul:

The body is a mixture of wind, water and fire;
Within it is the changeful play of the intellect.
The body hath nine gates and a tenth door;
O wise man, understand and reflect on this.
God *speaketh, preacheth* and *listeneth;*
He who reflecteth on himself is a wise man.
The body is earth, the wind *speaketh* therein.
Consider, O wise man, what it is that dieth—
It is the quarrelsome and proud understanding.
The conscious soul dieth not.
The precious jewel, for which men go on pilgrimages,
Dwelleth within the heart.
Pandits read and argue.
But know not that which is within themselves.
When my spiritual ignorance dieth, I die not myself.
He who is everywhere contained dieth not.
Saith Nanak, when the Guru showed me God,

No one seemed to me to die or to be born.

One Sant Das propounded six questions to Guru Nanak :

Is it known whence man hath come,
Whence he hath sprung, in what he shall be absorbed,
How he is bound, how he *obtaineth* emancipation,
And how he shall be easily absorbed in the Imperishable?

The Guru replied :

The Name is nectar in the heart as well as in the mouth:
Though it man is freed from worldly desires.
Man cometh in the course of nature and goeth in the course of nature.
Man is born according to *the desires* of his heart, and he is absorbed in the same way.
The pious man is emancipated and *falleth* into no entanglements:
He is delivered by meditation on the Word and by God's name.
Many birds roost by night on a tree—
Some happy, *others* unhappy—they whose minds have worldly love perish.
When night hath passed away, they gaze upon the sky:
They fly in every direction according to the destiny recorded for them.
They who are associated with the Name *deem the world* like a meeting-place of cowherds:
The poisonous vessels of lust and wrath have burst for them.
To those without the capital of *the Name* houses and shops are empty;
But by meeting the Guru the adamant doors *of their understanding* are opened.
A holy man is met by primal destiny.
God's perfect people are rendered happy by truth:
They barter their souls and bodies for divine knowledge and God's love.
Nanak toucheth their feet.

The following is a conversation between soul and body:

The Soul : 'O body, *thou thinkest* thyself immortal, and that thou shalt be *always* happy—*know that* this world is a play.
Thou practisest avarice, covetousness, and excessive falsehood, and bearest many burdens.
I have seen thee, O body, trodden as ashes on the ground.'
The Body : 'Hearken, hearken to mine instruction.
If thou have done good works, they shall abide with thee;
O my soul, thou shalt not again find such opportunity.'
The Soul : 'I address thee, O my body, hearken to my instruction.
Thou slenderest and bearest false witness against others.'
The Body : 'Thou covetest another's vine, O soul; thou committest theft and evil deeds.'
The Soul : 'When the soul *departeth,* thou shalt remain behind like an abandoned woman.

Thou, O body, halt remain but as a dream—what *good* deeds hast thou done?'

The Body : 'Whatever I took by stealth was pleasing to thee.

Thou hast no honour in this world, and thou shalt be rejected in the next; thou hast lost thy human dwelling in vain.'

I am very unhappy, O father, saith Nanak, no one careth for me.

Arabian and Turkish steeds, gold, silver, and loads of raiment.

No one taketh with him; they leave him *in this world*, O fool.

Sugar, fruit, all have I tasted; it is only thine ambrosial Name *which is sweet.*

Man diggeth deep foundations and constructeth edifices on them, *but they shall become at last* heaps of dust.

He hoardeth, and hoardeth, and giveth to no one; the fool thinketh that all is his own.

Rawan nominally possessed a golden Lanka and a golden palace, but they were no one's property.

Hear, O foolish and ignorant soul :

What pleaseth *God* shall be done.

My Lord is a great Merchant, we are His retail-dealers.

Our souls and bodies are all his capital; He it is who killeth and re-animateth.

The Guru reflects on the power of the deadly sins which lead men to destruction :

The others are five, I am but one; how shall I protect my house?

They ever assail and plunder me; to whom shall I complain?

Utter God's holy name, O my soul;

Before thee is Death's army fierce and numerous.

God erected a palace, put doors to it, and the woman sitteth within.

Deeming the world sweet, she ever sporteth, but these five men rob her.

When Death destroyeth the palace, her chamber is sacked, and she being alone is captured.

She is beaten by Death's mace, and his chains are riveted on her neck; the five men have taken flight.

The housewife wanteth gold and silver; friends want banquets.

Nanak, they who commit sin for these things shall go bound to Death's city.

Kinganath Jogi pressed Guru Nanak to become his disciple; the Guru replied that he had already learned the science of Jog. He composed the following hymn on the occasion :

Make restraint of thine in most heart thine earrings, thy body the patches coat;

Reduce the five senses to subjection, O Jogi, and make a *pure* heart thy staff.

In this way shalt thou obtain the way of jog.

Make the fact that there is but one World and none other thy devotion to tubers and roots

If God could be obtained by merely shaving the head, we should make a god of the Ganges.

It is the one Lord who *saveth* the three worlds; thou thinkest not of Him, O fool.

If thou apply thy mind to words through hypocrisy, thy doubts shall never leave thee.

If thou turn thy thoughts to the feet of the one God, why pursue avarice and greed?

If thou repeat the Name of the Bright One, thy soul shall be absorbed in Him.

O Jogi, why utterest thou so much deceit?

They *body is mad,* thy mind is silly, thou passest thy life talking of thy property.

Nanak *representeth,* it is after the naked body is burnt the soul regretted *lost opportunities.*

Man's precious life should not be wasted, but should be devoted of God's service and not to the acquisition of wealth:

Man loseth his nights in sleeping and his days in eating :
His human life, valuable as a diamond, the parteth with for a kauri.
Thou knowest nor God's name; O fool, thou shalt here after regret.
Thou buriest endless wealth in the earth, yet thy desire for it *departeth* not.
They who departed desiring endless wealth lost the Endless One.
If all were to obtain according to their desires, they would be happy.
Whatever all may desire, a man's fate is decided by his acts.
Nanak, He who fashioned creation *taketh* care of it.
It is not known on whom God's order will confer greatness.

The Gervour of the Guru's devotion:

Were I to become a fawn, live in the forest, and gather and eat tubers and roots,

I should ever and ever be a sacrifice to my Lord, who is obtained through of favour of the Guru.

I am a retail-dealer of Thine, O god;

The Name is my stock-in-trade and my merchandise.

Were I to become a koil and live in a mango-tree, I should still tranquilly meditate on the Word.

Through my love my Lord, whose form *appeareth* unequalled, would naturally meet me.

Were I to become a fish and dwell in the water, *I should still remember Him* who *watcheth* over all animals.

My Spouse dwelleth on this side and on that; I shall stretch forth mine arm to touch Him.

Were I to become a serpent and dwell in the ground, I should still abide in the Word and my fears would depart.

Nanak, they are ever the happy married wives whom God hath absorbed in His light.

Gauri Ashtapadi

Without a religious guide man would run riot in evil and haste to perdition :

The heart is an elephants, the body a forest,
The Guru the goad; when the mark of the true Word is *made on the elephant,*

He shall obtain honour in the King's court.
God cannot be known by cleverness.
Without chastening the mind how can God be appraised?
In the house is nectar which the thieves are taking away :
No one tried to restrain them.
If any one guard the nectar, God Himself will confer greatness on him.

Worldly wealth, comforts, and pleasures would never satisfy the Guru without devotion to God.

I may apply distilled aloe wood and sandal to my body, I may wear silks and satisn,
But without God's name how shall I obtain happiness?
What shall I wear ? in what dress shall I show myself? How shall I obtain happiness without the Lord of the world?
I may have rings in mine ears and a necklace of pearls on my neck,
A red coverlet, flowers, and red powder;
But where should I search for happiness except with the Lord of the world?
A beautiful woman with expressive eyes
May make the sixteen decorations and *render herself* very lovely,
Yet without worshipping the Lord of the world she would ever be despised.
One may have in his house or palace a comfortable couch;
A flower-girl may scatter flowers on it day and night,
Yet without God's name its owner would be unhappy.
Excellent horses, elephants, lances, musical instruments,
Armies, mace-bearers, and attendants are worthless and vain shows without the Lord of the world.
I may be called a Sikh, and I may summon wealth and supernatural power to me;
I may make for my head a crown, a regal hat, and an umbrella,
Yet how should I obtain real happiness without the Lord of the world?
I may be styled a lord, an emperor, or a king.
I may say 'Now then' *to inferiors; all this* would be false displays.
Without the Guru's instruction my business could not be adjusted.
Egotism and selfishness are forgotten under the Guru's instruction.
Through the Guru's instruction it is known that God is in the heart.
Nanak supplicateth, I *seek* Thy shelter, O God.

The Guru describes the condition of the holy and the means of salvation:

He who *serveth* the one God *knoweth* not others:
He layeth aside the bitter things deceit and evil.
By love and truth shalt thou meet the Truests of the True.
If there be any such saint of God,
His filth shall be washed away, and he shall meet God by singing His praises.
Reversed are the lotuses of all men's hearts :
The fire of evil inclinations burneth away the world,

While those who meditate on the word of the Guru are saved.
The bumble-bee, the month, the elephant, the fish,
And the deer suffer the consequences of their acts and die.
Absorbed in worldly desires man *knoweth* not the Real Thing;
He *thinketh* of lust and love for woman,
Which with wrath ruin all sinners.
He who forgetteth the Name, loseth his honour and his senses.
The perverse being who *alloweth* his mind to covet another's house,
Hath a halter round his neck, and is entangled in difficulties;
While the pious shall be delivered by singing God's praises.
As a widow, who *giveth* her body to a stranger,
And through lust or money *falleth* into another's power,
Is never satisfied without a lover;
So man readeth books and *reciteth* the Simritis;
He also *readeth, heareth* and *expoundeth* the Veds and the Purans;
But without being dyed with *God's* essence his mind is very unstable.
As the chatrik *loveth* and *thirsteth* for the rain-drips,
As the fish is delighted with the water,
So Nanak is satisfied quaffing God's essence.

There was a hill king called Amar Singh who was dethroned by his brother. On being expelled he went to Guru Nanak for advice. The following was given him :

They who wear religious garbs are full of pride and know not *God.*

Few are they whose minds are reconciled to devotion under the Guru's instruction.

The True One is not obtained by the practice of egotism. When pride departeth, the supreme dignity is obtained. Kings under the influence of pride make many expeditions :

They are ruined by pride and remain subject to transmigration.
He who *meditateth* on the Guru's word shall lose his pride;
He shall dismiss his wandering thoughts, and destroy his deadly sins.
He in whose heart is the truth shall easily arrive at God's court,
And, Knowing God, shall obtain the supreme state.
The Guru dispelleth the doubts of those whose works are true;
And they shall obtain a fixed seat in the court of the Fearless.
What do they retain who die talking of their possessions?
He who *meeteth* a perfect Guru *putteth* an end to his contentions.
What there is, is nothing *in reality*—
The pious who are saturated with divine knowledge sing God's praises.
The fetters of pride cause man to wander in transmigration.
Nanak, it is the saint of God who *obtaineth* happiness.

Death impends over all, but cannot harm the holy :

Even Brahma was subject to death from the beginning.

He found not *the end* of Visnu's lotus in the nether regions;
He accepted not God's order, and was led astray in error.
Whatever is created Death destroyeth.
God hath preserved us by our meditating on the word of the Guru.
Maya deludeth all the gods and goddesses.
Death looseth not his hold on him who *serveth* not the Guru.
God is imperishable, invisible and inscrutable.
Emperors, rulers, and kings shall not abide.
Having forgotten the Name they shall undergo death's torture.
The Name is my support; I shall abide as Thou Keepest me, O Lord.
Chiefs and kings have no abiding-place.
Bankers die after accumulating wealth and money.
O God, grant me Thine ambrosial name as my wealth.
Subjects, lords, headmen, sovereigns—
None is found permanent in this world.
Irresistible death striketh false mortals on the head.
One alone, the Truest of the true, is immovable.
All those whom He created He will again destroy.
Man obtaineth honour when he *knoweth* God under the Guru's instruction.
Qazis, shaikhs, and faqirs in religious garbs
Call themselves great, but through pride their bodies are in pain.
Death will not release them without *receiving* the true Guru's consolation.
The net of Death is over man's tongue and eyes;
It is over his ears when he listeneth to unchaste language.
He is robbed day and night without the Word.
Death cannot espy him in whose heart
God's true name dwelleth, and who singeth God's praises—
Nanak, the pious shall be absorbed in the Word.

A prayer to God for protection :

As a herdsman *guardeth* and *keepeth* watch over his cattle,

So God day and night *cherisheth* and guardeth man and keepeth him in happiness.

O Thou compassionate to the poor, I seek Thy protection; look on me with favour.

Preserve me in this world and the next.

Wherever I look there art Thou contained; guard me, O guardian.

Thou art the Giver, Thou art the Enjoyer, Thou art the support of the soul.

Man must supplement his prayers by good acts :

Without meditating on divine knowledge, man *ascendeth* or *descendeth* according to his acts.

Without praising the Lord of the world the darkness of ignorance shall not be dispelled.

We see that the world is perishing through covetousness and pride.

By serving the Guru, God and the true gate of salvation are attained.

What hath man brought into the world?
What shall be take away when he is entangled in Death's noose?
Like a well-bucket firmly attached to a rope, he is now in heaven, now in hell.

A spiritual guide is necessary for salvation:

His account is settled who through the Guru's favour *knoweth* God.
God, called the Pure One, who is in every heart, is my Lord.
Man shall not be emancipated without the Guru's instruction; see and ponder upon this.
Even though man performed hundreds of thousands of ceremonies, all would still be darkness without the Guru.
What shall we say to those who are blind and devoid of wisdom?
Without the Guru the way cannot be seen; how shall we reach the goal?
Man calleth the counterfeit genuine; but he *knoweth* not what the genuine is.
A blind man he *calleth* an assayer; wonderful is this age.
Man saith, the sleeper is awake, and he who is awake *sleepeth;*
He saith, they who are alive are dead, and he *weepeth* not for those *who are really dead*;
He saith, that he who is coming hath gone, and that he who hath gone is coming;
He calleth another's property his own, and with his own he is not satisfied;
He calleth what is sweet bitter, and what is bitter sweet;
He slandereth those who love God—such is what I have seen in this age.
Man serveth a handmaiden, but the Master he seethe not.
He churneth tank water, and no butter is produced.
He who can explain this it the Guru for me.
Nanak, he who *knoweth* himself is unequalled and unrivalled.

Gauri Chhant

The longing of the pious for God is compared to the longing of the young bride for her spouse :

Painful is the night for the young bride; *without her Beloved* she sleepeth not.
She pineth away through grief *at His absence* :
The woman pineth away through grief at *his absence, saying* 'How shall I look upon Him?
Ornaments, dainty food, sensuous enjoyments are all vain and of no account for her.
Intoxicated with the wine of youth and melting with pride milk cometh not to her brest.
Nanak, she meeteth her Spouse when He *causeth* her to meet Him; without Him no sleep cometh to her.
The bride is unhonoured without her beloved Lord.
How shall she be happy without embracing Him?
Without a spouse there is no domestic happiness; ask thy friends and companions.

Without the Name there is no love or affection; but, with the True One, woman abideth in happiness.

They in whose hearts there is truth and contentment, meet and Friend; under the Guru's instruction the Bridegroom is recognized.

Nanak, the woman who abandoneth not the Name shall be easily absorbed in God through it.

Come, friends and companions, let us enjoy our Beloved. I will ask my Guru and write His words of love.

The Guru hath communicated to me the true Word; the perverse shall regret *they have not received it.*

When I recognized the True One, my roaming mind became fixed.

The wisdom of the True One is ever new, so is the love of His word.

Nanak, true peace of mind is obtained from His look of favour; meet Him, my friends and companions.

My desires have been fulfilled; the Friend hath come home to me.

A song of rejoicing was sung at the union of Husband and wife.

His praises and a song of joy were sung; the bride is happy in His love and her heart is in raptures.

Her friends are also happy, her enemies unhappy; true profit is obtained by repeating the name of the True One.

With clasped hands the woman *prayeth* that she may night and day be steeped in God's love.

Nanak, the Beloved and His spouse unite in dalliance; my desires have been fulfilled.

Rag Asa

The Creator bestows good gifts :

If a beggar at God's gate cry aloud, God *heareth* him in His palace.

God may give him consolation or repulse him; He alone *bestoweth* greatness.

God *knoweth* man's virtues and *inquireth* not his caste; in the next world there is no caste.

God *acteth* Himself and *causeth* to act.

Thou, O Creator, prayest heed to man's complaints.

Since it is Thou alone who actest,

Why should we be dependent *on any but Thee?* What is the world to us?

Thou Thyself didst create; Thou Thyself dost bestow;

Thou forbiddest evil inclinations.

If Thou by the Guru's favour dwell in the heart,

Suffering and the darkness of ignorance shall depart therefrom.

Thou givest truth to those whom Thou lovest;

Thou givest truth to none besides.

If Thou give truth to any one, saith Nanak, there shall be no inquiry made of him hereafter.

The following was addressed to a votary of Krishan, who was worshiping his god with music and dancing:

Make understanding thy fife, the love of God thy drum;
By these joy and earnest desire are ever produced in thee heart.
This is devotion; this is austerity—
In this wise dance beating time with thy feet.

Deem knowing how to praise God as beating time:
Other dances are sensuous pleasures.
Play truth and contentment as thy pair of cymbals;
Make the perpetual vision *of God* the bells for thy feet;
Make love for none but God thy measures and songs—
In this wise dance beating time with thy feet.
Ever make the fear of God in thy heart and soul,
Whether sitting or standing, thy gyrations.
Make the knowledge that thy body is ashes thy recumbent posture—
In this wise dance beating time with thy feet.
Thine audience shall be the disciples who love instruction,
Who hear the true Name from the Guru's lips,
And repeat it again and again—
Nanak, in this wise dance beating time with thy feet.

The following was intended to show God's superiority to His creatures Ram and Krishan, who are now adored as gods by the Hindus:

God have created the atmosphere supported the whole earth and set bounds to water and fire.

The fatuous Rawan had his ten heads cut off; what greatness was obtained by slaying him ?

What praise of Thine, O God, shall be uttered?

Thou pervadest everything; Thou lovest all Thy *creatures.*

Having created living beings, Thou holdest their ways in Thy hand. What greatness was obtained by putting a nose-ring on the black serpent of *the Jamna?*

Whose husband art Thou? Who is Thy wife? Thou pervadest all things.

Brahma, the granter of favours, with his progeny went to ascertain God's greatness,

But could not find His limits; what greatness was obtained by slaying Kans?

When the sea of milk was churned and its gems brought forth, the *demigods and demons* each claimed the merit thereof.

What greatness was obtained by the distribution of the gems to each? Saith Nanak, if men try to conceal Thy greatness, *O God*, how can it be concealed?

The Guru in is anxiety to meet God compares himself to a bride who rejoices in her approaching marriage:

When the *Bridegroom* kindly came to my house,
My female companions met me and arranged for the marriage.
My heart was glad as I gazed upon the play; the Bridegroom came to wed me.
Sing sing, O ladies, *the bridal song* with wisdom and reflection.
The Life of the world hath come to my house as my Bridegroom.

My marriage having been brought about though my Guru, when I meet him I recognized my Spouse.

Whose Word filleth the three worlds; when my pride departed my heart was glad.

God arrangeth His own affairs; they are not arranged by others;

They consist in bestowing truth, contentment, mercy, and faith—a few pious persons know this.

Saith Nanak, God alone is the Spouse of all.

She on whom He *looketh* with favour is the happy wife.

In the opinion of the Guru human life is worthless without holiness:

A cow without milk, a bird without wings, and tillage without water are of no avail.

What is an emperor to whom no obeisance is made?

Dark is the chamber in which Thy name, O God, is not.

Why shouldest Thou forget me when I am in great affliction?

When affliction befalleth me, forget me not.

Man's eyes grow blind, his tongue loseth its taste, his ears hear not;

He can only move by being supported—these are the fruits of non-service.

Make the Word the garden tree, plant it in good soil, and irrigate with love.

The one Name is the fruit of all such trees; how shall men obtain it without *good* works?

All creatures are Thine, O Lord; none *obtaineth* his reward without devotion to Thee.

Woe and weal are distributed according to Thy will; without Thy name real life *remaineth* not.

How may man live except by dying by the Guru's teaching? If one live otherwise, he shall not know the way.

Saith Nanak, Thou, O Lord, restorest life; Thou preservest man as Thou pleasest.

The following was addressed by way of admonition to a Brahman:

Making my body the loin-cloth, my heart the Brahman,

Divine knowledge my sacrificial thread, meditation my grass and leaves,

I shall beg for God's name and praises *instead of the alms of the Brahmans*;

And by the favour of the Guru be absorbed in God.

O Brahman, so meditate on God

That His name my become thy purification, His name thy learning, and His name thy wisdom and good acts.

The sacrificial thread is only on thy body as long as thou hast life.

Make the remembrance of the Name thy loin-cloth and frontal mark,

And it shall abide with thee in this world and the next.

Search for nothing but the true Name;

Make God's love thy worship, the burning of *the love of* wealth *thine incense*.

Look only on the one God, search for none other.

He who repeateth God's name with his mouth and *pondereth* on it,
Beholdeth Him at the tenth door of the firmament.
His doubt and fear who *liveth* upon the love of God flee away.
If the sentry be on he alert, thieves will not break in.
Deem the knowledge of the one God thy frontal mark,
And the consciousness that God is within thee thy discrimination.
God cannot be overcome by other ceremonial acts.
He who merely *redeth* religious books hath not found His worth.
His secret is not known from the eighteen Purans or the four Veds.
Nanak, the true Guru hath shown me God.

The following was addressed to a pandit who inquired how salvation could be obtained:

The body like a frail earthen vessel in miserable; in birth and death it suffereth *further* pain.

How shall the dangerous ocean of this world be crossed?

It cannot without the divine Guru.

There is none but Thee O my Beloved; there is none but Thee, O god.

In all colours and forms art Thou; Thou pardonest him on whom Thou lookest with favour.

My mother-in-law is perverse; she will neither let me dwell at home, nor meet my Beloved.

Since I have worshipped the feet of my companions and friends, my Beloved through the kindness of the Guru hath looked on me with favour.

Reflecting on myself and chastening my heart I see that there is no friend like Thee.

At thou keepest me so I live; I endure woe and weal as Thou bestowest them.

I have dispelled hopes and desires, and I no more long for mammon.

The holy main who hath found shelter in the society of the saints, *obtaineth* the fourth state.

He in whose heart the invisible and inscrutable God dwelleth, *possesseth* all divine knowledge, meditation, devotion and penance.

Nanak, he whose heart is dyed with God's name shall readily obtain devotion under the Guru's instruction.

The following is supposed to have been composed by the Guru on the death of his father:

Abandon love of family and love of everything.
Abandon worldly love; it is all sinful.
Abandon worldly love and superstition, O my friends.
Repeat the true Name with your tongues and your hearts.
His children weep not and his mother *afflicteth* not herself for him.
Who possesseth the nine treasures of the true name.
The world is ruined by such love *as the worldly feel*;
Only some rare pious man may be saved.

Through such love *as that* one is born again
He who *feeleth* such love *goeth* to the city of Death.
Practice acceptance of the Guru's instruction as thy devotion and penance.
He who *breaketh* not with worldly love shall not be accepted.
If God look on man with favour such love shall depart,
O Nanak, and he shall be absorbed in God.

When Guru Nanak went to Gorakhmata—the present Nanakmata—he found religious men of several sects assembled there. The following was composed after a discussion with them:

He who meditateth on knowledge *conferreth* favour on others;
When he *correcteth* his evil passions he *dwelleth* at a place of pilgrimage;
The thinking bells of ecstasy resound for him when he *turneth* his heart to God.
What can Death do to me in the next world?
When man hath abandoned desires he is a Sanyasi.
If a Jogi be continent, he *enjoyeth* his body.
He who in his heart *meditateth* mercy, is a Digambar :
He *tortureth* himself, but not others.
Thou, O Lord, art one, but many are Thy manifestations.
Nanak *knoweth* not Thy wonderful play.

As a wife fears that she is forgotten by her spouse, so the holy man fears that he is neglected by God:

I am not possessed of one virtue to cleanse my polluted body.
My Lord awaketh; I sleep the livelong night.
How shall I thus become dear to my Spouse?
My Lord awaketh; I sleep the livelong night.
Even though I approach His couch smitten with desire,
I *know not* if I shall then please Him or please Him not.
How know I what shall occur, O mother?
Without beholding God I cannot abide.
I have not tasted love; my thirst is not quenched;
My youth hath fled, and I mourn *for what is lost.*
Even now I awake smitten with desire :
I have become sad, and remain without hope.
If woman adorn herself with the rejection of pride,
Her Spouse will enjoy her on the couch.
Then, Nanak, shall she please her Spouse's heart;
She will abandon pride and be absorbed in Him.

It is necessary to fear as well as love God so as to keep His commandments:

In this world woman is very silly.
I know not the worth of my Spouse;
He is one, there is none Spouse;

He is one, there is none other.
If He cast a glance of favour on me, I shall meet Him.
In the next world woman shall know the truth,
And easily recognize her Beloved.
If she obtain such wisdom by the Guru's favour,
She shall please her Spouse's heart.
Saith Nanak, if she adorn herself with fear and love,
Her Spouse will ever enjoy her on the couch.

When man has parted with all worldly love, he has prepared himself for deliverance:

No one hath a son, no one hath a mother.
Through deceitful worldly love man *wandereth* in doubt.
O my Lord, I am Thy creation;
I utter Thy name when Thou givest it me.
Man may wail aloud for his many transgressions,
But he shall only be pardoned if it be God's will.
By the Guru's favour evil inclinations depart—
Wherever I gaze there is only one God—
Saith Nanak, if man attain such wisdom,
The True One will absorb that true one in Himself.

The following was addressed to a worldly-minded Raja:

Thou mayest have lakhs of armies, lakhs of musical instruments and lances; lakhs of men may rise to do thee homage;

Thy dominion may extend over lakhs *of miles*; lakhs of men may rise to do thee honour—

All that would be fruitless, wert thou not credited in God's account.

Without God's name the world is only trouble.

If the fool be never so much admonished, he *remaineth* the blindest of the blind.

Thou mayest earn lakhs of rupees; thou mayest amass and spend lakhs; lakhs may come and lakhs may go;

But, if thy soul obtain not credit in God's account, where else shall I obtain it?

Lakhs of Shastars may be explained to thee; lakhs of Pandits may read the Purans for thee—

All would be unacceptable didst thou not obtain credit in God's account.

From the true Name—the kind Creator's name—honour is obtained.

It is dwell day and night in the heart, O Nanak, man shall be delivered by God's favouring glance.

The temptations to which man is exposed by his sense:

The five evil passions dwell concealed within the heart;
Wherefore it *remaineth* not fixed, but *wandereth* like a pilgrim.

My mind *remaineth* not fixed on the Merciful One:
Avaricious, deceitful, sinful, and hypocritical, it is excessively attached to worldly love.
When I meet my Beloved I will adorn myself,
And put on necklaces of flowers.
I have five companions and one husband.
It is ordained from the beginning that the soul depart.
The five senses shall weep in unison,
Saith Nanak, when the soul is arrested to give its account.

Asa Ashtapadi

Guru Nanak expatiates on the advantage of the Guru's instruction and the repetition of God's name :

Man may perform all devotion, all penance, *and resort to* every expedient;
Yet he is as if he wandered in a wilderness, and could not find the way.
Without knowing God, no one is acceptable.
Without the Name man is despised.
The Lord is permanent; the world *cometh* and *goeth*.
Mortals shall be emancipated by being the holy man's slaves.
The world is bound by worldly love and many desires;
Yet some reject it under the Guru's instruction.
The lotuses *of the hearts* of those who have the Name within them bloom,
And they fear not Death
The world which loveth women is overcome by them.
Men attached to sons and wives forget God's name.
They waste in vain their human lives and lose their game.
To serve the true Guru is the best thing.
They who utter words of pride in public,
Never apply the function of salvation to their hearts
They who burn worldly love under the Guru's instruction,
And ever meditate on the pure Name in their hearts,
Hold and restrain their wandering minds.
By God's favour the Guru *associateth* such persons with the congregation of the Sikhs.
Without a guru man *forgetteth* God and *suffereth* transmigration.
Him whom God *regardeth* favourable He *blendeth* with Himself.
If I speak of the beautiful One, I cannot describe Him.
If I discourse of the Ineffable, I canot find His worth.
All pain and pleasure depend on Thy will, O God.
All pain shall be erased by the True Name,
And men shall hear instruments *played* without hands and anklets without feet.
If man understand the Word, he shall behold the True One.
When the True, One is in the heart, all happiness is there also.
The Preserver *preserveth* men by His favouring glance.

He who *effaceth* himself *knoweth* the three worlds.
He who *understandeth* the Word, shall be absorbed in the True One.
Nanak, the Creator will congratulate him
Who without respite *meditateth* on the World.

How deliverance may be obtained:

He who burneth his hopes and desires by the Word,
Who *uttereth* and *causeth* others to utter God's name,
Shall by means of the Guru find the way to God's own abode.
His body shall become gold by God's incomparable light,
And he shall behold God's form in the whole three worlds.
I possess God's true name as wealth which shall never fail.
God *pervadeth* the five *elements*, the three *worlds*, the nine *religions*, and the four *quarters of the universe*.
The Almightly *supporteth* the earth and the heavens.
The wandering *mind* He bringeth back.
Whoever is a fool seeth not with his eyes;
His language *giveth* not pleasure, and he *understandeth* not what is told him.
Intoxicated with evil passions, he *quarrelleth* with the world;
While on the other hand a man *becometh* good by association with the good,
Pursueth virtue and *purifieth* himself from vice.
Without serving the Guru peace is not obtained.
The Name is diamonds, jewels and rubies;
It is the pearl of the heart, God's own wealth.
Nanak, God *assayeth* man, and *maketh* him happy with a glance.

The following was addressed to a hypocritical Jogi :

Men sing songs while meditating evil;
They in tone measures and style themselves knowing.
Without the Name the heart is filthy and *meditateth* evil.
Whither goest thou? O man, remain at home.
The pious are satiated with God's name, and by searching easily find Him.
The bodily sins of lust, wrath, and worldly love are in the mind;
So are painful greed, avarice and pride.
How can the mind be satisfied without God's name?
They who lave their hearts know the True One.
The holy man *knoweth* the condition of his heart.

The mind obtains composure by devotion :

The apostate's mind is a furious elephant
Which *wandereth* distracted in the forest of worldly love.
Impelled by Death it *rusheth* here and there,
While the pious search and find God in their hearts.
Without the Guru's word the mind is not at rest.
Remember God's very pure name and relinquish bitter pride.

Say how shall this stupid mind be happy:
Without understanding, it shall suffer the torture of Death.
God will cause man to meet the true Guru, and will pardon him.
The True One will thrust aside the tortures of Death.

Wealth is perishable; devotion to God an abiding gain:

When the body perisheth, whose shall be its wealth?
Without the Guru how shall God's name be obtained?
God' name is wealth which *accompanieth* and *assisteth* us.
Day and night he is pure who *fixeth* his attention on God.
What have we but God's name?

Treating pleasure and pain as the same I forsake not the Name: God will pardon and blend me with Himself.

The fool loveth gold and woman;
Attached to mammon he *forgetteth* the Name.
Him whom Thou, *O God*, pardonest Thou causest to repeat Thy name.
Death's myrmidons cannot overtake him who *singeth* Thy praises.
O Hari, who art God, the great Giver,
Mercifully preserve us as Thou pleasest.
Under the Guru's instruction God is pleasing to my mind;
Disease is removed and pain averted.
There is no other medicine, charm or spell.
By remembering God, sin is destroyed.
As I behold creation I am amazed and astonished
God is contained in the hearts of demigods and men.
God who filleth every place, I hold in my heart.
There is none equal to Thee, O Lord.
He who *loveth* worship hath God's name in his mouth.
In the Company of such saints and worshippers
Man *breaketh* his shackles and *meditateth* on God.
Pious men are emancipated by a knowledge of God through the Guru.
Death's myrmidons cannot inflict pain on him
Who *awaketh* in the love of God's name.
God to whom His saints are dear, *abideth* with them.
Nanak, salvation is obtained by bearing love to God.

The following on the disregard of worldly things was addressed to a selfish Brahman:

He who serveth the Guru *knoweth* the Lord;
His pain is erased who *recognizeth* the True Word.
Repeat God's name, my friends and companions.
On serving the true Guru ye shall behold God with your eyes.
Entanglements are mother, father, and the whole world;
Entanglements are sons, daughters and women;
Entanglements are religious ceremonies performed through ostentation;

Entanglements are sons, wives, and worldly love in the mind;
An entanglements is the tillage done by the tiller—
He suffereth for his selfishness when the King *demandeth* revenue--
An entanglements is traffic without meditating on God.
Man is never satisfied; worldly love is everywhere diffused.
An entanglement is the perishable wealth which merchants amass.
Without devotion to God man findeth no place.
Entanglements are Veds, religious discussions, and pride.
By the entanglements of worldly love and sin man perisheth—
Nanak *taketh* shelter in God's name—
He whom the true Guru *preserveth* is freed from his entanglements.

The following was addressed to a mixed assembly of professedly religious men:

I have searched in every direction, but found no friend.
If it please Thee, O Lord, Thou art mine and I am Thine.
I have no other gate than Thine; whom Shall I salute?
I possess Thee alone, O Lord; Thy true name is in my mouth.
The Sikhs strive for supernatural power; Pirs also desire wealth and supernatural power.
May I not forget the one Name under the true Guru's instruction!
Why do the Jogis, the Bhogis, and the Kaprias wander in foreign lands?
They heed not the Guru's instruction or the Real Thing that is within them.
Pandits, preceptors, and astrologers ever read the Purans,
But know not the Thing within them—God who is concealed within the heart.
Some anchorets perform austerities in forests, others ever dwell at places of pilgrimages.
Those benighted people know not themselves; why have they become ascetics?
Some who are called Jatis try to restrain their seed:
Without the word of the Guru they shall not be saved, but shall wander in transmigration.
Different persons are family men, worshippers, penitents; but it is only they who are attached to the Guru's instructions,
Who hold fast the Name, charity, and ablutions, and who awake in God's service.
Through the Guru the gate of Thy house, O Lord, is known; when men go there they recognize it.
Saith Nanak, may I not forget Thy name, and may my heart be reconciled with the True One!

Precepts for salvation:

By restraining is mental desires man shall assuredly cross the terrible ocean.
Thou, O Lord, was in the beginning and in the primal age;
Thou art the Merciful; *I have entered* Thine asylum.

Thou art the Giver; we are Thy beggars; O God, grant us a sight of Thee.

O man meditate on the Name under the Guru's instruction, and thou shalt be happy in the temple of thy heart.

Renounce falsehood and avarice; and then shalt thou recognize the True One.

Be absorbed in the Guru's instruction, and thou shalt know what is best for thee.

This mind is a grasping tyrant enamoured of greed:

Under the Guru's instruction greed is removed, and man *arriveth* at an understanding with God.

If man sow a barren field, how shall he obtain profit?

The obstinate man is not pleased with the truth; he is buried in falsehood.

Renounce avarice, ye blind; it *bringeth* great unhappiness.

If the true Lord dwell in the heart, the poison of pride shall be removed.

Forsake the evil way of mammon, my brethren, or ye shall be plundered.

Day and night praise the Name under the protection of the true Guru.

The mind of the perverse is a stone or a rock; accursed and vain in his life.

However much a stone by put into the water, it is dry at the core.

God's name is wealth, the true Guru hath given it.

Nanak, he who *forgetteth* not God's name *drinketh* distilled nectar.

The advantage of domestic devotion :

Why should I go searching in the wood? My heart is a verdant forest.

The true Word hath come quickly to my heart and *abideth* there.

Wherever I look there is God; no one else is seen.

Whosoever doeth the Guru's work shall find God's court.

The True One blendeth with Himself him who is pleasing to His mind;

He *blendeth* with Himself him who ever *walketh* according to His will.

If the true Lord dwell in the heart, it *becometh* fixed.

God then *granteth* greatness in which naught is wanting.

How shall one reach God's court by occasional service?

He who *embarketh* in a boat of stone shall be drowned with his cargo.

An inculcation of devotion regardless of worldly opinion :

He whose mind is imbued with God's name *discourset* of the True One.

What care I for men if I please Thee?

As long as there are life and soul, meditate on the True One.

The profit of singing God's praises is that man obtaineth happiness.

True is Thy work; grant it me, Thou Merciful One.

I live by praising Thèe; Thou art my prop and my support.

I am the servant and the porter at Thy gate; Thou knowest my pain.

I am astounded at Thy service which hath removed my pain.

Holy men through Thy name shall reach Thy court and Thy presence.

That time is auspicious when man recognizeth the true Word.

Practise truth, contentment, and love; and then the worship of God's name shall be thy viaticum.

Banish sin from thy mind, and the True One will bestow truth:

The True One *bestoweth* true love on the true.

What *pleaseth* Thee, O God, is the real justice.

True are the gifts which the true and merciful One *granteth*.

Serve Him day and night whose Name is priceless.

Thou, O God, art the most high; I who am Thy servant am low.

Saith Nanak, O True One, look on me with favour that I who am separated *from Thee* may meet Thee.

Asa Chant

It is said that Bhai Buddha and Mula, a Sikh went to the Guru and asked him what afforded the highest gratification. His reply was the following :

O woman is the prime of youth, my Beloved is playful.

When a wife *entertaineth* great love for her Spouse, He mercifully *taketh* delight in her and *enjoyeth* her.

The wife shall meet her Spouse if the Lord God Himself show her favour.

Her bed is pleasant in the company of her Beloved; her seven tanks are filled with nectar.

Show me compassion and kindness, O Compassionate One, that I may obtain the true Word and sing Thy praises.

Nanak, the young woman, having seen God her Spouse, is delighted and her heart is enraptured.

O young woman, beautiful without art, pray only for the love of the one God.

God is pleasing to my soul and body, and I am charmed with His companionship.

She who is dyed with God's love and *prayeth* to Him, shall abide in happiness through His Name.

When thou embracest virtue thou shalt know God; virtue shall abide with thee vice be put to flight.

Without Thee I cannot abide for a moment; I derive no satisfaction from merely conversing of Thee.

Nanak, she whose tongue and heart are moistened with God's essence, calleth for her Beloved

O my friends and companions, my beloved is a merchant.

I have purchased from him God's name whose sweetness and value are infinite.

If woman's house be pleasing to the inestimable, true, and beloved God, she shall be happy.

Other women enjoy dalliance with God; I cry aloud standing at His door.

Thou, Cause of causes, Omnipotent, Harbinger of prosperity, arrangest man's affairs.

Nanak, she on whom God *looketh* with favour is a happy wife; she *treeasureth* up the Word in her heart.

In my house is a true song of rejoicing; God my lover hath visited me.

Imbued with love He enjoyed me; I have exchanged hearts with Him.

I gave God my heart and took Him as my Spouse; He *enjoyeth* me as He *pleaseth*.

She who *offereth* her soul and body to the Beloved is supremely happy through the Word, and *obtaineth* the ambrosial fruit in her own home.

It is not obtained by intellect, or study, or by great cleverness; what the heart *desireth* is obtaineth by love.

Nanak, God is my Beloved; I belong to none besides.

As the deer is snared, the bumble-bee caught by the lotus, and the fish *falleth* into the net, so man's soul becomes the prey of Death.

Hear, O black deer, why art thou enamoured of the garden?

The fruit of sin is sweet, but only for four days; it then growth bitter.

The fruit for which thou greatly cravest, shall become very bitter without the Name.

That fruit is as a wave of the ocean, or as a flash of lightning.

There is no protector but God; yet He hath been forgotten by thee.

Verily, saith Nanak, think of it, thou shalt die, O black deer.

O bumble-bee, thou wanderest among the flowers, and very great shall be thy suffering, *when the lotus closeth on thee.*

I have inquired of my Guru regarding the true knowledge of God.

I have inquired of the true Guru regarding the knowledge of God; O bumble-bee, thou art enamoured of the flowers.

When the sun *riseth*, the body *falleth,* and souls hall be boiled in hot oil.

O demon, without the Word thou shalt be bound and punished on the road of death.

Verily, saith Nanak, thank of it, thou shalt die, O black bee.

My soul from a strange land, why fallest thou into entanglements?

When the true Lord dwelleth in thee, why shouldest thou be entangled in Death's net?

When the fisherman *casteth* his net, the fish *leaveth* the water with tears in its eyes.

The love of mammon is dear to the world; all doubts on the subject shall at last be set aside.

Serve God heartily, and dispel thy mental anxieties.

Verily, saith Nanak, think of it, O my soul from a strange land,

Rivers which separate in their course can only meet again by chance.

In every age what is şweet is full of poison: some rare holy man *knoweth* this.

Some rare person who thinketh of true Guru *knoweth* divine knowledge and *recognizeth* God.

Without God's name the fools and the heedless wander in superstition and are ruined.

They whose hearts contain not God's true name and service at last groan and weep.

Verily, saith Nanak, they have been long separated meet by the True Word.

Rag Gujari

Guru Nanak orders man to repeat God's name and engage not in idol worship:

If the heart be made the scraper, the Name the sandal,

And good acts be mixed with it as kungu, that shall be the real worship of God in the heart.

Worship God by meditating on His name, for without the Name there is no worship.

If any one were to wash his heart as the surface of the idol is washed,

He impurity should be removed, his soul should become pure, and he should depart to deliverance.

Even beasts have their merits; for the oil-cake they at they give milk, *but the Brahmans make no return for the offerings made them.*

Without the Name accursed is man's life and the acts he *performeth.*

God is near, think Him not distant; He ever careth for and *remembereth* us.

Eat what He *giveth,* said Nanak verily.

The Guru's God is superior to the demigods of the Hindus:

Brahma sprang from the lotus of Vishnu's naval, and having attuned his throat began to recite the Veds;

Yet he could not see God's limits, and remained in the darkness of transmigration.

Why should I forget the Beloved who is the support of my soul,

Whom the perfect worship, whom munis serve, on whom gurus meditate,

Whose lamps are the sun and moon, and whose one light pervadeth the three worlds?

The pious have light day and night, but for the perverse there is only sable darkness.

The Sikh sitteth in meditative posture and ever argueth, but can be see God even with both his eyes?

They in whose hearts there is light are awakened by the sound of the Word; the true Guru *decideth* their arguments.

O Lord of demigods and men, infinite, unborn, Thy true palace is unrivalled.

Saith Nanak, O Life of the world, grant me peace and save me by Thy favouring glance.

Gujari Ashtapadi

The Guru's heart is ever filled with devotion:

I ask Thee, O God, for nothing at any time but the love of Thy pure name; grant it to me, O Bright One.

The Chatrik Nanak *prayeth* for the nectareous water *of Thy name;* mercifully grant him to sing Thy praises.

There is no happiness without true devotion:

O Sire, how many people wear religious garbs to beg and fill their bellies!

O mortal, there is no happiness without God's service; without the Guru pride *departeth* not.

O Sire, what shall I ask? Nothing *appeareth* permanent; in this world are the ebb and flow of life.

Saith Nanak, grant me the Name as my wealth, that I may wear it as a necklace on my heart.

The Guru only claims to be a religious instructor from the ranks of the people:

O Sire, I am not high, or low, or middling; I am of God's people, and I seek His protection.

It is only they who are dyed with the Name who are free from worldly love and forget mourning, separation and disease.

My brethren, by the favour of the Guru God's service *is obtained.*

He in whose heart is the Word of the true Guru, obtaineth the Pure God, *heedeth* not Death and owneth him nothing.

The following instruction was addressed to pandit Ram Chand at Banaras :

The saints worship God with love; they thirst for the truth, and hear it with excessive love.

They who cry aloud in trouble obtain rest by prayer and heartily loving God.

O man, repeat God's name and seek His protection.

Repeat God's name and do *good* works; thus shalt thou cross over the ocean of the world.

O mortal man, to repeat God' name under the Guru's instruction is a happy thought.

By mentally repeating God's name one's mind *obtaineth* a treasure of real divine knowledge and peace.

In this world man's fickle mind *pursueth* wealth and *becometh* intoxicated with worldly love;

But, on being imbued with the Guru's word and teaching, God's name and service become firmly implanted in the heart.

Doubts which ruin the world by the disease of transmigration, cease not by wandering *to paces of pilgrimage.*

The place of God is the abode of unmixed happiness; he who is truly wise repeateth God's name as his penance.

Every one is saturated with worldly love, and *therefore endureth* the great pain of birth and death.

Man shall be saved by hastening to the asylum of the true Guru and repeating God's name in his heart.

Man's mind *becometh* stable, and he *practiseth* divine meditation under the Guru's instruction.

Pure is the heart which *containeth* truth and the excellent jewel of divine knowledge.

O man, by fear, love, and service, and by fixing thine attention on God's feet shalt thou cross the terrible ocean.

O God, put into my heart Thy name which is the purest of the pure; my body is in Thy sanctuary.

Extricate me, O God, from the waves of avarice and covetousness, and put Thy name as capital into my heart.

Chasten my mind, Thou spotless One, saith Nanak, I seek Thy protection.

Bihagre ki War

Reflection on the Hindu Idol-worshippers :

The Hindus have forgotten God, and are going the wrong way.
They worship according to the instruction of Narad.
They are blind and dumb, the blindest of the blind.
The ignorant fools take stones and worship them.
O Hindus, how shall the stone which itself *sinketh* carry you across?

Rag Wadhans

The Guru enjoyed a vision of God in his dreams, and on awaking felt the pain of separation from Him :

The peacocks are crying *with joy;* O sisters, the rainy season hath come.

The fervent woman, O God, is enamoured of Thy glances *which blind her like* a rope..

I am a sacrifice to a sight of Thee, O God; to Thy name I am a sacrifice.

Since Thou art *my Master* I am proud; without Thee what pride should I have?

O woman, break thy couch with its frame and thine arm with their bracelets,

Since, notwithstanding thy decorations, the Lord is enamoured of others.

Thou needest not a bracelet-dealer, or silver, or glass bracelets:

Burn the arm which *embraceth* not the Bridegroom.

All my companions went to enjoy the Bridegroom; whose door shall I, wretched that I am, approach?

O Lord, *I think myself* well behaved and very clever, yet I have no charm to please Thee.

I plaited my tresses with cosmetic and filled thee parting of my hair with vermilion;

Yet when I went before Thee I was not accepted; I shall die of excessive grief.

I am weeping; the whole world weepeth; yea, even the birds of the forests weep for me.

One thing weepeth not for me, the separation which parted me from my Beloved.

He came to me in my dreams and again vanished, upon which I wept my fill.

I cannot go to Thee, O Beloved, or send any one to Thee.

Return, O happy sleep, perhaps I may again behold my Lord.

What shall I give him, saith Nanak, who telleth me of Thee, O God?

I will cut off my head and give it to him to sit on; without my head I will perform his service.

Why do I not die and give up my life since my Lord hath chosen another?

Wadhans Chhant

The following was addressed to the Hindus, who set the highest religious value on ablutions:

Why wash the body defiled by falsehood?
The practice of truth is the acceptable obtain.
When there is truth in the heart, then man *becometh* true and *obtaineth* the True One.
Understanding is not obtained without favourable destiny; man *ruineth* himself by vain babbling.
Wherever thou sittest speak civilly, and fix thine attention on God's word.
Why wash the body defiled by falsehood?
When Thou, O *Lord,* didst cause me to speak, I spoke.
Thine ambrosial name is pleasing to my soul.
Thy name is sweet to my soul; a load of sorrow hath fallen from off me.
When Thou gavest the order, happiness came and took its seat in my heart.
I pray to Thee, who didst create the world, for Thy favour.
When Thou didst cause me to speak, I spoke.
The Master *granteth* man his term of human life according to his past acts.
Fall not into a quarrel by calling any one evil.
Enter not into a quarrel with the Lord; thou shalt only ruin thyself.
Why be jealous and vex him with whom thou associated?
Bear what God *giveth* thee; it is forbidden to remonstrate; speak not nonsense regarding it.
The Master *granteth* man his term of life according to past acts.
God created all things and *looketh* on them with favour.
Nobody *desireth* what is bitter; every one *desireth* what is sweet.
Everybody may ask for what is sweet, but God will do as He *pleaseth*.
Alms-offerings and various good works are not equal to the Name.
Nanak, they who are the objects of God's favour from the beginning, have obtained His name.
God created all things and *looketh* on them with favour.

Wadhans Alahanian

Some one inquired why God, who is ever present, is never visible. The Guru replied :

The Lord who created the world and again drew it within Himself, is known by His omnipotencee.

Search not for the True One afar off; He is in every heart, and is known by the Guru's instruction.

By the Guru's instruction know the True One who made creation; think Him not distant.

Meditate on the Name and thou shalt obtain happiness: without the Name man is not victorious in the arena of the world.

He who established the world *knoweth* its ways; what shall any one say?

He who established the world spread the net of mammon; accept that Lord *with thy heart.*

Wadhans ki War

Guru Nanak as usual pays no attention to ceremonial :

Perish the ritual by which I forgot my Beloved!
Nanak, that is the true love which *preserveth* me in honour with the Lord.

Rag Sorath

The Guru's reflections on death and future punishment:

Death must come to all and all must part company;
Go and ask the wise if men shall meet hereafter or not.
They who have forgotten my God shall suffer great pain.
Certainly praise that true Being,
From whose glance of favour happiness ever resulteth.
Praise Him, for He is Great. He is, was and ever shall be.
Thou alone, O God, art the Benefactor of all; no gifts are obtained from man.
What *pleaseth* Thee *taketh* place; what avail womanly tears?
How many kings have departed having exercised sovereignty over millions of fortresses on earth?
They whom the world could not contain have had rings put on their noses.
If man thought of future torments why should he devote himself to enjoyment?
Nanak, man shall have to wear on his neck as many chains as he hat sins.
If he possess virtues, which are as brothers and friends, his chains shall be cut off.
They who have no Guru shall not be accepted hereafter; they shall be beaten and expelled.

The following is in opposition to all except deistic forms of religion:

There *appeareth* no partner of Thine; then whom shall I praise *but Thee*?
Nanak, the slave of slaves *representeth,* God is known by the Guru's teaching.

The Guru's conception of God :

The Unseen, Infinite, Inaccessible, Inapprehensible God is not subject to death or destiny.
He is on no caste, unborn, self-existent, without fear or doubt.
I am a sacrifice to the Truest of the true.
He hath no form, or colour, or outline; He *becometh* manifest by the true Word.
He hath no mother, father, son, or kinsman; He *feeleth* not lust, and hath no wife.
Or family; He is pure, endless and infinite; all light is Thine, O Lord.
God is concealed in every heart; His light is in every heart.
He whose understanding's adamantine doors are opened by the Guru's instruction, fixeth his gaze on the Fearless One.

God having created animals made them subject to death, and retained all contrivances in his own power.

He who serveth the True Guru obtaineth the real boon, and is delivered by repeating the Word.

Truth is contained in pure vessels; few there are whose acts are pure.

By seeking Thy protection, saith Nanak, the soul *blendeth* with the Supreme Soul.

The condition of a man who has no Guru to communicate God's name :

As a fish without water, so is the infidel—dying of thirst.

If thy breath be drawn in vain, O man, thou shalt die without God.

O man, repeat God's name and praises;

But how shalt thou obtain this pleasure without the Guru? It is the Guru who uniteth man with God.

Meeting the society of holy men is as a pilgrimage for the holy.

The adventages of bathing at the sixty-eight places of pilgrimage are obtained by beholding the Guru :

As a Jogi without continence, devotion, truth, or contentment,

So is the body without the Name; Death will punish it since it *containeth* sin in its heart.

God is not found by loving the infidel; He is found by loving the true Guru.

Saith Nanak, he who is absorbed in God's praises *obtaineth* the Guru who is the dispenser of weal and woe.

Man should cultivate true piety in his own home:

The nectareous water of life, for which thou camest into the world, is with the Guru.

Abandon garbs, disguises, and cleverness; this water *is* not *obtained by devotion to* mammon.

O man, remain at home; go nowhere, my friend.

By searching abroad thou shalt suffer much affliction; the water of life is in thy heart at home.

Forsake vice and pursue virtue; thy vice thou shalt regret.

Thou knowest not good for evil; thou shalt again and again wallow in the mire.

Inside thee is the great filth of covetousness and falsehood; why washest thou thine outside?

Ever repeat the Pure Name under the Guru's instruction, then shall thy heart by pure.

Abandon covetousness and slander, forswear falsehood and thou shalt obtain the true fruit through the Guru's instruction.

O God, preserve me as Thou pleasest; Nanak *praiseth* Thy Word.

God is the invisible Benefactor and is pleased when men obey His behests:

All creatures are subject to destiny from the beginning; there is none not subject to it.

God alone is not subject to destiny; He beholdeth the work of His own omnipotence; He causeth His order to be executed.

O man, repeat God's name and thou shalt be happy;

Day and night worship the feet of the Guru and Giver and the Enjoyer.

Behold Him without thee as he is within thee; there is none other.

Under the Guru's instruction regard all men as equal, since God's light is contained in the heart of each.

Restrain in its place thy wandering mind; thou shalt know how to do this on meeting the Guru.

On beholding the Invisible thou shalt be astounded; thou shall forget thy misery and obtain happiness.

Quaff nectar and thou shalt obtain supreme happiness and abide in thine own home.

Sing His praises who *destroyeth* the fear of birth and death, and thou shalt not be born again.

God the First Principle, the Pure One, is in all things; of this there is no doubt.

Nanak hath obtained God the Infinite Supreme Being as his Guru.

Sorath Ashtapadi

The Guru deprecated idolatry and then gives his notion of an ideal Bairagi, or renouncer of the world:

May I not fall under the power of mammon, worship any but God, or visit tombs and places of cremation!

May I not enter the strange house impelled by greed! may the Name extinguish my greed!

The Guru showed me God in my own home; my heart became easily enamoured of Him, my brethren.

Thou art wise, Thou art far-seeing; it is only Thou, O Lord, who givest wisdom.

My heart hath no love for the world; it is tinctured with its hate; the World hath penetrated my heart, O my mother.

He who loveth the true Lord and continually repeateth His hymns, beholdeth His light in his own heart.

Countless persons call themselves Bairagis, but only he who is pleasing to God is a Bairagi.

Such a Bairagi treasureth the Word in his heart: he is ever absorbed in the fear of God and serveth the Guru.

He thinketh on the one God, his mind wavereth not, and he *restraineth* its wanderings.

He is intoxicated with God's love, ever absorbed in divine pleasure, and he singeth the praises of the True One.

In the mind, which is like the wind, dwell even for a little on the name of Him who liveth at ease, happiness shall result, my brethren.

My tongue, eyes, and ears are tinctured by the True One;

Thou, O Lord, hast Extinguished the fire that consumed me.

He is a Bairagi who *abandoneth* desires and *assumeth* an attitude of contemplation in his own him.

He who is filled with the alms of the Name is contented and quaffeth nectar at his ease.

As long as there is a practice of worldly love, their is no contempt of the world.

All the world is Thine, O Lord; Thou alone art the Giver; there is none other, my brethren.

Perverse creatures ever abide in misery; God conferreth greatness on the holy.

Infinite, endless, inaccessible, inapprehensible, Thy worth cannot be obtained by speaking.

Sun Samadh, Mahaparamarath, and Lord of the three worlds are names of Thine.

All animals born in the world have their destinies recorded on their foreheads, and must bear what is destined for them.

It is God who causeth man to perform good acts and maketh them steadfast in His service.

When mean feareth God, the filth of his soul and body departeth, and God Himself *giveth* him divine knowledge:

Only he who hath tasted it, knoweth its flavour, as a dumb man enjoyeth sweets.

How describe the Indescribable, my brethren? Ever walk according to His will.

If God cause man to meet the generous Guru, understanding is produced; he who hath no Guru hath no understanding.

Walk as God *causeth* you to walk, my brethren; what other device can man adopt?

Some are led astray in error, others love God's service; The play, O Lord, is incomprehensible.

Men obtain the result of what Thou hast applied them to; Thou leadest them by Thine order.

We can serve Thee if we have anything of our own; our souls and bodies are Thine.

God is merciful to him who hath met the true Guru; the ambrosial Name in his support.

He to whom the attributes of God, who *dwelleth* in heaven, become manifest, shall obtain divine knowledge and meditation from them.

God's name is pleasing to him; he *uttereth* it himself and *causeth* others to utter it; and he only *speaketh* of the Real Thing.

The Deep and Profound is obtained by the instruction of the Guru and priest; without such instruction the world would go mad.

Nanak, he whose heart is pleased with the True One is a perfect Bairagi, and naturally fortunate.

The following was the Guru's instruction to a Brahman:

Hopes and desires are entanglements, my brother; thy religious ceremonies are also entanglements.

May, my brother, is born in the world as the result of bad and good acts; he *perisheth* when he *forgetteth* the Name.

Maya *bewitcheth* the world, my brother; all thy religious ceremonies are worthless.

Hear me, thou Pandit with the religious ceremonies—

Meditation on the Supreme Being is the only religious ceremony, my brother, from which happiness is derived.

Thou standesth chattering of the Shastars and Veds, my brother, and makest it a worldly affair.

The filth of sin which is within thee shall not be washed away by hypocrisy.

Like the hypocrite, the spider is ruined when her *web* is blown by the wind and she falleth headlong.

By evil inclinations many are ruined; by love of mammon they are lost.

Without the true Guru the Name is not obtained, and without the Name doubt *departeth* not.

My brother, serve the true Guru and thou shalt be happy, and released from transmigration.

True peace is obtained from the Guru. When the mind is pure, man shall be absorbed in the True One.

He who *serveth* the Guru *knoweth* the way; without the Guru it cannot be found.

What *religious* acts can be perform who hath greed in his heart? He *uttereth* falsehood and *eateth* poison.

O Pandit, if thou churn coagulated milk, butter shall be produced;

If thou Churn water, thou shalt obtain but water; this is the way of the world.

The unseen God *dwelleth* in every heart, by without the Guru man is ruined by wandering.

Maya hath bound this world on all sides with her cable:

Without a guru its knot cannot be united; man growth weary in striving.

This world is led astray by superstition; words are of no avail.

By meeting the Guru, my brother, the fear of god *entereth* the heart. To die in the fear of God is man's true destiny.

In God's court the Name is superior to ablutions, alms, and *similar* religious acts.

He who, by the Guru's goad, hath driven the Name into his heart to abide there, shall become free from hypocrisy.

Man is a banker's shop, the unrivalled Name is his capital.

The merchant who *meditateth* on the Guru's instruction *secureth* the capital.

Nanak, blest are the merchants who on meeting *the Guru* engage in such traffic.

Deprecation of idolatry:

My brethren, you worship goddesses and gods; what can you ask them? and what can they give you?

Even if a stone be washed with water, it will again sink in it.

Rag Dhanasari

The Guru reposes his hopes in God and confirms his devotion to him:

My soul is in fear; to whom shall I complain?

I have served Him who causeth us to forget our sorrows; He is ever and ever the Giver.

My Lord is ever young; He is ever and ever the Giver.

Night and day serve the Lord, and in the end He will deliver thee.

Hark, hark, my friend, thus shalt thou cross over.

O Merciful One, by Thy name shall I cross over; I am ever a sacrifice unto Thee.

In the whole world there is only one True Being; there is no second.

He on whom God looketh with favour will serve Him.

How shall I, O Beloved, abide without Thee?

Grand me the favour to remain attached to Thy name.

There is none other, O my Beloved, to whom I may go to address myself.

I serve my Lord, I beg from no other.

Nanak is His slave and ever a sacrifice unto Him.

O Lord, I am ever a sacrifice to Thy name, for which I could bear to be cut to pieces.

Life is but brief, and man ought to make the best use of it:

We men live but for a moment; we know not *if we shall live* the space of two gharis.

Nanak *representeth,* serve Him to whom belong our souls and lives.

O fool, consider how many days thy live shall last.

O Lord, my breath, body, and soul are all Thine; Thou art very dear to me.

The poet Nanak thus *speaketh;* O True Cherisher,

If Thou give nothing to any one, what pledge can be give Thee?

Nanak *representeth,* he who is destined from the beginning to obtain something shall obtain it.

The deceitful person who, instead of thinking of God's name, *practiseth* deceit,

Shall be led captive to the gate of Death, and shall then as he is led along regret *lost opportunities.*

As long as we are in this world, Nanak, hear somewhat and speak somewhat *of God.*

I have searched and found no resting place; wherefore in the midst of life be in death.

The Guru moralized as follows on seeing a thief arrested:

If a thief praise *the magistrate,* the mind of the latter is not pleased thereby;

If he revile the magistrate, it cannot displease him in the least.

Nobody will be surety for a thief.

How can what a thief doeth he good?

Hear, O fool, dog, and liar,

The True One *knoweth* thee, O thief, without thy speaking.

A thief may be well dressed, a thief may be ingenious,

Yet he is only worth a double paisa, the price of a bad rupee.

If thou put a bad coin with others,

It will be found counterfeit on being assayed.
As man acteth, so shall be his reward:
He himself *soweth* and he himself *eateth* the fruit.
Even though man praise himself,
Yet will he act according to his understanding.
If he tell hundreds of lies to *conceal the truth*,
He shall still be false even though the whole world call him *good.*
If it please Thee, even a fool is acceptable.
Nanak, God is clever to know man's secret.

A Brahman, a Qazi, and a Jogi entered into discussion with the Guru, and he gave them the following instruction :

The body is the paper, the mind the order written thereon.
Silly man readeth not the lines of destiny on his forehead.
In God's court there destinies are engraved.
Lo! what is counterfeit is there of no avail.
Nanak, if there be sterling silver within us,
Everybody will say that it is real.
The Qazi telleth lies and eateth filth.
The Brahman *taketh* life and then *batheth*.
The ignorant Jogi *knoweth* not the way of *union with God*—
The whole three ruin the world.
He is a Jogi who knoweth the way to God,
And who by the Guru's favour only *recognizeth* the One.
He is a Qazi who *turneth* away men *from the world*,
And who by the Guru's favour while alive in dead.
He is a Brahman who *reflecteth* upon God:
He shall be saved himself and shall shave all his relations.
Wise is he who *cleanseth* his heart:
A Musalman is he who *cleanseth* his impurity.
He who *readeth* and *acteth* on what he *readeth,* is acceptable.
He shall bear on his forehead the stamp of God's court.

Dhanasari Ashtapadi

God is pleased with love and service, not with idolatry or pilgrimages:

God *maketh* Himself manifest and *beholdeth* men.
He is not pleased by obstinate penance nor by many religious garbs.
He who fashioned the vessel *of the body* and pured into it His ambrosial *gifts,*
Will only be satisfied with man's love and service.
They who, though ever reading, forget God's name shall suffer punishment,
And notwithstanding their great cleverness undergo transmigration.
He who *repeateth* the Name and thus *eateth* the food of fear,
Shall become a pious worshipper and be absorbed in God.
He who *worshippeth* stones, *visiteth* places of pilgrimage, *dwelleth* in forests,
And *renounceth* the world, *wandereth* and *wavereth*.

How can his filthy mind become pure.?
He who *meeteth* the True One shall obtain honour.

Dhanasari Chhant

They who utter falsehood are unhappy:

If a woman please her Spouse, she shall be honoured in His house:
If she utter falsehood it is of no avail:
If she utter falsehood it is of no avail; Her spouse will not look at her.
Without merits, forgotten by her Spouse, and false, painful are her nights.

Rag Suhi

Man ought to practise devotion at home :

Man dwelleth not at home, but *wandereth* abroad.
Why doth he forsake ambrosia and eat poison?
Embrace such knowledge, O my soul,
As may make thee a servant of the True One.
Although every one *speaketh* of divine knowledge and meditation,
Yet the whole world wandereth bound by its own entanglements.
He who performeth service is a servant of Him.
Who pervadeth the water, the dry land, the nether regions, and the firmament.
I am not good; there is nobody bad:
The representation of Nanak is—*he who thinketh* so is saved.

Suhi Ashtapadi

The Guru depreciates himself, and utters a prayer to the Almighty:

In me are all demerits; I have not one merit:
How shall I meet my Spouse?
No beauty or lustrous eyes are mine,
No family, no manners, or sweet speech.
The woman who cometh adorned with divine knowledge,
Shall be a happy wife if she please her Spouse.
O God, mercifully attach her to Thy feet
Who hath neither beauty nor good features,
Who remembereth not God at the last moment,
Who hath no wisdom, understanding, or cleverness.
The woman, who though very wise *pleaseth* not her Spouse,
Who attached to mammon is lost in superstition,
Shall, if she dismiss her pride, be absorbed in her Beloved,
And obtain Him who is her nine treasures.
I suffered through being separated from God in many births.
O Beloved Sovereign, take my hand.
Saith Nanak, the Lord is, was, and shall be.

The Beloved will enjoy her who is pleasing to Him.

Miscellaneous instruction of the Guru:

False and fleeting is the dye of the safflower, *lasting* for only four days.
Without the Name man *wandereth* in error; the evil passions rob him, false that he is.
He who is tinctured with the True One shall not be born again.
How canst thou who art dyed with the love of God, be *otherwise* dyed?
Serve *the Guru* who *giveth* God's dye, and apply thy heart to the True One.
Even though man wander in every direction, he shall not obtain spiritual wealth without good fortune.
If robbed by vice thou wander *in the forest* like a huntsman, thou shalt not find shelter.
They whom the Guru *protecteth* are saved; their hearts are dyed with his instruction.
They who wear white clothes, but whose hearts are filthy and hard,
Never uter the Name, but like thieves become absorbed in mammon.
They who know not their own *humble* origin are beasts and cattle.
Man though ever and ever engaged in pleasures, ever and ever *desireth* more enjoyment.
He *thinketh* not of the Creator, so misery *attacheth* to him again and again.
How shall he in whose heart the Dispenser of weal and woe *dwelleth*, want for anything?
They whose accounts are not adjusted shall be summoned; the executioner shall smite them on their heads.
When the account is called for it must be given; it will be examined and considered.
Man shall be saved by his love for the True One; the Pardoner will pardon him.
If he make any one else *than God* his friend, he shall die and he blended with the dust.
Man beholding various phases of life is led astray, and going astray *suffereth* transmigration;
But he shall be emancipated by a favouring glance from God, and God will blend him with Himself.
O listless man who possesses not divine knowledge, search not for it without the Guru.
Man is ruined by allowing himself to be drawn in different directions; *the effects of* both evil and good acts remain with him.
The god of death spieth everyone who is without the Word, and who feeleth not the fear of God.
He who made and sustained the world giveth support to all.
Why forget Him who is ever and ever the Benefactor?
May Nanak not forget the Name which is the support of the supportless!

Subi Chhant

The following is now sung by Sikhs at marriages and other festivities:

Friends have come to my house:

The True One hath caused me to meet them.

When it pleased God He caused me to meet them without mine own effort; by meeting the elect happiness is found.

I have obtained what I set my heart on.

When I meet the *saints* my soul is happy; night and day my hearth and home look bright.

The unbeaten sound of the five musical instruments playeth since saints have come to my house.

Come, beloved friends,

Sing a song of rejoicing, O women.

Sing a true song of rejoicing; then shall you be pleasing to God and rejoice through the four ages.

The Spouse hath come to my house, the place is adorned by Him. His instruction hath adjusted mine affairs.

I applied the great salve of divine knowledge to mine eyes, and saw God's from which *filleth* the three worlds.

Meet me, O companions, sing with zest a song of rejoicing since my Spouse hath come home to me.

My soul and body are bedewed with nectar,

And in my heart is the jewel of love:

In my heart is the precious jewel, and I ponder on the Primal Essence.

To animals Thou art the opulent Giver; Thou givest to every individual.

Thou art wise; Thou possessest divine knowledge; Thou art the searcher of hearts; Thou Thyself didst create the world.

Listen, my friends, the charming Bridegroom hath fascinated me, and my soul and body are bedewed with nectar.

O Supreme Spirit of the world,

True is Thy play;

True is Thy play, O Incomprehensible and Infinite One; who can cause us to understand but Thee?

Without Thee how many can call themselves Sikhs, Strivers, or wise?

The Guru hath stayed the soul which was maddened with the misery of death.

Nanak, he who *removeth* his demerits by the Word, *obtaineth* God through his aggregate of merits.

The Guru is waiting for God as a found wife for her husband:

Come, my Friend, that I may behold Thee.

Standing at my door I am watching for Thee; in my heart is excessive longing;

In my heart is excessive longong; hear me, my Lord, I have reliance on Thee.

On beholding Thee I have become free from desire; the pain of birth and death is at an end.

In all things is Thy light; from it art Thou known, but Thou art found by love.

Nanak, I am a sacrifice to the Friend; the True One is found *when my mind cometh* home.

Suhi ki War

God will assay man's qualities:

Nanak when a man *bringeth* and *putteth* money in his house he *examineth it*;

So in the Lord's court the counterfeit and the genuine shall be tested.

Bathing at places of pilgrimage only renders men more impure:

Men of evil minds and thievish bodies go to bathe at places of pilgrimage.
One part of their filth *departeth* by bathing, by they contract double more.

A gourd may be externally washed, but it containeth undiluted poison within.
Holy men are good without bathing; a thief is always a thief *whether he bathe or not*.

Men should traffic in God's name from their earliest years:

There are two lamps for fourteen shops,
And as many shopkeepers as souls:
When the shops are opened, the traffic *beginneth*.
Every one who *cometh* into the world is transient.
Religion is the broker who *putteth* a mark *on the goods*.
Nanak, they who profit by the Name are acceptable.
For those who obtain the greatness of the true Name.
Gratulations resound on their arrival at their own homes.
In evil association there is no hope of amendment:
It is the habit of thieves, adulterers, prostitutes and pimps.
To contract friendship with the irreligious and dine with them.
They take no through for God's praises; the devil ever dwelleth *in their hearts*.
If sandal be rubbed on a donkey, he will still roll in the dust.
Nanak, by spinning falsehood the web of falsehood is woven.
False is the cloth therefrom and its measurement; false the raiment and the pride thereof.
The repetition of God's name is superior to the call of the Muazzin or the horn of the Jogi,
Whether the Muazzin *repeateth* the call to prayer or *the Jogi bloweth* horns, and the bards join the chorus,
Some are givers, others are beggars; to me Thy name alone is acceptable.
Nanak, I am a sacrifice to those who have heard and accepted it.

The following sloks in the Suhi ki War contain miscellaneous instruction and reflections of the Guru:

I am a sacrifice to those whose words consist to God's praises.
Every night is for the married woman; let me who am separated from Thee, O God, obtain even one night.

They who have not obtained the sweets of love or the delights of the Bridegroom,

Are like the guest of an empty house who goeth as he cometh.
A curse on the lives of those who eat to distant their bellies
Nanak, without the true Name all love is turned into hate.
You say, *O Pandits*—' As darkness is dispelled when a lamp is lighted,
'So by reading the Veds sinful inclinations are destroyed.'
I say, 'When the sun riseth, the moon is not seen.
'Where divine knowledge appeareth mental ignorance is dispelled.
'You, O Pandits, read the Veds and study them,
'But the reading of the Veds is a secular occupation.
'Without understanding this every one shall be disgraced,
'Nanak, the man who *listeneth* to the Guru's instruction shall be saved.
'They who delight not in the Word and who love not God's name,
'Speak offensively with their tongues, and shall ever be disgraced.
'Nanak, they act according to their destiny which none can erase.'

Rag Bilawal

It would not redound to God's glory to call Him by the names of the Hindu incarnations.

Thou art an emperor; if I call Thee Lord, how will that be to Thy greatness?

If Thou inspire me, I will praise Thee, O Lord; I am foolish myself and can say nothing.

Give me understanding to sing Thy praises,
That I may abide in truth according to Thy will.
All that there is *cometh* from Thee; Thou lovest all.
I know not Thy limit, O my Lord; what skill have I, a blind man?
What shall I say? while talking I see that I cannot describe the Indescribable.

I speak as it *pleaseth* Thee; and this is only in the smallest degree for Thy greatness.

Among so many dogs I, a strange dog, bark for my belly's sake.
Even though Nanak perform no service, he will still bear his Master's name.

The Guru's faith in God.

My body I have clothed with a Qalandar's dress, I have turned my heart into a temple, and I bathe in that place of pilgrimage.

The one Word dwelleth in my heart, and I shall not be born again.
My soul is pierced by the Compassionate One; O my mother,
Who knoweth another's pain?
I think of no one but God,

O inaccessible, imperceptible, unseen, and boundless God, take thought for me.

Thou fillest sea and hand, the upper and lower regions; Thy light is in every heart.

My faculty of learning and my understanding are all Thine; I have built my heart as a temple to Thee.

I know none but Thee, O my Lord; I ever sing Thy praises.

Men and lower animals all seek Thy protection; all anxiety for them *resteth* with Thee.

What pleaseth Thee is good; this is Nanak's sole representation.

Lunar Days

The Guru counsels disregard of mammon:

What name shall I repeat except that of the Lord of the world?
Under the Guru's instruction God's court is seen in one's own home.
They who are attached to mammon shall regret it;
They shall go in fetters to Death's gate and suffer transmigration.
What have they brought, and what shall they take away?
They shall receive blows from the god of death on the head.
No one can be emanicapted without the Guru's instruction.
No one can be saved by the practice of hypocrisy.

Heartfelt devotion is superior to all offerings and ablutions:

On the tenth day of the lunar month repeat the Name as your offerings and ablutions.

Night and day lave yourselves in the attributes and knowledge of the True One.

When doubts and fears have fled, impurity shall not cling to the true heart.
A frail cord will soon snap:
Know that the world is as the cord.
Fix thy mind firmly on the True One and thou shalt be happy.

Ramkali

In his devotional enthusiasm the Guru indulges in self-depreciation:

Some read the Veds, some the Purans:
Some repeat names on their rosaries and meditate on them.
I know not and never knew anything; I recognize only Thy name.
I know not, O God, what my lot shall be.
I am ignorant and devoid of divine knowledge; O Lord, I seek Thy protection, mercifully preserve my self-respect and honour.
The mind sometimes riseth and sometimes falleth to the nether regions.
The greedy mind remaineth not still; it searcheth for *mammon* in all directions.
Man entered the word doomed to die; yet he ammasseth wealth for long life.
While others depart, O Lord, we see the burning fire approaching us also.
No one hath a friend, no one hath a brother, no one hath a father or mother.
Nanak representeth, if Thou give *Thy name*, it will assist me at the last hour.

After the death of a Hindu a lamp is kept burning for several days to light the soul of the departed to the next world. It is then floated on water. Guru Nanak indites the following homily on the custom:

Adore God in the following way
Make thy body into a raft by which thou mayest cross over.

Put on it the fire of thy heart,
And the lamp shall burn untiringly day and night.
Float such a lamp on the water
As shall procure thee all knowledge.
The knowledge of God is a good material;
God will accept a lamp made out of it.
Make good deeds thy wheel, and mould *thy lamp on it*;
It will accompany thee in this world and the next.
When God *looketh* on him with an eye of favour,
Some rare pious man *knoweth how to make this lamp.*
This lamp shall be permanent in his heart,
And shall not be extinguished when the dieth.
Float such a lamp on the water
As shall not be shaken or put out by the wind,
And by whose light God's throne may be seen.
Khatris, Brahmans, Sudars and Vaisyas
Find not *such a lamp* by thousands of researches and calculations;
But if any *of them* light such a lamp *as I have described*, He shall, O Nanak, obtain deliverance.

The following was addressed to a Jogi:

The Jogi runneth about begging for clothes and food;
He burneth with the pangs of hunger, and he shall also have misery hereafter.
He who hath not received the Guru's instruction, loseth his honour by his own stupidity.
Some rare man obtaineth God's service by the Guru's teaching.
The Jogi who *knoweth* the way *dwelleth* in a peaceful home.
He who is satisfied with the alms of love and the Word *beholdeth* all men with an equal eye.
The five oxen draw the carriage of the body:
The whole goeth well by the contrivance of God.
When the axle breaketh, the carriage turneth over
Its timber is scattered and it is burnt in the fire.
Meditate, O Jogi, on the Guru's instruction.
Consider weal and woe, union and separation of friends as the same.
Let the Name and meditation on the Guru's instruction be thy dainties.
The wall of thy body shall remain permanent by repeating God's name.
By the practice of sahaj jog thou shalt be freed from entanglements,
And shalt repress lust and wrath under the Guru's admonition.
Make the protection of God and the Guru earrings for thy heart.
Nanak, it is by devotion to God man shall be saved.

Ashtapadi

God is in man's heart and ought not to be sought for elsewhere:

O Nanak, may I obtain the greatness of the Name! there is no religious work superior to it.

If man go elsewhere to ask for what he hath at home, he shall be received with reproaches.

It is said that Guru Nanak on his excursion to the Himalayas met a Jogi called Chetnath, who reproached him with not being a Jogi, a Sanyasi, or a saint, but only a pretended guru. The following was Guru Nanak's reply :

O Jogi, thou buildst a hut and preachest to the world:

If, abandoning thy devotional attitudes, *thou beg from door to door,* how shalt thou obtained the True One?

Thou lovest mammon and woman,
And art neither an anchoret nor a worldly man.
O Jogi, keep thy seat, and the pain of thy worldly love shall depart.
Thou art not ashamed to beg from door to door;
Thou singest songs but knowest not thyself.
How shall the great fire which burneth thee be extinguished?
If the love of God attach to thy heart under the Guru's instruction,
Thou shalt easily enjoy the alms of contemplation.
Thou hypocriticaly appliest ashes to the body,
And shalt be punished for thy worldliness by Death's mace.
The impure vessel of thy heart cannot hold the alms of love.
Thou art bound by bounds and shalt suffer transmigration.
Thou dost not restrain the seed, and yet thou callest thyself continent.
While saying 'Mother', thou biggest and fallest in love with woman.
Thou art without compassion and God's light shineth not in thee.
Thou art immersed in every species of entanglement.
With a patched coat and a bag thou assumest many guises.
Like a conjurer thouperformest many tricks to deceive men.
The fire of anxiety burneth thy heart—
How shalt thou be saved without good works?
Thou makest rings of crystal for thine ears.
Without the highest divine knowledge there is no emancipation.
Thou art beguiled by the pleasures of the tongue and sensual organs.
Thou hast become a beast, and the mark of it shall not be erased.

Appendices

APPENDIX - I

GURU NANAK

Place of Birth-Talwandi

Date of Birth-21th Oct 1469

Married to Mata Sulakhni Daughter of Moolchand, Patwari of Batala Engagement 1485; Marriage 1487

son
Sri Chand
(1494-1612)
Not Married
Founded Udasi Sect

son
Lakhmi Chand
(1497-1555)
Married ; Children-one son

EDUCATION

Talwandi
(1474-1485)

Subjects—Arabic, Persian, Sanskrit Punjab, Religions, Arithmetic, Music

Teachers-Copal (Patti, Arithmetic) Pt. Brijnath (Sanskrit, Religion, Music) Mulla Qutab Uddin (Arabic Persian, Religion)

EMPLOYMENT

Self-employed/farmer worked with father at Talwandi (1485-1504)

Store-keeper with Daulat Khan Lodi Governor of Jullundar Doab at Sultanpur, capital of Jullundur Doab (Nov 1504-August 1507)

THE CALL

(23rd August 1507)*
Return—26 August 1507

Place of Ascent—River Bein
The Messenger—anger Gabriel
Place—Destination—Kingdom of God
Appointment—God's prophet

*Many authors give this date in 1496.

MISSIONARY WORK

First and Second Journeys	Third Journey	Fourth Journey
(1507-1515)	(1515-1517)	(1517-1521)
Area—East and South of India, Sri Lanka	Himalayas, Tibet	West Asia—Bagdad, Mecca, Medina
Approx distance-6400 miles	1000 miles	6000 miles

THE LAST 17 YEARS

Founded Kartarpur in 1521
Constructed first Gurdwara (called Dharamsala)
Started the tradition of Langar
Started the tradition of Taksal (school)
Breathed his last on 22nd September 1539.

TEACHINGS

Fatherhood of God
Brotherhood of mankind
Truthful living
Love and equality
Bhagti/Meditation on the name of God
Sharing each other's sorrows and happiness.

IMPORTANT NAMES

Daulta—Midwife
Pundit Hardyal—The household Pundit (He prepared the Horscope)
Teachers— Gopal, Pt Brijnath, Mulla Quatab-Uddin

The Executives—Rai Bular—Revenue officer Talwandi, Daulat Khan Lodi—Governor of Jullandur Doab stationed at Sultanpur, various Qazis.

The king, Emperors—Babaur, King Shivnabh of Ceylon.

The priests—The Heads of all important Hindu Temples, The Yogis, Sikhs, Gorakh Nath's followers, the head of Jains and Buddhist temples, the Imams of important Muslim moques.

COMPANIONS

Bala—Hindu, Sandhu Jat
Mardana—Muslim mirasi—Rebeck player.

RELATED GURDWARAS

Total number—41

The location

Nanakana Sahib = 7 ; Batala = 3 (10); Sultanpur = 5 (15); Eminabad = 2 (17); Kurukshetra = 1 (18); Dipalpur = 1 (19); Sialkot= 2 (21); Lahore = 1 (22); Delhi= 2 (24) ; Haridwar = 1 (25); Gorakhmata (Pillibhit, Up) = 1 (26); Varanasi = 1 (27); Gaya = 1 (28); Dhanpur (Assam) = 1 (29); Dacca = 1 (30); Chaittagong= 1 (31); Calcutta = 1 (32); Jaganath Puri = 1 (33); Bidar = 1 (34); Matia Kalam (Sri Lanka) = 1 (35); Muttal 9kashmir) = 1 (36); Bagdad = 1 (37); Hassan Abdal= 1 (38); Kartarpur = 1 (39); Dera Baba Nanak = 1 (40); Mecca (No Gurdwara—But there should be one to commemorate the visit of the great prophet).

HYMNS

Total = 974

Raags used = 19

The Hymsn to be read every day—

By an individual — Morning time — Moolmantar, Japji Sahib, evening time — 4 Shabads included in Rehras, bed time — 3 Shabads included in Sohila.

In a Gurdwara — Asa Di Var (24 Pauris + 46 Sloaks)

Other hymsn read regularly — Baramah (4 opening stanzas, 12 months, 1, closing stanzas) Patti, Sidh Ghost.

Languages used — Punjabi, Sanskrit, Persian, Lehndi.

SAKHIS — HAGIOGRAPIES

1. Purantan/Vallayatwali/Hafizabadwali/Cole-wali Janam Sakhi. Total Sakhian = 57
2. Bala wali Janam Sakhi. Total Sakhian = 300
3. Mehrban wali Janam Sakhi. Total Sakhian = 153

4. Bahi Gurdas Dian Varan. Var No. = 1 (Stanzas 23-45) and Var No = 11 (Stanzas 13-14)
5. Bhai Mani Singh dian Sakhian known as Gian-Ratnawli.

GURU NANAK — THE FIRST GURU OF THE SIKHS

		Guru's Age
1469	Born at Talwandit	
1474-1482	Education at Talwandi	5-13
1487	Marriage with Mata Sulakhni	18
1494	Birth—Sri Chand	25
1497	Birth—Lakhmi Chand	28
1485-1505	Work at home with father	16-35
1504	Employment at Sultanpur (where sister Nanki and brother-in-law Jai Ram Uppal lived)	35
1507	Resigned from the job	38
23 Aug	Angels took Nanak to the house of God from riven Bein	38
1507 26 Aug	Came back from God — First Commandment at Sultanpur	38
1507-1521	**Travels (for 14 years)**	
1507-1510	**First journey**—accompanied by Bhai Mardana	38-41
	Multan—conversion of Sheikh Sajjan	
	Panipat—discourse with Shah Sharif	
	Delhi—revived a dead elephant; meeting With Sultan Ibrahim	
	Banaras—discourse with Pundit Chatur Das	
	Nanakmata—discourse with Yogis	
	Assam (Kamrup)—conversion of Nur Shah	
	Orissa—Puri—hymn of Aarti	
	Talwandi—meeting with parents	
	Goindwal—healing of a leper	
	Saidpur—Emanibad, Babur's attack, Guru Nanak's arrest; Mallick Bhago and Lalo	
	Lahore—Duni Chand	
	Talwandi—meeting with parents	

1510-1515	**Second journey (5 years)—South of India and Ceylon** Madhya Pradesh— conversion of Kauda Ceylon—enlightenment of Raja Shivnabn	41-46
1515-1517	**Third journey (2 years)—North of India** Kashmir—discourse with Pandit Brahma Das. Mount Sumer-discourse with Siddhs Achal Batala—festival of Shivratri; discourse with yogis	46-48
1517-1521	**Fourth Journey—West of Asia** Mecca—discourse with Qazi Rukundin Bagdad—discourse with Pir Dastgir Hasan Abdal—discourse with Wali Qandhari	48-52
1521	End of missionary Journeys—settlement at Kartarpur, on the banks of Ravi	52
1532	Meeting with Bhai Lehna	63
1539	Anointment of Lehna as the second Guru of the Sikhs 14th July	70
1539 22nd-September	Death of Guru Nanak (2 months and 8 days after the anointment of Guru Angad)	

APPENDIX - II

GURU NANAK'S TEACHINGS

At a time when Hindus were frustrated and dismayed. Guru Nanak appeared to elevate the spirit of religion and man. His object was to regenerate the suffering humanity from superstition, ritualism, casteism, persecution and social industice. He wished to build a community of self-respecting men and women, devoted to God, and to fill them with a sense of religious liberty, social equality and brotherhood for all. His followers were called Sikh, a local form for Sanskrit word Shishya, meaning student, disciple, learner or seeker. The main tenets of his teachings are given below :

God

Guru Nanak' exposition of God is summed up in the basic formula called *Mul Mantra*:

Ik Omkar, Satnam, Karta Purakh, Nirbhau Nirvair, Akalmurti, Ajuni, Saibhang, Gurprasad.

There is one God. God is truth. He is the Creator. God is without fear. He is without animosity. He is the immortal being. He is unborn. He is self-existent. God is realized by the grace of the Guru. Guru Nanak says :

By uttering the Lord's Name, the *Mal Mantra*, provides elixir leading to the attainment of God. God to Guru Nanak was a fact and reality. He could argue about God. He could affirm God. His vision was cosmic. God is formless and omnipotent. He acts independently. He knows all and everything. He alone is the bestower of gifts. He is an ocean of mercy, friend of man, healer of sinner, cherisher of the poor, and destroyer of sorrow. He is wise, generous, beautiful and bountiful.

Nanak says even if he knew God, he could not describe Him. He is great and His bounties are great. He looks after everything. God is absolutely just. His grace is for all, but he gives as He wishes. He is omnipresent. The individual self is in God, and God is in the individual self. God and his devotees are one and there is nothing between them.

Atam mahi ram, Ram mahi atam

God and the individual souls are related like the ocean and its waves. The drop of water is in the sea, and the sea is in the drop of water.

Sagar mai bund, Bund mai sagar

In Christianity God is considered father and man as a son. Father and son seldom remain together during whole life. Nanak went a step further. He considered man as wife and God as man. In Nanak's time husband and wife could be separated only by death. There was no divorce, and desertion was rare.

God as husband

Guru Nanak considered himself a girl wedded to God. The Guru says :

1. "My Guru-God has brought me into union with Himself. I, a mere girl, have thus obtained the spouse in my home."
2. "The Beloved delights in me day and night, for, God is my husband and I am ever a bride."
3. God is the only spouse, all other beings are His brides.

Eka pursh nar sabai

Nanak says : A woman may be stupid, dirty, black and impure-minded; yet if she possesses merit, she meets her beloved; otherwise Nanak, the woman is to blame.

(In the *Adi Granth* the word Mohila for the Guru became Mohalla.) God pervades the whole universe.

Kudrat diseh, kudrat suniye, kudrat bhau sukh sar,
Kudrat patali, akasi, kudrat arb akar.

In nature we see Him. In nature do we hear Him speak.
In nature lies the essence of joy and peace.
The lower and upper regions, comprise nature,
The entire nature is His embodiment.

Nanak proclaimed that God never appeared in human form.

1. Nanak's God is both *Nirgun* (absolute) and *Sagun* (personal). He is spread over the whole universe. He can also be loved as a being.
2. God is one and cannot be represented as Brahma, Vishnu, Shiva, Rama and Krishna.
3. He belongs to all living beings.
4. He can be realized through love, devotion and good deeds.
5. He can be worshipped only by singing His praises and constant repetition of His Name.

A question might arise who created God, and whether God could be seen. Nanak put a limit to reasoning in matters spiritual. Intuition or a spontaneous and a sudden flash of light revealed the truth more easily than long arguments, disputations, and reasoning of cold intellect. There was an unseen spiritual presence beyond the visible universe. Nanak did not consider religion as a mental exercise. It was faith, a practical way of life for the realization of God and self. God could not be seen, but his presence could be felt like the pain in body or pleasure in the heart or the fragrance in a flower, air in the atmosphere, or electricity in various forms. Butter cannot be located in milk, but it is there. Thus God could be see through His creation. The creed of Nanak was not monotheism (belief in one God), but pantheism (belief that the whole universe is God).

Nam marg

Hinduism prescribed three-fold path of Gian Marg (knowledge), Karam Marg (action), and Bhakti Marg (devotion) to attain salvation. Buddhism believed in Karam Marg (action) alone. Islam laid emphasis on belief is one God, Prophet Muhammad and the *Quran*. Nanak does not seem to have come into contact with Christianity. Nanak rejected all the high roads laid down by older religions. He adopted an independent path, the simplest possible. It was *Nam Marg* or *Simran* or dedication to the Name, the True Name. Nanak said that God was not a distant deity. "The beloved is not far from thee, behold Him in thy heart." One could call Him for guidance and help as one would call a relative or a friend in time of need. By *Simran* God becomes a constant companion of every individual. Nanak therefore sang the Name. He preached the Name. He dwelt in the Name. He said the world was ailing. The Divine Name was the medicine. Without the Name life was barren. This conception gave new hope, new faith, new life and new expectations to the depressed, dejected and downcast people of Punjab. They found that the Name, the True Name, was the cure of all the ills and sufferings of humanity. In the light and beauty divine one transcended all worldly woes and worries. It was a simple, sublime and serene message.

Nanak's God was personal and merciful. He helped those who believed in Him sincerely. True devotion, complete surrender of the self and thoughtful, constant *Namsimran* as opposed to mechanical repetition and ritualism, would enable an individual to realize God. "Efface thyself so that you may obtain the Bridegroom." *Sat Nam* (the True Name) was the remedy for all human ills and for all human happiness in this world and hereafter. Mohsin Fani writes: "The *bani* of Nanak, viz., his hymns serve the purpose of prayer, admonition and counsel. Most of his sayings are on the greatness of God and His holiness." He further says that the vocabulary of Nanak is that of the Punjabi Jat or villager or rustic. "His disciples have no regard for the Sanskrit language." Thus repetition of the Name silently and inwardly was the beginning of spiritual life. The Name brought one into harmony with the universe. A healing process would start to cure one's ills.

Repetition of the Name is called *Simran.* It is to be done with great care and thoughtfulness.

> Prabh ki ustat karoh sant mit
> *Savdhan ikagar chit.*
>
> (Holy man, friend praise God attentively and with an alert mind.)
> Nanak says : "Thinking good is thinking of God."

Nam marg can be practised in two ways, through words, by keeping it in mind all the time, and by actions, i.e., serving God's creatures. The Nam Marg produces threefold effect. It is purifying, as it keeps one away from vice. It is illuminating as it imparts knowledge and beauty, truth and virue. It is unifying as it draws the devotee nearer God.

The Guru

Guru is an ancient and common term in Hinduism. In Hindu thought Guru is both spiritual and temporal. A temporal Guru may be a Pandit, elderly scholar or teacher. A spiritual Guru is a religious guide or teacher quite different from all kinds of priests well-versed in sacred literature. Guru Nanak adopted this term, but gave it a special meaning and significance. In Sikkhism Guru is a divine master, saviour, prophet, spiritual enlightener, who is as perfect as God, but not God. The guru is a God-illuminated person through whom God reveals Himself.

The Guru's association gives peace, tranquility and harmony with everything in the universe. The true guru leads his disciples to the presence of God. He is a bride between man and God. He is the stair-case to life a person to god. He is illuminating like the sun which never rises and never sets. The Guru raises the falling spirit of his followers and inspires them with hope and confidence. Gurbani is God's voice. It is the living fountain. It enables a person to enter the realm of truth, beauty and amity. In Sikh religion the Guru does not bestow boons and benediction. Nor does he plead in favour of his disciples.

Nanak claimed neither divinity nor prophethood, yet he regarded the Guru essential for the realization of God. It was only through him that an individual could have common with God. "Men shall not be emancipated without instruction by the Guru, even though he performed hundreds and thousands of ceremonies, all would still be darkness without the Guru." There was no necessity to worship any gods or goddesses. The Guru says in Japji:

"The word of the Guru is the inner music;
The word of the Guru is the highest scripture;
The word of the Guru is all pervading;
The Guru is *Shiv,* the Guru is *Vishnu* as well as *Brahma*;
The Guru is the mother of goddess."

In Sri Rag Nanak says :

"Everybody else is subject to error, only the Guru and God are without error."

The Guru in Sikhism is both human and divine.

Ram Ram sabh ko kahae,
Kahia Ram na hoe,
Gurparsadi Ram man vasde, Tan phal pavae koe.

(All utter Ram Ram, but one cann't get Ram by saying. Ram can live in heart with Guru's grace, only then one can get the fruit)

"His knowledge is acquired
Under the Guru's instruction;'
Man learns that Guru is everywhere."

The problem of how to find the True Guru (Sat Guru) is thus solved by Guru Nanak:

"Only that man finds peace of mind,
Who meets the true Guru.
And enshrines the Name of God in his heart;
And that too, Nanak, if God sends his Grace."

In *Asa ki Var Nanak* says :

"If a hundred moons rise,
And a thousand suns shine;
There would still be pitch darkness,
Without the Guru's light."

Nanak declared that his own Guru was God. He said : "I speak as the words of God come to me." "I have said what He commands me to speak." "Listen, the Eternal God Lord is my Guru." "My Satguru is eternal. He is neither born nor dies." Nanak demanded complete surrender from his disciples who could attain salvation through the superior spiritual power of the Guru.

Nanak says : "The Guru's instruction is jewels and gems; by serving him his disciples find them.

There is no place of pilgrimage equal to the Guru; The tank of consolation is contained in the Guru.

The Guru is a river whence pure water is ever obtained, and by which the filth of evil inclination is washed away.

He who findeth the True Guru hath obtained perfect bathing, which *maketh* him a god out of a beast or a ghost.

He who is inbued with the true Name *obtaineth* it; that Guru is called sandal.

Fix thine attention on His feet by whose odour vegetables are perfumed.

Through the Guru man *obtaineth* real life, and through the Guru man *departeth* to God's home.

Nanak, through the Guru man is absorbed in the True One; through the Guru man *obtaineth* the special dignity of deliverance."

Creation of universe

About the Creation of universe Nanak says :

Sache te pavana bhaiya
pavanai te jalu hoi, jal te
tribhavan sajiya ghat ghat
joti samoi

(From Truth emanated air, From air emanated water, From water emanated the three worlds. Then He merged Himself in His creation)

Guru Nanak in Maru Sohila holds that nobody knows the hour of creation. There was complete darkness.

Nanak says the universe is not self-existent. The universe was created by God. It is dependent upon Him. Whatever is in existence it is there by His will.

Heaven and hell

Hinduism and Islam mention seven regions of heaven and seven of hell. Nanak considers them countless. He says :

There are lakhs of regions; Upper and nether both, There cannot be any count of them.

Mohsin Fani wrote : Nanak in his hymns says that there are many skies and earths.

Nanak's conception of Karma

Nanak believed in the Law of *Karma.* He asserted that good deeds bore good fruit and bad deeds bore bad fruit. As a man soweth so shall he reap. God has created virtue as well as vice. A man should pursue the path of virtue and struggle against evil. Everything is not preordained. Man is free to choose between virtue and vice. Vice gives temporary pleasure. Virtue provides lasting happiness, but vice is more attractive than virtue.

On seing a rich Shaikh travelling in a planquin, Mardana asked Guru Nanak:

"Who created this man who rideth in a cost sadan chair, while the bearers have no shoes to their feet? Their legs are naked while they shampoo and fan him." The Guru replied:

"They who performed austerities in their former lives are now kings and receive tribute on earth. They who were then wearied, are now shampooed by others."

The Guru further observed : "O Mardana, whosoever is born hath come naked from his mother's womb and joy or misery is the result of actions in previous states of existence."

In *Japji* Nanak says :

"Words do not the saint or sinner make,
Action alone is written in the book of fate,
What we sow that alone we take,
O Nanak, be saved or for ever transmigrate."

Nanak held that *kam* (lust), *karodh* (anger), *lobh* (greed), *moh* (attachment) and *ahankar* (conceit) were the five diseases from which all living beings were suffering. But man was endowed with the capacity to overcome them. "Ego is a chronic disease, but its cure is to be found within it."

The Guru defines a truly religious person thus:
Religion *consisteth* not in a patched coat,
or in a Jogi's staff, or in ashes smeared over the body;
Religion *consisteth* not in earring worn,
or in a shaven head, or in the blowing of horns.
Religion consisteth not in mere words;
He who *looketh* on all men as equal is religious;
Religion consisteth not in wandering to tombs
or places of cremation or sitting in attitudes of contemplation.
Religion *consisteth* not in wandering in foreign countries,
or in bathing in places of pilgrimages.
Abide pure amidst the impurities of the world;
Thus hall thou find the way of religion."

Nanak preached that law of Karma could be modified by the grace of God and the Guru. God can destroy Karma.

Grace

The law of Karma is strict and hard. But the Lord is not cruel or barbarian. He is generous and gracious. He sends his grace through the Guru, who prescribed the worship of the Name. In case of a sinner's repentance, the Guru procures him God's grace and mercy. Blind are not those who have no eyes. Nanak, blind are they who go astray from the path of virtue.

The Guru laments at the wastage of precious life.

Raini gavai soi kai,
Divasu gavaia khai,
Hire jaisa Janamu hai
Kaudi badle jae.

(Night is lost in sleep, day in eating; The diamond-like life is given away for a kauri).

Transmigration of soul, Nirvan or Sach Khand

Like Hindustan Nanak believed that soul did not die. It neither grows nor decays. It is neither old nor young. It is as pure and luminous as God, but with a difference: Soul lives in a body which is dependent upon material things. Soul is influenced by five senses. Hence it acquires some impurity. On the death of the body soul gets into a new body, but it carries some impurity of the previous life with it. This impurity can be washed away by Guru's guidance and God's grace.

Nanak declared that soul emanated from the absolute, the fountain of light, the pure source. There were eighty-four lakhs souls or forms of existence. This number neither increased nor decreased. According to the old belief the number of souls was as follows :

17 lakhs immovable creatures like trees
10 lakhs aquatic animals
11 lakhs creeping animals
10 lakhs feathered animals
32 lakhs quadrupeds
4 lakhs human beings

Thus the number of human souls is only a fraction of creation. Death does not mean extinction. It marks a stage in the journey of the soul. Life, says Nanak, is as the shadow of the passing bird, but the soul of man is, as the potter's wheel, ever circling on its pivots. Soul being a part of God never dies. It cannot be destroyed. The body perishes, but the soul survives. It assumes various forms in different bodies according to one's deeds. It never changes through numerous births and deaths. The wall of selfishness or egoism stands between soul and God. According to Guru Nanak salvation or deliverance from the transmigration can be attained through good deeds and by the grace of the personal, absolute God. Grace can be invoked by *Namsimran* or worship of God with love and devotion.

The soul is a divine spark. It should reunite with the source from which it emanated. As long as this goal is not achieved, it remains unhappy, because it is separated from the source. During its union with the body the soul become impure. This impurity or duality or second love hinders the return of the soul to the eternal fountain of light. There is good and bad, virtue and vice in this world. The body is attracted towards *maya,* illusion, evil and vice.

The ultimate goal of soul in Sikhism is not heaven, a land of wealth, wine and women. In his hymns Nanak held *Nirvan* or *Sach Khand* or absorption in the immortal as the highest goal of human life. It is a state of ever-lasting bliss and beauty and eternal happiness. *Nirvan* can be attained by constant meditation on God, by upright character, and service of all living beings. The human soul then blends with God as water mixes with water.

As water blends with water, when two streams their waves unite,
The light of human life doth blend with God's celestial light.
No transmigrations then await the weary human soul;

It hath attained its resting place,
Its peaceful crowning goal.

According to Nanak all living beings have two bodies, tangible and intangible, touchable and untouchable, visible and invisible. The former is the body and latter is the soul. The soul separates from the body at death. It goes on taking birth after unless *Nirvan* is attained.

In *Japji* Nanak lays down five stages in the spiritual progress of man:

(i) *Dharam Khand* in which a man tries to realize his connection with God and disciplines his mind.

(ii) *Gian Khand* in which the disciple acquires knowledge and tries to understand why God has sent him into the world.

(iii) *Sharam Khand* in which the disciple attempts advancing towards God to meet Him. This is the beginning of action.

(iv) *Karam Khand* in which the disciple's godly life and his desire to meet God is appreciated by the Almighty, and He confers Her grace on the disciple who fully devotes himself to action.

(v) *Sach Khand* in which the disciple arrives at the destination, meets his Beloved and merges himself into eternity.

Thus Nanak says : In the soil of your mind sow the seed of good deeds and water the soil with God's name.

Nanak's attitude towards avatars and divinities

Nanak did not believe in divinities and incarnations. He did not believe that God took human form to protect the good and destroy evil. Nanak's God was formless and birthless. He sang the glory and greatness of only One True Lord. Mohsin Fani says : "He had no faith in idols and idol temples. Nanak praised Musalmans. He also praised *Avatars*, gods and goddesses of Hindus. But he did not consider all of them creator (*khaliq*), but declared them the created (*makhluq*)." In *Japji* he says : "One maya in union with God gave birth to three acceptable children. One of them is creator, the second the provider, the third performeth the function of destroyer."

This is Hindu Trinity pure and simple. But his says that these are not independent beings because "as it pleaseth God, He directeth them by this order." Nanak further says : "By hearing the Name man *becometh* as Shiva, Brahma and Indra."

Nanak mainly attacked not these divinities so much as those who only concentrated upon them by ignoring the True Lord.

The Vedas and the Quran

Nanak did not denounce the scriptures such as the *Vedas* and the *Quran* He said : "The four books and the four *Vedas* which were promulgated in the world, came down from high under the orders of the Lord God." Nanak further said :

> *"Ved Kitab kaho mat jhute,*
> *Jhuta so jo na vichare."*

(Do not call the *Vedas* and the *Quran* false. False is not who does not follow them.)

Nanak condemned the mechanical recitations from these scriptures without realizing the Immortal Lord.

Pilgrimages, penances, fasts, and renunciation and superstitions

Nanak was not opposed to pilgrimages of holy places. A visit to a sacred shrine and meeting pious people did ennoble the mind. But it did not wash away one's past sins. If the pilgrimage was made with the object, it was in vain. The real pilgrimage implied bathing in the holy Name.

Nanak denounced penances and fasts, He was opposed to the torture of body to get salvation. He said that human body was the sublime temple of God. He placed infinite light within it. It was not to be tortured to realise Him. Guru Nanak says :

> 'Let Jogis practise jog, let gluttons practise gluttony;
> Let penitents practise penance, and rub and bathe themselves at places of pilgrimages;
> But let me listen to Thy songs; O Beloved, if anyone will sit and sing them to me."
>
> Nanak declared : "Through fasting and penance the mind is not softened."

In *Japji* the Guru says :

> "Pilgrimage, austerities, mercy, and alms-giving on general and special occasions,
> Whosoever performeth may obtain some little honour;
> But he who *heareth* and *obeyeth* the *loveth* God in his heart,
> Shall wash off his impurity in the place of pilgrimage within him."

At another place the Guru says :

> "Burnt offerings, sacred feasts, and the reading of the *Puranas*.
> If pleasing to God, are acceptable."

The obvious conclusion is that these things by themselves are of no value and that they can be useful only when they are performed in a spirit of true devotion. He denounced the perversions, not the practices.

Nanak declared that nobody was high and nobody was low. Only fools and idiots claimed superiority over other.

The people who renounced the world appeared to Nanak unfit to face the challenge of life. He declared that such man were not doing any good or justice either to themselves or to society.

Nanak criticised useless yogis and ignorant mullan:

Makhattu hoi kai kan parae

(Unfit to earn livelihood many got their ears split.)

Gian vihuna gawe git

Bhukha mullan ghare masit.

(Without knowledge the hungry Muslim priest sing songs and converts his home into a mosque.)

Nanak regarded ancestral worship through *sharadhs*, evil eye, *mahurat*, omens and worship of graves, idols, statues, and tombs as superstitious. Nanak says : One does not serve his ancestors when they are alive, but offers them feasts when they are dead. Tell me what will the poor parents get when crows and dogs have eaten the feast offered.

Caste system

In Nanak's time Hindu society was based on caste and was divided into countless watertight compartments. Men were considered high and low on account of their births and not according to their deeds. Equality of human beings was a dream. There was no spirit of national unity except feelings of community fellowship. In Nanak's views a man's love of God was the criterion to judge whether a person was good or bad, high or low. As the caste system was not based on divine love, he condemned it. "Preposterous in caste, vain the distinction of birth. The Lord gives shelter to all beings." Nanak aimed at creating a casteless and classless society similar to the modern type of socialist society in which all were equal and where one member did not exploit the other. Nanak insisted that every Sikh home should serve as a place of love and devotion, a true guest house *(Sachdharamshala)*. Every Sikh was enjoined to welcome a traveller or a needy person and to share his meals and other comforts with him. Bhai Gurdas says :

"Wherever the holy feet of Guru Nanak touched, dharamshalas sprang into existence."

The sacred thread

The sacred thread had a strong link with caste. Some writers are of the opinion that Nanak tried to abolish this custom. They quote a hymn of Nanak which he uttered at the time of thread-wearing ceremony at the age of nine:

> "Out of the cotton of mercy make threads of temperateness and twisting
> them with righteous zeal tie in them the knot of continence.
> The sacred thread thus formed will be for the soul, if thou hast it,
> O Pundit, put it one me.
> It will not break, or get soiled, or be burnt or lost.

Blessed is the man, O Nanak, who goes about with such a thread on his neck."

It is not clear whether Nanak sought to abolish the custom altogether at that young age. This much is certain that he denounced the wearer's claim to superiority on the basis of the thread alone.

The middle path

Between the ascetic and the epicurean, Nanak chose the middle path or the *Gribastha Ashram* of the life of a householder. It was an ideal path as it offered opportunities for social, material and spiritual growth of an integrated man. Even the ascetics had to knock at the door of a householder for food and clothing, etc. The life of a householder offered a purposeful living and was conducive to social welfare. The family life was thus declared as an essential part of the Sikh way of life. Guru Nanak himself led the householder's life. He had not renounced family ties after enlightenment when he went on extensive tours. At the end of every great journey he joined his family, parents, wife, children and other relatives. His parents died before he had finished his travels. He settled down at Kartarpur with his wife and two sons. Nanak condemned asceticism and renunciation of the world. A householder was equally acceptable to God as a hermit. The secular business did not stand in the way of emancipation. Live in the world, but lead a good life, and help others to do so, he asserted. *Sadh sangat* or association with virtuous and holy men would help people in doing so. Work, worship and entertain others (*kirt karo, Nam japo* and *wand chhako*) was the motto placed before his disciples. Earn by honest labour and share the earnings with the needy.

Nanak believed in the unity of mankind and stood for the lofty ideal of the greatest good of all. This was his socialism and international justice based on righteousness. He believed in universal spiritual republicanism in which poverty was banished and war outlawed. By his own personal example he taught the people to live together as brothers. He himself denied with people of all castes and classes, great and small, Hindus and Muslims alike. In his *langar* all sat together and ate the same food by sitting on the floor.

Education

Nanak was clear in his mind as to the nature of education which should be imparted to the nation's youth. As the educational institutions of Hindus had been suppressed, Nanak considered spiritual instruction essential to retain peace of mind. He condemned purely secular education: "One may read cartloads of books. He may read camel-loads. He may read boatfulls. He may read books which will fill a cellar. One may read for days, even for months. One may read for his whole life, even for all his breaths. Nanak, only one thing will count. The rest is all an exercise in egoism." It is love of humanity.

Nanak lays down the qualifications of a teacher: "A teacher may be termed educated when he dispenses knowledge spontaneously. He digests what he reads and arrives at the reality and fixes his attention on the Name of God. The egoist sells knowledge, earns poison and eats poison. The fool does not understand the word and is steeped in ignorance. But if an educated man is greedy, avaricious and vain, he is to be termed as a fool."

Nanak denounced teachers who lived on the offerings of their pupils. "Do not fall at the feet of him, who calls himself a *Guru* or *Pir* and goes a begging."

Nanak expected high standards of morality, spirituality and intellectual attainments from a teacher. He must practise what he taught. Only when he could inspire his disciples. "The egoists indulge in mere talk; they do not practise what they say," declared Nanak.

Nanak observed : "Comprehension of learning consists in doing good to others. Mere reading of religious texts without understanding and without acting up to them is not of much avail. Nothing approaches the knowledged of Truth but true conduct excels it." Learning without realising the purpose of life and singing the praise of God increased egoism. God and man lived together with the partition wall of egoism between them.

Charity

Giving away something in the service of others was a necessary part of a Sikh's life. He was expected to make offering to the Guru, to Guru's community mess and to the needy. Nanak insisted that one should earn one's living by the sweat of one's brow. In Sarang ki Var he says :

Ghal, khae, kichh hathon de,
Nanak raho pachhani se
(Earn by toil, eat and something give away. O Nanak! such a person knows the real way).

Control over pleasures of senses

Nanak advocated control over five base elements in man—*kam, karodh, lobh, moh* and *ahankar*. He strongly pleaded against the glamour and glitter of wealth, wine, women and war, as these things kept man away from God.

Yoga

Guru Nanak was not against yogi. He wanted to adjust it to meet the needs of a householder. In his view Hat hyoga did not suit family men. He favoured Sahaj yoga. It gives mental poise. It keeps the balance of mind. It helps the householder to perform his duties properly. Nanak says:

Jo kichu karae bhala kari mano
Sahaj jog nidhi pawo
(Whatever He does, accept that as good and gain the treasure of Sahaj Yoga.)

Nanak further says :

Dekhi acharaju rahe bismadi
Ghati ghati sur nar sahaj samadhi.

(Through sahaj samadhi one beholds wonders and is elevated to the realm of sublimity.)

Love of humanity

Nanak loved all human beings, irrespective of religious or geographical limits or barriers. He said :

"Among the low my caste in lowest,
Among the lowly I am the lowest,
Sayeth Nanak, I keep company of such men,
And have no ambition to emulate great men;
Because where the lowly are looked after,
Is the place blessed by the Supreme Master."
He stressed the principle of service of mankind:
"In the world service of the people is supreme,
That will secure a seat for you in God's esteem."

Nanak proclaimed that the cultivation of humility was necessary for the elimination of the ego. God had created everybody and therefore nobody should malign anybody else. He said :

"Know that God dwells in all souls,
So become the dust of the feet of all,
In this may practise the love of God,
Regard your live, soul, body and wealth as His property."

Nanak held the sanctity of human life in high esteem. He said life originated from a pure source, the light of the lord, and therefore it remained essentially pure. "O mind, thou has emanated from the light of Lord." He said that in the course of life all the sins committed by man could be washed away. A sinner was not doomed for ever nor was he saved till eternity. He was rewarded and punished according to his deeds. Nanak says :

"The virtuous and the vicious are not mere echoes,
For, one carriers along all that one does."

Manmukh and Gurmukh

Guru Nanak aimed at converting manmukh Sikhs into gurmukh Sikhs. A manmukh believes in enjoyment of physical pleasure. Soul has no meaning for him. A manmukh person is selfish. He is centred in himself alone. He is not interested in his fellow beings. He is full of pride and arrogance. He frowns upon lower class people, and flatters his superiors. He is full of envy, jealously, and hatred and cannot tolerate praise of others. He has no love for God and godly persons.

A gurmukh controls his ego. He follows the path leading to the Guru and God. He keeps his five senses in check and is above temptations. A gurmukh shuns falsehood and loves truth. He believes in doing good to others.

Guru Nanak is Sikh Ghost lays down the following four qualities of a gurmukh:

Gurmukh shastar simrit Ved,
Gurmukh pawe ghat ghat bhed,
Gurmukh vair, virod gwawe
Gurmukh sagli ganat mitawe.

(A gurmukh knows Vedas and other holy scriptures. A gurmukh realizes the presence of God in everything. A gurmukh is free from hatred and malice. A gurmukh never thinks that anybody has wronged him.

The ideal man

Guru Nanak's ideal man must possess the following qualifications :

1. He is a householder and discharges his duties towards himself, his family and society. He is friendly and sympathetic towards the welfare of others. He is a *yogi* and *bhogi.*
2. He is a man of God. He repeats God's name all the time silently and attentively. They are not pure who keep their bodies clean. Pure are they in whose heart God dwells. By associating with holy men they curb anger, greed, lust, passion and conceit.

Uttam sangat uttam hoe.

3. He should resist evil, injustice, tyranny and wickedness.
4. He should took upon others as his superiors.

Manda jane ap ko awer Bhola sansar.

5. He should earn living by labour and should share his earnings with the needy.
6. *He believes in Nam (God), Dan (charity), Ishnan (cleanliness).*
7. *Hak praya Nanaka us sour us ghae*
   Gur pir hama tan bhare jan murdar na khae.

(What belongs to others is like pork and beef. The Guru and a Muslim saint will consider ill-gotten wealth as eating a corpse.)

Women

Woman was held in an inferior position. She was kep in *purdah.* Child marriage and *Sati* were common due to the exigency of times. No education was imparted to them.

Women, therefore, received great consideration from Nanak. They were allowed to attend his sermons along with men. *Purdah* was discouraged. Women joined in the chorus in singing hymns. For *langar* men brought provisions and fuel wood, while women cooked food. Men and women both served meals to the *pangat.* Nanak condemned *Sati* or the custom of self-immolation of widows on funeral pyres of their dead husbands. Guru said : "How can they be inferior when they give birth to men? Women as well as men share in the grace of God and are equally responsible for their actions to Him."

Nanak raised the status of women by asserting that as a wife won over her husband by her beauty, accomplishments, chastity, love, service and devotion, so could God be attained. Nanak declared:

"In a woman we are conceived, of a woman we are born. To a woman we are betrothed and married. Through a woman new relationships are formed. The woman continued the race. When one woman dies, we look for another. The woman carries on the tradition. Why should we call her evil of whom are born kings. *Manda kiyon akhiye jo jamme rajan.* A woman is born of a woman. There is no human being who is not born a woman. Nanak, True God alone is independent of a woman."

Guru Nanak condemned the practice of *Sati*. He declared :

A *Sati* is not one who burns himself on the funeral pyre of her husband. A *Sati* is one, O Nanak, who dies with the sheer shock of separation.

Nanak believed in monogamy. On his return home from his tour of the east after twelve years, Nanak stayed in the jungle five kilometres away from his home town Talwandi. The Guru's father and mother waited on him and tried their best to persuade him to stay at home and stop from wandering any longer. Nanak refused all the imploring of his parents, because the comfortable living was not his idea of what life demanded of him. In this course of arguments it was suggested that they would get him another more attractive and younger wife. Nanak replied : "Father dear, it is God who *arrangeth* marriages. He maketh no mistake, and those whom He hath once joined He *joineth* for ever." The obvious inference is that Nanak was a believer is monogamy. Bhai Gurdas also drew the same conclusion when he wrote : "Be chastte with one wife."

Sikhism different from other reform movements

Although Nanak was a saint of the Bhakti school, yet in certain respects Nanak's religion differed from other reforms movements as of Ramanand, Kabir, Chaitanya and Gorakhnath:

1. The latter laid stress on fundamentals of Hinduism, believing that their acceptance would ultimately bring about social readjustment. Sikhism from the very beginning concentrated on social reform and repetition of the Name.

2. Conception of God in Sikhism is different from that of other Bhakti leaders. The Sikh God is Akal Purakh. He is without body, formless and timeless. The other leaders believed in Rama and Krishna being incarnations of God. Nanak objected to it as the human body was subject to deterioration and death. Besides Nanak's emphasis on love of God was stronger and deeper than that of other Bhakti leaders. To Nanak God's love was whole existence.

3. Many bhaktas though firmly believing in the unity of God could not oppose the worship of Shiva or Vishnu often represented by some idol or picture. They felt it was easier for the simple-minded and illiterate people to concentrate on something concrete which they could see with their own eyes. Nanak rejected idol worship because the idols were considered as God rather than as His representation for the purpose of concentration.

4. Sikh religion had no mythology, no traditions and no ambiguity. It was plain and simple. Believe in one God, have faith in the Guru and lead a good life. Then success in this world and salvation after death is yours. The other reformers mainly concerned themselves with salvation of the soul.

5. In Sikhism renunciation of the world was prohibited, while the other sects advocated it. Nanak also rejected celibacy.

6. It was Nanak alone who founded the institution of Guruship for the spread of Bhakti movement.

7. At several places Guru Nanak established *sangats* or *dharamshalas* and *pangats* or *langars* to serve as an association of his disciples to meet regularly to sing the praises of God. No such thing was done by others.

8. No other Bhakti leader dislodged Sanskrit from the position of its being the sacred language of Hinduism, though they preached in the local tongue. Nanak cut himself off absolutely from Sanskrit as it was not understood by the common people.

9. Guru Nanak aimed at upliftment the individual as well as building a nation. The other Bhakti leaders laid emphasis on individual alone. The result was that whereas the Sikh developed themselves into a powerful community and ruled in the country for nearly a hundred years, the other sects either disappeared to remained where they were in the lifetime of their founders.

10. Sikhism laid great stress on interdining and recitation; the others on individual dining and on modes of ecstasy like dancing or performing *Arti*, etc.

11. Nanak wanted to establish union of the individual with the universal. His conception of union transcended the union between male and female. He considered man as wife and God as man. It was the spiritual union.

12. The mysticism and Sant traditions of other Bhaktas had some tinge of Buddhism, Nath Yogis, Hathyoga and Sufism. Nanak's mysticism was plain and simple, clear and precise. It was devotion to God alone.

13. In matter like birth, marriage, death, and pilgrimage, etc. Nanak rejected the old priestly practices and rituals and insisted on simple and economical ceremonies, which could be performed by non-Brahmans.

14. Nanak travelled more extensively than others inside the country and abroad, which no other Bhakti leader did. It widened his outlook.

15. Kabir was a mystic. His thoughts and ideas appealed to the people in isolation. Kabir's popularity depended upon his witty remarks, wise sayings, and striking examples. Guru Nanak's principles had a continuity, and his words and expressions could be understood more easily by illiterate peasantry and working classes.

16. The essential quality of a bhakta was love. This love was directed towards avatars of Vishnu and tantric yoga by most of the bhaktas. Nanak directed it to the Supreme Almighty Lord. The former involved difficulties and sufferings. Nanak's love of God was simple.

17. The idea of Guruship was well-established in India, but its transformation into a living faith had not been a familiar feature. A religious institution disintegrated after the death of its founder. Sikhism escaped this fate.

Was Nanak a reformer or a revolutionary?

A social and religious revolutionary destroys the existing social institutions held dear by the people. He strives to build a new order on the ruins of the old. He censures and casts off the important customs and performances prevailing in his age. He calls upon people to adopt the new ways preached and propagated by him, ignoring the common practices and traditions then in use. His pace is fast and he has no patience to wait for a long time. He puts something dazzling and blazing before the masses. A revolutionary does not care for the sentiments of other people. He boldly incurs the displeasure of the supporters of old institutions and fears no opposition to his plans. Lenin introduces communism in Russia by sacrificing fifty lakhs Russain people.

A reformer makes an attempt to remove the corrupt practices and customs and modifies them to meet the needs of changed times and environments. He simplifies old beliefs and gives the people a slogan which consoles the afflicted hearts and gives them fresh hopes of deliverance from sufferings and misfortunes. In his reforming zeal he does not injure the feelings of others and advances slowly by winning their cooperation and goodwill.

In the light of these remarks he will try to analyse Guru Nanak's personality and work to determine whether he was a revolutionary or a reformer.

Some writers like Macauliffe, Bhai Kahan Singh and Teja Singh are of the opinion that Guru Nanak was a revolutionary because he tried to destroy all the prevalent religious institutions as well as the structures of society of his time. They hold that Guru's bitterest attack was aimed at the annihilation of caste system, and that he tried to build a new society in place of the old one. Payne and Gokul Chand Narang are of the view that Nanak belonged to the great family of Bhakti reformers. Ganda Singh says that "The Guru was not a mere reformer but the founder of a new religion." Indubhushan Banerjee deals with this topic at length in 33 pages, but he mainly dwells on caste system, pilgrimages and divinities. Kirpal Singh Narang in his *History of Punjab* has not gone beyond Indubhushan. G.S. Chhabra has casually discussed this subject in a separate section.

We will now examine it somewhat in detail.

1. Nanak's denunciation of caste was not revolutionary in character. His opposition to caste was so milk and appealing that no Brahman or any other high caste Hindu organised and resistance against Nanak. On the contrary, he was loved by one and all. Malik Bhago of Sayyidpur simply resented Nanak's refusal to accept his invitation. He considered it a personal insult, but he did not persecute the Guru. He quietly bore the humiliation and proceeded no further. The reason was that nobody objected to his reform scheme for the removal in a peaceful manner of what was harmful to society. Kabir had already denounced it is equally strong terms. The German traveller, Baron Hugel, writing three hundred years later, says that the Sikhs worship one God, abhor images, and reject castes, at least in theory. Nanak married a Khatri girl, and chose a Khari disciple as his successor.

2. The study of the Vedas was permitted to the two upper classes—Brahmans and Kshatriyas according to Alberuni. This privilege was denied to Vaishas and Shudras. Nanak broke this barrier by throwing up Name to all persons irrespective of birth. No body protested against it.

3. Similarly, Nanak's denouncement of fasts, penances and pilgrimages implied attacks on perversions, formalism and ritualism, and not on their basic conception. He considered these practices of limited utility. He declared that they had not much to do with divine love.

4. Nanak did not deprecate the holy scriptures such as the *Vedas* and the *Quran.* He never questioned the wisdom and philosophy contained in them. He criticised the blind and mechanical readings of these texts without realising God through them. "What availeth thee to read the Vedas and Puranas? It is like loading a donkey with sandal whose perfume he availeth not." Bhai Gurdas declared that the superstitions prevailing at Guru Nanak's time were due to the ignorance of the Vedas by people.

5. Even the sacred thread was not wholly condemned. Nanak denounced the ignorance of the implications of its use, and wearing of it only for the sake of form. One hundred years after Nanak wrote Mohsin Fani: "It is said he (Nanak) held in his hand the rosary of Muslims and wore the sacred thread around his neck." Moshin Fani further says that a devoted and true disciple of Guru Hargobind named Sadh, perhaps abbreviation of Sadhu Ram, accompanied him from Kabul to Panjab. He had been sent by the Guru to purchase Irani or Iraqi horses. He had the sacred thread on. He tore it off and gave it to the author of the *Dabistan* to tie up his broken coat belt. According to Malcolm, "the family of Govind, proud of their descent, had not laid aside the Zunnar, or holy cord, to which they were, as belonging to Kshatriya race entitled." On one occasion Guru Gobind Singh wanted some thread to fasten his sword belt. Daya Singh, the first member of the newly created Khalsa, a Khatri of Lahore, broke his sacred thread and gave it to the Guru.

6. While challenging the predominant position of Hindu deities, Nanak did not

hold them to any disrespect or cast any aspersion on them. He simply wanted to show that they were not superior to God, but were His creation. Mohsin Fani says : "Nanak praised Musalmans as well as the *Avtars* and gods and goddesses of the Hindus; but he held that all these had been created and were not creators, and he denied their incarnation."

7. Nanak's first slogan after enlightenment, "There is no Hindu and no Musalman," might appear revolutionary in its nature. But it was said so innocently that it gave offence to no one, not even to a fanatic Mullan or a bigoted Brahman. His explanation that both had forgotten their original religions, that both being the children of the same God had no difference between them, was satisfying and soothing.

8. People were tired of meaningless ritualism and forcible extortion of money from simple, illiterate people under grab of sacred scriptures. Consequently they welcomed Nanak's plain formula of *Nam Simran* or constant repetition of God's Name, to get deliverance from the ills of this life and salvation hereafter. Nanak's God was the creator of Hindus and Muslims alike. Ram and Rahim, Kartar and Karim were different names of the same God. Nanak held the holy books of Hinduism and Islam in high esteem and regard.

9. Like Hinduism the Buddhism Nanak believed in the law of *Karma* and transmigration of soul. As a matter of fact, he Guru applied the whole weight of his soul force on good living.

10. Nanak pleased only the discontented and the distressed people. His songs and sermons soothed their afflicted minds and restored their confidence in the joy of living. Like his contemporary Martin Luther he preached no new faith. His only contention was that through centuries religion had been polluted and contaminated by numerous superstitions and improper practices. Like a river-which is pure at source, but dirty and muddy at mouth, religion must be reformed and its purity restored to meet the needs of the time. Cunnigham says : "His reform was in its immediate effect religious and moral only."

11. The Hindu society of Nanak's time was on the whole vegetarian, while the Muslims, one and all, were a nation of meat-eaters. Nanak had no objection to meat diet, but he did not encourage this habit among his disciples. Mohsin Fani writes : "He considered flesh, wine and hog as unlawful *(haram shamuradah)*. He gave up meat eating and enjoined not to injure animals. Meat eating became popular among his disciples after him. Arjan Mal, one of the Guru, on knowing the evil effect of this habit, forbade men from animal diet. He said this practice was against the wishes of Nanak. Eventually Hargobind, son of Arjan Mal, ate meat and took to hunting. Most of his disciples adopted this practice."

12. The institution of the *Sangat* was not new or a revolutionary innovation. It had its forerunner in the Buddhist Sangha and in the congregations of Islam. Similarly the foundation of the office of the Guru which resulted in the gradual building up of the Sikh community was not unknown. Numerous religious *maths*

and other bodies have had a succession of Gurus even up to the present days. The four *maths* established by Shankaracharya in the eighth century have been under Gurus up till now.

13. Further, Nanak suggested no change in the civil institutions of Hinduism or Islam. He preached no civil or criminal laws. Cunningham observes : "He left the progress of his people to the operation of time; for his congregation was too limited, and the state of society too artificial, to render it either requisite or possible for him to become a municipal law-giver, to subvert the legislation of Manu, or to change the immemorial usage of tribes or races."

14. The founder of every religion is honoured by his followers only. Nanak is universally loved and revered by people of all religions. You may go to a church, mosque or temple, everywhere they will speak about Nanak with respect. Christ by his bold teachings had annoyed the Jews and the Roman Emperors who hanged him. Muhammad was forced to flee from Mecca to Medina where he was in constant danger to his life. This was the treatment meted out to these great leaders in their own homelands. Nanak on the other hand visited great leaders in their own homelands. Nanak on the other hand visited great centres of Hindu and Muslim lore and learning. In those wild days the sword of Muslim fanaticism flashed on the heads of all non-Muslims. Nobody could utter a word against Islam. Nanak pointed out the defects existing in Hinduism and Islam. But such was Nanak's sweetness that nobody felt offended. He acted as a friend of all. He brought peace and happiness to everybody so imperceptibly as dew dropped from heaven unseen.

15. As a child Nanak's genius confounded his teacher by eloquently speaking on the existence of God. As a young boy of nine he delivered a homily to the Brahman priest on the meaning of the sacred thread. As a lad he disappointed his father by neglecting to perform worldly duties assigned to him. As a youth his mind could not be diverted from God towards enjoyment of conjugal pleasures. As a young man he dismayed his employers by absorption in the Name of God. As a fully grown-up man he distressed his sister and brother-in-law by disappearing from home from time to time. This was inded revolutionary conduct.

17. In conclusion it might be pointed out that Nanak did not wish to destroy the existing institutions of his time. Like Buddha he wished to live in peace with Hindus and Muslims alike. His chief aim was to condemn the form which had been substituted for the worship of the True Lord. His main concern was not to pull down the old institutions and build up an entirely novel structure on the ruins of the old. He provided his contemporaries with a new viewpoint which could enable them to find the fundamental truth. In its immediate effect, his reform was religious, social and moral and in its intensity, it was moderate, mild, slow and steady, and peaceful an pacifying. To us it appears that Guru Nanak was a reformer of a high order. Sir Lepel Griffin says : "He was a reformer in the best and truest sense of the word."

The office of the Guru perpetuated

Nanak realised that his life's work would come to an end at his death if steps were not taken to provide perpetual and enduring guidance to the simple and illiterate disciples whose number was daily increasing. He had seen how Hindus lay scattered, disunited and corrupted for want of a central authority to bind them together and to preserve the purity of pristine principles of Hinduism. He had also witnessed how the work of other Bhakti leaders was suffering and decaying without such an institution. He had observed at Baghdad that it was the office of the Caliph which was keeping Islam as vigorous and strong as it was in its nascent stage. He was therefore determined to perpetuate the office of the Guru, and was on the look-out to find a suitable person to succeed him. He indirectly and unsuspectingly without giving out his mind to anybody tested the spirit of devotion and sense of discipline, service and self-sacrifice. His discipline, Bhai Lahna, alone, came out successful in every trial and test.

Nanak held a big congregation on Asuj Vadi 5, Samvat 1596 (September 2, 1539), 20 days before his death. He delivered a stirring address. He praised Lahna for his single-minded devotion and service. He invited Lahna to come near him, placed five paise and a coconut before him, put his head at Lahna's feet, gave him *Bani Pothi* or a collection of his own hymns and a rosary, called him Angad or a part of his own body, appointed him his successor, and declared that the new Guru shared his spirit and soul as well. By doing so he established the unity of Guruship, based on the principles of impersonality, indivisibility and continuity. In consequences the succeeding Gurus used the name Nanak in their compositions, correspondence, etc. The hymns of each Guru are distinguished by the number of Mahalla. Mahalla one is Guru Nanak and Mahalla two is Guru Angad.

Guru Nanak excluded his sons from succession of Guruship. His younger son Lakhmidas was a worldly man and had no desire for this office. His elder son Srichand was keen on it. But his ideas differed from those of his father. He was deeply disappointed at his elimination. He was a sad man. He renounced the world in mortification. A considerable number of Sikhs followed him, and were called Udasis or the disappointed ones with the world. They believed that the world was illusory, and that the religious leaders should not be family men. Nanak was a householder and so was Angad. Nanak excluded renunciation from Sikhism and made it a religion of householders. Further, Guruship is Sikhism provided a living ideal for its followers. The life of a Sikh entred round the personality of the Guru, whom he adored and emulated and with whom he lived in close personal spiritual union.

His death

Guru Nanak passed away on September 22, 1539, at Kartarpur. Such was the love of both communities for him that he was called : *Nanak Shah Faqir, Hindu ka Guru, Musalman Ka Pir*. A *Samadh* or tomb was built at the site of his cremation on the bank of river Ravi. Annual fairs were held at this place of great ceremonies were performed in his memory. Later on the tomb was washed away by the floods in the Ravi, and the village went to Pakistan in 1947.

Conclusion

Nanak separated religion from ritualism and politics. He determined the place of religion in social context. His aim was to create a homogeneous society free from class conflict. The worship of God and repetition of Name, he thought, would eradicate all differences between man and man. His emphasis ws on adoration of God and devotion to Guru.

Economically, Nanak was not against riches. Wealth should be distributed and not accumulated. *Kirt karo, Nam Japo, wand chhako,* should be the ideal.

Politically he pointed out what kind of rulers the country should have. They should be honest, liberal—minded, just and sympathetic.

The country's foundation rested on the poor and not on the rich. The former were many, very many, and the latter were few, very few. Thus he favoured the rule of the masses. The community meals and community living set an example. He wanted to make the life of the common people easy and happy.

Human life was governed jointly by saint and satan present all the time in a person. Listen to the voice of the saint, and avoid the temptations offered by the satan. He laid emphasis on gurmukh.

Nanak believed in universal good, *Sarbat da bhala* through full development of the individual in body and soul. Body implied robust health. Mind signified wisdom through holy sangat. Soul denoted meditation and communion with God.

Nanak's religion consisted in the love of God, love of man and love of godly living. His religion was above the limits of caste, creed and country. He gave his love to all, Hindus, Muslims, Indians and foreigners alike.

His religion was a people's movement based on modern conception of secularism and socialism, a common brotherhood of all human beings. Like Rousseau, Nanak felt 250 years earlier that it was the common people who made up the human race. They had always toiled and tussled for princes, priests and politicians. What did not concern the common people, was hardly worth considering.

Nanak's faith was simple and sublime. It was the life lived. His religion was not a system of philosophy like Hinduism. It was a discipline, a way of life, a force, which connected one Sikh with another as well as with the Guru Nanak portrayed his ideas in simple and crisp poetry abounding in subtle wit and wisdom,

Nanak's work to begin with assumed the form of an agrarian movement. His teachings were purely in Panjabi language mostly spoken by cultivators. They appealed to the down-trodden and oppressed peasants and petty traders as they were ground down between the two millstones of government's tyranny and the new Muslims brutality.

Did Guru Nanak found a new religion?

1. The philosophy of Guru Nanak is not new. It is generally borrowed from ancient Hindu scriptures. He gave it a new turn and fresh meaning according to his own ideas of communion with God.

2. Hinduism believed both in monotheism and polytheism. Nanak retained the former and rejected the latter. He held that God was immortal and he could not be incarnated into mortal human beings like Brahma, Vishnu, Shiva, Rama and Krishna.

3. The idea of guruship was well-established in Hinduism, but its transformation into living faith had not been so strong and intimate as was insisted upon by Nanak.

4. Nomination of a successor to a departing Guru was not unknown in Hinduism. Nanak added a new and revolutionary feature by declaring that his own soul joined the soul of his successor. Thereby the new Guru commanded the same respect and reverence of his followers as the founder of the movement. All the succeeding Gurus became the embodiment of the founder, and they assumed his name. For distinction they called themselves Nanak II, III and so on. This step definitely gave greater solidarity than it was prevalent in Hinduism. A Hindu religious institution disintegrated after the death of its founder. Sikhism survived with vitality.

5. Religious worship in Hinduism consisted of visits a temple in the morning and evening, in witnessing the *Arti* and in listening to *Katha*, or sermons from sacred scriptures. In Sikhism it was to sing Guru's hymns in praise of God.

6. Hinduism is based on individualism. Congregations are held, but there is little love and affection binding them. Nanak planned to give his followers a close bond of unity and cohesion through *sangats, pangats* and personal attachment of the Guru. This unity has come down to our own times as it had existed in its earliest days.

Guru Nanak's aim appears to be to lay the foundation of a reform movement which should serve as a bridgehead between Hinduism and Islam.

APPENDIX - III

GURU NANAK'S FAMOUS COMPOSITIONS

The Japji

It is believed that *Japji* was composed by Guru Nanak about 1520 at Baghdad, and it was reduced to writing at Kartarpur on the Ravi. It consists of two shalokas, one in the beginning, the other at the end and 38 *pauris* or stanzas. Its first 14 lines are called *Mul Mantra.* The whole poem discusses communion with God through Karma and Bhakti, action and devotion. It is in Panjabi language and now in Gurmukhi script. There are some Persian and Arabic words in Japji.

Guru Nanak explains the prevailing religious usages and practices. He does not believe in Hindu Trinity of Brahma, Vishnu and Shiva. He says that the three different functions of creation, protection and dissolution represent only one Supreme Being. Nanak describes numerous gods and goddesses, and holds they are all God's creation. He does not believe in the theory of evolution. God uttered one word, and the whole universe came into being at once. Everything in this world happens under His *hukam.* Nothing is beyond His *hukam.* God grants His grace to those who sincerely repeat His Name. God is sormless. He is spirit. His image cannot be conceived. Nanak denounces *Naths* and *Yogis,* and their way of living.

In 21st stanza Nanak says alms-giving, austerities, pilgrimages and religious gifts have little merit.

In 26th stanza he explains that numerous gods, goddesses, *avatars* and holy books have described God in His different aspects, but none has given an adequate description of Him. In stanza 27 Nanak says that God alone is the object of prayer and worship.

In the 28th stanza the Guru declares :

"He who conquers his desires conquers the universe." In the 30th stanza he states : "God sees all, Himself is unseen."

In stanzas 34-37, Guru Nanak lays down five stages of spiritual progress :

(i) In Dharma Khand the devotee realizes that God is the creator of all things. (ii) In Gian Khand he gains wider knowledge of universe. He feels certain that God is creator, preserver and destroyer. (iii) Sharam Khand is the realm of action and effort. (iv) Karam Khand lays emphasis on good deeds. Up to the fourth stage, the devotee retains his individuality. (v) Sach Khand is the realm of truth. The devotee attains union with God. Atma merges into Parmatma, and loses its individuality.

Dharma, Artha, Kama, and Moksha are the four main interests of human beings. Dharma and Moksha are the two banks of the river of life. They contain the flood of Artha and Kama.

In stanza 38 the Guru says in order to attain union with God, a person should follow eight stages like the minting of a gold coin. "Let chastity be the Smithy, patience the Smith, understanding the Anvil, knowledge the Tools, discipline the Bellow, austerity the Fire, devotion the Pot, immortality the Mould. Thus in the mind of Truth, World—Name is coined. Those who catch his sight and find acceptance, succeed in their toil. They by His grace achieve salvation."

Japji lays great stress on the oneness of God, repetition of the Name, and complete surrender to His will in thought, word and deed. His essence is Truth, Beauty and Love. Prayers and good deeds are essential, but they are not enough. Without Lord's grace they cannot bear fruit.

In the Epilogue of the *Japji* Guru Nanak says : "Those who meditate on the

Name wholeheartedly attain the goal of life."

Asa di Var

Asa is a musical measure, and Var is a heroic measure. It is to be recited before dawn. It consists of *pauris* and *shalokas*, which may be called stanzas and staves. There are 24 stanzas and 46 staves. Stanzas are sung in chorus and staves singly with or without an instrument. This ode lays emphasis on oneness of God, importance of the repetition of Name, and complete surrender of oneself to God's will.

God lives in nature, but he is above nature. He is one and cannot be divided. He is a combination of the holy trinity of creation, preservation and dissolution. He is both nirgun or absolute and sagun or personal.

Nanak says : "Everybody else is subject to error; only the Guru and God are without error." The only why to worship God is to sing His praises, and to meditate on His Name.

The disciple is made to believe that world is a reality and not a dream. To meditate on the Name will guide him along the right path. When the devotee is saturated with the Name, the Guru would begin to mould his life in the godly way. He is required to shun any feeling of pride, and to live in truth, love and beauty. Sweetness, love and humility constitute truth and beauty. God is not pleased with rites and ceremonies. He needs faith alone.

The substance of 24 *pauris* or stanzas is given below :

1. God is self-existent and self-luminous. He first originated Himself, and then created Nature. He knows all and understands everything. He looks on with kindness.

2. He has a Dharma Raja to keep record of everybody's actions. The virtuous are treated kindly and are retained in heaven. The sinners are conveyed to transmigration cell for punishment.

3. The souls of sinners at death are fettered and produced before Dharma Raja. A record of their deeds is shown to them. Severe punishment is inflicted upon them. They have wasted their lives.

4. The True Guru is obtained through God's grace. He creates love of the Lord in our minds. The Guru saves his disciples from the chain of births and deaths.

5. The Guru instructs his disciples to repeat the Name, to share their meals with others. They should practise charity without disclosing it to others. They should be humble. The period of youth does not last for ever. It leads to old agé and then to death.

6. True Guru alone enables one to realize God. God manifests Himself in True Guru, and speaks through him. Man is freed for ever when he meets the True Guru.

7. The faithful disciples of True Guru worship God patiently and with contentment. They shun evil. They eat and drink moderately. Their meals are simple. They do not care for the world. God bestows greatness on such persons.

8. God alone is the bestower of Truth. Truth is obtained through the Guru. The foolish persons waste away their human life in vain.

9. God's devotees obtain real joy. God's beauty is reflected in them. Love had humility are the essential qualities of Divine worship.

We should seek the holy dust of the sacred felt of the devotees. If luck favours us to get it, we should apply it to our forehead. We obtain fruit according to our actions.

11. A true devotee worships God as his only Beloved. In reality we act as God directs us. It is God who unites us with Him.

12. God's justice is impartial for all, rich or poor, high or low, Everyone is judged in accordance with his deeds. Only the wayward will be punished.

13. We remember God only through Guru's grace. He opens our spiritual eyes, and then we see the world in a different colour. The True Guru is the boat, graciously to ferry us across the ocean of the world.

14. We reap fruit sweet or bitter for our actions. For bad deeds we will be dragged to hell for punishment. Then we will weep over our past misdeeds.

15. God through His kindness draws some people to His service. They reach their goal if they carry out His will. They get the fruit of their soul's desires.

16. God has His eyes on all of us. Some are blessed with the gift of Name. He gives work to all and everybody acts according to His pleasure. In His wrath even kings are reduced to beggary.

17. Worldly men enjoy life to the full. They live in splendid mansions, work in magnificent buildings, ride on finest horses, possess bewitching harems. In the midst of these pleasures they forget the Lord, and even death.

18. The True Guru alone possesses all the virtues. If we are united with the Guru, we will be united with God. Guru through his kindness will enshrine God in our hearts. Thereby we will obtain nine treasures of excellence.

19. Human life is transitory. After a while, we will depart. Why should we then act in pride? The Guru says we should not call anyone bad or low.

20. God is source of all creation. He looks at all of us at work. We should not forsake the Lord who is the master of our life and soul.

21. We must always remember God who alone can give us happiness. His service alone is beneficial. We should act in such a way that we don't lose the Lord.

22. A true servant works according to his master' will. Then he will be respected. His wages will be doubled. If he claims equality with his master, he will arouse his indignation and will get shoe beating in the face. We should be grateful to the Lord whose bread we eat.

23. God creates and He destroys. Some labour hard in bonds. While others ride on fine horses. We must submit to the Lord. He causes things to be done. He will take care of us.

24. God is the creator. He ministers to the needs of His creatures. God has assigned our work to us. Nobody can go outside it. We must submit to His will and willingly should carry out his wishes.

Bara Maha

Bara Maha is said to be the last composition of Guru Nanak composed at Kartarpur on the Ravi towards the close of his life. It is a poem of love. The topic of God realization. Guru Nanak considers himself as a bride and God the bridegroom. It embodies the deepest passion for the divine. The twelve months indicate the changes in Nature and the changes in the moods of the divine lover. The Guru describes the various changes through which is bride passes before the union takes place.

The poem contains 17 stanzas. The first four stanzas have no reference to months. The Guru says that human life is governed by one's good or bad deeds. Happiness and grief depend upon them. The law of Karma operates according to the law of justice. But God can modify it through His grace and mercy. Absorb yourself in the love of the Lord. Live in the Name. The next twelve stanzas give the message of each month. The last stanza relates the joy in union.

Bara Maha is an allegorical poem. The twelve months refer to the Hindi months of the Bikrami year. It begins with the first month of Chait and ends with the last month of Phagun.

Chait (March-April); It is the spring season. All is green. Flowers are blooming everywhere. Cuckoo sings on the mango trees. The black bee flits from flower to flower. The bride is separated from his spouse. She pines to meet him. Her loneliness is painful. The bride suffers from pangs of separation. This is the beginning towards God realization.

Baisakh (April-May): Trees are covered with green leaves. The bride stands at the door of her house waiting restlessly for her husband. O Lord, have mercy upon me. Come into my home. Without you I my useless. With Name in her heart and on her tongue she looks charming and happy.

Jeth (May-June): The earth is burning. Water is scarce. Moisture dries up. Bride suffers from loneliness. She wishes to meet her Lord. If her mind is pure and heart is full of real love, true devotion and virtue, He will certainly bless her with His grace.

Asarh (June-July) : Earth and sky are hot. All creatures feel miserable. Crickets chirp in the evening in woods. Everybody looks for a shady place. If truth and virtue abide in the bride's mind and he possesses a loving heart, the Lord will be with her in life and death.

Sawan (July-August) : Dark clouds appear in the sky. It rains in torrents. Bursts of thunder and flashes of lightning frighten the bride. My spouse has gone abroad. I feel lonely in bed. I am in agony. I cannot bear pangs of separation. O Mother, how can I have appetite and sheep without the Lord? I do not like my fine clothes. She will be happy when her Lord comes and she merges in Him.

Bhadon (August-September) : There is water everywhere. Pools and ponds are full. It is a dark night and rain has been falling incessantly. Frogs are croaking, peacocks dance and scream Mosquitoes are stinging. Snakes are hissing. How can I have peace without the Lord? She will meet Him if she follows Guru's advice. Then the Lord will come to live with her.

Asu, Asvin or Asauj (September-October) : Summer is departing. Winter is approaching. Trees are green and bushes are in flower. But I am restless. I am growing old, my black hair is growing grey. My Lord does not care for me, because I did not love Him. I loved worldly things. Can I win His love? If you change your way of living under the guidance of True Guru, you will be united with the Lord.

Katak or Kartik (October-November) : Love is the source of happiness. Love depends upon right knowledge and right actions. This makes life harmonious. The lamp of life must be kept burning with the oil of love. Discard ego. Get the grace of True Guru. O Lord, open the door and let me in. A moment of separation is equal to six months to me. Have mercy upon me.

Maghar or Mangsar (November-December); I am grieved that I did not love the Lord. I did not have a pure heart. I must cherish genuine love for Him. I must meditate upon His Name. He is the only True helper. I must offer Him my sincerest devotions.

Poh or Posh (December-January) : It is winter. Snow is falling. Trees have shed their leaves. The bride has followed the path shown by the Guru. She is absorbed in the Lord. O Lord, bless me with Thy vision and liberate my soul from bondage. Let me unite with Thee.

Magh (January-February) : Her mind is purified. Her heart has become a place of pilgrimage. Meeting with the Lord is like bathing in the Ganga, the Yamuna, and at their confluence with Sarasvati, nay in seven seas. In the month of Magh worship of the Lord is blissful, like bathing in sixty-eight sacred places of pilgrimage.

Phagun or Phalgun (February-March): The bride has obtained union with the Lord. The Lord is living in her house. She has attained complete joy and happiness. The bride thanks the Guru for bestowing his grace upon her, and guiding her to unite with the Lord.

Other works.

Among Nanak's other works is *Sidh Gosht*. It contains discussions held by Guru Nanak with Nath yogis living in mountains. They are given in question-answer form. *Majh Ki Var, Malhar Ki Var and Dakhni Omkar* are also his compositions. Nanak composed his poetry in many dialects and languages, such as Hindi, Multani, Punjabi, Pothohari and Purabi.

There are numerous Persian and Arabic words in Nanak's compositions. For example :

1. *Asa di Var* contains :
   Pak (pure), *Qadir* (God) and *Qudrat* (Nature).
2. *Dakhni* Omkar has :
   Bina (one who can see) and *Dana* (wise).
3. *Japji* includes :

Bakhshish (gift), *Batil* (false, absurd), *Bina* (who can see with eyes), *Dana* (wise), *Dar* (gate, entrance), *Dargah* (court), *Darya* (river), *Gubar* (darkness), *Hukam* (command), *Husan* (beauty, elegance), *Jaur* (force), *Kalam* (the word of God, book of revelation), *Pairhan* (clothes), *Salah* (consultation), *Shumar* (calculation), *Sift* (qualification).

4. In *Patti Rag Asa* the following words occur :
   Alam (world), *Shair* (poet), *Sultan* (king).

Nanak composed a quatrain in Persian :

Yak 'arj guftam pesh-e-to,
Dar gosh kun Kartar;
Haq kabir, karim to,
Be aib Parwardgar.

(I am making one supplication to Thee, Almighty!, listen to it carefully. O Lord! you are Truth, High, Benevolent and Sinless.)